Adventist Theological Society
Dissertation Series 11

THE PRINCIPLE OF ARTICULATION IN ADVENTIST THEOLOGY

An Evaluation of Current Interpretations and a Proposal

Roy E. Graf

Adventist Theological Society Publications
P. O. Box 86
Berrien Springs, MI 49103
Phone: 269–471–1704
Email: info@atsjats.org
Website: https://www.atsjats.org

Copyright © 2019 by Roy Edgar Graf Maiorov
Copyright © 2019 by Adventist Theological Society
First published 2019, reprinted 2020

Cover design by Marco Bojorquez
Text layout by Joel Iparraguirre

All right reserved. No part of this book may be used or reproduced in any manner or translated into other languajes without written permission from the publisher except in the case of brief quotations embodied in critical articles and reviews.

ISBN: 978-0-9831147-3-4

Scripture quotations marked "KJV" are taken from the Holy Bible, King James Version (Public Domain). Scripture quotations marked "NASB" are taken from the New American Standard Bible®, Copyright © 1960, 1962, 1963, 1968, 1971, 1972, 1973, 1975, 1977, 1995 by The Lockman Foundation. Used by permission. THE HOLY BIBLE, NEW INTERNATIONAL VERSION®, NIV® Copyright © 1973, 1978, 1984, 2011 by Biblica, Inc.™ Used by permission. All rights reserved worldwide. Scripture quotations marked "NKJV" are taken from the New King James Version. Copyright © 1982 by Thomas Nelson, Inc. Used by permission. All rights reserved.

Dedicated to my beloved wife Cinthya
and my daughters Emily and Melissa,
God's most precious gifts
in my life.

TABLE OF CONTENTS

List of Abbreviations xiii
Acknowledgments xiv

Chapter One—Introduction 1
  Background 1
  Statement of the Problem 8
  Purpose of the Study 9
  Justification of the Study 9
  Scope and Delimitations 10
  Presuppositions 10
  Methodology 10
  Procedure 15

Chapter Two—Understanding the Principle of Articulation: Methodological Considerations 19
  Introduction to the Notion of Principle of Articulation 20
  The Phenomenological Description of the Principle
  of Articulation in Theology 29
    Parts 32
    The Articulating Agent 35
    The Articulating Action 37
    The Whole 39
  The Hermeneutical Method and the
  Principle of Articulation 42
    Presuppositions in Theology 43
    Basic Presuppositions of Reason 45
    Basic Interpretations of the Ontological and
    Epistemological Presuppositions in Theology 48
    The Principle of Articulation as a Presupposition
    and as an Ontological Reality 51

The Principle of Articulation and
the Sources of Theology 52
The Model Method and the Principle of Articulation:
Additional Remarks 55
The *Sola Scriptura* Principle as a Criterion of Evaluation
for the Models 56
Conclusion 58

**Chapter Three—The Principle of Articulation in Christian
and Adventist Theological History 61**

Introduction 61
The Greek Philosophical Background 62
   Parmenides 62
      Ontology and Epistemology 62
      The Principle of Articulation 64
   Plato 64
      Ontology and Epistemology 65
      The Principle of Articulation 66
   Aristotle 67
      Ontology and Epistemology 67
      The Principle of Articulation and Cosmology 69
   Summary 70
The Principle of Articulation in Medieval Christianity 71
   Augustine 71
      Ontology and the Interpretation of God 71
      The *Via Negativa* and Epistemology 72
      The World 73
      The Human Being 74
      Articulating Agent and Articulating Action 75
      The Whole 77
   Thomas Aquinas 77
      Ontology 77
      Epistemology and the *Via Negativa* 78
      God and the Analogical Language 79
      The World 80
      The Human Being 82
      Articulating Agent and Articulating Action 83
      The Hierarchy as the Whole 87
   Summary 88

The Principle of Articulation in the Protestant Reformation ... 89
   Martin Luther 90
      Ontological and Epistemological Presuppositions 90
      The Interpretation of God 90
      The Interpretation of the World 92
      The Interpretation of the Human Being 93
      The Articulating Agent 94
      The Articulating Action 95
      The Whole 99
   John Calvin 100
      Ontological and Epistemological Presuppositions 100
      The Interpretation of God 101
      The Interpretation of the World 102
      The Interpretation of the Human Being 103
      Articulating Agent and Articulating Action 104
      The Whole 107
   Summary 108
The Principle of Articulation in Modern Theology 109
   Friedrich Schleiermacher 111
      Ontological and Epistemological Presuppositions 111
      The Interpretation of God and the World 113
      The Interpretation of the Human Being 115
      The Articulating Agent and the Articulating Action 116
      The Whole 117
   Process Theology 118
      Ontological and Epistemological Presuppositions 118
      The Interpretation of God and the World 121
      The Interpretation of the Human Being 124
      The Articulating Agent and the Articulating Action 126
      The Whole 126
   Summary 127
The Principle of Articulation Among the
Adventist Pioneers 129
   Ontological and Epistemological Presuppositions 130
   The Interpretation of God 131
   The Interpretation of the World 134
   The Interpretation of the Human Being 134
   The Articulating Agent and the Articulating Action 135
   The Interpretation of the Whole 138

    Changes in the Understanding of the
    Principle of Articulation 138
    Conclusion 143

Chapter Four—The Principle of Articulation in Current Adventist Theology 145

    Introduction 145
    Evangelical Adventist Model 146
        Ontological and Epistemological Presuppositions 148
        The Interpretation of God 151
        The Interpretation of the World 158
        The Interpretation of the Human Being 161
        The Interpretation of the Articulating Agent 164
        The Interpretation of the Articulating Action 164
        The Interpretation of the Whole 172
        Critical Evaluation 173
    Modern Adventist Model 182
        Ontological and Epistemological Presuppositions 183
        The Interpretation of God 192
        The Interpretation of the World 197
        The Interpretation of the Human Being 200
        The Interpretation of the Articulating Agent 202
        The Interpretation of the Articulating Action 203
        The Interpretation of the Whole 206
        Critical Evaluation 207
    Adventist Theodicy Model 216
        Ontological and Epistemological Presuppositions 218
        The Interpretation of God 221
        Interpretation of the World 227
        The Interpretation of the Human Being 229
        The Interpretation of the Articulating Agent 232
        The Interpretation of the Articulating Action 237
        The Interpretation of the Whole 239
        Critical Evaluation 240
    Conclusion 246

Chapter Five—The Principle of Articulation: Toward a Scriptural Interpretation 249

    Introduction 249

Ontological and Epistemological Presuppositions 250
The Interpretation of God 256
The Interpretation of the World 262
The Interpretation of the Human Being 268
The Interpretation of the Articulating Agent 273
The Interpretation of the Articulating Action 279
   The Sanctuary/Temple Structural
   Pattern of Relationship 279
   Pre-Articulating and General Articulating Actions 290
   Specific Articulating Actions... 293
The Interpretation of the Whole 306
Conclusion 309

Chapter Six—Summary, Conclusions, and Recommendations 311

Summary 311
Conclusions 321
Recommendations 325

Bibliography 329

LIST OF ABBREVIATIONS

AB	Anchor Bible
AUSDDS	Andrews University Seminary Doctoral Dissertation Series
AUSS	*Andrews University Seminary Studies*
DTIB	*Dictionary for Theological Interpretation of the Bible*
fr.	fragment
GC	General Conference
JATS	*Journal of the Adventist Theological Society*
KJV	King James Version
LW	*Luther's Works*
NAC	The New American Commentary
NASB	New American Standard Bible
NIV	New International Version
NKJV	New King James Version
NPNF	The Nicene and Post-Nicene Fathers
SCG	*Summa Contra Gentiles*
SDA	Seventh-day Adventist
ST	*Summa Theologica*
WBC	Word Biblical Commentary

ACKNOWLEDGMENTS

Journeys such as writing a dissertation cannot be possible without the help and support of great people. Thanks to all who dedicated their time and talents to help me in this academic and spiritual endeavor.

First and most importantly, let all the glory and honor be to God, the Source of all Truth and Life. May this work be a small contribution to the progress of His cause.

Dr. Remwil Tornalejo, my dissertation advisor, many thanks to you. Thank you for your time, dedication, and suggestions. May God continue using your talents for His cause!

Dr. Raúl Kerbs, your insightful comments and sharp ideas helped me model my own. Thanks for your always prompt feedback. Thanks for the interviews. Most of all, thanks for your generosity in sharing your expertise and time with me. It has been an honor working with you.

To Dr. Fernando Canale, thank you very much for your mentoring, especially at the beginning of this process. Thanks for the generosity of your time and ideas, as well as for appreciating the change of paradigm proposed in this work.

To the readers of this work, Dr. Teófilo Correa and Dr. Francisco Gayoba, thanks for your time and for bringing new perspectives to the discussion. I really appreciate your time and disposition.

To the editors, Ms. Ellen Compuesto and Mr. Donnie Ver Medalla, thank you for improving this paper. Thank you for being so patient and kind with all my questions.

To my sponsor, Peruvian Union University, thanks for providing me and my family with this wonderful opportunity to get ready for a better service. Special thanks to Dr. Maximina Contreras, Dr. Víctor Choroco, and Dr. Edgard Horna for their vision, trust, and encouragement along the way.

To my friends, Dr. Marcos Blanco, Dr. Sergio Celis, Dr. Carlos Mora, Dr. Miguel Patiño, and Dr. Alvaro Rodríguez, thanks for the hours spent in fruitful, stimulating conversations. Your ideas, support, spirituality, and passion for God's work have had a tremendous impact on my life.

To my mother Adita as well as to my parents-in-law Iván and Mirta, thank you for your patience, support, and prayers. Thanks for bearing with having your grandchildren so far from you. I also want to honor the memory of my late father Neldo, whom I will see at the Second Coming, for his life of dedication, perseverance, and commitment to serve God. I cannot wait to hug him on that glorious day.

To my dear daughters, Emily and Melissa, thanks for being a comfort every day. I could not have asked for more understanding girls. Thanks for your smiles, hugs, and prayers. I love you.

To my best friend, my lovely wife Cinthya, thank you! I could not have done it without you. Thanks for not only providing stability and organization in our home but also for reading the manuscript, correcting mistakes, and asking questions. You are the best partner I could have dreamed of having in this life. Thank you from the bottom of my heart.

CHAPTER ONE

Introduction

Background

The principle of articulation is a basic type of presupposition of human reason that allows the systematization of knowledge in general and—which is the main interest of this study—of theological knowledge in particular. It articulates the previous knowledge of the knower, with the new one. As such, it is an *a priori* principle of reason that provides systematicity, unity, and wholeness to knowledge.

Every system of thought, whether philosophical or theological, is structured regarding a principle of articulation. This principle can be explicit or implicit, but is always present because it is a pre-condition or basic assumption of human understanding. As such, it is unavoidable. Actually, while the term *principle* is appropriated from a hermeneutical perspective, from an epistemological view, it operates as a *presupposition*. This means that the existence of the principle of articulation is not merely a hypothetical affirmation that depends on some particular theory of the operation of reason. It is not part of an interpretation or assumption regarding the way in which reason works. It is evident from a phenomenological depiction of the functioning of human reason in general. The identification and understanding of the principle of articulation, therefore, requires an analysis of the presuppositions implicit in the system.

The notion of a principle of articulation has an epistemological foundation. The first thinker who identified and conceptualized the existence of this principle explicitly as a presupposition of reason was the modern philosopher Immanuel Kant. Indeed, he was the first to offer an analysis and interpretation of the structure of reason. According to him, reason structures knowledge in a systematic way producing a unifying or articulating system. The systematization of knowledge is defined as the "coherence according to one principle" or "unity of reason."[1] Kant holds that this coherence or unity implies that the knowledge of the whole precedes the knowledge of the parts and determines the position of each part regarding the whole. The unity of reason, then, implies "the complete unity of the knowledge of our understanding, by which that knowledge becomes not only a mere aggregate but a system."[2] Kant considers that the supreme idea, articulating the understanding of reality as a whole, is the idea of God. As an idealist, Kant does not see this idea as based on experience but as "a regulative principle of reason, leading us on to the highest systematical unity."[3]

Other thinkers also recognize that the operation of reason involves a principle of unity. Hans-Georg Gadamer, a postmodern philosopher,[4] thinks that the understanding of texts in general involves a principle, which he denominates the *fore-conception of completeness*. This is a formal condition of the functioning of understanding because "it states that only what really constitutes a unity of meaning is intelligible."[5] In other words, "The reader assumes an immanent unity of meaning."[6] While Gadamer speaks of this fore-conception of completeness or immanent unity of meaning regarding the understanding of texts, it is

---

1. Immanuel Kant, *Critique of Pure Reason*, trans. Max Müller (London, UK: Macmillan, 1922), 518-519 [645]. Bracketed pagination refers to the first German edition.
2. Ibid., 519 [645].
3. Ibid., 552 [688]. See also p. 562 [700-701].
4. Gadamer can be considered as a postmodern philosopher because, according to him, in the production of meaning that takes place in the relationship between the knower and the object—for example, in the interpretation of texts—the knower has a contribution to do based on his/her presuppositions or prejudices (hermeneutical understanding of reason). In the acquisition of these presuppositions, language plays a fundamental role. Reason is a historical-temporal phenomenon, not a timeless one, in contrast to the modern understanding of reason. See Hans-Georg Gadamer, *Truth and Method*, rev. Joel Weinsheimer and Donald G. Marshall, 2nd rev. ed. (London, UK: Continuum, 2004). Gadamer, however, does not subscribe to the position assumed by many postmodern philosophers in the sense that there is no meaning to search in the text. For that reason, some may consider him as a precursor of—or someone who preluded—postmodernism. See Stanley J. Grenz, *A Primer on Postmodernism* (Grand Rapids, MI: Eerdmans, 1996), 108-111.
5. Gadamer, *Truth and Method*, 294. Gadamer holds that the fore-conception of completeness is determined by the content that the reader expects to find.
6. Ibid.

clear that nothing prevents the application of this epistemological principle to the understanding of reality as a whole.

The idea of articulation, then, is basic to the concept of system and particularly to the concept of theological system.[7] Timothy Watson defines a theological system, from the perspective of its cognitive organization, as "a cognitive whole of *articulated* theological doctrines."[8] From the perspective of the reality described by the system, a theological system is also an ontological system. In this sense, a theological system is "an ontological whole of theologically significant parts articulated in time and space."[9] The principle of articulation is the central structuring element of the system.

In each theological system, the articulating principle is found in an assumed or explicit interpretation of God, His actions, or His way of relating to the world. This principle is fundamental to the system. Christian theology, however, seems to be far away from some agreement regarding the interpretation of this articulating principle. Millard J. Erickson illustrates this by saying that

> many see Luther's theology as centering on salvation by grace through faith. Calvin seemed to make the sovereignty of God basic to his theology. Karl Barth emphasized the Word of God, by which he meant the living Word, Jesus Christ; as a result some have characterized his theology as Christomonism. Paul Tillich made much of the ground of being. Nels Ferré and the Lundensian school of such Swedish thinkers as Anders Nygren and Gustaf Aulén made the love of God central. Oscar Cullmann stressed the "already but not yet." Some postmodern theologies stress community.[10]

The specific interpretation of the principle can vary depending on the data sources admitted into the system.[11] Furthermore, the iden-

---

7. Watson proposes an intentional definition of system: "A system is a whole of articulated parts." Timothy Watson, "The Meaning and Function of System in Theology" (PhD diss., Andrews University, Berrien Springs, MI, 2011), 85.

8. Ibid., 86. Emphasis mine.

9. Ibid.

10. Millard J. Erickson, *Christian Theology*, 3rd ed. (Grand Rapids, MI: Baker, 2013), 63. Erickson considers that the center of his own system is "the *magnificence of God*." Ibid., 64. Emphasis in original. Norman R. Gulley has also identified centers, poles, or central issues in several systems of theology. Norman R. Gulley, *Systematic Theology*, vol. 1, *Prolegomena* (Berrien Springs, MI: Andrews University Press, 2003), 147-148.

11. For example, the interpretation of the principle of articulation in a given system will be different if only Scripture is admitted as a source or other sources are

tification of the principle may be very imprecise or vague. In theology, the principle is often described as *center*. This term, however, suggests that some elements of a given theological system are peripheral or not so well integrated.[12]

Historically, Seventh-day Adventists (SDAs) have affirmed the *sola Scriptura* principle by which "Seventh-day Adventists accept the Bible as their only creed"[13] or data source for theology. This fact does not mean, however, that the interpretation of the principle of articulation in Adventist theology has been homogeneous or self-evident. In the context of Adventist thought, it is also possible to find different positions regarding the central structural principle of its theology, in spite of the historical affirmation of the *sola Scriptura* principle. The Adventist pioneers frequently identified the heavenly sanctuary as the articulating center of Adventist theology. John N. Andrews affirms that the "sanctuary subject is the great central doctrine in their [Adventists] system; for it inseparably connects all the points in their faith, and presents the subject as one grand whole."[14] Regarding the position of the pioneers, Alberto R. Timm believes that "the founders of the Seventh-day Adventist Church emphasized the foundational nature of the sanctuary and of the three angels' messages to their theology."[15]

More recently, during the 20th and 21st centuries, Adventist systematic and biblical theologians have interpreted Adventist and biblical theology[16] in the light of different doctrinal topics. Among these

---

admitted as well, whether tradition, philosophy, reason, or experience. For a discussion regarding the potential sources of theology, see John Macquarrie, *Principles of Christian Theology*, 2nd ed. (New York, NY: Charles Scribner, 1977), 5-18. John Macquarrie prefers the expression *formative factors* rather than *sources*. See also Chapter 2, pp. 52-54.

12. For a discussion regarding the difference between *principle of articulation* and *center* in a system of thought, see Chapter 2, pp. 35-37.

13. General Conference (GC) of SDAs, *Seventh-day Adventist Church Manual*, 19th ed. (Silver Spring, MD: GC of SDAs, 2016), 162.

14. John N. A[ndrews], "The Sanctuary," *Advent Review and Sabbath Herald*, June 18, 1867, 12.

15. Alberto R. Timm, *The Sanctuary and the Three Angels' Messages: Integrating Factors in the Development of Seventh-day Adventist Doctrines*, Adventist Theological Society Dissertation Series 5 (Berrien Springs, MI: Adventist Theological Society, 1995), 4.

16. It has been suggested that "the center of a theological system must be the same as the underlying center of Scripture, if the system is to be true to Scripture." Gulley, *Prolegomena*, 146.

proposed motifs or central themes, it is possible to find the following issues: justification by faith,[17] the reign of God,[18] the great controversy,[19] Christ,[20] God-Christ,[21] the Trinity,[22] the sanctuary,[23] and Atonement.[24] In this context, moreover, Rolf J. Pöhler has even suggested that several approaches are simultaneously possible. There may "be as many useful approaches as there are valid perspectives on revealed truth. The choice we make will, and should, depend on the audience we are trying to reach."[25] This proposed solution implies that the concept of system does not have any epistemological foundation and the articulating center is only a question of choice according to the communication needs.

Generally speaking, all these suggestions work on the basis of an exegetical or a doctrinal approach to the topic that does not take into

---

17. Arthur G. Daniells, *Christ Our Righteousness: A Study of the Principles of Righteousness by Faith as Set Forth in the Word of God and the Writings of the Spirit of Prophecy* (Washington, DC: Review & Herald, 1941), 71-73.

18. Richard Rice, *Reign of God: An Introduction to Christian Theology From a Seventh-day Adventist Perspective*, 2nd ed. (Berrien Springs, MI: Andrews University Press, 1997), 13.

19. Herbert E. Douglass, *Messenger of the Lord: The Prophetic Ministry of Ellen G. White* (Nampa, ID: Pacific Press, 1998), 256-277.

20. This topic in particular has been interpreted in several ways. From a systematic perspective, see Fritz Guy, *Thinking Theologically: Adventist Christianity and the Interpretation of Faith* (Berrien Springs, MI: Andrews University Press, 1999), 132; Gulley, *Prolegomena*, 148. From a biblical-exegetical perspective, see Richard M. Davidson, "The Eschatological Literary Structure of the Old Testament," in *Creation, Life, and Hope: Essays in Honor of Jacques B. Doukhan*, ed. Jiří Moskala (Berrien Springs, MI: Old Testament Department, SDA Theological Seminary, Andrews University, 2000), 363.

21. Gerhard F. Hasel, *Old Testament Theology: Basic Issues in the Current Debate*, 4th ed. (Grand Rapids, MI: Eerdmans, 1995), 204; Gerhard F. Hasel, *New Testament Theology: Basic Issues in the Current Debate* (1978; repr., Grand Rapids, MI: Eerdmans, 1993), 164.

22. Gerhard F. Hasel, "Proposal for a Canonical Biblical Theology," *Andrews University Seminary Studies (AUSS)* 34, no. 1 (1996): 32.

23. For example, Carmelo Martines, "Principios epistemológicos para la comprensión de la doctrina del santuario," *DavarLogos* 11, no. 1 (2012): 2. See also Gerald A. Klingbeil, "El santuario, el ritual y la teología: En busca del centro de la teología adventista," *Theologika* 27, no. 1 (2012): 66-85.

24. Norman R. Gulley, *Systematic Theology*, vol. 3, *Creation, Christ, Salvation* (Berrien Springs, MI: Andrews University Press, 2012), 601.

25. Rolf J. Pöhler, "Does Adventist Theology Have, or Need, a Unifying Center?" in *Christ, Salvation, and the Eschaton: Essays on Honor of Hans K. LaRondelle*, ed. Daniel Heinz, Jiří Moskala, and Peter M. van Bemmelen (Berrien Springs, MI: Andrews University, 2009), 31.

consideration the role of the most basic presuppositions of the knower. In other words, these interpretations of the principle of articulation operate at a *micro* or *meso* hermeneutical level of interpretation. The micro hermeneutical level is the level of the textual or exegetical interpretation, while the meso hermeneutical level is the level of the doctrinal-theological interpretation. Fernando L. Canale, however, has proposed discussing the central structural principle of theology at the *macro* hermeneutical level; namely, at the level of the basic presuppositions of the mind.[26] In his phenomenological analysis of the structure of reason, Canale identifies these basic presuppositions as the ontological, epistemological, and systematic assumptions of the knower. Canale explains that human reason operates—in the context of the subject-object relation—based on three presuppositional frameworks. The first one is the ontological framework, which involves the assumptions about the nature of reality. The second one is the epistemological, which involves the assumptions regarding the nature of knowledge. The third one is the systematic (metaphysical) framework, which implies that reason understands reality as a unity or as an articulated whole, namely, as an articulated system. From a hermeneutical perspective, this systematic framework or type of presupposition is the principle of articulation. This principle is susceptible of several interpretations.

Canale, therefore, proposes to interpret the principle of articulation in Adventist theology based on his previous analysis of the presuppositional frameworks of reason. This interpretation entails a different methodology in comparison with the exegetical or the doctrinal approaches. The reason is that the application of the *sola Scriptura* principle also involves the presuppositional frameworks on the base of which

---

26. The micro-meso-macro categories come from Hans Küng, who applies Thomas Kuhn's concept of scientific paradigms to theology. Hans Küng, *Theology for the Third Millennium: An Ecumenical View*, trans. Peter Heinegg (New York, NY: Doubleday, 1988), 134-135. Canale, in turn, adapted this micro-meso-macro categorization to talk about the hermeneutical levels. See Fernando L. Canale, "Evangelical Theology and Open Theism: Toward a Biblical Understanding of the Macro Hermeneutical Principles of Theology?" *Journal of the Adventist Theological Society (JATS)* 12, no. 2 (2001): 20-26; Fernando L. Canale, "Deconstrucción y teología: Una propuesta metodológica," *DavarLogos* 1, no. 1 (2002): 13. Raúl Kerbs defines the macro hermeneutical presuppositions as "the most basic presuppositions the mind needs to be able to function and to get acquainted with reality as such." Raúl Kerbs, "Philosophical Assumptions of the Church Fathers: God and Creation," *Enfoques* 26, no. 1 (2014): 36.

the theological task interprets Scripture and builds its doctrines.[27]

Canale has suggested some possible preliminary identifications of the principle of articulation. He states that "the sanctuary-covenant relational structure"[28] is the key to understanding the redemptive activities of God through history, which assumes the great controversy metanarrative. Consequently, he concludes, "As biblical metanarrative, the great controversy is the hermeneutical principle of articulation in Biblical Adventist theology."[29] At the same time, Canale thinks that "the principle of articulation deals with the way in which God, human beings, and the world interact."[30] In this interaction, Christ plays a central role.[31] He considers, therefore, that "Adventists have always assumed that the historical, incarnated, resurrected, and ascended Christ is the principle of articulation of all realities in the vast universe from past to future eternity."[32]

On the basis of Canale's work, Raúl Kerbs has also proposed that in the Bible, "the historical mediation of Christ between the analogically temporal, transcendent, and infinite reality of the Trinity and the finite and temporal reality of creation is the way in which the Scriptures interpret in a temporal way the principle of articulation and the connection of all things in one unity."[33] He thinks, however, that even though biblical clusters of meaning—such as the sanctuary and the great controversy—are crucial in the biblical interpretation of the principle of articulation of reality as a whole, it should not be forgotten that the actual relation developed between the being of God and the

---

27. See Fernando L. Canale, *A Criticism of Theological Reason: Time and Timelessness as Primordial Presuppositions*, Andrews University Seminary Doctoral Dissertation Series (AUSDDS) 10 (Berrien Springs, MI: Andrews University Press, 1987), 19-159.

28. Fernando L. Canale, "From Vision to System: Finishing the Task of Adventist Theology; Part III Sanctuary and Hermeneutics," *JATS* 17, no. 2 (2006): 61-62.

29. Ibid., 62. Actually, what Canale seems to be presenting here is an identification of the principle of articulation that is usual in Adventist theology in general.

30. Fernando L. Canale, *Basic Elements of Christian Theology: Scripture Replacing Tradition* (Berrien Springs, MI: Andrews University, 2005), 27.

31. Ibid., 150-153, 222.

32. Fernando L. Canale, "The Message and the Mission of the Remnant: A Methodological Approach," in *Message, Mission, and Unity of the Church*, ed. Angel Manuel Rodríguez (Silver Spring, MD: Biblical Research Institute, 2013), 277.

33. Raúl Kerbs, *El problema de la identidad bíblica del cristianismo: Las presuposiciones filosóficas de la teología cristiana; desde los presocráticos al protestantismo* (Libertador San Martín, Entre Ríos, Argentina: Editorial Universidad Adventista del Plata, 2014), 284-285. See also ibid., 281-287.

being of humans through the role of Christ as Mediator is what articulates everything.[34]

Canale's work introduces a useful approach in order to clarify the interpretation and operation of the principle of articulation in Adventist theology. He makes a pioneering methodological contribution in this field when he introduces the necessity of considering the basic presuppositions of reason in order to identify the principle of articulation. However, he does not offer a comprehensive interpretation of the principle of articulation. Moreover, it is not clear if all his specific enunciations of possible principles of articulation such as the sanctuary-covenant structure, the great controversy, or Christ are equally valid or not, or what is the compatibility or possible interrelationship among them.

This previous scenario reflects a high level of disagreement regarding the understanding of the articulating principle of Adventist theology. The situation involves the necessity of a clear interpretation of the articulating principle, its structural elements, and the way in which that principle operates in Adventist theology in relation to the *sola Scriptura* principle. This task requires an explanation of the principle of articulation and its basic components in theology, from the perspective of the basic presuppositions of reason. This explanation would provide a conceptual tool allowing an evaluation of the various proposals regarding their conformity to *sola Scriptura* at the level of their basic presuppositions. At the same time, in order to understand the diversity of proposals regarding the articulating principle in the context of Adventist theology, it is necessary to situate them in the wider context of Christian theological pluralism in general.

Statement of the Problem

As mentioned, there is a high level of disagreement regarding the interpretation of what or who provides systematic articulation to Adventist theology. The previous background shows that there are multiple interpretations about which element has the articulating role in Adventist theology. Thus, this role has been attributed to various centers, the compatibility or possible interrelationship of which is not clear. Usually, these proposed centers are based on an exegetical or doctrinal approach (micro or meso hermeneutical level) without neither considering the presuppositions involved in each case nor the analysis of the

---

34. Ibid., 287.

basic components of the principle of articulation in theology (macro hermeneutical level).

In order to overcome this divisive multiplicity, it is imperative to analyze the existing proposals from the perspective of their assumed ontological and epistemological presuppositions, and their interpretation of the basic components of the principle of articulation in theology, as well as their evaluation in the light of the *sola Scriptura* principle. Such a study would pave the way for a biblical[35] systematic interpretation of the principle of articulation in Adventist theology.

Purpose of the Study

In harmony with the statement of the problem, the purpose of this study is to (1) explain the principle of articulation and its basic components in theology; (2) describe, analyze, and evaluate critically the various interpretations of the principle of articulation in Adventist theology, considering their possible connections with Christian tradition; and (3) propose an interpretation of the principle of articulation for Adventist theology, grounded in the *sola Scriptura* principle.

Justification of the Study

The clarification of the Adventist understanding of the principle of articulation is not only a theoretical discussion. It has practical consequences. Different understandings of the principle of articulation in Adventist theology imply theological disunity and different theological identities. In turn, different theological identities naturally convey that the church is divided regarding its message. In other words, practical disunity reflects theological pluralism and disunity. Therefore, a review of the status of this issue in Adventist theology is necessary.

Moreover, the discussion regarding the principle of articulation in Adventist theology—and in Christianity in general—has been carried out from the perspective of the notion of center. This is a reductive and abstractive view of the principle, where the basic macro hermeneutical presuppositions of reason are not under discussion. This study searches to cover this lack as a way to contribute to the clarification of the Adventist theological identity.

---

35. The expression *biblical* here is not referring to the methodology of what is named *biblical theology*. Rather, the idea is that the interpretation is biblical in its foundation although the approach is systematic.

Scope and Delimitations

The principle of articulation necessarily relates to each aspect of Adventist theology. For that reason, an exhaustive discussion of the interpretation and structural interconnections of the principle of articulation in the Adventist theological system is beyond the scope of this study. Instead, the proposed interpretation and operation of the principle in Adventist theology in Chapter 5 attempts to be more like a wide outline. Based on that outline, an extensive additional discussion, expansion, and building is possible. Moreover, this study does not attempt to present a detailed inductive demonstration of the existence of this principle and its structural elements in the Bible, although biblical evidence is introduced when necessary.

Presuppositions

This study includes some discussion about the *sola Scriptura* principle as a presupposition and as a criterion of evaluation for the interpretations of the principle of articulation in Adventist theology. However, the study does not claim any exhaustive demonstration of the validity of *sola Scriptura*. Rather, it assumes its validity. *Sola Scriptura*, in the context of this study, means that Scripture is the only authoritative source of theological knowledge or doctrines. Other sources of knowledge can provide auxiliary information to theology but they do not have normative theological authority and are under the authority of Scripture.

At the same time, *sola Scriptura* also entails that only Scripture provides data and principles of interpretation coming from the object of theology—God. This fact meets the epistemological principle according to which the knowledge of every object has to come from the object itself, not from the knower. Although the knower assumes presuppositions, the knower has to re-evaluate these presuppositions in the light of the new information that the object shows (data, presuppositions). This re-evaluation is indispensable for understanding the object rightly.

Methodology

In order to provide a biblical interpretation of the principle of articulation in Adventist theology, it is necessary to point out the methodological tools to be used. A mere historical description of each interpretation of the principle of articulation would be impractical because it would not help to distinguish with clarity the essential elements of continuity and discontinuity between different models. For that reason, a systematic approach to the analysis of the diverse interpretations of the principle of articulation is preferable.

First, the study needs to clarify what the principle of interpretation is. This clarification requires a brief phenomenological description of what the principle of articulation is in its nature and basic operative components. As the focus of this study is on theological systems, the principle of articulation in its operative components refers here to the principle of those theological systems. Those components are present in every theological system. However, the interpretation of the components is different in each system. The phenomenological method,[36] then, through the phenomenological description of the principle of articulation in theology, provides the structure to organize the analysis and discussion of the different interpretations of the principle of articulation.

Second, in order to understand the reasons why the various models interpret the principle in different ways, it is necessary to apply the

---

36. Martin Heidegger explains the task of the phenomenological method—or simply phenomenology—as grasping "its objects in *such a way* that everything about them which is up for discussion must be treated by exhibiting it directly and demonstrating it directly. The expression 'descriptive phenomenology' . . . has the same meaning." Martin Heidegger, *Being and Time*, trans. John Macquarrie and Edward Robinson (Oxford, UK: Blackwell, 2001), 59. Emphasis in original. Phenomenology, therefore, studies phenomena. The concept of phenomenon, however, requires clarification. Phenomenon is derived from the Greek word *phainomenon*, middle passive participle of *phainō*, the basic meaning of which is bringing to light, revealing, or exhibiting. The idea of *phainomenon* is which is apparent to the senses or to the mind; which is manifest. Henry George Liddell and Robert Scott, *A Greek English Lexicon*, 8th rev. ed. (1901), s.v. "*phainō*." The meaning of this term seems to imply that there is something of what appears that is not accessible to the knower, as Heidegger seems to admit in his discussion of the term phenomenon. Heidegger, *Being and Time*, 51-54. In any case, Heidegger understands phenomenology as an ontological discipline. Phenomena appear to the knower by an ontological action; namely, phenomena are external to the knower or the mind. Kant, on the other hand, makes a distinction between phenomenon and *noumenon*. In Greek, the term is a middle passive of *noeō*, to perceive, observe. *Noumenon* refers to an object of perception. Liddell and Scott, *A Greek English Lexicon*, s.v. "*noeō*." Kant, however, interprets *noumenon* as the thing in itself but on which the knower cannot know anything. Kant, *Critique of Pure Reason*, 208-209 [255-256]. In contrast, phenomenon is the thing but subject to the *a priori* mind structures or forms of space and time. See ibid., 16-17. For Kant, therefore, it is the mind that makes the phenomenon appear, and not an external object to the mind. These distinctions are useful in order to understand the phenomenological description of the principle of articulation.

hermeneutical method.[37] This method addresses the task of specifying the necessary conditions for the interpretation of the principle of articulation in its basic components. In order to interpret the principle of articulation, reason assumes macro-presuppositions regarding the nature of the components of the principle. The most fundamental and all-inclusive type of presupposition refers to the understanding of being in general, that is to say, the ontological presupposition. At the same time, the understanding of being is inseparable from the understanding of knowledge in general, namely, the epistemological presupposition. In order to understand the interpretation of the principle of articulation, the hermeneutical method seeks to determine the ontological and epistemological presuppositions involved in the understanding of this principle in its basic components. This task entails the identification of the sources that theologians use to build their theological systems. The specification of the ontological and epistemological presuppositions involved in the interpretations of the principle of articulation allows the evaluation of the models regarding their conformity to the *sola Scriptura* principle.[38]

---

37. For an application of this method, see Kerbs, *El problema de la identidad*. Kerbs applies this method in order to make the basic presuppositions of reason and their impact on the constitution of Christian theology explicit. See also Canale, *A Criticism of Theological Reason*, 160-284.

38. This principle involves the associated principles of *prima Scriptura* and *tota Scriptura*. John C. Peckham explains those principles in these terms: "Sola Scriptura signifies that the Bible and the Bible alone is the correct foundation for theology. *Prima Scriptura* upholds that the Bible is the supreme truth. *Tota Scriptura* teaches that the whole of the Bible be taken into account for any belief, thus explicitly rejecting a 'canon within a canon.' Consequently, the canon of Scripture functions authoritatively as the foundation, critic, and corrective of all theology and practice. The canon stands above the community and tradition as the final arbiter of truth because of its divine authority." John C. Peckham, "The Canon and Biblical Authority: A Critical Comparison of Two Models of Canonicity," *Trinity Journal* 28, no. 2 (2007): 248-249. Emphasis in original. Regarding the *prima Scriptura* principle, one clarification is in order. *Prima Scriptura* does not mean here that the Bible is the main source of theology among other sources of divine revelation—as some theologians consider tradition, reason, or experience, for example. The principle means that Scripture, the only divinely revealed source of theological knowledge, is the exclusive authoritative norm to evaluate any other auxiliary source of knowledge that can work as a resource for theology but without being normative. For a useful discussion of the *sola Scriptura* principle, see also John C. Peckham, "*Sola Scriptura: Reductio ad Absurdum?*" *Trinity Journal* 35, no. 2 (2014): 195-223; John C. Peckham, *Canonical Theology: The Biblical Canon, Sola Scriptura, and Theological Method* (Grand Rapids, MI: Eerdmans, 2016), 140-165.

Third, in order to organize the main lines of interpretation of the principle of articulation, it is necessary to apply the model method.[39] This method has been used in natural or social sciences.[40] In theology, models are useful to categorize or to group similar interpretations of a particular issue. In the case of this study, for example, similar interpretations of the principle of articulation constitute a pattern or model. That pattern or model is applicable to the thinking of several theologians who follow a similar interpretation of this principle.[41]

The model method is currently applied in systematic theology, sometimes with different names.[42] It is different from historical meth-

---

39. Avery Dulles explains the advantages of this method by saying that "in an ideal world it might be desirable to enter into dialogue with every theologian as an individual. To do this, however, one would have to compose lengthy historical disquisitions that would be distracting in a work of systematic theology. What was essential for theology was to identify the major points of view and to grasp the inner logic behind the characteristic positions. By giving a general overview of what significant groups of believers had held on different questions, it would be possible to exhibit where the principal agreements and disagreements lay." Avery Dulles, *The Craft of Theology: From Symbol to System* (New York, NY: Crossroad, 1992), 47.

40. Ibid., 46. A *model* has been defined as "a way of representing a phenomenon so as to illustrate some of its basic properties and their interconnections. . . . It provides an arrangement of concepts that delineates a specific vision of a phenomenon from a particular perspective." Francis Schüssler Fiorenza, "Systematic Theology: Task and Methods," in *Systematic Theology: Roman Catholic Perspectives*, ed. Francis Schüssler Fiorenza and John P. Galvin, 2nd rev. ed. (Minneapolis, MN: Fortress, 2011), 1:38-29. In other words, models do not claim to be "copies" of a phenomenon but rather general *representations* of a phenomenon in order to facilitate its analysis and explanation. For the understanding of *model* as *representation*, see Marx W. Wartofsky, *Models: Representation and the Scientific Understanding* (Boston, MA: Reidel, 1979). Marx W. Wartofsky considers that models, theories, and analogies in sciences are "species of the genus representation." Ibid., 1. That is to say, all of them are representations that interpret particular realities.

41. Dulles defines a model as "a schematic construction that enables one to make statements potentially applicable to an indefinite number of individuals. . . . The theologian's models can be helpful for speaking about classes of theologians, even though every individual will have distinguishing characteristics." Dulles, *The Craft of Theology*, 47.

42. Dulles says that what he names *models* is called *types* by other theologians and the methodology is also called typological approach or simply *typology*. Ibid. Dulles and Küng have also equated *model* to Kuhn's concept of *paradigm*. See, for example, Küng, *Theology for the Third Millennium*, 132, 134. Dulles suggests that "a dominant model is . . . a paradigm." Avery Dulles, *Models of the Church*, expanded ed. (New York, NY: Doubleday, 1987), 29. Dulles has applied the model method to the study of the church and the revelation. See ibid.; Avery Dulles, *Models of Rev-*

odology in the sense that historical details are secondary to the necessity of representing theological tendencies.[43] This fact, however, does not preclude that the models may be presented in historical order—as it is the case in this study. In this sense, the models are historical.[44] The analysis within each model, however, follows the systematic organization emerging from the phenomenological description of the principle of articulation in its basic components.

The models can be better understood with the help of a discussion of some typical or paradigmatic representatives of each one of them, although these representatives not necessarily meet every aspect of the model and sometimes, additional names may need to be mentioned. In this sense, it is important to remark that none of the thinkers pertaining to particular models uses the concept of principle of articulation *explicitly*, although all of them offer an *implicit* interpretation of this principle. Nor are the models used by theologians explicit. These models must be discovered or made explicit.

Regarding the proposed interpretation of the principle of articulation for Adventist theology, its presentation follows a biblical systematic approach. The general outline for the discussion is the one resulting from the phenomenological analysis of the principle of articulation in its basic operative components. These components are interpreted in the light of the biblical ontological and epistemological presuppositions, in explicit contrast to the traditional interpretation of the same

---

elation (New York, NY: Doubleday, 1983). Küng has applied the model method to the study of the change of paradigm in theology. See Küng, *Theology for the Third Millennium*. David Tracy has applied the system of models to the study of the various tendencies in contemporary theology. See David Tracy, *Blessed Rage for Order: The New Pluralism in Theology* (Minneapolis, MN: Winston-Seabury, 1975).

43. "The typologist cannot replace the critical historian who presents and analyzes the work of individuals. The systematician's aim is rather to identify issues and options. Thus, systematics can work at a level of generality that for history would be unacceptable." Dulles, *The Craft of Theology*, 47. Tracy explains that "models do not provide an exact description of particular historical phenomena. They do provide intelligible interlocking sets of basic terms and relations that aid us to understand the point of view expressed in particular historical positions." Tracy, *Blessed Rage for Order*, 23.

44. The historical order does not intend to suggest that the models are not valid or current today anymore. They are presented in the order in which they emerge historically but they are still "alive" and influencing contemporary theology. This is not only the case for the historical chapter of this study (Chapter 3) where the main models of Christian tradition are described, but also for the systematic chapter discussing the current models in Adventist theology (Chapter 4).

presuppositions. The proposed interpretation of the principle of articulation, therefore, aims to articulate the Adventist system of theology detached from philosophical interpretations and in commitment to the *sola Scriptura* principle.

Procedure

Chapter 1 introduces the background of the problem. In that context, it draws attention to the multiple proposed centers for Adventist theology. The chapter calls for a different approach to this issue from the perspective of the hermeneutical concept of the principle of articulation.

Chapter 2 works as a methodological chapter. First, it presents an introduction to the notion of principle of articulation. Second, it offers a phenomenological description of the principle of articulation in its basic operative components as it emerges in theological systems. Third, in relation to the hermeneutical method, the chapter explains (1) the role and levels of presuppositions in theology; (2) the most basic presuppositions of reason; and (3) the basic interpretations of the ontological and epistemological presuppositions as the presuppositions of reason that are operative in the interpretations of the principle of articulation in theology. In this context, the chapter distinguishes between (4) the principle of articulation as a presupposition of reason and as an ontological reality and it clarifies (5) the role of theological sources regarding the origin of the ontological and epistemological presuppositions that determine the interpretation of the principle of articulation. Fourth, the chapter briefly discusses the criteria to classify the interpretations of the principle of articulation based on the model method—already discussed in the methodology section of Chapter 1—as well as the way to structure the analysis of the models based on the phenomenological description. Finally, the chapter explains the role of the *sola Scriptura* principle as the basic criterion for the evaluation of the models. In this way, the chapter establishes the necessary philosophical background and provides some conceptual tools to understand the procedure in the following chapters.

The plurality of interpretations of the principle of articulation in current Adventist theology requires familiarity with the plurality of interpretations in the broader context of Christian theology. The understanding of the diversity of interpretations of the principle of articulation in Christianity facilitates determining the possible connections of those interpretations with some of the interpretations of this principle in current Adventist theology. Therefore, Chapter 3 presents a brief review of the main models of interpretation of the principle of articulation in Christian theological history preceded by a succinct exposition of the Greek philosophical background of Christian theology. The exposition of the main models is based on the leading representatives of those models. Augustine and Thomas Aquinas are representatives of the hierarchical model of medieval Catholicism. Martin Luther and John Calvin are representatives of the soteriological model of the Protestant Reformation. Friedrich Schleiermacher and process theology are representatives of the panentheistic model of modern theology. In general, the presentation of the historical interpretations of the principle of articulation follows the "outline" provided by the phenomenological description of the principle of articulation in Chapter 2, but with some flexibility, considering the limitations of a historical chapter. This description includes the identification of the assumed ontological and epistemological presuppositions involved in each interpretation. Chapter 3 also summarizes the interpretation of this principle among the Adventist pioneers. In this way, this chapter allows seeing the conflict of interpretations regarding the principle of articulation between Christian theological tradition and the Adventist pioneers. Additionally, the chapter succinctly introduces some changes in relation to the interpretation of the principle of articulation through Adventist theological history until the beginning of the 20th century.

Chapter 4 analyzes the main interpretations of the principle of articulation in contemporary Adventist theology according to three basic models: the evangelical Adventist model, the modern Adventist model, and the Adventist theodicy model. In each model, it is necessary to discover the assumed ontological and epistemological presuppositions involved in the interpretation of the principle of articulation. The central part of the discussion of each model analyzes the principle of articulation in its basic components in harmony with the "outline" provided for the phenomenological analysis of Chapter 2. The main representative theologians chosen for each model are the following: for the Adventist evangelical model, Desmond Ford;[45] for the modern Adventist mod-

---

45. The selection of D. Ford is virtually unavoidable considering that he is the main representative and crystallizer of the evangelical Adventist thought.

el, Fritz Guy;[46] and for Adventist theodicy model, Norman R. Gulley.[47] In any case, although the models are basically explained based on the selected representatives, some secondary exponents are mentioned in order to complement the exposition of the models and to understand their potential implications in Adventist theology. Adventist models are briefly evaluated from the perspective of the *sola Scriptura* principle at the level of their basic interpretations of the presuppositions of the mind and regarding the impact of those presuppositions on the interpretation of the principle of articulation. In this sense, the background provided by the discussion of the interpretations of the principle of articulation in Christian historical theology—Chapter 3—is useful to determine if the Adventist models presented in Chapter 4 did adopt one of those interpretations.

Chapter 5 of this study proposes a biblical systematic interpretation of the principle of articulation, which aims to meet the basic characteristics of this principle based on the *sola Scriptura* principle. The chapter highlights the ontological and epistemological presuppositions involved in the biblical understanding of the principle of articulation in contrast to the philosophical interpretations of those presuppositions. The central part of the chapter addresses the specific interpretation of the components of the principle in harmony with the "outline" provided for the phenomenological analysis of the components of the principle of articulation in theology described in Chapter 2. The discussion is developed in dialogue with Adventist and non-Adventists representative writers who deal with the various aspects of the topic, and in dialogue with Christian tradition in general. Chapter 6 offers a general summary and the conclusions of the study, as well as some suggestions for further research.

---

46. Guy is probably the main representative of what it is denominated as *progressive Adventism*. He has written texts explaining the methodological foundation of their theological projects.

47. Gulley has published the most important systematic theology in the history of the Adventist Church, written from the perspective of the cosmic controversy (Great Controversy) as its integrative element. He is, therefore, an adequate representative of this model.

CHAPTER TWO

Understanding the Principle of Articulation: Methodological Considerations

The purpose of this chapter is to present some methodological considerations that facilitate the understanding of the work in the rest of this study. The presentation of these methodological considerations involves five sections. The first section of this chapter introduces the notion of principle of articulation in general, in order to allow its more specific interpretations in the context of theological systems later. The second section offers a brief phenomenological description of the principle of articulation and its basic operative components in the specific case of theological systems.

In connection with the hermeneutical method and the interpretation of the principle of articulation, the third section of the chapter presents (1) an introduction to the role and levels of presuppositions in theology. The section follows with (2) a brief explanation of the most basic presuppositions of reason—particularly the ontological and epistemological presuppositions—operative in the interpretations of the principle of articulation and (3) the basic possible interpretations of those presuppositions in the context of theology. The section ends with (4) a discussion of the difference between the principle of articulation as a presupposition and as an ontological reality, and (5) the relationship between the interpretation of the principle and the sources of theology.

The fourth section of the chapter clarifies the criteria to classify the interpretations of the principle of articulation in connection with the model method, already explained in Chapter 1, and the way to structure the analysis of the models based on the phenomenological description of the second section. Finally, the last section of the chapter explains the role of the *sola Scriptura* principle as the basic criterion for the evaluation of the Adventist models at the level of the basic

Introduction to the Notion of Principle of Articulation

An understanding of the principle of articulation requires some familiarity with the way in which human beings are able to know. Tillich has explained the general understanding of the structure of knowledge as composed of three basic elements. The first one is the knower or subject. The second one is that which is known, the object. The third element is the union between the knower or subject and the known or object. "Knowing is a form of union"[1] or relationship between the subject and the object.[2]

In this relationship, the human mind can know different kinds of objects, either material or physical ones, texts or oral language, ideas, emotions, and others.[3] During this process, "the gap between subject and object is overcome,"[4] at least, to some extent. This means that "the subject 'grasps' the object, adapts it to itself, and, at the same time, adapts itself to the object."[5] Evidently, this fact also implies that the object has something to "offer" and that it can be "grasped" by the subject.

The nature of this union or relationship has been extensively discussed over time. Tillich suggests that the union entails some previous detachment in order to make the process of knowledge possible. That

---

1. Paul Tillich, *Systematic Theology: Three Volumes in One* (Chicago, IL: The University of Chicago Press, 1967), 1:94. Tillich has been considered as showing a "clear Kantian filiation." José Luis Illanes Maestre, *Sobre el saber teológico* (Madrid, España: Rialp, 1978), 167. There is no intention in this study to endorse Tillich's specific theory on the interpretation of reason or his panentheistic ontology. Tillich is quoted rather as a general reference in order to explain what the different interpretations of reason have in common. To the extent that Tillich is useful for this purpose, he is quoted here.

2. In a similar way, Canale suggests that "the structure of knowledge always involves three components—*subject*, *object*, and their *relationship*." Fernando L. Canale, *The Cognitive Principle of Christian Theology: A Hermeneutical Study of the Revelation and Inspiration of the Bible* (Berrien Springs, MI: Andrews University Lithotech, 2010), 75. Emphasis in original.

3. Ibid., 74.

4. Tillich, *Systematic Theology*, 1:94.

5. Ibid.

is to say, there must be some distance between the subject and object or some inequality, something that they do not have in common. At the same time, the unity between both implies some equality or similarity; namely, something that they have in common.[6]

From the perspective of the structure of reason, the relationship between the knower and the object of knowledge is possible because the knower is able to integrate or systematize the new knowledge with the previous one according to some basic idea or presupposition. This basic presupposition is the *principle of articulation*.[7] As said in Chapter 1, the first thinker to identify and conceptualize the principle of articulation is Kant.[8] Kant explains this principle, precisely, in the context of his analysis and interpretation of the structure of reason, including subject, object, and the relationship between both. He refers to that principle as the systematic unity of reason.

According to Kant's theoretical philosophy, human reason,[9] ultimately, organizes ideas[10] in three general kind or classes: (1) the unity of

---

6. Classical philosophy emphasized the element of union. Reality is organized according to a *logos* or universal reason, which is "graspable" by the human *logos* or mind. Both are in an implicit essential harmony. In recent times, some postmodern philosophers (and theologians) emphasize the element of separation. According to Peter C. Hodgson, "Recent deconstructive philosophy has stressed the aspect of distance . . . to the point where union is no longer possible. If so, this is a loss of the dialectical insight that union in fact occurs in knowledge although always only fragmentarily and ambiguously." Peter C. Hodgson, *Winds of the Spirit: A Constructive Christian Theology* (Louisville, KY: Westminster John Knox, 1994), 124. The problem with the total denial of this element of union or articulation is that knowledge and communication become impossible at all, something that the defenders of this position denies in practice when they communicate the idea that the union is not possible and they assume that they are understood.

7. The expression *principle of articulation* has been coined by Canale. See references in Chapter 1, p. 7. The notion of *articulation* (Latin *articulatio*), however, is already explicit in Kant. See, for example, Kant, *Critique of Pure Reason*, 667-669 [832-834].

8. "We find in Kant for the first time an explicit, systematic reflection on the nature of system and a determination of his concept in terms of the nature of reason." Martin Heidegger, *Schelling's Treatise on the Essence of Human Freedom*, trans. Joan Stambaugh (Athens, OH: Ohio University Press, 1985), 36.

9. Kant speaks about *pure reason* that for him, who is an idealist philosopher, refers to reason in total detachment from the experience or as *a priori* to the experience. See Julián Marías, *History of Philosophy*, trans. Stanley Appelbaum and Clarence C. Strawbridge (New York, NY: Dover, 1967), 287.

10. From his idealist perspective, Kant denominates these ideas as *transcendental*. For Kant, transcendental ideas are those concepts of reason that do not have their

the subject knower; (2) the unity of the phenomena of the world; and (3) the unity of the two prior classes of ideas, namely, the unity of the "*objects of thought in general.*"[11] These classes of ideas are *a priori* concepts or presuppositions of reason trying to "grasp" reality as a whole. Kant interprets that they correspond or are equivalent to three basic unifying universal ideas to which every other idea refers: (1) the idea of soul or knower; (2) the idea of world or universe—the known—and (3) the idea of God, the Supreme Being giving systematic unity to the two previous ideas. The idea of God is the base of the systematic unity for reason, which provides a systematic relation among these three basic ideas.[12]

Beyond his particular interpretation of the principle of articulation, Kant, then, holds that reason structures knowledge in a systematic way in accordance with, ultimately, a unifying or articulating principle. Reason is, therefore, a systematization or coherence of knowledge according to one principle of articulation or idea of the whole. This systematization provides unity and structures knowledge as a whole. As the articulating idea of the whole is *a priori* to experience, the whole determines the place of the parts of the system and not the opposite.

---

origin in the sensory experience. Kant, *Critique of Pure Reason*, 266 [327]. "No objective deduction . . . is possible with regard to these transcendental ideas; they are ideas only, and for that very reason they have no relation to any object corresponding to them in experience." Ibid., 273 [336]. As these ideas do not have origin in sensory experience, they are subjective. However, they are universal because they are the same for all individuals.

11. Ibid., 271-272 [334]. Emphasis in original. This study is following Kant's theoretical philosophy, rather than his practical one. In his practical philosophy, Kant assumes these articulating ideas as *if* they were realities. See Marías, *History of Philosophy*, 294. For Kant's practical philosophy, see Immanuel Kant, *Kant's Critique of the Practical Reason and Other Works on the Theory of Ethics*, trans. Thomas K. Abbott, 6th ed. (London, UK: Longmans, Green, 1903).

12. Kant, *Critique of Pure Reason*, 272 [334]. "We can perceive, that there is among the transcendental ideas themselves a certain connection and unity by which pure reason brings all its knowledge into one system. There is in the progression from our knowledge of ourselves (the soul) to a knowledge of the world, and through it to a knowledge of the Supreme Being." Ibid., 274 [337]. For Kant, there is a tendency of the mind to interpret reality as a whole using these three unifying ideas. Kant also explains that, traditionally, these three ideas are studied by different metaphysical disciplines: psychology (the study of the soul), cosmology, and theology. Ibid., 272 [334]. Kant, however, considers that it is impossible to demonstrate the existence of the soul, the world as a unified entity, and of God. See Benjamin A. G. Fuller, *A History of Philosophy*, vol. 2, rev. ed. (New York, NY: Henry Holt, 1947), 232-233. Consequently, he rejects the ontological and cosmological argument. See ibid., 233-241.

The system is, then, the whole articulated by the principle of articulation or idea of the whole.[13] The articulating principle is "the form of the whole,"[14] which means that it is the formal category of reason systematizing or providing structure to the whole.

The universality of the principle of articulation—as well as the general ideas of the unity of the world and the unity of the knower—always remains as a *problematical* or *hypothetical* principle because it is only an idea, not a knowledge of something real, external to the mind. This knowledge has connection with experience. Consequently, only particular objects of knowledge are certain or "real." In contrast, the principle of articulation operates as a universal rule of the mind used to introduce articulation and unity in the system but it remains always hypothetical. This rule is what Kant names "the hypothetical use of reason."[15] The principle of articulation, consequently, "*is regulative only*, and intended to introduce, as much as possible, unity into the particulars of knowledge, and thus to *approximate* the rule to universality."[16] This unity, therefore, is only a *projected* unity because it is always hypothetical. It is not possible to postulate a *real* systematic unity, whether among the objects or as an *a priori* unity of reason.[17]

---

13. "If we review the entire extent of our knowledge . . . we shall find that it is the *systematising* [sic] of that knowledge, that is, its coherence according to one principle, which forms the proper province of reason. This unity of reason always presupposes an idea, namely, that of the form of a whole of our knowledge, preceding the definite knowledge of its parts, and containing the conditions according to which we are to determine *a priori* the place of every part and its relation to the rest. Such an idea accordingly demands the complete unity of the knowledge of our understanding, by which that knowledge becomes not only a mere aggregate but a system. . . . We ought not to say that such an idea is a concept of an object, but only of the complete unity of concepts, so far as that unity can serve as a rule of the understanding. Such concepts of reason are not derived from nature, but we only interrogate nature, according to these ideas, and consider our knowledge as defective so long as it is not adequate to them." Kant, *Critique of Pure Reason*, 518-519 [645]. Emphasis in original.

14. Ibid., 667 [832]. Again, the articulating idea is not "a concept of an object, but only of the complete unity of concepts, so far as that unity can serve as a rule of the understanding." Ibid., 519 [645].

15. Ibid., 520 [647].

16. Ibid. First emphasis is mine. Second emphasis is in original.

17. Ibid., 520-521 [647]. "Such a unity, however, is only an [sic] hypothesis of reason. It is not maintained that such a unity must really exist, but only that we must look for it in the interest of reason, that is, for the establishment of certain principles for the various rules supplied to us by experience, and thus introduce, if it is possible, systematical unity into our knowledge." Ibid., 522 [649-650].

The three basic ideas of God, world, and soul (knower), then, serve "as a rule for possible experience, nay, as heuristic principles in the elaboration of experience."[18] While they do not correspond to any *schema of sensibility* (i.e., they are not based on experience), they work as *maxims* of reason, allowing the interpretation of reality as a united and systematic whole.[19] These three basic ideas, then, work "as *regulative* principles for the systematical unity of the manifold of empirical knowledge in general."[20] They are not real except in the sense of "the reality of a schema of a regulative principle for the systematical unity of all natural knowledge."[21]

According to Kant, then, it is not possible to postulate the systematic unity of reason objectively but only subjectively. This subjectivity is not equivalent to individuality, however, because for Kant—as an idealist philosopher—this subjectivity is universal. The three ideas of God, world, and soul are mental but they are the same for everybody.[22] In any case, reason has the tendency to think this systematic unity by attributing an object to its idea. The first object is the concept of *ego* or soul—considered only as a thinking nature. The second one is the concept of universe—nature in general.[23] The third one is God. As mentioned, God works as the articulating principle of reality as a whole.[24] Kant reiterates, however, that this principle is only "a regulative principle of reason, leading us on to the highest systematical unity, by the idea of an

---

18. Ibid., 533 [663].
19. Ibid., 534-535 [664-666]. In this sense, for example, the idea of a highest or supreme intelligence can help to understand reality as a systematic unity when "we are led to say, for instance, that the things of the world must be considered as if they owed their existence to some supreme intelligence; and the idea is thus a *heuristic* only, not an ostensive concept, showing us not how an object is really constituted, but how we, under the guidance of that concept, should look for the constitution and connection of the objects of experience in general." Ibid., 539 [670-671]. Emphasis mine.
20. Ibid., 539 [671]. Emphasis in original.
21. Ibid., 541 [674].
22. In other words, they are transcendental. See also footnote no. 10 in this chapter.
23. For these two first ideas, see ibid., 547-550 [681-685].
24. "The highest formal unity, which is based on concepts of reason alone, is the systematical and purposeful unity of things, and it is the speculative interest of reason which makes it necessary to regard all order in the world as if it had originated in the purpose of a supreme wisdom. Such a principle opens to our reason in the field of experience quite new views, how to connect the things of the world according to teleological laws, and thus to arrive at their greatest systematical unity." Ibid., 551 [686-687].

intelligent causality in the supreme cause of the world, and by the supposition that this, as the highest intelligence, is the cause of everything, according to the wisest design."[25]

To summarize, for Kant, reason is essentially systematic and at the same time, hypothetical. The system of knowledge is articulated around the transcendental idea of a supreme cause or being (God) that allows the knower to interpret knowledge as a whole. This articulating element, however, remains hypothetical because it does not have a relation to experience. It is not a knowledge of what is real.

In spite of Kant's important contribution to the understanding of the principle of articulation as the systematic unity of reason, it is clear that his idealism did not allow him to develop a phenomenological understanding of that principle. His interpretation of the principle of articulation as referring to God is idealistic because he understands that phenomena are transcendental. Namely, phenomena are a projection of the mind, not ontological realities external to the knower. In consequence, Kant's understanding of the principle of articulation or systematic unity of reason is purely a projected system or unity, without connection with the experience of the subject knower. For him, the idea of articulation is not a knowledge of what is real, which is also applicable to the regulative ideas of the world and the soul. These ideas are universal or transcendental but they do not have real existence beyond the mind of the knower. It is the mind that makes the principle of articulation appear, without relation to any external reality. Here Kant allows seeing his *innatism*; namely, for him, these ideas are innate to the mind and consequently, reason imposes them on the objects of experience.[26]

Kant's idealist bias regarding his analysis of the principle of articulation finds a useful corrective in the phenomenological approach used

---

25. Ibid., 552-553 [688]. Kant adds that "in admitting this fundamental idea of a Supreme Author, it is clear that I do not admit the existence and knowledge of such a Being, but its idea only, and that in reality I do not derive anything from that Being, but only from the idea of it, that is, from the nature of the things of the world, according to such an idea." Ibid., 562 [700-701].

26. Heidegger makes a useful observation regarding this point. "Why are these Ideas necessary and why just these Ideas? And how should their own connection be grounded if these Ideas are not drawn from the beings themselves which they mean and from the corresponding immediate comprehension of these beings? For all this, Kant has no answer other than claiming that these Ideas necessarily belong to the nature of human reason. There is still a remainder here of the old doctrine of *ideae innatae*." Heidegger, *Schelling's Treatise*, 40. Emphasis in original.

by Heidegger and particularly Gadamer. Kant rightly proposes that the principle of articulation or unity of reason provides systematicity to knowledge, is hypothetical, and, consequently, has an anticipatory character.[27] However, Kant's idealism leads him to an essentialist or abstractive understanding of human knowledge. Phenomena, in Kant, are not ontological with a real existence external to the mind. They are fundamentally a projection of universal structures or schemes of the knower, in total detachment from his/her own personal experience. Knowledge is essentially subjective—although not individual but universally mental—because there is no real contribution of an external object.[28]

In contrast, Heidegger and Gadamer propose that knowledge involves a subjective and an objective component.[29] Knowledge is an interpretation of real objects—phenomena external to the mind—in the light of the subjective background of the knower. The knower involves his/her personal background in the act of knowledge. The personal background that the knower involves in the act of knowing is a knowledge of what is real, and thus, it is an individual knowledge. It is not universal and mental as in the case of Kant. The personal background is based on his/her prior experience with real phenomena. Heidegger considers that "in every case interpretation is grounded *in something we see in advance—in afore-sight.*"[30] That is, a previous concept that the knower has about the object. In this interpretation, the interpreter

---

27. "According to Kant, reason posits a *focus imaginarius*, a focus in which all the rays of questioning things and of determining objects meet, or, conversely, in terms of which all knowledge has its unity. Reason is the faculty—we can say—of anticipatory gathering—*logos, legein.*" Ibid., 37. Emphasis in original.

28. See Canale, *Cognitive Principle of Christian Theology*, 77-78.

29. Heidegger and Gadamer talk about subject-object relationship in critical terms, possibly because they see it as an abstraction related to the idealistic interpretation of that relationship—as in Kant. Heidegger, for example, holds that the subject-object relationship is a superficial and formal way to talk about the *Dasein* and the world. Heidegger, *Being and Time*, 86-87. This study, however, does not intend to elaborate interpretations or philosophical theories of reason but a phenomenological depiction of human reason or knowledge in general. From this perspective, Heidegger and Gadamer can provide useful insights considering that their criticism goes against a particular interpretation of the subject-object relationship. Moreover, although Heidegger speaks about the relationship between the man or *Dasein* and the world instead of the subject-object relationship, in reality there is no *Dasein* and world as abstract entities but as concrete actual entities and individuals in particular situations. The same applies to Gadamer's view of the relationship between the reader and the text. See footnotes 40 and 41 in this chapter.

30. Heidegger, *Being and Time*, 191. Emphasis in original.

can draw the previous ideas from the object itself or can try to force its understanding into previous concepts, which do not have relation to the object.[31] In any case, these previous structures exist and are unavoidable. While they can be changed, modified, or re-elaborated through successive interaction with the object of knowledge, the previous structures or presuppositions of reason cannot be eliminated.[32] Consequently, as Heidegger affirms, "Whenever something is interpreted as something, the interpretation will be founded essentially upon fore-having, fore-sight, and fore-conception. An interpretation is never a presuppositionless apprehending of something presented to us."[33]

---

31. "Anything understood which is held in our fore-having and towards which we set our sights 'foresightedly', becomes conceptualizable through the interpretation. In such an interpretation, the way in which the entity we are interpreting is to be conceived can be drawn from the entity itself, or the interpretation can force the entity into concepts to which it is opposed in its manner of Being. In either case, the interpretation has already decided for a definite way of conceiving it, either with finality or with reservations; it is grounded in *something we grasp in advance—in* a *fore-conception.*" Ibid. Emphasis in original.

32. According to Heidegger, the structure of understanding is a circular structure where the fore-structure (presuppositions) can be re-elaborated based on the interaction with the object of knowledge itself. He refers to this successive approach to the object of knowledge as the "circle of understanding." Ibid., 195. An illustration can help to understand the role of presuppositions in the act of knowledge. It is possible to imagine a person who starts reading a new book. The topic is completely new for the reader, and he/she does not have enough background to understand the content. Consequently, the reader may have serious problems to understand the new terminology, concepts, and, even more, the presuppositions assumed by the author. This fact is inevitable because the reader will try to "connect" the new information with the old information that he/she has stored in his/her mind, which is not necessarily directly related to the content of the book. The presuppositions of the reader may be very different from the presuppositions of the writer. In these circumstances, the reader can try to force the understanding of the text in terms of his/her own previous ideas or presuppositions. Other option, however, is to allow the text to inform the reader. The reader can try to understand the new terminology, concepts, and presuppositions, contrasting them with their own previous ideas. In this process, the reader probably will need to approach the text or to read it several times (circle of understanding) in order to increase his/her own understanding of it. Furthermore, the reader will need to make an effort to understand the book in the light of the presuppositions of the text, instead of understanding the text in the light of his/her own presuppositions. Finally, the reader can even internalize the new ideas found in the text and, therefore, change or at least modify his/her own presuppositions. In one sense, this process never ends, as explained below. For some illustrations about the role of presuppositions in theology in particular, see the discussion in the third section of this chapter (p. 42ff) on the hermeneutical method and the principle of articulation.

33. Ibid., 191-192.

Gadamer explains that the previous structures of reason—this fore-conception, or set of presuppositions that implies an anticipatory element in the act of knowledge[34]—include the *fore-conception of completeness*. In the process of knowledge, the knower *projects* his/her presuppositions on the object of knowledge[35] that includes the *fore-conception of completeness*, which is Gadamer's equivalent of the principle of articulation. Gadamer applies this concept to the understanding of texts, where the reader assumes a unity of meaning but, as he clarifies, the fore-conception of completeness "is obviously a formal condition of all understanding."[36]

Gadamer uses a Heideggerian concept, the structure of the understanding as a circular structure.[37] He explains that in the successive approaches of the knower to the object, there is a progressive realization of the circular understanding of the whole and the parts.[38] In other words, the *grasping* or knowledge of the object by the knower is susceptible of additional realization. The understanding *situates* the object in the context of the whole that essentially belongs to the prior knowledge that the knower has of the object. This process requires an articulation that is constantly "improved" in every approach to the object. While this circular process of understanding can create rival interpretations, it is possible to arrive at a unity of meaning.[39]

At the same time, Gadamer points out that the circle of understanding is not a mere projection upon the object by the knower. The successive approaches to the object produce changes in the fore-conception of the knower, including the understanding of the fore-conception of completeness or principle of articulation.[40] That is to say, the object has a "contribution" in the process of knowledge that goes beyond the

---

34. Gadamer, *Truth and Method*, 270, 272, 293.
35. Ibid., 269.
36. Ibid., 293.
37. See footnote 32 in this chapter.
38. Gadamer, *Truth and Method*, 293.
39. "Rival projects can emerge side by side until it becomes clearer what the unity of meaning is; interpretation begins with fore-conceptions that are replaced by more suitable ones." Ibid., 269.
40. "A person who is trying to understand a text is always projecting. He projects a meaning for the text as a whole as soon as some initial meaning emerges in the text. Again, the initial meaning emerges only because he is reading the text with particular expectations in regard to a certain meaning. Working out this fore-projection, *which is constantly revised in terms of what emerges as he penetrates into the meaning*, is understanding what is there." Ibid., 269. Emphasis mine.

mere imposition of the knower's projection upon the object.[41]

In summary then, it is possible to affirm, in harmony with Kant, that the principle of articulation is a presupposition that provides systematicity to human knowledge and is hypothetical and anticipatory in character. On the other hand, however, it is necessary to admit, in line with Gadamer, that the principle of articulation is a knowledge of the real—in the sense of external to the mind of the knower. It is not only an imposition or static projection of the knower upon the object; it also involves a "participation" of the object of knowledge by "shaping" the knower's knowledge of that principle. The element of articulation is not only a reality in the mind of the knower that he/she projects; it is also external to the mind; it is part of reality itself.[42]

The Phenomenological Description of the Principle of Articulation in Theology

The explicit identification of the principle of articulation as a presupposition of reason is a relatively recent fact in the philosophical field. As such, however, the principle of articulation or principle of unity of reason has been interpreted—although not necessarily explicitly identified—in every system of thought; for example, in philosophical or theological systems.[43] Traditionally in philosophy, the principle can be found in relation to the central metaphysical issue of *the one and the many* or *the whole and the parts*.[44] The *one* is the articulating

---

41. Gadamer explains this fact in terms of the relationship between a reader and a text. "When we read a text we always assume its completeness, and only when this assumption proves mistaken—i.e., the text is not intelligible—do we begin to suspect the text and try to discover how it can be remedied. . . . The important thing to note is that applying them properly depends *on understanding the content*.The fore-conception of completeness that guides all our understanding is, then, always *determined by the specific content*. Not only does the reader assume an immanent unity of meaning, but *his understanding is likewise guided by the constant transcendent expectations of meaning* that proceed from the relation to the truth of what is being said [in the text]." Ibid., 294. Emphasis mine.

42. The third section of this chapter, about the hermeneutical method and the principle of articulation, briefly discusses this issue of the principle of articulation as an ontological reality. See pp. 51-52 in this chapter.

43. For some historical examples, see the next chapter in this study.

44. Traditionally, metaphysics has been identified with the study of general and particular ontologies—God, world, and human being. Metaphysics was subdivided in general metaphysics or ontology, and special metaphysics, encompassing the disciplines of natural theology, rational cosmology, and rational psychology (anthropolo-

element or agent that allows the *many*, through an *articulating action*, to be articulated or united as a totality. In other words, this element articulates the *parts* of a system in a *whole*. The principle of articulation is the essence of a system.[45]

In its operability, the principle of articulation is inseparable from the concept of cognitive system and from the elements that constitute a cognitive system.[46] *Parts* or *many*, *one* or *articulating agent*, *articulating action*, and *whole* are operative components of a phenomenological description of the principle of articulation. Without parts, there is no need or possibility of an articulating agent performing an articulating action in a system. In turn, without articulating agent or action, the parts cannot be a whole and there is no possibility of knowledge in general and scientific, philosophical, or theological knowledge in particular.[47] This inseparability of articulation and system becomes

---

gy). This is the structure of the classical metaphysics of Christian Wolff (1679-1754), and it is the classification used by Kant. See Julián Marías, *Idea de la metafísica* (Buenos Aires, Argentina: Editorial Columba, 1954), 23-25. See also John J. Haldane, "A Thomist Metaphysics," in *The Blackwell Guide to Metaphysics*, ed. Richard M. Gale (Oxford, UK: Blackwell, 2002), 87. In this traditional view, metaphysics is the study of that which is beyond the physical world. Here, however, metaphysics is understood as dealing with the key philosophical problem of the relationship between *the one and the many* or *the whole and the parts*. For an understanding of metaphysics as dealing with this issue, see Edward C. Halper, *One and Many in Aristotle's Metaphysics: The Central Books*, 2nd ed. (Las Vegas, NV: Parmenides, 2005), xxvi; Helena De Preester, "Part-Whole: Metaphysics Underlying Issues of Internality/Externality," *Philosophica* 73 (2004): 27-50; Wolfhart Pannenberg, *Metaphysics and the Idea of God*, trans. Philip Clayton (Edinburgh, Scotland: T. & T. Clark, 1990), 130-152.

45. As Heidegger explains, in relation to the Kantian understanding of reason, "Reason [articulating agent] itself is nothing other than the faculty of system, and reason's interest is concerned with making evident [articulating action] the greatest possible manifold of knowledge [parts or many] in the highest possible unity [whole]. This demand is the essence of reason itself." Heidegger, *Schelling's Treatise*, 37.

46. A cognitive system means a system of knowledge that offers an interpretation of reality. Cognitive systems can take the form of intentional or explicit disciplinary systems such as philosophical, scientific, or theological systems. In this study, theological systems are the focus of interest. As the principle of articulation or systematic presupposition is, however, a presupposition of reason, it is always operative in the process of structuring knowledge in general. Other ways of speech or communication, then, such as literary works, myths and legends, religious texts, such as the Bible, and even oral and written daily ways of communication are implicitly cognitive systems to the extent that they are products of human reason and assume an interpretation of reality as a whole.

47. The principle of articulation provides epistemological and methodological legitimacy to theology. It is not possible to talk about *systematic theology* without

evident in the way in which Kant defines system and identifies the operative components of a system, "By *system* I mean the unity of various kinds of knowledge under *one* idea. This is the concept *given by reason of the form* of the *whole*, in which concept both the extent of its *manifold contents* and the place belonging to each *part* are determined *a priori*."[48] In a system, a principle of articulation (the unity of various kinds of knowledge under one idea) involves parts (manifold contents), an articulating agent (reason with the unifying idea), articulating action (giving the form of a whole), and a whole. Summarizing, then, a phenomenological depiction of the principle of articulation in theology (from the perspective of its operability) involves the parts that have to be articulated, the articulating agent, the articulating action, and the whole that is the result of the articulation.

What are the essential parts that require articulation in a theological system? What is the articulating agent? What is the articulating action of that agent? Finally, what is the whole of a theological system? In the context of this section, the answers do not intend to expose particular interpretations of these basic operative components of the principle of articulation—although in every particular system these elements always appear as already interpreted. The section searches, rather, a

---

some specific understanding of *system* as a fundamental methodological element, providing inner consistency, rationality, and articulation. Tillich suggests, in this sense, "The final expression of consistency in applying methodological rationality is the theological system. If the title 'Systematic Theology' has any justification, the systematic theologian should not be afraid of the system. It is the function of the systematic form to guarantee the consistency of cognitive assertions in all realms of methodological knowledge." Tillich, *Systematic Theology*, 1:58. The systematic character of theology is important because that characteristic connects with its claim of being truth. "The systematic investigation and presentation itself entails also a very specific understanding of truth, namely, truth as coherence, as the mutual agreement of all that is true. Systematic theology ascertains the truth of Christian doctrine by investigation and presentation of its coherence as regards both the interrelation of the parts and the relation to other knowledge." Wolfhart Pannenberg, *Systematic Theology*, vol. 1 (Grand Rapids, MI: Eerdmans, 1991), 22-23.

48. Kant, *Critique of Pure Reason*, 667 [832]. Emphasis mine except in the last case. For an additional exposition of the concept of cognitive system in Kant, see Nicholas Rescher, *Kant and the Reach of Reason: Studies in Kant's Theory of Rational Systematization* (Cambridge, UK: Cambridge University Press, 2000), 64-98. Watson's phenomenological definition of system is simpler than the one of Kant: "A System is a *whole* of *articulated parts*." Watson, "The Meaning," 85. Emphasis mine. Watson's definition, however, does not distinguish between the articulating agent and the articulating action performed by the agent.

phenomenological depiction of the principle[49] to the extent that their basic operative components are "self-evident."[50]

Parts

The description of the theological task, particularly the task of systematic theology as a discipline, involves the study of Christian doctrines. David K. Clark, for example, considers that systematic theology involves the description, interpretation, and application of "Christian doctrines in a comprehensive manner."[51] Similarly, Wolfhart Pannenberg considers that systematic theology deals with Christian doctrine, particularly the "truth of Christian doctrine."[52] Consequently, doctrines are parts that require articulation in a theological system.[53] From a Catholic perspective, Thomas G. Guarino also believes that in spite of the challenges posited by postmodernity to the classical epistemological approach to doctrines, they are still an object of study for systematic theology.[54] Consequently, as Watson summarizes, "In cognitive theological systems, the parts are theological doctrines, ideas, or theories."[55]

Doctrines in theology are not interrelated in an arbitrary way. They have logical connections. Some of them are the foundation for understanding others. Said in another way, some of them work as presuppo-

---

49. By introducing the phenomenological method, Heidegger says that it "does not subscribe to a 'stand-point' or represent any special 'direction'; for phenomenology is nothing of either sort, nor can it become so as long as it understands itself." Heidegger, *Being and Time*, 50. Phenomenology, then, is a descriptive methodology where *phenomenon* means "*that which shows itself in itself*, the manifest." Ibid., 51. Emphasis in original.

50. Ibid., 50.

51. David K. Clark, *To Know and Love God: Foundation of Evangelical Theology; Method for Theology* (Wheaton, IL: Crossway, 2003), 34. In a similar way, Erickson defines theology as "*that discipline which strives to give a coherent statement of the doctrines of the Christian faith*." Erickson, *Christian Theology*, 8. Emphasis in original.

52. Pannenberg, *Systematic Theology*, 48. See also ibid., 17-19. Pannenberg seems to suggest that theology should not simply presuppose the truth of the doctrine but demonstrate it. Still, in doing this demonstration, systematic theology involves the study of Christian doctrines and their interrelationship.

53. As mentioned in the first chapter, a theological system is "a cognitive whole of articulated *theological doctrines*." Watson, "The Meaning," 86. Emphasis mine.

54. See Thomas G. Guarino, *Foundations of Systematic Theology* (New York, NY: T. & T. Clark, 2005).

55. Watson, "The Meaning," 94.

sitions for others. For example, if a given theological system includes a doctrine of sin (hamartiology) and a doctrine of salvation (soteriology), its study is not possible without a previous understanding of the human being (doctrine of man or anthropology), and an understanding of God (doctrine of God or theology proper). The human being is the one who is affected by the problem of sin and is in need of salvation. In turn, God is usually the One who performs salvation.

In a similar way, if a system of theology includes a general doctrine of the last things (eschatology), this doctrine assumes a particular understanding of God and the world, and probably an understanding of the human being too because all of them are "actors" in the development of the last events. A doctrine of revelation, if such a doctrine is part of a theological system, also involves an understanding of God (the Revealer) and of the human being (the one who receives the revelation). In turn, an understanding of the human being cannot be possible in disconnection from a view of the world or understanding of the world as a whole, given the fact that humans are part of the world.

On the other hand, a central issue in theology has always been the study of God (doctrine of God or theology proper).[56] The doctrine of God and His existence work as presuppositions for every other doctrine in Christian theology. Without God, there is no theology at all. The doctrine of God, however, cannot be the only doctrine in theology because in that case, it is not possible to talk about *parts*, and consequently, there is no need or possibility of articulation with other doctrines. In theology, God always relates to the world and human beings.[57] These three elements—God, the world, and the human being—are the basic parts of the system. The specific interpretations about God, the world, and human nature in a theological system are essential to the operation of the system. Any other possible doctrine necessarily relates to or amplifies the interpretation of these three basic *parts* of theology.[58]

---

56. See Erickson, *Christian Theology*, 8; Pannenberg, *Systematic Theology*, 4-8.
57. See Pannenberg, *Systematic Theology*, 49; Erickson, *Christian Theology*, 8.
58. The fundamental role of the interpretations of God, the world, and the human being in theology can explain why from the time of Peter Lombard's *Sentences* (12th century), if not even before, systematic expositions of Christian doctrine have frequently followed a sequence of God-creation (world)-human being. See Gale Heide, *Timeless Truth in the Hands of History: A Short History of System in Theology*, Princeton Theological Monograph Series 178 (Eugene, OR: Pickwick, 2012), 70-72. Something similar occurs with the first part of Aquinas's *Summa Theologica*. After his introduction to sacred doctrine in question 1, Aquinas dedi-

In theological systems, doctrines are interpretations of what is assumed as real. In this sense, theology, as philosophy, searches to provide an understanding of reality as a whole. In philosophy, however, God is only a possible interpretation of what is called the *one* or the principle of articulation, which is susceptible of several different interpretations. In theology, instead, God is assumed as a reality, which is essential in order for theology to be theology. If there is no God, there is no theology. The interpretations of God can vary, but His existence cannot be put into question. The same is valid for the world and the human being.[59] The world and the human being are assumed as realities necessary for theology, although they can be interpreted in different ways. They are not only regulative ideas or presuppositions of the mind.

---

cates questions 2-119 to discuss issues related to the mentioned sequence. Thomas Aquinas *Summa Theologica* (*ST*) (trans. Fathers of the English Dominican Province). In this sense, Guy's appreciation regarding the way to organize systematic theology can be misleading when he affirms that "there is no theologically 'right' way to slice the [theological] pie. . . . Nor is there any proper 'first piece'; one could legitimately begin with the human predicament, the Christian hope, or the mission of Jesus." Guy, *Thinking Theologically*, 207.

59. The fact that Kant (and other philosophers) also considers these three elements as the fundamental parts of an articulated cognitive system is not casual. Classical and modern philosophy have searched to offer an understanding of reality as a whole. In this search, an understanding of the human being, the world, and the articulating element of reality as a whole—the *one*—has been always present. Postmodern philosophy, however, has frequently rejected this possibility of understanding reality as a systematic whole. Nevertheless, from the perspective of the analysis of the structure of reason, it is clear that an implicit understanding of reality as a whole is always present in every product of human reason. See the discussion of the "Whole" in pp. 39-42 in this chapter. In this sense, it is interesting how Tillich defines philosophy. He suggests that the problem with the question about philosophy "lies partly in the fact that there is no generally accepted definition of philosophy. Every philosophy proposes a definition which agrees with the interest, purpose, and method of the philosopher." Tillich, *Systematic Theology*, 1:18. Under these circumstances, he proposes a very broad definition of philosophy as "*that cognitive approach to reality in which reality as such is the object*. Reality as such, or reality as a whole, is not the whole of reality; it is the structure which makes reality a whole and therefore a potential object of knowledge." Ibid. Emphasis in original. It should be said here, however, that in Kant's theoretical philosophy (see footnote 11 in this chapter) the idea of God works as an interpretation of the principle of articulation that other philosophers would refer to only as the *one*. In contrast, in theology, God is not a possible interpretation of a part of the system but a necessary existing reality. Without an understanding of God, there is no *theological* system.

The Articulating Agent

The articulating agent of a system is the element providing articulation and unity. As mentioned, the articulating agent in Kant is reason, particularly the unifying idea of God. Reason is, however, only an interpretation of the principle of articulation in Kant's theoretical philosophy, not a phenomenological fact. In theological systems, instead, given their *theo*-logical character, the articulating agent is necessarily linked to God, who is, in turn, a part of the system. God is the principle of articulation as a phenomenological fact. "No matter how mysterious the connections of things in history and the universe [are], the eternal given of theology is that the man behind the curtain has a name, 'God.'"[60] Of course, in theology there are several possible interpretations of God's reality. Consequently, the particular conception of the articulating agent can vary substantially from one theological system to another. In any case, "the doctrine of God is always the most decisive thing in every theology."[61]

In theology, the articulating agent is frequently named *center*. However, *center* and *articulating agent* are not necessarily the same. While they can match, this is not necessarily the case. As the discussion in the first section of this chapter has shown, the principle of articulation in general is an *a priori* presupposition of reason. As such, it may not be immediately apparent, even for the author of a given theological system. In contrast, centers are frequently conscious—and sometimes arbitrary—elections of the author of a cognitive system. Usually, a center is only a prominent central theme selected in order to present the entire set of doctrines in an organized way.[62] The idea is that the system

---

60. Watson, "The Meaning," 98.
61. Paul Tillich, *A History of Christian Thought: From Its Judaic and Hellenistic Origins to Existentialism* (New York, NY: Simon & Schuster, 1968), 263.
62. Thomas N. Finger, for example, seems to suggest this idea when he explains that "since all of God's acts are interrelated and since theology seeks to correlate them, to some degree, in *synthetic* fashion, all of its doctrines are also interconnected. This fact means that systematic reflection, in principle, may begin with any doctrine. Consequently when we propose an eschatological starting point, *we are merely arguing that it is especially apt for our times, not that it is the only valid one*." Thomas N. Finger, *Christian Theology: An Eschatological Approach*, vol. 1 (Nashville, TN: Thomas Nelson, 1985), 103. First emphasis in original. Second emphasis mine. Curiously, Finger does not see that he himself is suggesting that God is the key element to systematize theology given the interrelation and correlation of His acts. In a similar approach, Erickson suggests that "each theologian must decide on a particular theme

of doctrines should be presented and communicated in an understandable way.[63] As this center does not necessarily derive from an analysis of the presuppositions of reason implicit in a given theological system, the center can be distractive when trying to identify the real articulating agent. Moreover, as an arbitrary selection, a center may disregard certain elements in a system considering them as peripheral, elements that a real articulating agent would be able to include.

In this context, Kant's distinction between *articulation* and *aggregation* is useful. According to Kant, a system is *articulated*, not *aggregated*.[64] The articulating agent, as the core of the principle of articulation, is not an arbitrary choice but an *a priori* assumption. As such, it is not merely a choice. It must be discovered. According to Kant, this articulating idea is frequently very difficult to determine or define even for the creator of a system. This idea, "like a germ, lies hidden in reason."[65] In theological systems, although the articulating agent is always related to God—or even identified with God—the particular interpretation of God involves aspects that are not necessarily obvious for the interpreter.[66]

---

which, for her or him, is the most significant and helpful in approaching theology as a whole." Erickson, *Christian Theology*, 63. Clearly, for Erickson, the central theme is a question of election by the theologian. "What is being pled for here is conscious and competent choice and use of an integrating motif." Ibid.

63. That is the idea of *ordo disciplinae* that Aquinas presented in the prologue to his *Summa*. See Aquinas, *ST*, prologue to the First Part. For a brief discussion of the *ordo disciplinae* see Bernard Lonergan, *Método en Teología*, trans. Gerardo Temolina, 4th ed. (Salamanca, España: Ediciones Sígueme, 2006), 333. The idea that a center is basically an organizing element to facilitate communication and organization seems to be common among several systematic theologians. Lonergan, for example, argues that the purpose of systematization in theology is the promotion of comprehension. Ibid., 324. More explicitly, Erickson suggests that a central motif provides "unity to the system, and thus power to the communication of it." Erickson, *Christian Theology*, 63. Even more, for Erickson, a center may be changed. "The integrative motif may have to be adjusted as part of the contextualization of one's theology." Ibid., 64.

64. Kant, *Critique of Pure Reason*, 668 [832-833].

65. Ibid., 669 [834]. "We shall often find that the originator of a science, and even his latest successors are moving vaguely round an idea which they have not been able to perceive clearly, failing in consequence to determine rightly the proper contents, *the articulation* (systematical unity), and the limits of their science." Ibid. Emphasis mine.

66. This difficulty in determining the articulating principle of a system and the way that this principle articulates the system is because such identification requires an analysis of the presuppositions operating in that system and its interrelationship with the parts. Particularly relevant are the ontological and epistemological assumptions subjacent to the interpretation of God. This identification of the presuppositions requires the application of the hermeneutical methodology, explained in p. 42ff in this

Of course, a so-called *center* can be a valid interpretation of the articulating agent of a given theological system. In that case, however, this center should be able to articulate all the elements of that system. This center or articulating agent should be able to provide a structural articulation at the deepest possible level for all the parts of the system.[67] At the same time, it should be able to articulate the variety in the system. Such an articulating system would avoid a contrived "flattening" of the parts of the system in order to "adjust" them to the articulating agent, or an artificial distinction between center and periphery.[68]

The Articulating Action

These considerations regarding the characteristics of the articulating agent lead directly to the discussion of the articulating action,

---

chapter. According to Kant, the detection of the articulating idea cannot depend on the description of the author of a system, who is not necessarily aware of that idea. "It is necessary, therefore, to explain and determine all sciences, considering that they are contrived from the point of view of a certain general interest, not according to the description given by their author, but according to the idea which, from the natural unity of its constituent parts, we may discover as founded in reason itself." Ibid.

67. In this sense, if the articulating element is understood as part of an *a priori* set of presuppositions, it is not possible to talk about articulation at two levels as Watson suggests, one at the level of external presentation (such as the one observable in the table of contents), and another at the level of the internal structure. A real principle of articulation involves the inner structure of the system, beyond its external organization. See Watson, "The Meaning," 99.

68. The fear of this "flattening" or distinction between *central* and *peripheral* frequently appears among biblical theologians who feel uneasy with the possibility of finding a system in the Bible, or a unifying center, except, maybe, through an inductive methodology. Gerhard F. Hasel, for example, considers that those intending to systematize the Old Testament from the perspective of a specific center, "have to superimpose that center upon the diverse and manifold encounters between God and man over so long a period and are able to deal adequately only with those parts of the rich Biblical witness that fit into the framework of that center, no matter what it is." Hasel, *Old Testament Theology*, 158. In assessing proposed centers for the New Testament, Hasel evaluates them as arbitrary, subjective, and reductionist because they imply a "selective principle in the form of a center either from without Scripture (tradition) or from within Scripture on the basis of which value judgments are made with regard to the content of Scripture as a whole or in its parts." Hasel, *New Testament Theology*, 169-170. In the same line, Gerald A. Klingbeil, another biblical theologian, suggests that "the notion of a central theme tends to 'flatten' the theological panorama and often invites to produce superficial or 'biased' interpretations." Klingbeil, "El santuario, el ritual y la teología," 84. Regarding the rejection of the distinction between *center* and *periphery* in biblical theology, see Hasel, *New Testament Theology*, 142.

as part of the depiction of the principle of articulation. In cognitive systems, the articulating action is the particular "action," function, or role that the articulating agent performs in the system in order to produce articulation. Kant explains the articulating action of reason—the articulating agent—as providing the form of the whole.[69] In a theological system, the articulating action is closely related to the articulating agent. They are inseparable in every theological system. However, they are not the same. It is necessary to distinguish between them because in two different theological systems, the articulating agent can be the same while the articulating action attributed to that agent can be different.

From a cognitive perspective, the articulating action of the articulating agent produces inner consistency, coherence, and wholeness in theological systems.[70] The articulating action is what makes the parts or doctrines constitute a system. Namely, the articulating action is always a systematizing action.[71]

As mentioned above, the articulating agent in theology is always related to God. The diverse interpretations of God condition the interpretation of God's actions and consequently, the interpretation of the articulating action of the system. In theological systems, God articulates the relationship between Himself and the world-humanity.[72] God is a part of the system, but a key part, because He is the part that provides articulation.

The specific action/s that God performs to relate Himself to the world-humanity, according to the interpretation of a theological system, constitute the articulating action/s. In this sense, however, not every action of God regarding the world has the same importance in terms of its articulating role. Some actions are more encompassing than others in articulating a given theological system. Ultimately, the fundamental articulating action of God is the one that provides complete, comprehensive inner consistency, coherence, and wholeness to the theological system that interprets reality.

---

69. See p. 31 in this chapter.
70. See footnote 47 in this chapter.
71. See Kant, *Critique of Pure Reason*, 518-519 [645], 521 [647-648].
72. For an extensive compilation of historical texts regarding the nature of God and God's activities regarding the world, see parts one and two of William Madges, *God and the World: Christian Texts in Perspective* (Maryknoll, NY: Orbis, 1999).

The Whole

The product of the articulation or systematization of the parts or doctrines is a *whole*. The whole is a totality, perceived as such as a result of the articulation, which determines the place of each part or doctrine in the whole. In turn, the parts also determine the whole.[73] In theological systems, the whole frequently remains without identification. However, "the whole is an implicit component of the notion of systems."[74] In theology, the understanding of the *whole* is also closely related to the interpretation of God, who is the one providing articulation and unity to the whole.[75] In other words, the interpretation of the nature of God conditions not only the interpretation of the articulating action but also the interpretation of the whole.

This whole is more than the mere addition or sum of doctrines. In the words of Kant, "The whole [of the system] is articulated (*articulatio*), not aggregated (*coacervatio*)."[76] The theological system is not just a set of doctrines but a united whole. There is a real—systematic—whole when an articulating agent is performing an articulating action. In Kantian terms, this is an *architectonic unity*.[77] It means that this unity or articulation is the result of an *a priori* principle operating as a presupposition.[78] When there is no *articulation* but only *aggregation*, it is only possible to talk about a *technical* unity but not about an

---

73. "The anticipation of meaning in which the whole is envisaged becomes actual understanding when the parts that are determined by the whole themselves also determine this whole." Gadamer, *Truth and Method*, 291.

74. Pannenberg, *Metaphysics and the Idea of God*, 136.

75. Ibid., 142-144. Strictly, Pannenberg believes that in theological systems, God provides unity to the whole, but God is not part of that whole because, according to him, that would mean that God is not infinite. God is the infinite source of unity for the world and the source of the world itself through creation. Consequently, God pre-exists to the finite world. Pannenberg seems to identify the whole of theological systems with the whole of the parts of the world. The problem is, however, that once God has created the world, it is necessary to face the issue of the relationship between God and the world. In this context, God is necessarily a part of the whole of the system, without excluding His infinitude. Of course, here Pannenberg has in mind a particular interpretation of God and the world.

76. Kant, *Critique of Pure Reason*, 668 [832-833]. Emphasis in original.

77. Ibid.

78. Apparently, Kant is appealing to the etymology of the word *architectonic*. As Heidegger explains, for Kant *architectonic* means "*tectonic*—built, joined and *arche*—according to leading and ruling grounds and principles." Heidegger, *Schelling's Treatise*, 37. Emphasis in original.

architectonic unity of the whole.[79] For example, a mere compilation of doctrinal expositions may have technical unity but they do not necessarily constitute a whole because they are not a real system. In a real system, the development of every doctrine assumes the same principle of articulation as a presupposition of reason.

A characteristic of the whole is that, as an articulated cognitive system, it can be more or less complex. The level of complexity of the whole depends on several factors, such as the complexity and quantity of the doctrines, the nature of the articulating agent, and the particular articulating action/s attributed to that agent.[80] Moreover, a cognitive system can be interpreted as *closed* or *open*. In a closed system, the circle of understanding—the interaction between subject and object—is interpreted as having an end. In this interpretation, after successive approaches, the circle finally ceases when the knower understands the object of knowledge in a perfect, complete, or absolute way, in the context of the whole.[81] In contrast, in an open system, the whole is never fully or completely grasped. The knower is not able to know all the

---

79. Kant holds that only when there is an architectonic unity of the whole, it is possible to talk about a scientific system. Kant, *Critique of Pure Reason*, 668 [833].

80. "A complex system is not constituted merely by the sum of its components, but also by the intricate relationships between these components." Paul Cilliers, *Complexity and Postmodernism: Understanding Complex Systems* (London, UK: Routledge, 1998), 2. For an additional discussion regarding complex systems in general, see ibid., 3-5.

81. In anticipation of the discussion of the hermeneutical method in the next section, as well of the application of this method in the following chapters, it is useful to clarify here that, in classical philosophical or theological cognitive systems, such as Aristotelian or Thomistic systems, there is an interpretation of the whole of reality as essentially timeless. This fact seems to be valid regarding modern systems such as the one of Hegel or Schleiermacher. From this perspective, the whole refers to a reality that is ultimately unchangeable and closed. In this case, it would be possible to reach a perfect and completed or finished abstractive (or timeless) understanding of the object of knowledge in the context of the whole. Gadamer refers to this view of the circle of understanding—applied to the interpretation of texts—when he says that "the circular movement of understanding runs backward and forward along the text, and ceases when the text is perfectly understood." Gadamer, *Truth and Method*, 293. He holds that this view is the "nineteenth-century hermeneutic theory." Ibid. Søren Kierkegaard, for example, illustrates this understanding of the notion of system as necessarily closed and timeless when he affirms, "System and closure are pretty much one and the same, so that if the system is not completed there is no system. . . . A half-finished system is nonsense." Søren Kierkegaard, *Concluding Unscientific Postscript to the Philosophical Crumbs* (New York, NY: Cambridge University Press, 2009), 91. Regarding open systems, see footnote 83 in this chapter.

reality encompassed by the whole. In this interpretation of system, the successive approaches of the knower to the object of knowledge—the circle of understanding—produce additional comprehension and realization of the whole as an articulated system.[82] In this sense, there is no point in the process of knowing where it is possible to affirm a perfect understanding of the whole.[83]

In summary, the phenomenological description of the principle of articulation, from the perspective of its operability or functioning in theological systems, involves four aspects. The first one is the *parts or doctrines* of the system, which work based on three basic doctrines that operate as assumed realities: an interpretation of God, the world, and the human being. The second one is the *articulating agent*, which in theological systems is always related or even identified with God. The articulating agent is more than a mere center or prominent topic chosen arbitrarily for the author of a system. The articulating agent may not be obvious and its identification usually requires an analysis of the basic presuppositions of reason, as well as an analysis of the cause of the articulation or coherence among the ideas of reason in general and theological doctrines in particular. The articulating agent

---

82. "The circle of whole and part is not dissolved in perfect understanding but, on the contrary, is most fully realized." Gadamer, *Truth and Method*, 293.

83. Postmodernism rejects the idea of closed and timeless systems because from a postmodern view, reality is essentially temporal, changeable, fragmentary, diverse, and very complex. In consonance, postmodernism rejects the epistemology behind the modern understanding of system according to which "one could supposedly inter-relate the various realms of knowledge into one final whole that depicted the patterns and themes of knowledge generally. The final product was absolute knowledge that was true regardless of circumstance, or 'objective.'" Heide, *Timeless Truth*, 187. See also Guarino, *Foundations of Systematic Theology*, 5-19. In this context, it is easier to understand the postmodern reaction against the great metanarratives of the modernity in general. See Jean-François Lyotard, *The Postmodern Condition: A Report on Knowledge*, trans. Geoff Bennington and Brian Massumi (Manchester, UK: Manchester University Press, 1984), xxiv. The postmodern rejection of closed and timeless systems opens the possibility of an open and temporal system that offers an interpretation of reality as a whole. A system like that, however, is necessarily more complex than a closed one. Paul Cilliers defends that possibility by affirming that the traditional and modern approaches to the systematic whole constitute "an *avoidance* of complexity. The obsession to find one essential [timeless] truth blinds us to the relationary nature of complexity, and especially to the continuous shifting of those relationships. Any acknowledgement of complexity will have to incorporate these shifts and changes, not as epiphenomena, but as *constitutive* of complex systems." Cilliers, *Complexity and Postmodernism*, 112. Emphasis in original.

is able to articulate all the doctrines of the system at the deepest level in spite of its variety.

The third operative component of the principle of articulation is *the articulating action*, closely linked to the articulating agent. This is the particular action or role performed by the articulating agent in order to articulate the system as such. In theology, God performs this action that articulates the relationship between Him and the world-humanity. The fourth operative component of the principle of articulation is the *whole*. It is the product of the articulation. It is more than a set or aggregation of doctrines. It is a systematic whole articulated according to one principle producing unity (architectonic unity). This whole can be very complex and it is possible to interpret it as closed or open. It is closed if its interpretation assumes that it is possible to reach a complete, perfect, or closed knowledge of the whole. It is open if the interpretation of the whole assumes that it is susceptible of additional understanding and realization.

The Hermeneutical Method and the Principle of Articulation

In order to understand the diversity of interpretations regarding the principle of articulation in its basic components—parts-doctrines, articulating agent, articulating action, and whole—it is necessary to apply the hermeneutical method. This method entails determining the presuppositions that operate as basic conditions to interpret the principle of articulation. However, the principle is in itself a basic presupposition of reason. Are there other presuppositions involved in the understanding of the principle of articulation? In that case, what are the presuppositions involved in the interpretation of that principle?

This section introduces the role and levels of presuppositions in theology. It also offers a brief explanation of the fundamental presuppositions of the mind and their basic possible interpretations, which are operative in the interpretation of the principle of articulation in theology. The section also clarifies the difference between the principle of articulation as a presupposition and as a reality. Then the section explains the role of theological sources in the determination of the basic presuppositions of the mind that in turn condition the interpretation of the principle of articulation.

Presuppositions in Theology

Presuppositions are a necessary condition of human knowledge. There is no *presuppositionless* knowledge. The knower has a fore-structure, fore-conception, or set of presuppositions that allow him/her to know. Using Gadamer's vocabulary, the knower has "prejudices."[84] These prejudices or presuppositions are not unmodifiable. An intentional modification of presuppositions implies, however, to be aware of their existence.[85] The knower has to be "open" to what the object of knowledge has to "say." At a technical level, this entails the application of a hermeneutical method.[86]

In theology, there is a growing awareness of the role that presuppositions perform in the development of the theological task. Clark, for example, defines *presupposition* as

> any belief—but especially a belief with a high depth of ingression within a system of thought—that is assumed to be true without an explicit justifying process. It is simply accepted as a given within a worldview, argument, or research program without explicit or previous argumentation or grounding.[87]

Presuppositions in theology are not all of the same kind.[88] As mentioned in Chapter 1, it is possible to talk about the micro, meso,

---

84. While this term usually has a negative sense or meaning, due to the discrediting of the concept during the Enlightenment, for Gadamer, "'prejudice' certainly does not necessarily mean a false judgment, but part of the idea is that it can have either a positive or a negative value." Gadamer, *Truth and Method*, 273. The Enlightenment has installed a "prejudice against prejudice." Ibid., 274. However, prejudices or presuppositions are a *pre-condition* of the understanding. In other words, knowledge is not possible without these pre-conditions. Ibid., 272, 278.

85. Ibid., 269, 270.

86. "A person trying to understand something will not resign himself from the start to relying on his own accidental fore-meanings, ignoring as consistently and stubbornly as possible the actual meaning of the text until the latter becomes so persistently audible that it breaks through what the interpreter imagines it to be. Rather, a person trying to understand a text is prepared for it to tell him something. That is why a hermeneutically trained consciousness must be, from the start, sensitive to the text's alterity. But this kind of sensitivity involves neither 'neutrality' with respect to content nor the extinction of one's self, but the foregrounding and appropriation of one's own fore-meanings and prejudices. The important thing is to be aware of one's own bias, so that the text can present itself in all its otherness and thus assert its own truth against one's own fore-meaning." Ibid., 271-272.

87. Clark, *To Know and Love God*, 309.

88. "The status of a belief as an assumption, however, could be of different kinds." Ibid.

and macro hermeneutical levels of interpretation. This classification implies that there are micro, meso, and macro presuppositions. Micro hermeneutical presuppositions are those operating at the textual or exegetical level of interpretation. For example, a preliminary step in the exegetical process is to establish what the most probable original text is when different manuscripts have divergent readings. A common assumption is the one expressed in the rule that says that "the more difficult reading is to be preferred."[89] Moreover, the identification of the historical and linguistic contexts also pertains to the micro hermeneutical level. A meso hermeneutical presupposition is a theological or doctrinal presupposition. Its scope is wider than the scope of micro hermeneutical presuppositions. Moisés Silva (a New Testament scholar), for example, suggests that biblical interpreters usually have systematic theological presuppositions. "Whether we mean to or not, and whether we like it or not, all of us read the text as interpreted by our theological presuppositions. Indeed, the most serious argument against the view that exegesis should be done independently of systematic theology is that such a view is hopelessly naive."[90] Silva even holds the view that the interpreter should use a conscious and intentional use of those theological assumptions.[91] He illustrates his points: "I would suggest . . . that a student who comes to a biblical passage with, say, a dispensationalist background, should attempt to make sense of the text assuming that dispensationalism is correct."[92]

---

89. Bruce M. Metzger and Bart D. Ehrman, *The Text of the New Testament: Its Transmission, Corruption, and Restoration*, 4th ed. (New York, NY: Oxford University Press, 2005), 302. In a similar way, in textual criticism "the shorter reading is to be preferred." Ibid., 303. For a summary of these rules, see Grant R. Osborne, *The Hermeneutical Spiral: A Comprehensive Introduction to Biblical Interpretation*, 2nd ed. (Downers Grove, IL: InterVarsity, 2006), 62-63.

90. Moisés Silva, "Systematic Theology and the Apostle to the Gentiles," *Trinity Journal* 15, no. 1 (1994): 25. Silva adds, "Exegetes who convince themselves that, through pure philological and historical techniques, they can understand the Bible directly—that is, without the mediation of prior *exegetical, theological,* and *philosophical* commitments—are less likely to perceive the real character of exegetical difficulties." Ibid., 25-26. Emphasis in original. "The very process of understanding depends on our prior framework of interpretation. If we perceive a fact that makes sense to us, the simple reason is that we have been able to fit that fact into the whole complex of ideas that we have previously assimilated." Ibid., 25.

91. "My systematic theology may—indeed, must—inform my exegesis. To put it in the most shocking way possible, my theological system should tell me how to exegete." Ibid., 23.

92. Ibid., 26. Silva does not want to suggest that the interpreter should inten-

Of course, theological presuppositions are also operative in the interpretation of doctrines. As mentioned in relation to the discussion of the parts of the principle of articulation, some doctrines work as assumptions for others. In this sense, the doctrine of God is essential for the interpretation of the rest of the doctrines.

The most encompassing level of presuppositions, however, is the macro hermeneutical one. This level of assumptions also constitutes the most basic level of presuppositions of the mind. Ultimately, every other presupposition in theology connects with this level of presupposition.

Basic Presuppositions of Reason

Probably the contemporary thinker who has better conceptualized the understanding of the basic presuppositions of reason is Canale. He discusses these basic presuppositions in the context of his phenomenological analysis of the structure of reason.[93] Knowledge is possible because there is a relationship between subject ("knower") and object ("known"). This basic relation is an *a priori* condition to any theory about knowledge.[94]

Canale explains the relationship between the subject and the object in terms of what he denominates as *frameworks*. A framework is a structural aspect of the relationship between the subject and the object. These frameworks, ultimately, relate to the most basic types of presuppositions that human reason needs to operate in order to produce knowledge and meaning. The most fundamental framework is the ontological one. This framework refers to the structural aspect of the relationship between the subject and the object whereby the properties of the object

---

tionally misinterpret the text. Instead, the interpreter should "become self-conscious about what we all do anyway." Ibid. However, Silva admits that "when we come across a fact that resists the direction our interpretation is taking, we are better prepared to recognize the anomaly for what it is: an instance in which our interpretive scheme is faulty and must be modified." Ibid., 25.

93. See Canale, *A Criticism of Theological Reason*, 28. Although he follows, to some extent, Nicolai Hartmann's analysis of the structure of reason, Canale also recognizes that at some point Hartmann abandons the rigorous "phenomenological analysis to work from the viewpoint of a particular ontological theory, while at the same time still claiming that his analysis is strictly phenomenological." Ibid., 33, n. 5. In this sense, Canale's phenomenological analysis of the structure of reason is an original contribution that deserves consideration.

94. Ibid., 28-29. See also the first section of this chapter, particularly p. 21.

are communicated to the subject.[95] The ontological framework is an indispensable component of the structure of reason because *thinking* and *being* cannot be separated. This fact means that thinking necessarily involves an understanding of *being in general*[96] or, in other words, an ontology as a presupposition of the knower, an assumed interpretation regarding being. Even more, reason turns around ontology.[97] This basic presupposition is fundamental in the constitution of meaning. Without ontology, there is no meaning. Ultimately, all meaning flows from this basic presupposition.[98] This basic understanding of *being in general* necessarily affects the understanding of *particular beings* or entities such as God, the world, and the human being. It is the most encompassing, universal, and basic presupposition.[99]

The second framework is the epistemological one. It is also a previous condition to any specific subject-object relationship, as an *a priori* condition. As such, it expresses itself in categories whose specific meanings are based on the ontological framework.[100] In other words, the epistemological framework refers to the structural aspect of the relationship between the subject and the object whereby the properties of the object that are communicated to the subject are "processed" by cognitive categories. The interpretation of those properties, through previous epistemological categories, becomes in turn part of the epistemological categories that are used by the knower to interpret objects.[101] These categories involve, besides the ontological presupposition al-

---

95. Canale, *A Criticism of Theological Reason*, 30.
96. Ibid., 35-36.
97. More technically, "Ontology is the center of gravity of reason." Ibid., 36.
98. Ibid., 37-38.
99. Kerbs, *El problema de la identidad*, 33.
100. Canale, *A Criticism of Theological Reason*, 39-40.
101. These categories, Oliver Glanz explains, "can be understood as schemes that are needed to place the properties communicated by the object." Oliver Glanz, "Investigating the Presuppositional Realm of Biblical-Theological Methodology, Part II: Canale on Reason," *AUSS* 47, no. 2 (2009): 223. Glanz also explains that the origin of these categories is found in the previous cognitive activity of the knower in the context of the subject-object relationship. They constitute all the presuppositions, in a broad sense, involving not only logical categories but also sensations, social memories, etc. The past experiences are projected to the present knowledge. At the same time, among the presuppositions within the epistemological framework are found specific interpretations of the ontological and epistemological frameworks (assumed interpretations of being and knowledge) and as it is shown below, of a third framework called the systematic framework. Ibid., 223-224.

ready mentioned, a specific interpretation of the act of knowledge or epistemological presupposition. In other words, the epistemological framework entails an interpretation of what knowledge is; namely, how the mind relates to what *is* (the object).[102]

The relationship between the ontological and epistemological frameworks implies that there is a unity, coherence, or articulation in the cognitive process as a whole. This articulation between the knower and the object is systematic. It produces a system of meaning or significations that are necessarily interrelated.[103] This principle of articulation is the systematic framework,[104] which assumes that the reality of the articulated elements is a whole. The study of the whole is one of the concerns of the discipline traditionally called *metaphysics*, by seeking to elucidate the way in which the different parts of reality are articulated in a unified whole.[105] If the principle of articulation, then, involves the relationship between the ontological and epistemological frameworks,[106] it means that the principle assumes the ontological and epistemological presuppositions that operate as cognitive categories along with the principle of articulation itself. In terms of the basic presuppositions of the mind, then, the understanding of the principle of

---

102. Kerbs, *El problema de la identidad*, 33.

103. Canale, *A Criticism of Theological Reason*, 44.

104. In his dissertation, Canale does not use the term *framework* for the principle of articulation but it is used by Glanz to describe Canale's understanding of reason. Glanz, "Investigating the Presuppositional Realm, Part II," 221ff.

105. Canale, *A Criticism of Theological Reason*, 47-48. See footnote no. 44 in this chapter.

106. The principle of articulation (systematic framework) "holds together the epistemological and ontological framework in unity and coherence." Glanz, "Investigating the Presuppositional Realm, Part II," 221. The principle of articulation or systematic framework is the one that "facilitates the coherent interrelation of the *logos* (i.e., the epistemological framework) and the *ontos* (i.e., the ontological framework)." Sven Fockner, "Reason and Theology: A Comparison of Fernando Canale and Wolfhart Pannenberg" (MA thesis, Andrews University, Berrien Springs, MI, 2008), 17. The frameworks do not exist in themselves, in an abstract way. They always co-appear with concrete interpretations of them. In other words, the distinction between the frameworks and their particular interpretations is only analytical. In practice, there are no frameworks separated from their specific interpretations. They always appear together. Moreover, the distinction between the different frameworks is also analytical. It is possible to distinguish between them in the analysis of particular systems of thoughts, in discourses, or in texts—including the Bible—but in concrete terms, they always appear together, not in a separate way. See Glanz, "Investigating the Presuppositional Realm, Part II," 221; Canale, *A Criticism of Theological Reason*, 46.

articulation or systematic presupposition involves the understanding of the ontological and epistemological presuppositions.

This fact means that the hermeneutical method, applied to the interpretation of the principle of articulation in theological systems, entails an identification of the ontological and epistemological presuppositions underlying the principle itself. Heidegger seems to think in this direction when he affirms, "The possibility of the thought of *something like a system* and the possibility of its starting point and development *have their own presuppositions*. This concerns nothing less than *the interpretation of Being and truth and knowledge* in general."[107]

As products of the human mind, the systems of thought or systems of meaning always assume different interpretations of these basic types of presuppositions, whether they are mythological, philosophical (Greek, modern, or postmodern), scientific, theological, or biblical. These interpretations express themselves in an oral way or in texts.[108] Consequently, this study, in order to understand the interpretations of the principle of articulation in theological systems, needs to do a preliminary identification of the ontological and epistemological presuppositions involved in those interpretations of the principle of articulation.

Basic Interpretations of the Ontological and Epistemological Presuppositions in Theology

It is possible to find two basic interpretations of the ontological presupposition throughout history: timelessness and temporality.[109] The interpretation of being as timeless implies that the interpretation of knowledge is also timeless: knowledge is the "grasping" of a timeless or non-historical abstractive essence or idea of the object of knowledge (timeless epistemological presupposition) by the timeless reason (or soul, as classical philosophy would say) or it is a "processing" of sensory data by timeless structures of the mind, as in Kant. The interpretation of being as temporal, on the contrary, links with an interpretation of knowledge as temporal, historical. The knower interprets the temporal object in terms of his/her own temporal historical background.

---

107. Heidegger, *Schelling's Treatise*, 29. Emphasis mine.
108. Kerbs, *El problema de la identidad*, 36-42.
109. Canale, *A Criticism of Theological Reason*, 74-153.

In turn, the interpretation of the ontological and epistemological presuppositions as either timeless or temporal implies, accordingly, an interpretation of the principle of articulation as timeless or temporal.[110] In theology, the interpretation of being as timeless has had a direct impact on the interpretation of God and His actions, in a departure from the biblical interpretation of God as temporal.[111] Under the leading influence of Greek philosophy, time has been put in virtual opposition with eternity. Eternity is not everlastingness but timelessness.[112] This fact has produced early instances in Christian history of an interpretation of God as unchangeable or immutable and impassible or emotionless. This God is sharply different from the biblical God who changes His mind, participates in history acting in space and time, and demonstrates His feelings.[113] As William C. Placher posits, "This [change] may

---

110. The following chapter illustrates these basic interpretations of the ontological and epistemological presuppositions and their impact on the interpretation of the principle of articulation with historical examples from philosophy and particularly from theology.

111. During the first centuries of Christianity, "theologians had appropriated philosophical ideas from middle Platonism and Stoicism, primarily the language of Being, essence, and substance as the means to designate the one God which was beyond the destruction of time and history. The language of Being led to the classical concept of God as an eternal essence or substance beyond the temporal world." Tyron Inbody, *The Faith of the Christian Church: An Introduction to Theology* (Grand Rapids, MI: Eerdmans, 2005), 93. See also Chapter 3 below.

112. "For Greek thinking in its Platonic formulation there exists between time and eternity a qualitative difference. . . . For Plato, eternity is not endlessly extended time, but something quite different; it is timelessness. Time in Plato's view is only the *copy* of eternity thus understood. How much the thinking of our days roots in Hellenism, and how little in Biblical Christianity, becomes clear to us when we confirm the fact that, far and wide the Christian Church and Christian theology distinguish time and eternity in the Platonic-Greek manner." Oscar Cullmann, *Christ and Time: The Primitive Christian Conception of Time and History*, trans. Floyd V. Filson, 3rd ed. (London, UK: SCM, 1962), 61. Emphasis in original.

113. "Israel worshiped a God who could grow angry, who changed his mind, a God involved in history, who cared so much about one group of people that their apostasies drove him to fits of impatience. The greatest philosophers of Greece spoke of an unchanging divine principle, far removed from our [spatio-temporal] world, without emotion, unaffected by anything beyond itself. Improbably enough, Christian theology came to identify these two as the same God." William C. Placher, *A History of Christian Theology: An Introduction* (Philadelphia, PA: Westminster, 1983), 55. Placher is not alone in his appreciation of this timeless God as non-biblical. Tyron Inbody, a systematic theologian, holds that classical theism supported a "concept of God who is timeless and unrelated to the world in any essential way. *Such a concept is not derived from Scripture or the doctrine of the Trinity*; it is deduced from the as-

be *the single most remarkable thing to have happened* in Western intellectual history."[114]

Cullman notes, in contrast, that in the New Testament, "time and eternity share this time quality. *Primitive Christianity knows nothing of a timeless God.* The 'eternal' God is he who was in the beginning, is now, and will be in all the future, 'who is, who was, and who will be' (Rev. 1:4)."[115] In the same line, Nicholas Wolterstorff, with a more philosophical-systematic approach, argues that in the Bible "it seems evident that the biblical writers regard God as having a time-strand of God's own on which actions on God's part are to be found. . . . The God who acts, in the way in which the biblical writers speak of God as acting, seems clearly to change."[116] The temporal interpretation of God—or at least partially temporal in some cases—has reappeared in modern times, as the following chapters illustrate, but not always from a biblical perspective. In any case, it is still valid to affirm that the two most basic interpretations of God in theology are timelessness and temporality.

In harmony with the two basic assumed ontologies of God, there are two basic methods of interpreting His nature, attributes, and actions. These two basic methods also correlate with the two basic assumed interpretations of knowledge as timeless or temporal. A timeless interpretation of God requires a methodology that denies every temporal-spatial characteristic in God. In this case, for example, biblical affirmations of God's temporality or similitude with His creation must be denied or interpreted in metaphorical terms. On the contrary, a temporal interpretation of God requires a more positive approach to biblical affirmations of God's temporal-spatial characteristics.

In turn, the two basic interpretations of God's ontology and the two basic methods of knowing Him have a significant impact on the interpretation of the principle of articulation in every theological system. A timeless interpretation of God and His actions implies that ultimately, the articulation of reality as a whole is understood from a timeless perspective. On the contrary, a temporal interpretation of

---

sumptions of Greek philosophy. Eternity means timelessness and changelessness, and as a result [classical] theists infer that God is not temporal in any sense and so cannot change in any sense. Time and change are less than real—the really real is beyond time." Inbody, *Faith of the Christian Church*, 94. Emphasis mine.

114. Placher, *A History of Christian Theology*, 55. Emphasis mine.
115. Cullmann, *Christ and Time*, 63. Emphasis mine.
116. Nicholas Wolterstorff, *Inquiring About God: Selected Essays, Volume I*, ed. Terence Cuneo (Cambridge, UK: Cambridge University Press, 2010), 145.

God's nature and actions necessarily entails a temporal understanding of the articulation of reality as a whole.[117]

The Principle of Articulation as a Presupposition and as an Ontological Reality

In the context of the discussion of the hermeneutical method, a brief clarification is useful. So far, the discussion of the principle of articulation has been mainly developed in terms of the principle as a basic presupposition of reason, operative in theology. The hermeneutical method contributes to identifying and clarifying the interpretation of the presuppositions involved in the interpretations of the principle of articulation in theological systems.

Here, however, it is necessary to highlight a fact that has appeared only almost implicitly. The principle of articulation is not only a presupposition of reason but also an ontological reality. From the perspective of the theological systems, the principle is a reality interpreted by the system.

As said, the principle of articulation is one of the epistemological categories "lodged" in the mind of the knower, along with the epistemological and ontological presuppositions. These categories, nevertheless, depend on, or originate in, the ontological framework. The principle of articulation is an interpretation of what is assumed as something actual, which organizes, structures, or articulates reality as a whole. In other words, the principle of articulation implies that the knower assumes that reality itself is articulated by a principle. Reality itself is a system.

Of course, the interpretations of reality can vary substantially from one theological system to another but they still imply that there is an actual *ontological principle* of articulation. The principle as a presupposition articulates what was mentioned before as a *cognitive whole or system*, while the principle as an ontological reality articulates what can be named as an *ontological system*.[118]

A theological system depicting the relationship between God and the world-humanity, then, describes not only imaginary components

---

117. Of course, this section implies certain degree of generalization and simplification. The following two chapters offer examples for qualifying these introductory remarks regarding the basic interpretations of the presuppositions of the mind.

118. See p. 3 in Chapter 1.

of a system but what is assumed to be actual components interpreted by the doctrines of the theological systems, as suggested in the phenomenological depiction of the principle of articulation. Theology is, consequently, an ontological discipline; namely, a discipline that tries to understand reality as a whole.[119] Although in the course of this study the emphasis is on the principle of articulation as a presupposition of theology, this clarification points out that theology deals with realities.

The Principle of Articulation and the Sources of Theology

In the context of the above discussion regarding the epistemological framework, a final important consideration in this section about the hermeneutical method and the principle of articulation is the relationship between the principle of articulation and the sources of theology. The sources of a theological system refer to the origin of theological knowledge. The matter of the sources is the most fundamental issue in the context of which it is necessary to interpret the epistemological presupposition. The interpretation of the epistemological presupposition relates systematically to the interpretation of the ontological presupposition and the principle of articulation. Consequently, the interpretation of the principle of articulation of a cognitive theological system, which in turn interprets reality as a whole, depends extensively on the sources involved in the development of that system.

Christian theology, throughout history, has admitted a variety of sources in the process of theological building. While Scripture has been considered as an important—and in some cases the only—source for theology, other sources have frequently played an important role in theology as well. "One characteristic of Catholic theology, as distinct from most Protestant theology, is its adherence to tradition as a divinely authoritative norm."[120] From Dulles's Catholic post-critical theological

---

119. This feature of theology is shared with philosophy. "Philosophy necessarily asks the question of reality as a whole, the question of the structure of being. Theology necessarily asks the same question, for that which concerns us ultimately must belong to reality as a whole; it must belong to being." Tillich, *Systematic Theology*, 1:20-21. "The structure of being and the categories and concepts describing this structure are an implicit or explicit concern of every philosopher and of every theologian. Neither of them can avoid the ontological question." Ibid., 21. Of course, Tillich has in mind a particular interpretation of ontology and of God's ontology.

120. Dulles, *The Craft of Theology*, 87.

perspective, tradition includes not only the so-called apostolic tradition but also liturgy and "the sense of the faithful,"[121] which is the result of the indwelling by the believer in the religious community. For Dulles, Scripture and tradition are inseparable from the magisterium of the church.[122] On the other hand, Dulles holds that "it is impossible to carry through the project of systematic theology without explicit commitment to particular philosophical options."[123]

However, this multiplicity of sources—Scripture, tradition, and philosophy—is far from being exclusive of Catholic theology. In line with John Wesley's quadrilateral, for example, Protestant theologian Alister E. McGrath considers the following as sources of theology: Scripture, reason, tradition, and experience.[124] Grant R. Osborne, an evangelical scholar, includes Scripture, tradition, community, experience, and philosophy among the components of systematic theological constructions.[125] Stanley J. Grenz, a postmodern evangelical scholar, proposes "the Bible as canonized by the church,"[126] tradition as shown in church history, and "the thought-forms of contemporary culture."[127] In a similar vein, Macquarrie includes experience, revelation, Scripture, tradition, and culture among the formative factors in theology.[128]

This landscape regarding the potential sources of theology suggests that the interpretations of the principle of articulation can be

---

121. Ibid., 8-9.

122. "Since the three are reciprocally coinherent, no one of them can be used as a totally independent source to judge or validate the other two. Scripture has no normative value except as read in the light of tradition and under the vigilance of the magisterium." Ibid., 98.

123. Ibid., 119. See also ibid., 119-133. Besides Dulles's discussion about the relationship of theology and philosophy, see Guarino, *Foundations of Systematic Theology*, 39-71.

124. Alister E. McGrath, *Christian Theology: An Introduction*, 2nd ed. (Oxford, UK: Blackwell, 1997), 181. See also ibid., 181-235.

125. Osborne, *The Hermeneutical Spiral*, 376-386. Regarding this list of components, Osborne comments, "Many factors intersect in theological decisions, and each plays an important role in the process. It is commonly assumed in evangelical circles that only the first—Scripture—is valid, and that the others are barriers rather than positive components of theological construction. Yet this is untrue. Each aspect is an important ingredient in the theological mix, and each one carries certain dangers that we must avoid." Ibid., 376.

126. Stanley J. Grenz, *Theology for the Community of God* (Grand Rapids, MI: Eerdmans, 1994), 16.

127. Ibid., 18, 19. See the entire discussion in ibid., 14-20.

128. Macquarrie, *Principles of Christian Theology*, 4-18.

as varied as the theological sources involved in a theological system. The theologian can combine the sources in various ways and proportions resulting in diverse theological systems, each one with different interpretations of the principle of articulation. Moreover, the variety is a result of the fact that those sources do not necessarily assume the same basic presuppositions of reason in the interpretation of the principle of articulation of reality as a whole—or they do not even share the interpretation of the basic presuppositions of the mind in general. Consequently, in order to articulate the data of the diverse sources in one system (with one principle) it is necessary that in the process of theological construction, those theologians using more than one source give practical priority to some sources (or even to one source) over the others. This priority is unavoidable because it is not possible to assume more than one principle of articulation at the same time by the same knower (theologian). More than one principle would imply more than one (theological) system of thought with diverse interpretations of reality as a whole.

In this sense, the affirmation of one source in a theological system as the only valid one or the affirmation of the priority of one source over others is not enough to determine the origin of the presuppositions involved in a theological system. An example can help. A theological system can claim the priority of Scripture over tradition or even the exclusivity of Scripture in the interpretation of the principle of articulation. However, it is necessary to clarify if the interpretation of Scripture is made in the light of its own ontological and epistemological presuppositions or in the light of the presuppositions involved in other sources such as philosophy or tradition. In the latter case, the theologian is able to articulate the data from more than one source in a whole, by re-interpreting the presuppositions of one source—in this case, Scripture—in the light of the presuppositions of another source, which for practical purposes implies that this source has the priority over Scripture. Moreover, for a system affirming the exclusivity of Scripture in the interpretation of the principle of articulation, the use of extra-scriptural presuppositions entails that Scripture is not really the only source of that theological system. In the context of the application of the hermeneutical method, therefore, it is necessary to consider the explicit or implicit use of sources in a particular system of theology. This consideration facilitates the identification and clarification of the interpretation of the principle of articulation operating in that system.

The Model Method and the Principle of Articulation: Additional Remarks

Although the model method in theology in general has been already explained in the methodology section of the first chapter, some additional remarks are necessary here. As said, the evaluation of the Adventist models interpreting the principle of articulation is carried out in relation to the *sola Scriptura* principle.[129] The first part of the historical chapter is intended to provide a background in order to understand the possible connections between the interpretations of the principle of articulation within the models in Christian theology in general and some of the interpretations of this principle in current Adventist theology. In this sense, the selection of the historical models in Christianity in general is not arbitrary. Besides covering the most representative interpretations of the principle of articulation in Christian theology throughout history, the hierarchical model of medieval Catholicism, the soteriological model of the Protestant Reformation, and the panentheistic model of modern theology represent—implicitly and explicitly—three different attitudes regarding the interpretation of the principle of articulation in the light of the *sola Scriptura* principle.[130] Additionally, the Adventist pioneers' reaction in relation to the traditional interpretations of the principle of articulation can be seen in the light of their positioning with respect to that principle.

Regarding the selection of the Adventist models evaluated in Chapter 4, the selection is not arbitrary either. They also cover the most important interpretations of the principle of articulation in current Adventist theology. Additionally, the evangelical Adventist model, the modern Adventist model, and the Adventist theodicy model represent different attitudes toward the *sola Scriptura* principle. The contrasting or comparing of the historical models can illuminate the origin of the interpretation of the principle of articulation in each model.

In connection with the organization of the discussion of each

---

129. See the following section in this chapter, pp 56-58.
130. Grenz, for example, suggests that the theological method during the Middle Age included the affirmation of Scripture—interpreted by the church's magisterium—and the tradition accepted by the church. The Protestant Reformation affirmed the *sola Scriptura* principle and post Reformation has gone in the direction of a pluralistic understanding of the sources of theology. See Grenz, *Theology for the Community of God*, 16. The landscape is more complex, however, than this schematic depiction, as the following chapter illustrates.

model, the phenomenological description of the principle of articulation offers the structure to follow in the discussion of each model. In each model, it is necessary to identify the interpretation of the operative components of the principle of articulation: parts, articulating agent, articulating action, and the understanding of the whole. At the same time, in the light of the background provided by the discussion about the hermeneutical method, it is clear that at least a summarized identification of the basic presuppositions of reason that underlay the interpretation of the principle of articulation is necessary. Namely, a discussion of the ontological and epistemological presuppositions must precede the identification of the operative components.

A warning is important here, however. In practice, the presentation of the order of the mentioned elements—ontological and epistemological presuppositions, operative components of the principle of articulation—is not the order in which they appear or manifest in the texts of the different thinkers or theologians. Sometimes, there is some overlap in the presentation of these issues in a given author. In theology, for example, the ontological presuppositions are usually detected in connection with the doctrine of God. This is only natural considering that "the doctrine of God is the most important from the standpoint of ontology, since God is the ultimate reality, the source and sustainer of all that is."[131] For that reason, the description of those elements—presuppositions and components of the principle—is necessarily flexible in its organization, and some overlap may appear.

The *Sola Scriptura* Principle as a Criterion of Evaluation for the Models

The *sola Scriptura* principle is the chosen criterion of evaluation for the models that interpret the principle of articulation in theological systems. This principle assumes that only Scripture is the authoritative foundation for theology in its totality (*tota Scriptura*). Any other source of knowledge lies under the authority of the Bible (*prima Scriptura*).[132] Moreover, its authority resides in its unique divine authorship,[133]

---

131. Erickson, *Christian Theology*, 424.
132. See footnote 38 in Chapter 1.
133. See Richard M. Davidson, "Biblical Interpretation," in *Handbook of Seventh-day Adventist Theology*, ed. Raoul Dederen (Hagerstown, MD: Review & Herald, 2000), 60-64.

which results in its inner systematic consistency as a whole.[134] This inner consistency implies that there is only one principle of articulation underlying biblical theology.

The application of the *sola Scriptura* principle as a criterion for the evaluation of the models in this study requires some additional clarification in the context of this chapter. As said, this study does not follow an inductive or exegetical approach. This study, rather, concentrates on the macro hermeneutical level and uses a systematic approach. Considerations at the theological level of interpretation (meso) or even at the exegetical one (micro) appear but mainly in connection with the discussion regarding the macro hermeneutical level. This is particularly true regarding Chapter 3, the historical chapter, and Chapter 4, which analyzes and evaluates the interpretation of the principle of articulation in current Adventist theology. Chapter 5 offers a proposal of interpretation of the principle of articulation in Adventist theology; it also focuses on the macro level but has a broader interaction with the findings of biblical and systematic theology that contribute to the elaboration of a proposal in harmony with the *sola Scriptura* principle.

As the principle of articulation is in itself a presupposition of reason that involves other presuppositions—ontological and epistemological—the evaluation of the models in Chapter 4 fundamentally encompasses those presuppositions, in order to determine if they have a scriptural origin. The application of the hermeneutical method allows tracing back the origin of the presuppositions involved in the interpretation of the principle of articulation and, consequently, determining if they derive from Scripture or from other sources. Given the systematic relationship among the three basic presuppositions, the eventual assumption of extra-biblical presuppositions at the ontological or epistemological level necessarily leads to a non-biblical interpretation of the principle of articulation in its operative components. In this sense, the historical chapter provides a useful background in order to determine the potentially non-biblical origin of the presuppositions involved in the interpretation of the principle of articulation in Adventist theology and the potentially non-biblical origin of the interpretations of the principle itself. On this basis, it is possible to evaluate the Adventist models in the light of the *sola Scriptura* principle in Chapter 4. At the

---

134. "The consistency of Scripture is an essential part of the inherent canonicity of the books of Scripture as the canon is viewed as a whole." Peckham, "The Canon and Biblical Authority," 243.

same time, the findings achieved regarding the study of the Adventist models and their conformity (or not) to the *sola Scriptura* principle allow clarifying what elements of those models can be integrated or must be rejected in order to propose a biblical interpretation of the principle of articulation.

A last remark is necessary here. In the process of analysis and evaluation, it is also possible to find some inconsistencies that distort the harmonic interrelationship among presuppositions. From the perspective of the *sola Scriptura* principle, those inconsistencies in a model suggest that the model is not biblical or at least not completely biblical because the *sola Scriptura* principle itself assumes the consistency and coherence of Scripture as a whole.

Conclusion

This chapter has elaborated some introductory concepts and presented some methodological remarks in order to clarify the discussion in the following chapters. As a result, it is possible to make some conclusive comments. First, the chapter shows that the principle of articulation has an essential role in the context of the structure of knowledge in general.

Second, the articulating principle in theology is more than a mere center imposed by the author of a theological system. The phenomenological description of the principle of articulation in theology allows perceiving that the principle is a complex structure. As mentioned in this chapter, the structure of the principle involves four basic operative components: parts or doctrines (God, world, and human being), articulating agent (related to God), articulating action (a divine action articulating the relationship between God and the world), and the whole (resulting from the articulating action).

Third, the discussion about the hermeneutical method leads to conclude that the role of presuppositions in theology cannot be ignored. At the macro hermeneutical level of interpretation, the identification of the ontological and epistemological presuppositions is basic to understanding the interpretation of the principle of articulation in theological systems. In connection with the epistemological presuppositions, a first issue to be solved is the sources of theological knowledge, which condition the interpretation of the principle of articulation. As said in this chapter, throughout history, theologians have used diverse sources to elaborate theology that may involve extra-biblical macro hermeneutical presuppositions. As *sola Scriptura* works as the basic criterion for the evaluation of Adventist theological models of interpretation of the principle of articulation in this study, it is necessary to establish if these models have borrowed extra-biblical presuppositions from the historical models in Christian theology. The findings of this course of action are important to pave the way for the elaboration of an interpretation proposal that aims to be more consistent with Scripture.

Finally, considered as a whole, this chapter shows the necessity of multiple methods in order to facilitate the understanding and evaluation of the principle of articulation in Adventist theology, and the elaboration of a proposal in harmony with the *sola Scriptura* principle. The phenomenological method provides an accurate description of the principle of articulation in theology in its operative components. The hermeneutical method helps to discover the presuppositions involved in the interpretation of the principle of articulation. Finally, the model method simplifies the comparisons, contrasts, and correlations between the various interpretations of the said principle.

CHAPTER THREE

The Principle of Articulation in Christian and Adventist Theological History

Introduction

The purpose of this chapter is to present a brief review of the interpretations of the principle of articulation in Christian and Adventist early theological history. The first section offers a discussion of the Greek philosophical background operative in Christian theological history. The second section discusses the interpretations of the principle of articulation in medieval Christianity, particularly in Augustine and Aquinas. The third section discusses the interpretation of the principle of articulation in the Protestant Reformation, specifically in Luther and Calvin. The fourth section offers a brief landscape of the understanding of the principle of articulation in modern theology, based mainly on Schleiermacher and process theology. This discussion, however, is illustrative rather than exhaustive. It is intended to facilitate the understanding of the contrast to—or even the conflict with—the interpretation of the principle of articulation in Adventist theological history.

The last section offers a general view of the Adventist interpretation of that principle among the Adventist pioneers until the beginning of the 20th century. The main expositor referred to here—although not the only one—is Ellen G. White. In this way, it is possible to see the contrast between Christian tradition in general and the Adventist pioneers' interpretation. The section also highlights some attempts to change that interpretation. In the general context of this study, this chapter introduces the necessary historical background to perform the analysis and evaluation of the current Adventist interpretations of the principle of articulation. At the same time, the chapter involves the application of the methodologies already explained in Chapter 2.

The Greek Philosophical Background

While western philosophy as a discipline is considered as starting with Thales of Miletus,[1] the most important pre-Socratic philosopher from the perspective of metaphysics is, undoubtedly, Parmenides. Greek philosophy was interested since its inception about the relation between "the One and the Many."[2] Greeks could perceive that reality is changeable, mutable. Things not only change their location; there is also a change in quality, quantity, and substantiality (generation, corruption). What was the unifying factor of reality? The Greeks wanted to know what the permanent and immutable root of reality is, what the substratum of reality is, the unifying element.[3] The first philosophers tried to find that unifying element in different physical or cosmological elements such as water (Miletus), air (Anaximenes), or more abstract principles such as the *apeirón* (substance without limits according to Anaximander) or numbers (Pythagoreans).[4]

Parmenides

Ontology and epistemology. Parmenides (6th to 5th century BC), however, was going to propose the most influential solution in the history of philosophical and theological thought.[5] In his poem *On Nature*, Parmenides proposes that the solution is the *being*.[6] Parmenides discovered that things consist of or are something. All things have in common that they *are*. Being is the consistency of things.[7] Being is the real substratum of reality. Parmenides describes being and enumerates its *signs* or characteristics. However, in order to understand them, it is necessary to clarify the way to the knowledge that implicitly reveals something of Parmenides's understanding of reality as a whole. In the

---

1. Frederick Copleston, *A History of Philosophy* [three vols. in one book], vol. 1, *Greece and Rome* (Garden City, NY: Image, 1985), 24.
2. Ibid., 77.
3. Marías, *History of Philosophy*, 12-13.
4. Copleston, *Greece and Rome*, 22-37. See also Michael C. Stokes, *One and Many in Presocratic Philosophy* (Washington, DC: Center for Hellenic Studies, 1971).
5. Marías, *History of Philosophy*, 20.
6. Parmenides's poem has been reconstructed based on posterior quotations. Here, fragments (fr.) are quoted from Geoffrey S. Kirk, John E. Raven, and Malcolm Schofield, *The Presocratic Philosophers: A Critical History With a Selection of Texts*, 2nd ed. (Cambridge, UK: Cambridge University Press, 1983), 241-255.
7. See Marías, *History of Philosophy*, 23-24.

poem, a goddess says to Parmenides that there is a first *way of truth*, or persuasion, and a second way, which, strictly speaking, is impracticable for the simple reason that what does not exist cannot be known; namely, "what is not."[8]

But there is a third way that is the *way of opinion* which is followed by the unreliable mortals. This way is the one of those who believe that the first two ways are possible, not only the first one. It is the way followed by mortals who know nothing and for whom "to be and not to be are the same."[9] The way of truth is the way of reason (*nous* or mind), but the way of opinion is the way of the senses or sensory perception.[10] The way of truth is the only possible one in order to know being. The senses can perceive what is mutable, temporal, corruptible, and multiple. Being, though, has attributes that are only discernible by reason, which is akin to being.[11]

Parmenides explains being's attributes, signs, or *predicates* in opposition to or through the negation of what the senses perceive. Being is uncreated, imperishable, a homogeneous whole, immutable, and perfect. It is timeless or existing in an eternal *now*.[12] It cannot have a beginning or an end because that would imply that there is change in being and being is actually changeless. It is absolutely and completely, or it is not at all. It is undivided, full of being, unmoved, and all continuous. Being encompasses all and is like a homogeneous spherical bulk.[13]

---

8. See fr. 2, p. 245; fr. 1, p. 243; Marías, *History of Philosophy*, 21.

9. See fr. 1, p. 243; fr. 6, p. 247.

10. This is the most usual interpretation of Parmenides's two ways. See Marias, *History of Philosophy*, 21. This was also the interpretation of Simplicius, a Neoplatonic philosopher of the 6th century who quotes Parmenides's fragment 8. See Kirk, Raven, and Schofield, *The Presocratic Philosophers*, 254.

11. See fr. 8 (32-49), p. 252. In the words of Marías, being and the *nous* or mind "are seen to be essentially related, and the one does not occur without the other." Marías, *History of Philosophy*, 23.

12. See fr. 8 (1-4), p. 248; fr. 8 (5-21), p. 249. Parmenides states about being, "It never was nor will be, since it is now, all together, one, continuous." Ibid. Michael C. Stokes argues that Parmenides's being is temporal because the Greek for *now* is a time word. Stokes, *One and Many*, 129. See also Leonardo Tarán, "Perpetual Duration and Atemporal Eternity in Parmenides and Plato," *The Monist* 62 (1979): 43-53. However, being does not have a past or future. Against the temporality of Parmenides's being, see Richard M. Gale, "Time, Temporality, and Paradox," in *The Blackwell Guide to Metaphysics*, ed. Richard M. Gale (Oxford, UK: Blackwell, 2002), 67; Kirk, Raven, and Schofield, *The Presocratic Philosophers*, 250-251; Gwilym E. L. Owen, "Plato and Parmenides on the Timeless Present," *The Monist* 50 (1966): 317-340.

13. See fr. 8 (5-21), p. 250; fr. 8 (22-25), fr. 8 (26-31), p. 251; pp. 250-251; fr. 8

Parmenides is probably the first philosopher who explicitly provides an interpretation of being. It is timeless, one, simple, immaterial, and immutable. It is in sharp contrast to the apparent reality observable through the senses. This apparent reality is temporal, multiple, and changeable. Being is the denial of this reality. This basic understanding of being is, then, inseparable from the basic method for interpreting being. Parmenides's way of truth is what would be later denominated the *via negativa* or *negative way* used in Christian theological tradition to understand the being of God. This *via negativa* is the procedure according to which being is interpreted by denying the features of the things that are perceived by the senses.[14]

The principle of articulation. Parmenides's understanding of being as timeless and immutable would naturally lead to a hierarchical interpretation of the articulation of reality as a whole. Being, which is one, is what actually *is*. The sensory world, temporal and multiple, is virtually unreal.[15] As the real being is one, and there is no multiplicity, the problem of the articulation between the one and the many or the whole and the parts still does not emerge for Parmenides. However, "in Parmenides's thinking we see already beginning the division between the two worlds, the world of truth and the world of appearances (opinion or *doxa*); the latter world is false when it is taken as true reality. This division comes to be decisive in Greek thought."[16]

Plato

The hierarchical understanding of reality as a whole is even clearer for Plato (ca. 427-347 BC). Parmenides's understanding of being did not allow for a reasonable explanation of the possibility of multiplicity, change, and time. After him, then, Greek philosophy would try to find a solution to this problem.[17] Plato is a typical example.

(32-49), pp. 252-253.

14. Kerbs, *El problema de la identidad*, 71. For the use of the *via negativa* in Christian theology, see examples in Frederick Copleston, *A History of Philosophy* [three vols. in one book], vol. 2, *Augustine to Scotus* (Garden City, NY: Image, 1985), 26-27, 36, 93-95, 118-119, 348-350, 358, 394-395, and this chapter.

15. Parmenides's denial of the temporal world is so strong that it has been interpreted as virtually a monism rather than a dualism. Kirk, Raven, and Schofield, *The Presocratic Philosophers*, 249.

16. Marías, *History of Philosophy*, 23.

17. Ibid., 44.

Ontology and epistemology. Plato's Allegory of the Cave is very illustrative of his interpretation of being and knowledge.[18] Plato compares humans in general with those living in a prison in a subterranean cavern. The people there are immobilized during their entire lives in such a way that they can only see the bottom of the cave and the shadows projected there by an external light. This prison represents the world or region of sight, the corporeal or visible world. In turn, Plato compares the upper or external world—the one that an escaped prisoner discovered in the allegory—with the intellectual world or intelligible region.[19] The upper world is the world of ideas.[20] It is possible to know the world of the senses through the way of opinion (*doxa*), while the upper world is knowable through the way of the real knowledge (*episteme*).[21] The real knowledge is the knowledge of ideas.[22] This way of knowledge is opposite to the way of opinion, which is interested in sensible things.[23] For Plato, the knowledge of ideas implies—as in Parmenides—the denial of the information coming from the senses; that is to say, the application of the *via negativa* to the features of the world of appearances. The ideas are archetypes of particular things. They are the real being of things.[24] Plato attributes to the ideas the same characteristics that Parmenides attributes to being. They are *one*, *changeless*, and *eternal* or timeless.[25]

In harmony with his theory of ideas, Plato's cosmology affirms that the sensible world is a movable image of eternity and time is a

---

18. Plato *The Republic* 514-517 (trans. Shorey).
19. Ibid., 517b; 532d. In this allegory, it is clear that Plato's ontology and epistemology are inseparable—as in every system of thought. See Copleston, *Greece and Rome*, 142-143.
20. For an explanation of the theory of ideas, see Copleston, *Greece and Rome*, 163-206.
21. Plato emphasizes this distinction between the two worlds in his analogy of the divided line. Plato *The Republic* 509d-511e. See a discussion in Copleston, *Greece and Rome*, 151-154.
22. Plato describes this knowledge as "the soul's ascension to the intelligible region [the intellectual world]." Plato *The Republic* 517b. This *ascension*, however, is equivocal or non-literal language because the ideas are timeless and motionless as the following discussion shows.
23. Ibid., 509-511.
24. There are ideas of human beings, animals, geometrical shapes, and even values. Regarding living creatures, see Plato *Timaeus* 30-31 (trans. Bury) and Plato *Phaedo* 78e (trans. Fowler). In relation to geometrical shapes, see Plato *The Republic* 511c-d. Regarding values, see, for example, Plato *Parmenides* 130b (trans. Fowler).
25. Marías, *History of Philosophy*, 47. For Plato, *eternal* is equivalent to *timeless*.

creation of the Demiurge or God. Motion only exists in time, not in eternity.[26] The timeless ideas provided the model for the creation of the temporal things by the Demiurge. The physical world has a soul and the world is the body of that soul. This creation is not *creatio ex nihilo* but from previous materials. The Demiurge is more like an artisan working on the original matter.[27]

Plato's anthropology is dualistic. Humans are a compound of soul and body. The soul is preexistent. Before its incarnation in a body, the soul has been in the world of ideas where it contemplated them.[28] After death, the soul still survives in an independent way. The ideal life, then, is the life of the philosopher, whose life is a preparation for death. The philosopher searches real knowledge in total detachment from corporeal senses in order to reach the timeless and immaterial truth.[29]

The principle of articulation. The particular objects of the world of the senses have their unity in their correspondent ideas.[30] There is one idea for each kind of sensible thing. In turn, the ideas are organized in a hierarchical order where the ultimate idea is the idea of good. In this way, while the timeless ideas contain the *beings* of the particular temporal things, the good contains the being of the ideas. The good is the idea of the ideas by giving its being to the other ideas.[31]

While the notion of hierarchy refers to the principle of articulation of the Platonic system from the perspective of the whole, the ultimate agent producing articulation or unity is the supreme idea of good.[32] Particular things of the sensible world, however, only exist by *participation* or *imitation* of the ideas,[33] which is the articulating "action" of the ideas. Particular things, therefore, are not completely real in themselves. They are at the bottom of the hierarchy, while the idea of good is at the top of it. This hierarchy, then, goes from what is temporal and "less real" at the bottom part toward what is timeless

---

26. Plato *Timaeus* 37d-38a.
27. Ibid., 29a-c; 30c-36b; 47e-48a; 52d-53b.
28. Plato *Phaedrus* 245c-249a (trans. Fowler). Plato actually believes in cycles of reincarnation.
29. Plato *Phaedo* 64c-67d.
30. Plato *The Republic* 596a-b.
31. Ibid., 517b-c. See Marías, *History of Philosophy*, 46-47, 53.
32. In this sense, "Plato saw clearly that the plurality of Ideas needs some principle of unity." Copleston, *Greece and Rome*, 167, 175, 178.
33. See, for example, Plato *Parmenides* 132d.

and "more real" in the upper part, culminating with the idea of good.[34] This is Plato's answer to the question of the relationship between the one and the many.

Aristotle

Aristotle (384-322 BC), Plato's most important disciple, modified the Platonic hierarchical understanding of the principle of articulation of reality as a whole. Aristotle questioned the concept of participation or imitation as unclear. The ideas, as immutable essences, were unable to produce motion or change in sensible things. Aristotle also criticized that Plato separated the ideas from the things themselves.[35]

Ontology and epistemology. In contrast, Aristotle proposed interpreting the *idea* as the *form* or essence of the *matter* (hylomorphic theory). In other words, particular things are a compound of two basic inseparable elements: matter and form.[36] The form is the universal element in the particular thing, its essence, but instead of being separated from the particular thing—as in Plato's forms—form is in the thing itself, determining what the thing is. In this sense, all the particular elements of the sensory world are real beings, in contrast to Parmenides and Plato. Aristotle, then, is able to recognize a multiplicity of beings. All of them, however, are one in an *analogical* way because all of them are one regarding one principle. That principle is the *substance*.[37]

The matter and the form that make up particular things have their unity, thus, in the substance. The substance is, first, the concrete, individual thing.[38] In a more important way, however, substance is the form itself, the essence that gives to the form-matter compound its being. What makes the difference among beings of the same kind—for example, horses of different colors—is not the form but the matter, which is the prin-

---

34. The ideas are, for Plato, the "true being, [remaining] always the same." Plato *Phaedo* 78d.

35. Aristotle *Metaphysics* 987b, 1045b, 991a, 1039a-b, 1078b (trans. Tredennick).

36. Ibid., 1029a, 1039b, 1058b, 1070a.

37. "'Being' is used in various senses, but always with reference to one principle [substance]." Aristotle *Metaphysics* 1003b. Regarding the concept of substance in Aristotle, see William K. C. Guthrie, *A History of Greek Philosophy*, vol. 6, *Aristotle: An Encounter* (Cambridge, UK: Cambridge University Press, 1981), 100-105.

38. See, for example, Aristotle *On the Soul* 412a (trans. Hett). In his *Categories*, Aristotle calls this specific definition of substance as primary substance. Aristotle *The Categories* 5.2a (trans. Cooke).

ciple individualizing the concrete thing.³⁹ In living creatures, the form of the body is the soul—whether plants, animals, or human beings.⁴⁰

The form, however, can be "separated" from the matter only by an abstraction of the mind.⁴¹ This abstraction implies, once again, the *via negativa*, the negation of the material-temporal element of the compound that allows reaching the real knowledge, the knowledge of the essence or timeless element in the object: the form.⁴² The form has similar characteristics to the being of Parmenides and the ideas of Plato. It is indivisible, ingenerated, and incorruptible, which for Aristotle implies that it is eternal or timeless.⁴³ The matter changes but the form is unchangeable.⁴⁴

How the motion of particular things is possible if they contain an unchangeable form? For Aristotle, being is expressed in different *modes*.⁴⁵ Among them, being can be in potentiality (or potency) and in actuality (act). Potentiality refers to the possibilities of a particular being, while actuality is the realization of that possibility. For example, an egg is potentially a chicken but an egg in actuality. Potentiality is ascribed to the matter, while actuality is related to the form.⁴⁶ Motion is the passing from potentiality to actuality.⁴⁷ The potentiality that lies in the matter constitutes the principle of change or motion. Without potentiality—and matter—there is no motion.⁴⁸ Motion implies some incompleteness or imperfection because actualization is still not achieved.⁴⁹

---

39. Aristotle *Metaphysics* 1070a, 1034a, 1058b, 1069b, 1074a.

40. For Aristotle's explanation of his understanding of soul in plants, animals, and human beings, see Aristotle *On the Soul* 412a-416b, 432a-433b.

41. See, for example, Aristotle *Metaphysics* 1061a-b; Aristotle *On the Soul* 427a-432a. Regarding the Aristotelian theory of abstraction, see Copleston, *Greece and Rome*, 303; Ignacio Miralbell, "La teoría aristotélica de la abstracción y su olvido moderno," *Sapientia* 63, no. 223 (2008): 3-27; Guthrie, *Aristotle: An Encounter*, 100-105; Canale, *A Criticism of Theological Reason*, 93-95.

42. Strictly speaking, Aristotle considers that matter is unknowable in itself. It can be known to the extent that it is part of the compound matter-form. See Aristotle *Metaphysics* 1039b-1040a. See also Copleston, *Greece and Rome*, 305-306.

43. Aristotle *Metaphysics* 1034a-b, 1039b.

44. See, for example, ibid., 1070a; Aristotle *On the Soul* 412a.

45. For a good summary of the modes of being, see Marías, *History of Philosophy*, 66-69.

46. Aristotle *Metaphysics* 1019a-1020a, 1048a-b; Aristotle *On the Soul* 412a.

47. Aristotle *Metaphysics* 1065b, 1069b.

48. Ibid., 1049b, 1069b.

49. Ibid., 1048b.

At the same time, actuality is prior to potentiality in the sense that it constitutes the "goal" or finality of what is potential. For example, the adult is prior to the child that will become that adult in the sense that the adult is the "end" of the growing child. In a more important and fundamental sense, however, actuality is prior to potentiality because motion always requires a cause that ultimately refers to the necessity of a first cause of all motions or movements. That cause must be pure actuality.[50] The perishable substances or particular things that are in constant change (the passing from potentiality to actuality), require an ultimate unchangeable, eternal cause.[51]

The principle of articulation and cosmology. "The distinction of potency [potentiality] and act [actuality] leads to the doctrine of the hierarchy or scale of existence."[52] Reality as a whole is organized in a hierarchical way according to the degree of potentiality and matter (which implies motion) that exists in different things or entities. Aristotle holds that there are three basic types of substances constituting this hierarchy from bottom to top: sensible perishable substances; sensible eternal substances; and finally, the immutable substance.[53] The first group includes all those things pertaining to the sublunary or terrestrial world composed of matter and form, such as rocks, plants, animals, or human beings, subjected to generation and corruption.[54] In the superlunary world, it is possible to find the sensible eternal substances, the celestial spheres that have a circular eternal motion.[55] They are incorruptible. Their matter is called aether.[56] In turn, these spheres are moved by an immutable substance, the first cause of every motion, which is the first eternal unmoved mover that moves the other

---

50. Ibid., 1050a-b. See especially Aristotle *The Physics* 242a (trans. Wicksteed and Cornford). See also ibid., 256a-258b.

51. Aristotle *Physics* 258b-260a.

52. Copleston, *Greece and Rome*, 311.

53. Aristotle *Metaphysics* 1069a-b.

54. The exception here would be the active mind or intellect that apparently Aristotle considers as immortal. Aristotle *On the Soul* 430a. See also ibid., 413a; Aristotle *Metaphysics* 1070a. Regarding the scale of being or existence in Aristotle, see Copleston, *Greece and Rome*, 315-316; David Ross, *Aristotle*, 6th ed. (London, UK: Routledge, 1995), 95-100. For an excellent explanation of Aristotle's metaphysics and the chain of being, see Kerbs, *El problema de la identidad*, 147-154.

55. Aristotle *Metaphysics* 1072a.

56. In contrast to the four elements that constitute the matter of the sublunary substances: earth, fire, air, and water. Aristotle *On the Heavens* 269a-270b (trans. Guthrie).

substances because it is the object of love, desire, and thought.⁵⁷

Aristotle refers to this unmoved mover as *God*, an eternal or timeless living being, pure actuality without potentiality or matter.⁵⁸ The essence of this God is thought. He does not think about external objects but He thinks Himself. He is impassive, unalterable, and unmovable, without magnitude, parts, or divisions.⁵⁹ He is the supreme cause of order and motion.⁶⁰ He is the supreme form or substance, the one in which all the conditions of being are totally and completely realized.⁶¹ Aristotle's God is not a Creator. Aristotle's understanding of God assumes that the world is eternal (uncreated). In the depiction of the first cause, it is evident again that the application of the Parmenidean *via negativa* allows discovering the "real" nature of the supreme being through the progressive elimination of motion and matter in the successive instances of the hierarchy.

Summary

This short review of the Greek philosophical background shows that in Greek philosophy, the principle of articulation was understood based on the presupposition about being (ontology) as timeless, immutable, and unchangeable (Parmenides). The particular beings or things, such as the particular things of the world, the world itself, the human beings, and the articulating agent—the parts of the system—are understood from the perspective of timelessness (timeless ideas or forms).

The ultimate agent of articulation is the idea of good (Plato) or God as the first unmoved mover (Aristotle), with similar ontological characteristics to the being of Parmenides. The articulating "action" is performed by participation in the ideas and, ultimately in the idea of good (Plato) or by attraction through love in the case of the unmoved mover (Aristotle). This articulation is the cause of the hierarchical structure of the entire reality (the whole system). All the parts of the system participate in a hierarchy of being, where inferior beings are temporal and material, or with a higher proportion of the material

---

57. Aristotle *Metaphysics* 1072a-b.
58. Ibid., 1074a.
59. Ibid., 1072b-1073a; Aristotle *Physics* 266a. "Therefore Mind thinks itself, if it is that which is best; and its thinking is a thinking of thinking." Aristotle *Metaphysics* 1074b.
60. Aristotle *Metaphysics* 1075b.
61. Marías, *Idea de la metafísica*, 18-19.

component, while superior beings are timeless or with a higher proportion of the timeless component.

The Principle of Articulation in Medieval Christianity

Early after the apostolic period, Christianity began to suffer the effect of making contact with Greek-Latin culture, while Christian believers tried to present the Good News to the pagans. Imperceptibly, they assumed that it was easier to share the Gospel presenting the biblical God with similar characteristics to those of Parmenides's being, Plato's idea of good, and Aristotle's God or unmoved mover.[62] This process was a Hellenization of the original Christian experience[63] and its intellectual development. Several leading representatives of the Christian thought illustrate this process. The two most important are Augustine and Aquinas.

Augustine

Ontology and the interpretation of God. Augustine (354-430) takes from Greek philosophy the fundamental hermeneutical presuppositions regarding ontology and epistemology and applies them to the understanding of God, His actions, and His relation to creation, including human beings. For Augustine, the real being is what is unchangeable. However, the only absolutely unchangeable being is God Himself.[64] He affirms his sympathy for the Platonist and neo-Platonist philosophers. Augustine even considers that he can understand the nature of God thanks to the Platonists, who provide the necessary presuppositions to understand Him.[65]

Augustine, then, virtually identifies the being of Greek philosophical tradition with God Himself.[66] He applies to God the same characteristics that Parmenides sees in being, Plato sees in the ideas, and

---

62. See Placher, *A History of Christian Theology*, 55.
63. Enrique D. Dussel, *El dualismo en la antropología de la cristiandad* (Buenos Aires, Argentina: Editorial Guadalupe, 1974), 17.
64. Augustin, *On the Trinity* 5.2.3 (The Nicene and Post-Nicene Fathers; hereafter, NPNF, trans. Haddan).
65. Augustin *The Confessions* 7.20.26; 8.2.3 (NPNF, trans. Pilkington).
66. This identification is clear in Augustine's interpretation of Exod 3:14. See, for example, ibid., 7.10.16; Augustin *On the Trinity* 5.2.3.

Aristotle sees in his philosophical God. First, God is eternal or *timeless*. He lives in an eternal present, unrelated to time.[67] Second, God is *immutable* or unchangeable.[68] God does not experience variation even in His knowledge or emotions.[69] Third, God is *spaceless* or immaterial. Namely, He is simple.[70]

Augustine is aware that the Bible frequently describes God as having a physical aspect. However, he interprets all these descriptions as non-literal. Scripture employs a language suitable for babies from which it tries to elevate the mind toward what is divine. The Bible can say that God is jealous or He repents of something but this is not the case. Actually, biblical Revelation rarely describes God as He really is. One exception is, Augustine thinks, Exod 3:14 where the Lord introduces Himself as "I AM THAT I AM" that is understood by Augustine as a reference to the essence of God.[71]

Augustine believes that the Bible uses an analogical language whereby mutable and material things actually describe that which is timeless, immutable, and immaterial. There are almost no literal descriptions of God in the Bible. Accordingly, whenever the Bible refers to a theophany, as when God speaks to Abraham, Moses, or reveals Himself to Daniel, "those visions were wrought through the *changeable creature*, made subject to the *unchangeable God*, and *did not manifest God properly as He is.*"[72]

The *via negativa* and epistemology. Clearly, Augustine uses the *via negativa* in order to determine the primordial nature of God. Change, which involves time, space, multiplicity, and passibility, has to be denied

---

67. "In the Eternal nothing passeth away, but that the whole is present." Augustin *The Confessions* 11.11.13. See ibid., 11.13.16.

68. Augustin *The Confessions* 12.11.11. See also Augustin *On the Trinity* 1.1.2. For Augustine, God's will works in total simultaneity. There is no succession of time or change in His will. Ibid., 12.15.18.

69. Augustin *The Confessions* 11.31.41; 1.4.4.

70. That is to say, without parts as a body has. See Augustine's argument in this sense in Augustin *On the Trinity* 6.6.8. To these characteristics, Augustine adds God's invisibility because "there is nothing that is visible that is not also changeable." Augustin *On the Trinity* 3.10.21. In the context of his affirmation of God's simplicity, Augustine admits that He is a Trinity, but He is not triple. Augustin *On the Trinity* 6.7.9; 6.8.9. For a succinct but good exposition of Augustine's understanding of the Trinity, see Justo L. González, *Historia del pensamiento cristiano* (Barcelona, España: Clie, 2010), 273-277.

71. Augustin *On the Trinity* 1.1.2.

72. Ibid., 2.17.32. Emphasis mine. See also ibid., 2.18.35.

regarding God.⁷³ Augustine considers that "it is necessary . . . *to purge our minds*, in order to be able *to see ineffably that which is ineffable.*"⁷⁴ It should not be said of God that He is *unspeakable*. God condescends with human beings by accepting their worship with words but the fact is that they do not clearly know what the words referring to God mean.⁷⁵

For Augustine, then, real knowledge is the knowledge of what is timeless. The same is valid in the case of knowledge in the sensible world. Augustine adapts the Platonic theory of ideas by affirming that the timeless and immutable ideas of every particular temporal thing are in the mind of God.⁷⁶ As Augustine does not accept Plato's notion of the pre-existence of the soul, he proposes that the rational soul can know the ideas through a divine illumination. In this way, higher reason can know corporeal things thanks to the incorporeal and timeless ideas provided by God to human reason.⁷⁷

The world. As a result of his ontological assumptions, Augustine divides reality on a hierarchical structure with two basic parts. One is the realm of God, the timeless heaven. Although it has a beginning, because it is part of creation, it is eternal and spaceless. It participates of God's timelessness.⁷⁸

The other part is the realm of temporal creation in general. Particular things are, but they are not completely, because they are mutable, changeable. The time of this realm is a creation of God. Time is not co-eternal with God. Before Creation, there was no time.⁷⁹ Between the timeless and temporal realms, there is no direct contact. God created the temporal realm with His word but His word is co-eternal with Him. This means that God created the temporal world from timelessness, without direct contact with His creation. In spite of the several references to the words that God pronounced in the story of Creation (or in other biblical

---

73. Ibid., 5.1.2.

74. Ibid., 1.1.3. Emphasis mine. Augustine thinks that "a man who is resting upon faith, hope and love, and who keeps a firm hold upon these, does not need the Scriptures except for the purpose of instructing others." Augustin *On Christian Doctrine* 1.39.43 (NPNF, trans. Shaw).

75. Augustin *On Christian Doctrine* 1.6.6.

76. Agustín *Ochenta y tres cuestiones diversas* Cuestión 46.2 (trans. Madrid).

77. Augustin *On the Trinity* 12.2.2; 12.15.24.

78. Augustine describes heaven as "the house of God, not earthly, *nor of any celestial bulk corporeal*, but a spiritual house and a partaker of Thy eternity [timelessness]." Augustin *The Confessions* 12.15.19. Emphasis mine. See also ibid., 12.11.13.

79. Ibid., 7.11.17; 11.13.15-16; 11.14.17.

stories), God did not pronounce those words in time but out of time.[80] Augustine, then, is forced to postulate that the words of God in time are actually uttered by creatures, which he does not specify.[81]

Regarding the procedure of Creation, Augustine proposes his theory of seminal reasons. Augustine holds that Creation did not take six literal days. The elements mentioned in Gen 1 were created simultaneously, without succession of time. God created the *seeds* of everything and then, the elements started a process of development and growth. Augustine does not consider that a timeless God has to create in a sequence of six days. Time starts with the development of these seminal reasons. The order of the six days, for Augustine, is not temporal but causal.[82]

The human being. As Plato, Augustine clearly distinguishes between the soul and the body of the human being.[83] Soul and body, however, are creations of God. Still, the soul is superior to the body. The image of God lies in the soul, not in the body. The soul was breathed into the body.[84] The soul is incorporeal, spiritual, and immortal—subsistent to the death of the body—although it is able of some motion or mutability.[85] It can partake of the unchangeable nature of God's wisdom.[86]

Augustine tries to prevent making God liable for the problem of evil. Human beings had free will before the Fall.[87] The problem of evil or sin is a result of the wrong use of that free will.[88] Augustine believes that after the Fall, human beings still have freedom but it is only a "freedom" to commit sin,[89] which for practical purposes implies that after the Fall, humanity lost its free will. Adam transmitted original sin to

---

80. Ibid., 11.7.9; 13.29.44.

81. "There was already a corporeal creature before heaven and earth by whose temporal motions that voice might take its course in time." Ibid., 11.6.8. Augustine does not clarify what kind of corporeal creature he has in mind.

82. Agustín *Del Génesis a la letra* 5.1-12, 23; 6.5.8 (ed. Martín); Augustin *On the Trinity* 3.8.13. Regarding the seminal reasons in Augustine, see Eugene TeSelle, *Augustine: The Theologian* (London, UK: Burns & Oates, 1970), 218; Copleston, *Augustine to Scotus*, 75-77.

83. Augustin *On the Trinity* 15.7.11.

84. Agustín *Del Génesis a la letra* 5.12.21-22; 8.24.35.

85. Ibid., 7.28.43; Augustin *A Treatise on the Soul and Its Origin* 2.7 (NPNF, trans. Holmes and Wallis).

86. Augustin *On the Trinity* 3.2.8.

87. Agustín *Del libre albedrío* 3.18.52 (trans. Seijas).

88. Ibid., 1.1.1-2; 1.2.4; 2.1.3; 3.17.49.

89. Ibid., 3.18.52.

the successive generations. The solution, then, is God's predestination or election of some for salvation, who are attracted by God through His irresistible grace.[90] Augustine's understanding of the free will before the Fall, however, reflects an inconsistency with his understanding of God's absolute will and foreknowledge, as the following section shows.

Articulating agent and articulating action. For Augustine, God's will is the ultimate efficient cause of every motion. God's will, although unmoved, is the cause of motion in the rest of reality according to a hierarchical order: first, spiritual beings; then, corporeal creatures; and finally, at the bottom, the inferior inanimate beings.[91] If God's will is timeless and immutable, it is impossible that intelligent creatures possess real free will. This affirmation is valid not only for Augustine's soteriology but also for his view of the human condition before the Fall. In other words, Augustine understands the relationship between God and His creation, including human beings, in the light of the absolutely timeless, unchangeable, and unconditional providential decisions of God's will.

This deterministic view of the way in which God articulates His relationship with His creatures relates to Augustine's understanding of God's foreknowledge. What God timelessly foreknows will happen by necessity; namely, it cannot be changed, including human "free" choices.[92] However, he emphatically declares, "God's foreknowledge is no cause of sin."[93] He tries to conciliate God's timeless and immutable foreknowledge with human free will by affirming that the reason for the existence of free actions is that God foresees them.[94] In this way, however, Augustine is also admitting that "future" events, actions, or facts are already real in the mind of God.[95] God's fore-

---

90. See Augustin *A Treatise on the Predestination of the Saints* (NPNF, trans. Holmes and Wallis); Augustin *A Treatise on the Grace of Christ, and on Original Sin* (NPNF, trans. Holmes and Wallis).

91. Augustin *On the Trinity* 3.2.7-8; 3.4.9.

92. See Augustine's whole discussion about the relationship between free will and God's foreknowledge in Agustín *Del libre albedrío* 3.2.4 to 3.5.12.

93. Augustin *A Treatise on the Soul* 1.7.

94. Agustín *Del libre albedrío* 3.3.7-8. See also Augustin *The City of God* 5.9-10 (NPNF, trans. Dods). For an extensive discussion regarding Augustine's defense of human free will in spite of his understanding of God's foreknowledge, see Gareth B. Matthews, *Augustine* (Oxford, UK: Blackwell, 2005), 96-104. Apparently, Augustine understands that God's foreknowledge is the cause or guarantee of the existence of free will.

95. From Augustine's perspective, "God is the ultimate controller (whether or not he is the ultimate cause) of the human will, and his giving of grace is not respon-

knowledge is the cause of those events and not the opposite. Augustine actually admits this fact when he says that, in God, being and knowing are identified.[96] What God knows is what already exists as a reality in His mind.

For Augustine, then, there is no new knowledge in God. God's knowledge comes from His own mind, not from anything external to Himself.[97] In one sense, then, the particular temporal things have already *existence* in God's mind as timeless archetypical ideas. As ideas, they are not created but eternal. The particular temporal things are created, and they exist thanks to their *participation* in those timeless ideas.[98] Like Plato, Augustine believes that temporal reality is a movable image of eternal ideas. As such, they cannot be in another way than in the way in which they are in the mind of God.[99]

Ultimately, God—as the articulating agent—articulates the relationship between God Himself and His creation—including human beings—in terms of an absolute providence-predestination pattern understood from the perspective of God's timelessness. Everything is determined by God's will.[100] Based on God's immutable will and God's timeless foreknowledge—or simply knowledge—of the ideas and actions of His creatures, Augustine goes in the line of a virtually deterministic understanding of God's articulating action. The temporal elements participate in the ideas in the mind of God, which is what God really knows, not the objects and actions of the temporal realm.

In this context, it is important to say that Augustine does not deny the role of Christ as Mediator but this role is minimized in the light of his understanding of salvation in terms of predestination. Christ's sacrifice in time allows God's application of His timeless predestination

---

sive to anything in the human will. . . . I don't see how he can be saved from the imputation of theological determinism with all its infelicitous consequences." Eleonore Stump, "Augustine on Free Will," in *The Cambridge Companion to Augustine*, ed. Eleonore Stump and Norman Kretzmann (Cambridge, UK: Cambridge University Press, 2001), 142. Although Eleonore Stump presents this statement mainly in the context of Augustinian soteriology, nothing prevents to see the same determinism in the relationship between God and human beings before the Fall.

96. Augustin *On the Trinity* 7.1.2. See also 6.10.11; 7.1.1; 7.2.3.
97. Augustin *The Confessions* 11.31.41; Agustín *Del Génesis a la letra* 5.14.29.
98. Agustín *Ochenta y tres cuestiones diversas* Cuestión 46.2.
99. Augustin *On the Trinity* 6.10.11. In this context, it is only natural for Augustine to believe that creatures have some traces of the Trinity. Ibid., 6.10.12; 15.2.3.
100. See Augustin *On Christian Doctrine* 3.34.49.

to the elect. He is the supreme example of predestination.[101] But the ultimate cause of salvation is God's election, not Christ's sacrifice.

The whole. As in the case of Greek philosophical systems, Augustine's system interprets that reality as a whole is a hierarchy. The top of the hierarchy is God Himself who is the Supreme Being, the one who is timeless and has never changed. Created things, however, participate in timelessness on different degrees and consequently, they have different levels of being.[102]

Thomas Aquinas

Aquinas (c. 1225-1274) was probably the most influential Christian theologian during the Middle Ages. He proposes developing Christian theology based on Aristotelian philosophy, but at the same time, he takes elements of neo-Platonism. Augustine also has an important influence on Aquinas's theology.[103]

Ontology. Aquinas re-edits the Aristotelian hylomorphic theory according to which common things, or composite substances, consist of matter and form.[104] In these things, the essence includes matter and form. The form is the timeless element of compound things and the cause of their existence. But Aquinas distinguishes between essence and being. Essence does not necessarily imply *the existence* of an object or concrete thing as an entity in reality.[105] The essence of the composite substances can be found in the idea of the object that is in the mind of God.[106] The relationship between the essence and the existence of a composite substance is the relationship that exists between potenti-

---

101. Regarding Christ as Mediator in Augustine, see Augustin *On the Trinity* 4.8.11 to 4.14.19; Augustin *Treatise on the Predestination* 30-31; Augustin *A Treatise on the Gift of Perseverance* 67 (NPNF, trans. Holmes and Wallis).

102. "The things that He made He empowered to be, but not to be supremely like Himself. To some He communicated a more ample, to others a more limited existence, and thus arranged the natures of beings in ranks." Augustin *The City of God* 12.2.

103. González, *Historia*, 546, 530; Copleston, *Augustine to Scotus*, 323.

104. See, for example, Thomas Aquinas *Summa Contra Gentiles (SCG), Book 1: God* 51-52.3 (trans. Pegis); Aquinas *ST* I q. 3 a. 2 resp.; Thomas Aquinas *Concerning Being and Essence* 2 (trans. Leckie). Every treatise in the *ST* uses these subdivisions: question (q.), article (a.), objection (obj.), "on the contrary" (s.c.), "I answer that" (resp.), and replay to the objection (ad.).

105. Aquinas *Concerning Being and Essence* 2.

106. Aquinas *ST* I q. 44 a. 3 s.c. and resp.; q. 16 a. 3 resp. and ad. 3.

ality and actuality.¹⁰⁷ God creates the matter with the form—without which matter cannot exist or be known.¹⁰⁸ In fact, a form, according to Aquinas, can exist (1) as a timeless idea in the mind of God;¹⁰⁹ (2) in the object composed of matter and form; and (3) in the mind of the knower of such object that *abstracts* the form in order to know the object.¹¹⁰

Aquinas also holds that there are simple substances that are not composed of form and matter, such as the souls alone and the intelligences (angels). These simple substances only have form and being (or existence), without matter. It is still possible to distinguish between essence (in this case, only form) and existence in simple substances.¹¹¹ For Aquinas, this distinction implies that the efficient cause of the existence of the substances—whether composed or simple—is external to them. He then concludes that there must be a first cause of everything, where the distinction between essence and existence does not exist. That cause is God.¹¹²

Epistemology and the *via negativa*. Aquinas's abstractive understanding of form and his essentialist understanding of entities is in consonance with Aristotelian ontology, which assumes the timelessness and immutability of being in general. Consequently, Aquinas interprets knowledge basically as an abstraction of the temporal-material element of the object.¹¹³ Aquinas reedits Aristotle's metaphor of *tabula rasa* and rejects the innate ideas.¹¹⁴ The mind of the knower discovers the universal timeless form of the object in order to elaborate a universal concept, which is in turn used to understand the individuals corresponding to that universal concept.¹¹⁵ Aquinas's epistemology, then, implies the de-

---

107. Ibid., I q. 3 a. 4 resp.
108. Ibid., I q. 15 a. 3 ad. 3. In this way, "a form is nothing else but the act [actuality] of matter." Ibid., I q. 105 a. 1 resp. "By the form, which is the actuality of matter, matter is made being in act and a this somewhat." Aquinas *Concerning Being and Essence* 2.
109. Aquinas *ST* I q. 15 a. 3 resp. Aquinas, following Augustine, explains that the ideas of the objects are not separated from God but are contained in His divine essence. See ibid., I q. 15 a. 3 s.c. See also ibid., I q. 15 a. 3 resp.; I q. 44 a. 3 resp.
110. Aquinas *SCG* 1.65.3; Aquinas *ST* I q. 85 a. 2 ad. 2; Aquinas *Concerning Being and Essence* 3.
111. Aquinas *Concerning Being and Essence* 4.
112. Ibid., 4, 5.
113. Aquinas describes this abstraction following Aristotle. See Aquinas *ST* I q. 85 a.1 s.c.
114. Ibid., I q. 84 a. 3 s.c. and resp.
115. See González, *Historia*, 542.

nial of the mutable and changeable features of the objects, namely, the application of the *via negativa*.¹¹⁶

God and the analogical language. Aquinas explains the divine nature in harmony with the *via negativa* method. Aquinas ascribes to the Christian God almost the same ontological characteristics that Aristotle ascribes to the first unmoved mover. God is bodiless for three reasons: (1) bodies have motion and God is the first unmoved mover; (2) He is pure actuality and has no potentiality (which is present in the matter of bodies); and (3) as animated souls are nobler than bodies, God, who is the noblest being, is incorporeal. God's incorporeity implies that He is not a matter-form compound. He is a form, absolutely simple, without accidents.¹¹⁷ God is absolutely one, not multiple or divided.¹¹⁸ God is also altogether immutable and eternal in the sense of timeless.¹¹⁹ God's eternity, then, is not an everlasting duration but timelessness.¹²⁰

Apparently, God and creation in general are totally different, and nothing affirmative can be said about Him. However, Aquinas says that God and His creation have some similarities. There is an analogy between them because both are beings.¹²¹

According to Aquinas, then, it is possible to affirm something about God by using an analogical language.¹²² This language is an intermediate between univocal and equivocal language. It is not possible to affirm something univocally of God and the creatures—with the same meaning—because they are different. Nor is it correct to say some-

---

116. Aquinas *ST* I q. 12 a. 4 resp.; I q. 84 a. 6, 7; I q. 85 a. 1; I 85 a. 3; I q. 86 a. 3.
117. Ibid., I q. 3 a. 1 resp.; I q. 3 a. 2 resp.; I q. 3 a. 6 resp. See ibid., I q. 3 a. 7; I q. 3 a. 8.
118. See ibid., I q. 11.
119. Ibid., I q. 9 a. 1 resp. "The idea of eternity follows immutability, as the idea of time follows movement." Ibid., I q. 10 a. 2 resp. See also ibid., I q. 10 a. 1 resp.
120. Aquinas, following Boëthius, clarifies the difference between eternity and time: "Eternity is simultaneously whole. But time has a *before* and an *after*. Therefore time and eternity are not the same thing." Ibid., I q. 10 a. 4 s.c. Emphasis in original. "Eternity is the measure of a permanent being; while time is the measure of movement." Ibid., I q. 10 a. 4 resp.
121. Aquinas explains that this similitude consists in an imperfect *participation* or *similitude* with the divine being and goodness. Aquinas *ST* I q. 6 a. 4 resp. This similarity is "according to some sort of analogy.... In this way all created things, so far as they are beings, are like God as the first and universal principle of all being." Ibid., I q. 4 a. 3 resp.
122. For the following explanation, see ibid., I q. 13 a. 5.

thing equivocally about God because they are not absolutely different.[123] However, someone can say that God and His creatures are wise, for example, according to an analogous meaning. It is possible, then, to affirm some things about God based on what is known about Him through His creatures because He is their principle and ultimate cause.[124]

Aquinas, however, applies this analogical way assuming God's timelessness and spacelessness. As a result, when the biblical revelation describes God as a physical, temporal being who can experience change, these descriptions must be interpreted in a metaphorical way.[125] This hermeneutical criterion is also applicable to other realities related to God; for example, the concept of eternity. "As God, although incorporeal, is named in Scripture metaphorically by corporeal names, so eternity though simultaneously whole, is called by names implying time and succession."[126] In practice, then, Aquinas's analogical way builds based on the *via negativa* method, which in turn operates based on the presupposition that God is timeless, immutable, and absolutely simple.

The world. Aquinas's understanding of the world assumes the timelessness and immutability of being, God, and God's actions. Aquinas thinks that God is the necessary Creator or Cause of everything that exists. Following Plato, he believes that things exist because they participate in God's being. The degree of participation in God determines the degree of perfection. Things find their unity in God.[127] God's creation includes matter (primary matter), although matter is close to nothing. It is at the bottom of the hierarchy of created beings and it depends on the form in order to exist or be known. In contrast, angels, as beings without matter, are closer to the top of that hierarchy.[128]

---

123. Ibid., I q. 13 a. 5 resp. This was the problem with the neo-Platonic theologian known as Pseudo-Dionysius (6th century AD) who is a typical expositor of the *via negativa*. See Dionysius the Areopagite *On the Divine Names and the Mystical Theology* (trans. Rolt).

124. Aquinas *ST* I q. 13 a. 5 resp.

125. Ibid., I q. 1 a. 9 ad. 3. When Scripture describes movement or change in God, "these things are said of God in Scripture metaphorically." Ibid., I q. 9 a. 1 ad. 3. In the same way, Scripture uses sensible material objects to teach timeless spiritual and immaterial truths. "In Holy Writ spiritual truths are fittingly taught under the likeness of material things." Ibid., I q. 1 a. 9 s.c.

126. Ibid., I q. 10 a. 1 ad. 4.

127. Ibid., I q. 44 a. 1 resp.

128. Ibid., I q. 44 a. 2 s.c. and resp. See also ibid., I q. 15 a. 3 ad. 3; I q. 50 a. 2 s.c. and resp.

Aquinas understands Creation as a timeless and immutable action of God. Creation is making something out of nothing, *ex nihilo*.[129] Creation from nothing does not imply change or movement because there is nothing pre-existent. Creation is only a change according to human understanding that has the impression that passing from nothing to something is a change. Creation, however, is an instantaneous fact, without implying a real change in God.[130] Actually, while creatures are related to God, "in God there is no real relation to creatures, but a relation only in idea."[131] As God is timeless, He cannot relate directly to His temporal creatures except through the ideas or knowledge of them that are included in His being.[132] Creation means, therefore, dependency on God,[133] but not the direct involvement of God with His creatures. If God had direct contact with His creatures in time, that would imply a novelty in God, namely, a change from timeless to temporality in His knowledge and relationships. Instead, God knows and relates to His creatures as they are in His ideas of those creatures.[134]

Consequently, "creation can be called *a change only in a metaphorical sense*, that is, only so far as the created thing is thought of as having being after not being."[135] God's will to create is eternal, immutable. There was no moment where He decided to create. From His timeless eternity, He had the will or desire to create.[136] Thus, God is *prior* to His creation in terms of the causal order but not in a temporal sense. His relation to the world *after* Creation is also timeless.[137]

In fact, Aquinas seems to believe that Creation in itself does not imply duration. It is an instantaneous or timeless event. There is no real

---

129. Ibid., I q. 45 a. 1 s.c. and resp.; I q. 45 a. 2 resp.; I q. 45 a. 6 resp.

130. Ibid., I q. 45 a. 2 ad. 2 and 3. See also ibid., q. 45 a. 5 resp.; I q. 45 a. 3 resp.

131. Ibid., I q. 13 a. 7 resp.

132. "In God relation to the creature is not a real relation, but only a relation of reason; whereas the relation of the creature to God is a real relation." Ibid., I q. 45 a. 3 ad. 1. See also Copleston, *Augustine to Scotus*, 364.

133. Vittorino Grossi et al., *Historia de los dogmas*, vol. 2, *El hombre y su salvación*, trans. Alfonso Ortiz García (Salamanca, España: Secretariado Trinitario, 1996), 61. See Aquinas *ST* I q. 8 a. 3.

134. "It cannot be said . . . that these relations exist as realities outside God." Thomas Aquinas *SCG, Book 2: Creation* 13-14.1 (trans. Anderson). See ibid., 12.3; 13-14.3-4.

135. Ibid., 37.4. Emphasis mine.

136. Aquinas *ST* I q. 46 a. 1 resp. and ad. 6. See Copleston, *Augustine to Scotus*, 367.

137. Aquinas *ST* I q. 46 a. 1 ad. 6 and 8.

temporal succession in Creation.[138] Although Aquinas is aware that the Bible describes Creation as lasting six literal days,[139] he believes that God created heaven, earth, time, and angels simultaneously.[140] Aquinas seems to endorse—with some modifications—the Augustinian theory of the seminal reasons regarding the creation of corporeal creatures.[141] This instantaneous timeless creation occurred in the beginning, according to Gen 1, but the six days registered in the biblical story refer to a work of distinction or diversification (first three days) and adornment (last three days), developed in time.[142]

God's preservation of the world is not a temporal action either. "The preservation of things by God is a continuation of that action whereby He gives existence, which action is without either motion or time."[143] As the first unmoved mover, God *moves* the creatures or created things indirectly through a virtual contact by providing the timeless form that in turn produces the movement or actualization. This virtual contact is only one-way, from God toward creature. The world cannot produce changes in God.[144]

The human being. According to Aquinas, the soul is the incorporeal principle of life. It is subsistent and incorruptible because it is the seat of the intellect or mind. The body finally disappears. The soul, then, is the essential aspect of the human being. It is the form of the body, simple, without any material element in its constitution.[145] Nevertheless, the human being includes soul and body together because the soul, through the body, operates sensations.[146]

The human soul is different from the souls of other living creatures. Plants have a nutritive soul and animals a sensitive one. Human souls, however, are intellectual or rational—without excluding the nutritive

---

138. Ibid., I q. 46 a. 2 ad. 1. See also José María Barrio Maestre, *El Dios de los filósofos* (Madrid, España: Ediciones Rialp, 2013), 124-125.

139. See, for example, Aquinas *ST* I q. 74; I q. 105 a. 2 s.c.

140. Ibid., I q. 46 a. 3 resp.; I q. 66 a. 4 resp.

141. Ibid., I q. 62 a. 3 resp.

142. Ibid., I q. 74 a. 1 ad. 1; I q. 74 a. 2 ad. 1. See also the introduction to q. 65 and the discussion in qq. 66 to 74.

143. Ibid., I q. 74 a. 1 ad. 4.

144. Ibid., I q. 105 a. 3 resp. and ad. 1.

145. Ibid., I q. 75, introduction; I q. 75 a. 1 s.c. and resp.; I q. 75 a. 2 s.c. and resp.; I q. 75 a. 5 s.c. and resp.; I q. 75 a. 6 resp.; I q. 76 a. 1 s.c. and resp.

146. Ibid., I q. 75 a. 4 s.c. and resp.

and sensitive functions of the other types of souls.[147] The intellectual aspect is the one that avoids the corruption of the human soul.[148] Intellectual powers, as will and intelligence, remain after death. However, the nutritive and sensitive faculties of the soul disappear with death because they are attached to the soul-body composite.[149]

Aquinas holds that God created human beings in His image and likeness. This image and likeness, however, is only regarding the soul, not the body.[150] Given God's immateriality and timelessness, for Aquinas, the notion that God's image and likeness involve the material body is unacceptable.[151]

Aquinas speaks about the beatific vision of God after death. Souls cannot rest until they have a vision of God's essence or beatific vision.[152] In this vision, the soul becomes partaker of God's happiness.[153] "This vision consists in a participation in eternity, as completely transcending time."[154] In other words, the soul is above matter because it participates in timeless activities as the vision of the divine substance. A soul separated from the body "has a greater freedom of intelligence, since the weight and care of the body is a clog upon the clearness of its intelligence in the present life."[155]

Articulating agent and articulating action. As said, if God is timeless, unchangeable, absolutely simple, and pure actuality, He cannot have direct contact with His temporal creation or be affected by something external to Himself.[156] How then can God articulate His relation-

---

147. Ibid., I q. 75 a. 3 resp.; I q. 76 a. 3 resp.
148. Ibid., I q. 76 a. 3 ad. 1.
149. Ibid., I q. 77 a. 8 resp. Regarding the powers of the soul, see ibid., I qq. 78-83.
150. Ibid., I q. 90 a. 2 s.c.; I q. 93 a. 1 s.c.; I q. 93 a. 2 resp.
151. "The image of God belongs to the mind only." Ibid., I q. 93 a. 6 s.c.
152. Thomas Aquinas *SCG, Book 3: Providence; Part 1* 50.3, 9, 10 (trans. Bourke).
153. Ibid., 51.6.
154. Ibid., 61.4. Aquinas additionally explains this participation by saying that the soul's "action, as joined to higher things which exist above time, participates in eternity. Especially so is the vision by which it sees the divine substance. And so, by this kind of vision it comes into the participation of eternity." Ibid., 61.5. Aquinas even affirms that "by the gift of grace men can merit glory in such a degree as to be equal to the angels, in each of the angelic grades; and this implies that men are taken up into the orders of the angels." Aquinas *ST* I q. 108 a. 8 resp.
155. Aquinas *ST* I q. 89 a. 2 ad. 1.
156. "Aquinas would find it absurd or even blasphemous to suppose that God is affected by or in need of anything other than what is divine." Brian Davis, *The Thought of Thomas Aquinas* (New York, NY: Oxford University Press, 1992), 150.

ship with the world? In order to answer this question, it is useful to explore Aquinas's understanding of God's knowledge and providence.

God does not know anything external to Himself. He is unchangeable, even regarding His knowledge. Consequently, in God, knowledge is knowledge of Himself. Subject and object are the same, without distinction.[157] "In God to be is the same thing as to understand."[158] In God, then, knowledge is timeless as He is. There is no succession of events or past, present, and future. God knows everything simultaneously, in a permanent present. Even future events are present for Him.[159]

As external things to God are not the cause of God's knowledge, Aquinas logically concludes that the opposite is correct. "The knowledge of God is the cause of things. For the knowledge of God is to all creatures what the knowledge of the artificer is to things made by his art."[160] God's will only follows His knowledge—as the cause of everything—that in turn is inseparable from His being.[161] This understanding of God's knowledge entails a highly deterministic view of the relation between God and the world.

In harmony with his understanding of God's knowledge, Aquinas holds that providence is the design of God's government of the world. The government itself is the execution of His providence. From the perspective of His timeless plan or providence, God controls everything immediately, but from the perspective of the application of His timeless plan, He rules or controls some things through others. In this way, God makes some things to be the cause of others in His government. In any case, "we must say that God has the design of the government of all

---

157. Aquinas *ST* I q. 14 a. 2 resp. "God understands Himself through Himself." Ibid.

158. Ibid., I q. 14 a. 4 s.c.

159. Regarding how God knows, see ibid., I q. 14 a. 4 resp.; I q. 14 a. 5 resp.; I q. 14 a. 6 resp.; I q. 14 a. 7 sc. and resp.

160. Ibid., I q. 14 a. 8 resp. See also ibid., I q. 14 a. 8 s.c. Regarding the causative knowledge of God, see the discussion in Davis, *The Thought of Thomas Aquinas*, 137-138.

161. "Now it is manifest that God causes things by His intellect, since His being is His act of understanding; and hence His knowledge must be the cause of things, in so far as His will is joined to it." Aquinas *ST* I q. 14 a. 8 resp. See also Aquinas *SCG* 1.61.7. According to Aquinas, God's will is inseparable from God's knowledge and being. God has an "inclination to put in act what His intellect has conceived appertains to the will. Therefore the will of God is the cause of things." Aquinas *ST* I q. 19 a. 4 resp. God's will needs to be fulfilled always and is as immutable as God. Ibid., q. 19 a. 6. resp. and a. 7 resp.

things, even of the very least,"¹⁶² and consequently He is the ultimate cause of everything. All beings, whether in general or individually, are subject to God's providence. God is the first causal agent of all beings. He directs the existence of everything toward an end or goal. Providence is, precisely, the ordering of things towards the end that God has established for them.¹⁶³

This understanding of the way in which God relates to created things, particularly His providence, implies that God seems to be responsible for evil and He does not leave room for the free will of intelligent creatures. Aquinas says that God does not want evil.¹⁶⁴ He also tries to explain how free will is possible although nothing escapes God's providence. Aquinas distinguishes between necessary and contingent events. Necessary events are those that, according to the will of God, will necessarily happen. Contingent events, instead, can happen or not. Necessary events are effects of necessary causes ordained by God,¹⁶⁵ while contingent events are the result of contingent causes also ordained by God. Human actions, for example, based on free will, are contingent events¹⁶⁶ and thus, only humans are responsible for wrong decisions.

However, Aquinas clarifies that God is who prepares the contingent causes because He wants the resulting events be contingent.¹⁶⁷ Aquinas holds that the contingency lies in the fact that there is no certainty that they will really happen. As long as they are future events, they are uncertain. Only when future contingent events become present events, they are not uncertain anymore because they are a reality.

Regarding God's knowledge, though, Aquinas argues that all events are present for Him, including contingent events. Contingency relates to time, but God's knowledge is timeless. Therefore, in spite of Aquinas's qualification in the sense that evil can be the result of contingent human decisions, the ultimate cause of evil is God's timeless

---

162. Aquinas *ST* I q. 103 a. 6 resp. See also ibid., q. 22 a. 3 resp.

163. Ibid., I q. 22 a. 2 resp.; I q. 22 a. 1. resp.

164. Ibid., I q. 19 a. 9 s.c.

165. These necessary causes ultimately refer to God because He is the Supreme Good of whom every good thing participates. He is also the first Unmoved Mover of everything. Finally, the forms of everything or archetypical ideas are in His mind as part of His being. See ibid., I q. 105 a. 5 resp.

166. "The works of men are contingent, being subject to free will." Ibid., I q. 14 a. 13 s.c.

167. Ibid., I q. 19 a. 8 resp.; q. 22 a. 4 s.c. and resp.

knowledge.[168] For practical purposes, contingency is applicable only to temporal beings and human temporal knowledge, but not to God's knowledge.[169] God has an absolutely necessary or causative knowledge of contingent events.[170]

In theory, then, although Aquinas defends the idea that human beings have free will, the fact is he also admits that "since the very act of free will is traced to God as to a cause, it necessarily follows that everything happening from the exercise of free will must be subject to divine providence."[171] Thus, salvation is a result of God's causative knowledge. For Aquinas, predestination is a part of God's providence—particularly applied to human salvation. As part of God's knowledge, predestination "pre-exists in God."[172] Following Augustine, Aquinas considers that God foreknows those who will receive salvation. The active application of God's predestination—which as a plan is part of God's providence, knowledge, and being—is part of God's active government but is passive in the predestined.[173] Something similar occurs with those condemned. "As predestination is a part of providence, in regard to those ordained to eternal salvation, so reprobation is a part of providence in regard to those who turn aside from that end."[174] Ultimately, predestination does not depend at all on something that human beings can do—whether doing good works or making right choices—but is only a question of God's decision.[175]

---

168. See Aquinas's discussion in Aquinas *SCG* 1.67.1-11. "Nothing prevents the divine intellect from having an eternal [timeless] and infallible knowledge of contingents." Ibid., 1.67.3.

169. "He knows with certitude whether contingent things are or are not." Ibid., 1.67.4. "God knows contingent things not successively, as they are in their own being, as we do but simultaneously. The reason is because His knowledge is measured by eternity, as is also His being; and eternity being simultaneously whole comprises all time. . . . Hence all things that are in time are present to God from eternity, not only because He has the types of things present within Him, as some say; but because His glance is carried from eternity over all things as they are in their presentiality. Hence it is manifest that contingent things are infallibly known by God, inasmuch as they are subject to the divine sight in their presentiality; yet they are future contingent things in relation to their own causes." Aquinas *ST* I q. 14 a. 13 resp.

170. Aquinas *SCG* 1.67.5.

171. Aquinas *ST* I q. 22 a. 2 ad. 4.

172. Ibid., I q. 23 a. 1 resp.

173. Ibid., I q. 23 a. 2 resp.

174. Ibid., I q. 23 a. 3 resp.

175. Ibid., I q. 23 a. 4 resp., a. 5 s.c. and resp. In fact, "whatsoever is in man disposing him towards salvation, is all included under the effect of predestination;

For Aquinas, even Christ's incarnation was predestined. As predestination is a divine eternal or timeless preordination of things that takes place in time, "we must needs [sic] admit that the union itself of natures in the Person of Christ falls under the eternal predestination of God. For this reason do we say that Christ was predestinated."[176]

The timeless providence of God orients everything toward the end of the divine goodness, of which everything created participates in different degrees.[177] God is the supreme perfection of being, completely simple, providing unity to the world.[178] He is immutable and unchangeable. In order to reflect divine perfection, the universe must show in its multiplicity different degrees of perfection in correspondence with different degress of being.[179] Aquinas considers that God's articulating action is a deterministic "movement" from multiplicity and mutability toward unity and immutability.[180]

The hierarchy as the whole. Aquinas believes that the result of God's articulation of reality as a whole is a complex hierarchy organized in different levels according to the degree of likeness or proximity that the different elements of the hierarchy have to the divine being. God is at the top of this hierarchy because He is immutable, immaterial, pure actuality, and timeless. He is the ultimate cause of every other cause, whether natural or voluntary.[181] God uses the highest intellectual creatures that are closer to Him to rule over all the lower creatures. The highest creatures, such as angels, participate in a higher degree of God's being, power, knowledge, and perfection. They are instruments of divine providence. Every level of the hierarchy rules over the immediate lower level.[182] The temporal and mutable creatures are at the bottom of the hierarchy. Aquinas put the heavenly bodies and angels

---

even the preparation for grace." Ibid., I q. 23 a. 5 resp. "Which flows from free-will is also of predestination." Ibid. Aquinas says that the exact number and identity of those destined to salvation are already a certainty in the mind of God. Ibid., I q. 23 a. 7 s.c. and resp.

176. Ibid., III q. 24 a. 1 resp.
177. Ibid., I q. 22 a. 1 resp.; I q. 22 a. 2 resp.; I q. 22 a. 4 resp.
178. Ibid., I q. 11 a. 3 resp.; I q. 44 a. 1 resp.
179. Ibid., I q. 22 a. 4 resp.
180. Kerbs, *El problema de la identidad*, 492.
181. Aquinas *ST* I q. 83 a. 1 ad. 3; q. 44 a. 1 resp.
182. Ibid., I q. 106 a. 3 resp. and ad. 1; Aquinas *SCG* 3.78.1-2; 79.5. For Aquinas, the heavenly part of the hierarchy is the model for the church hierarchy. Aquinas *ST* q. 106 a. 3 ad. 1.

in an intermediate position in this structure with different degrees of relation to/participation in timelessness and spacelessness.[183]

Summary

The hierarchical model of the principle of articulation followed by Catholic medieval theology explicitly assumes the presuppositions regarding being as timeless, immutable, and absolutely simple as found in Greek philosophy. The being of every particular thing is essentially timeless and unchangeable. Consequently, the hierarchical model assumes an interpretation of knowledge as a capturing of the timeless element of every object. It is necessary to "remove" the temporal, material, and mutable elements of the object to grasp the timeless essence, idea, or form—the *via negativa*.

Catholic medieval theology applied the *via negativa* to the interpretation of God, the world, and the human being, the essential parts of a theological system. Temporal-spatial biblical depictions of God and heavenly realities are interpreted metaphorically: namely, as timeless, immutable, and spaceless realities. The creation of the world is a timeless action of God, a creation out of nothing. There is no literal interpretation of the six-day story of Creation. Although the material world involves time—in contrast to a timeless heaven—temporality is only a creation of God. God Himself is timeless. Consequently, He does not relate in a direct way to the temporal part of creation. Human beings are also a dichotomy of soul and body. The image of God lies only in the soul, which is immortal, and akin to the timeless world, while the body is transient. The soul is able to participate in the timeless beatific vision of God after death.

Regarding the articulating agent and the articulating action, God is the ultimate cause of motion in the world, although He is unmoved. He moves the world according to a hierarchical structure where the superior beings, which have a higher degree of participation in God's timelessness and immutability, move the beings of the immediate inferior level and so on. God's articulating action relates to His unchangeable (fore) knowledge, will, and providential plan. God's knowledge and will regarding everything in the world are causative and necessary.

---

183. For an excellent summary of Aquinas's understanding of the hierarchical structure of reality from the perspective of timelessness, see Aquinas *ST* I q. 10 a. 5 resp.

Therefore, although the hierarchical model of the articulating principle has tried to admit the existence of free will in intelligent creatures, in reality, God's timeless and immutable articulating action is highly deterministic.

Every particular being in the world exists from the timeless eternity in the mind of God as an immutable archetypical idea or essence, which is included in God's being. God does not know anything external to Himself except through the ideas of the external things that are in His mind. Particular things exist and act because they participate in those unchangeable ideas or essences. Consequently, God's knowledge pre-determines every aspect of the reality of the world including salvation or damnation. Predestination is part of God's rigid providence applied to human beings. Even Christ's incarnation is understood from the perspective of God's immutable predestination.

Reality as a whole, then, is a hierarchy. God is at the top and all the other creatures participate in different degrees of God's timelessness and immutability. The greater the participation of a particular being in the hierarchy, the higher the position of that being in the hierarchy. God provides unity and articulation to the whole. There is a motion from mutability and temporality toward immutability and timelessness, from the inferior levels of the hierarchy toward the superior ones.

The Principle of Articulation in the Protestant Reformation

Augustine and Aquinas openly used Greek philosophical presuppositions in their theological constructions. Luther and Calvin, the main Protestant reformers during the 16th century, claimed to follow the *sola Scriptura* principle.[184] This section can help to ponder this claim.

---

184. According to Luther, faith "must rely on the Word of God alone." Martin Luther, *Luther's Works (LW)*, vol. 3, *Lectures on Genesis: Chapters 15-20*, ed. Jaroslav Pelikan and George V. Schick (Saint Louis, MO: Concordia, 1961), 325. See Hans Schwarz, *True Faith in the True God: An Introduction to Luther's Life and Thought*, rev. ed. (Minneapolis, MN: Fortress, 2015), 143. Calvin also affirmed that "it is impossible for any man to obtain even the minutest portion of right and sound doctrine without being a disciple of Scripture." John Calvin *Institutes of the Christian Religion* [two vols. in one] 1.6.2, trans. Henry Beveridge (Grand Rapids, MI: Eerdmans, 1989).

Martin Luther

Ontological and epistemological presuppositions. Luther's interpretation of the ontological and epistemological presuppositions is not explicit. Luther, however, as a former Augustinian monk, was highly acquainted with Augustine's works, which were a main influence in his theology.[185] In consonance, Luther distinguishes between temporal and timeless realities. The first one is God's creation. The second one is God's realm.[186]

The temporal realm is accessible to common human reason, even after the Fall. Human reason is "the essential difference by which man is distinguished from the animals and other things."[187] Human reason, however, is naturally hostile to God. In order to access the timeless realm of God, faith or theological reason is necessary.[188] A discussion of Luther's interpretations of God, the world, and the human being can reveal additional insights regarding Luther's ontological and epistemological presuppositions, particularly how they operate in the context of his theology.

The interpretation of God. Luther assumes God's timelessness, immutability, simplicity, and spacelessness.[189] He believes that God does not experience time.[190] In consequence, God does not know temporal

---

185. Albrecht Beutel, "Luther's Life," in *The Cambridge Companion to Martin Luther*, ed. Donald K. McKim (Cambridge, UK: Cambridge University Press, 2003), 5. In general, Luther has a negative attitude toward scholastic theology and Aristotle but a much more positive attitude toward Augustine. See, for example, Martin Luther, *LW*, vol. 48, *Letters I*, ed. Gottfried G. Krodel and Helmut T. Lehmann (Philadelphia, PA: Fortress, 1963), 42.

186. "It is undeniable that whatever is not temporal must be eternal, and whatever has no beginning cannot be temporal, and whatever is not a creature, must be God. For outside of God and creature there is nothing." Martin Luther, *LW*, vol. 52, *Sermons II*, ed. Hans J. Hillerbrand and Helmut T. Lehmann (Philadelphia, PA: Fortress, 1974), 42.

187. Martin Luther, *LW*, vol. 34, *Career of the Reformer IV*, ed. Lewis W. Spitz and Helmut T. Lehmann (Philadelphia, PA: Fortress, 1960), 137, 144.

188. Ibid., 144. Luther thinks that faith, not reason, is what is necessary to consider God's activity that "rushes beyond time and temporal matters." Martin Luther, *LW*, vol. 12, *Selected Psalms I*, ed. Jaroslav Pelikan (Saint Louis, MO: Concordia, 1955), 54.

189. See Veli-Matti Kärkkäinen, *The Doctrine of God: A Global Introduction; A Biblical, Historical and Contemporary Survey* (Grand Rapids, MI: Baker, 2004), 51-52, 100, 121.

190. "In God's case there is neither a past nor a future, but outside of time and in eternity everything is in present time." Luther, *Selected Psalms I*, 52. "For eternity has

events in a successive way but in a simultaneous way.[191] This understanding of God's knowledge is in line with Aquinas's idea that "which he created does not affect him."[192]

God's timelessness and immutability involve His will. God's will is the ultimate cause of the entire reality, even future events. Luther holds that it is necessary for Christians "to know that God foreknows nothing contingently, but that he foresees and purposes and does all things by his immutable, eternal, and infallible will."[193] Luther also affirms that God is absolutely simple.[194] God's simplicity implies that He is also spaceless. The biblical language that describes God as having eyes, ears, or arms does not correspond with God's spiritual essence but is a language adapted to human beings or a manner of speech. God is not literally sitting in a throne in a temple in heaven as biblical prophets frequently describe. God reveals Himself in Scripture through this kind of veil or wrapper.[195] Therefore, God is a hidden reality accessible

---

neither past nor future.... For God is ... outside time." Ibid. "God is outside time, a spiritual being." Ibid., 47.

191. Commenting on 2 Pet 3:8-10, Luther says that God does not see time or temporal events longitudinally but transversely. "In God's sight everything is in one heap." Martin Luther, *LW*, vol. 30, *The Catholic Epistles*, ed. Jaroslav Pelikan and Walter A. Hansen (Saint Louis, MO: Concordia, 1967), 196. For practical purposes, Luther's idea that God experiences time simultaneously means that God does not experience time at all because the successive element of time—past, present, and future—is eliminated. God perceives a logical succession in events but not a temporal one. See also ibid., 114.

192. Scott S. Ickert, "Luther on the Timelessness of God," *Lutheran Quarterly* 7, no. 1 (1993): 51.

193. Martin Luther, *LW*, vol. 33, *Career of the Reformer III*, ed. Philip S. Watson and Helmut T. Lehmann (Philadelphia, PA: Fortress, 1972), 37, 42, 43. Luther modifies Aquinas's notion that God foreknows because His knowledge is causative. In the case of Luther, God knows the future because He knows what He will do. God's immutable will is the cause of His foreknowledge. "God who causes all things is also the only causal agent.... God is the first or principal cause, all others are only secondary or instrumental causes." Paul Althaus, *The Theology of Martin Luther*, trans. Robert C. Schultz (Philadelphia, PA: Fortress, 1979), 107.

194. "God's power, arm, hand, nature, face, Spirit, wisdom, etc., are all one thing; for apart from the creation there is nothing but the *one simple Deity himself.*" Martin Luther, *LW*, vol. 37, *Word and Sacrament III*, ed. Robert Fischer and Helmut T. Lehmann (Philadelphia, PA: Fortress, 1961), 61. Emphasis mine.

195. Martin Luther, *LW*, vol. 1, *Lectures on Genesis: Chapters 1-5*, ed. Jaroslav Pelikan and George V. Schick (Saint Louis, MO: Concordia, 1958), 14-15; Martin Luther, *LW*, vol. 16, *Lectures on Isaiah: Chapters 1-39*, ed. Jaroslav Pelikan and Hilton C. Oswald, trans. Herbert J. A. Bouman (Saint Louis, MO: Concordia, 1969), 76.

only through faith.[196] Luther's understanding of God's nature shows that although he does not offer a technical explanation of his epistemological presuppositions, his implicit epistemology still supports the *via negativa*.[197]

The interpretation of the world. Luther believes that reality is divided into a timeless realm and a temporal one. The temporal world is God's creation out of nothing. There was no time before Creation.[198] Luther believes that the original creation was developed in six literal days. The story of Creation in Genesis is about the world and its creatures.[199] The six-day period involves the creation of new classes, species, or types of creatures. From God's timeless perspective, however, Creation is instantaneous. Through His timeless Word, God speaks and the creatures come to be in the temporal realm. Actually, the creation of those original species involves already the individuals of each kind that would appear throughout the time after the Creation week.[200]

Luther believes that this temporal-spatial world is only transient. "Men were not created to live permanently in this lowest part of the universe but to take possession of heaven."[201] Luther affirms a vision of reality that considers temporal-material reality as inferior to the timeless superior reality in which intelligent creatures will finally live.[202]

---

196. Luther, *Career of the Reformer III*, 62.

197. Regarding Luther's use of the negative way, see Mark Mattes, "Luther's Use of Philosophy," *Lutherjahrbuch* 80 (2013): 110-141.

198. Luther, *Lectures on Genesis: Chapters 1-5*, 10, 11.

199. Ibid., 5. Apparently, however, angels—also created during that week—are able to experience God's timelessness in His presence. See ibid., 10, 12, 22; Martin Luther, *LW*, vol. 2, *Lectures on Genesis: Chapters 6-14*, ed. Jaroslav Pelikan, Daniel E. Poellot, and George V. Schick (Saint Louis, MO: Concordia, 1960), 129-130.

200. Luther, *Lectures on Genesis: Chapters 1-5*, 76. "So God, through His Word, extends His activity from the beginning of the world to its end. For with God there is nothing that is earlier or later, swifter or slower; but in His eyes all things are present things. For He is simply outside the scope of time." Ibid.

201. Ibid., 46.

202. At least those who are part of the elect. Scott S. Ickert points out that the Reformation inherits from medieval theology the notion that temporal creation must be seen from the perspective of the timelessness of God. "It was necessary to distinguish time from eternity to keep the Creator distinct from his creation. In himself, the immutable God transcends temporality, and thus all that creation is heir to. Time, then, poses a profound threat to eternity as the domain of God's immortal divinity. Consequently, God displays his lordship over time, and therefore his supreme transcendence, by looking down on time from the perspective of the standing now, the eternal 'today' comprehending past and future." Ickert, "Luther on the Timelessness of God," 50-51.

The interpretation of the human being. Luther believes that the human being, although part of the temporal creation, was "created to inhabit the celestial regions and to live an eternal life when, after a while, he has left the earth"[203] when he/she dies. "That future life will be without time."[204] This view clearly implies a dualism regarding human nature. Only the body of a human being dies. Souls are immortal.[205] Normally, the souls of believers are sleeping in peace after death. However, they are also able to experience visions and hear angels and God. Before Christ's coming, they are in "the bosom of Christ."[206] In contrast, the souls of the wicked "have everlasting night and darkness."[207]

Luther thinks that original sin deeply affects the entire human condition. Sin involves the total corruption of the whole human nature.[208] Given this fact, the only hope of humanity is for God to work salvation without human intervention. Moreover, as God's will is the overwhelming cause of the entire reality, human beings do not have real free will and consequently cannot provide any solution for the problem of sin.[209]

The rejection of free will leads naturally to ask if God is in some way responsible for human sin. Luther admits, on the one hand, "that God works all in all [I Cor. 12:6] and that without him nothing is effected or effective; for he is omnipotent, and this belongs to his omnipotence."[210] On the other hand, however, Luther wants to avoid the ob-

---

203. Luther, *Lectures on Genesis: Chapters 1-5*, 46.

204. Ibid., 44.

205. Martin Luther, *LW*, vol. 51, *Sermons I*, ed. John W. Doberstein and Helmut T. Lehmann (Philadelphia, PA: Fortress, 1959), 234; Luther, *Lectures on Genesis: Chapters 1-5*, 44, 45.

206. Martin Luther, *LW*, vol. 4, *Lectures on Genesis: Chapters 21-25*, ed. Jaroslav Jan Pelikan and Walter A. Hansen, trans. George V. Schick (Saint Louis, MO: Concordia, 1964), 313. Regarding the sleep of the dead in Luther, see Althaus, *The Theology of Martin Luther*, 410-417.

207. Luther, *Lectures on Genesis: Chapters 1-5*, 44.

208. Luther, *Career of the Reformer IV*, 164; Luther, *Selected Psalms I*, 307-308.

209. Regarding Luther's view of free will, see John C. Peckham, "An Investigation of Luther's View of the Bondage of the Will With Implications for Soteriology and Theodicy," *JATS* 18, no. 2 (2007): 274-304, especially 277-282. "It is our function passively to receive God and His working within us, just as we see that a workman's tool is acted upon." Martin Luther, *LW*, vol. 27, *Lectures on Galatians, 1535, Chapters 5-6; Lectures on Galatians, 1519, Chapters 1-6*, ed. Jaroslav Pelikan and Walter A. Hansen (Saint Louis, MO: Concordia, 1964), 294.

210. Luther, *Career of the Reformer III*, 175. Bracketed in original.

vious conclusion that God is responsible for sin. He argues that to the extent that humans are evil instruments, "God works evil in us, i.e., by means of us, not through any fault of his, but owing to our faultiness, since we are by nature evil and he is good."[211]

However, it is still possible to ask if human sin is the result of God's will. If God's will and foreknowledge necessarily determine the destiny of the human being, why does God allow the fall of Adam? Luther answers that God's will is the superior rule for everything, its own standard, without another rule, reason, or cause governing over it. Thus, what God wills is always right and what happens as a result is right too.[212]

The articulating agent. Luther's approach to theology is through soteriology.[213] In that context, he grants a central role to Christ as the divine representative that articulates the relationship between God and the world, particularly humanity. Christ is the one who reveals the eternal and timeless God. There is no other way to know the infinite and incomprehensible God.[214] The hidden God revealed Himself in the incarnated Christ.[215] The believer can encounter God "under the mask, in the Word [Christ]."[216] Christ here on earth is a temporal manifestation of a timeless God.

For Luther, "the cross is the Word historicized making credible God's eternal promises."[217] Luther, however, still understands Christ's salvific work from an essentially timeless perspective. The cross and Christ's sacrifice is not the final cause of salvation but only an intermediate one. Christ's death is the way through which God makes possible His timeless decision to save some people from eternity based on His immutable will.[218] Everything that Christ thought, said, and wanted

---

211. Ibid., 178. God "makes good use of this evil [in His creatures] in accordance with his wisdom for his own glory and our salvation." Ibid.

212. Ibid., 180-181.

213. González, *Historia*, 727.

214. Martin Luther, *LW*, vol. 26, *Lectures on Galatians, 1535, Chapters 1-4*, ed. Jaroslav Pelikan and Walter A. Hansen, trans. Jaroslav Pelikan (Saint Louis, MO: Concordia, 1963), 29. See also Luther, *Selected Psalms I*, 54.

215. Martin Luther, *LW*, vol. 5, *Lectures on Genesis: Chapters 26-30*, ed. Jaroslav Pelikan and Walter A. Hansen (Saint Louis, MO: Concordia, 1968), 48.

216. Martin Luther, *LW*, vol. 24, *Sermons on the Gospel of St. John: Chapters 14-16*, ed. Jaroslav Pelikan and Daniel E. Poellot, trans. Martin H. Bertram (Saint Louis, MO: Concordia, 1961), 68.

217. Kenneth Hagen, "Luther on Atonement–Reconfigured," *Concordia Theological Quarterly* 61, no. 4 (1997): 264.

218. "Christ's work was done at a particular time in history. But in God's sight it

reflected God's will.²¹⁹ In fact, the "present" salvific activity of Christ is timeless. Although for Luther Christ is the heavenly High Priest in God's presence on behalf of the believers,²²⁰ he also holds that "in the existence in which Christ is, those who lived in the past and those who are living today are alike before Him. For His rule extends over both the dead and the living. And in that life the beginning, the middle, and the end of the world are all in one lump."²²¹

The articulating action. If Christ is the articulating agent in Luther's theology, justification by faith plays, in his perspective, a central role as the articulating action that restores the relationship between God and humanity.²²² Luther considers justification by faith as the central doctrine of Christianity. In this doctrine "*are included all the other doctrines of our faith*; and if it is sound, all the others are sound as well."²²³

Luther understands the doctrine of justification from his perspective of predestination. As God's immutable will and foreknowledge are the cause of everything in His creation, Luther affirms that God predestines the saved and the lost.²²⁴ Given Luther's soteriological emphasis, predestination is crucial in his thought.²²⁵

---

has existed from all eternity. . . . The work of salvation is . . . based on God's eternal will to save; and its significance therefore transcends time." Althaus, *The Theology of Martin Luther*, 211.

219. Luther, *St. John: Chapters 14-16*, 141.

220. Martin Luther, *LW*, vol. 29, *Lectures on Titus, Philemon, and Hebrews*, ed. Jaroslav Pelikan and Walter A. Hansen (Saint Louis, MO: Concordia, 1968), 217.

221. Luther, *The Catholic Epistles*, 114.

222. "Christology is . . . found right at the centre of his theology, linked with justification by faith alone." Matthieu Arnold, "Luther on Christ's Person and Work," in *The Oxford Handbook of Martin Luther's Theology*, ed. Robert Kolb, Irene Dingel, and L'ubomír Batka (New York, NY: Oxford University Press, 2014), 276.

223. Luther, *Lectures on Galatians, 1535, Chapters 1-4*, 283. Emphasis mine. Regarding the importance of this doctrine, Luther thinks that "if the doctrine of justification is lost, the whole of Christian doctrine is lost." Ibid., 9.

224. Predestination determines "who shall believe or not, who can or cannot get rid of sin—in order that our salvation may be taken entirely out of our hands and put in the hand of God alone." Martin Luther, *LW*, vol. 35, *Word and Sacrament I*, ed. E. Theodore Backmann and Helmut T. Lehmann (Philadelphia, PA: Fortress, 1960), 378. See also Martin Luther, *LW*, vol. 25, *Lectures on Romans*, ed. Hilton C. Oswald (Saint Louis, MO: Concordia, 1972), 373-378.

225. "Everything he taught, the whole range of his theology from eternity to eternity, and the complete sweep of his thought, religious or secular, stands upon God's eternal decree of predestination." William M. Landeen, *Martin Luther's Religious Thought* (Mountain View, CA: Pacific Press, 1971), 130.

Luther conceives of salvation as a creation work. There is no real participation of human will. God makes everything out of nothing.²²⁶ This understanding of salvation avoids the interference of meritorious works. In addition, Luther prevents any voluntary participation of human beings in their own salvation. For Luther, any participation of human beings in justification or salvation, in any possible way, is synonymous with justification by works. Luther develops a monergistic understanding of justification by faith.²²⁷ Faith "is *something that is done to us rather than something that we do.*"²²⁸ The Holy Spirit creates the capacity to believe but only in the elect. The rest will perish in unbelief because God implants faith in the elect but without their cooperation.²²⁹

The true righteousness of God, therefore, is completely passive because God is the One who declares the believer as righteous independently of any human work or action. For Luther, an active righteousness relates to civil legal requirements, ceremonial requirements, or works of the law. It is active because the human being has to do something in order to be considered righteous. The believer should abandon active righteousness and embrace only passive righteousness, the one of grace and forgiveness. Actually, believers should live as if the law did not exist. The only purpose of the law is to terrify, humiliate, and produce contrition among the unbelievers.²³⁰

Luther thinks that passive righteousness relates to the heavenly timeless realm of God, reached by faith, while active righteousness relates to the temporal-spatial realm, where justification is by the law or works.²³¹ Passive righteousness means that justification is, in essence,

---

226. Luther, *Selected Psalms I*, 377-380. See also Luther, *Lectures on Galatians, 1535, Chapters 1-4*, 66.

227. See Althaus, *The Theology of Martin Luther*, 125.

228. Luther, *Lectures on Genesis: Chapters 6-14*, 267. Emphasis mine.

229. Luther, *Career of the Reformer III*, 60-61. Martin Luther, *LW*, vol. 23, *Sermons on the Gospel of St. John: Chapters 6-8*, ed. Jaroslav Pelikan and Daniel E. Poellot, trans. Martin H. Bertran (Saint Louis, MO: Concordia, 1959), 23; Jan D. Kingston Siggins, *Martin Luther's Doctrine of Christ* (New Haven, CT: Yale University Press, 1970), 146.

230. Luther, *Lectures on Galatians, 1535, Chapters 1-4*, 4-7. The Ten Commandments are valid to the extent that they reflect the natural law. "We read Moses not because he applies to us . . . but because he agrees with the natural law." Luther, *Word and Sacrament I*, 173.

231. Faith is the way "through which we ascend beyond all laws and works. 'As, therefore, we have borne the image of the earthly Adam,' as Paul says, 'let us bear the image of the heavenly one' (1 Cor. 15:49), who is *a new man in a new world,*

imputed or forensic righteousness, not imparted. The sinner is declared or considered as righteous while he/she is still a sinner.²³² After being justified, though, a Christian remains a sinner. "A Christian man is righteous and a sinner at the same time [*simul iustus et peccator*], holy and profane, an enemy of God and a child of God."²³³ Justification removes sin forensically but not substantially.²³⁴

As Luther understands justification from the perspective of the absolute will and timeless predestination of God, the elect cannot receive forgiveness only for past sins. God's forgiveness necessarily covers the entire temporal experience of the believer: past, present, and future.²³⁵ Justification is ultimately salvation itself.²³⁶ From the perspective of the believer's temporal experience, the forgiveness of sins or justification is a continuous work of God.²³⁷ From God's perspective, however, salvation is something produced in one eternal, timeless instantaneous decision by the will of God in His predestination.²³⁸ Justification or forgiveness is a punctiliar fact (without duration), once and forever, springing from God's timeless predestination, will, and foreknowledge. In consequence, the ultimate cause of salvation is not the sacrifice of Christ on the cross but God's election.²³⁹ The cross is an intermediate

---

where there is no Law, no sin, no conscience, no death, but perfect joy, righteousness, grace, peace, life, salvation, and glory." Luther, *Lectures on Galatians, 1535, Chapters 1-4*, 8. Emphasis mine.

232. González, *Historia*, 630; Luther, *Career of the Reformer IV*, 167.

233. Luther, *Lectures on Galatians, 1535, Chapters 1-4*, 232.

234. Luther, *Career of the Reformer IV*, 164-167.

235. "The *forgiveness of sins* begins in baptism and *remains with us all the way to death*, until we arise from the dead, and leads us into life eternal. So *we live continually under the remission of sins.*" Ibid., 164. Emphasis mine. "When we consider the application of the forgiveness, *we are not dealing with a particular time, but find that it has taken place from the beginning of the world.* So St. John in the Book of Revelation [13:8] says that the Lamb of God was slain before the foundation of the world." Martin Luther, *LW*, vol. 40, *Church and Ministry II*, ed. Conrad Bergendoff and Helmut T. Lehmann (Philadelphia, PA: Fortress, 1958), 215. Emphasis mine. Bracketed in original.

236. Luther, *Lectures on Galatians, 1535, Chapters 1-4*, 223.

237. Luther, *Career of the Reformer IV*, 167.

238. Luther mentions as a possible interpretation of Rom 5:6, the following one: "When we were weak according to time, even though before God we were already righteous through His predestination. For *in the predestination of God all things have already taken place*, even things which in our reality still lie in the future." Luther, *Lectures on Romans*, 296. Emphasis mine.

239. Luther believes that God "saves us not by our own merits, but purely by *His own election and immutable will*. . . . He gives approval not to our will but to His

cause but not the final one. Christ's death is the way through which God makes His timeless decision from eternity possible in time.

In Luther's understanding of justification, good works are fruits that show if a tree is good. They are external evidence of justification.[240] Luther also thinks that there is a progressive transformation in the Christian life.[241] But he does not believe that good works or moral growth are really part of God's salvation. Salvation is already a reality in justification. Sanctification is a consequence of salvation, not part of it.[242] Imputed justification has the practical priority in human salvation.[243] There is no possibility of sanctification understood as perfection of character.[244]

The prior landscape strongly suggests that for Luther, justification by faith is the manifestation of the elect's predestination, which in turn springs from God's timeless supreme will and foreknowledge. In the final analysis, then, God articulates the relationship between Himself and His creation through the application of His overwhelming timeless will and His timeless predestination in the case of His intelligent creatures. Ultimately, God's will, foreknowledge, and predestination are essentially one and the same timeless action of God, ruling the entire creation, including intelligent creatures.[245]

Luther's understanding of the principle of articulation operates as an abstractive center that prevents him from including in his theological thinking biblical data that are not easy to interpret in the light of his view of predestination-justification and the underlying presuppositions. In his perspective, then, the Epistle to the Romans "is really the chief part of the New Testament, and is truly the purest gospel."[246] In

---

own *unchanging and firm will of predestination*." Ibid., 371. Emphasis mine.

240. Luther, *Career of the Reformer IV*, 161-162, 165, 166; Luther, *Word and Sacrament I*, 374.

241. Martin Luther, *LW*, vol. 31, *Career of the Reformer I*, ed. Harold J. Grimm and Helmut T. Lehmann (Philadelphia, PA: Fortress, 1957), 299; Luther, *Lectures on Galatians, 1535, Chapters 5-6*, 227.

242. See Althaus, *The Theology of Martin Luther*, 245-246.

243. Martin Luther, *LW*, vol. 32, *Career of the Reformer II*, ed. George W. Forell and Helmut T. Lehmann (Philadelphia, PA: Fortress, 1958), 239.

244. Luther, *Lectures on Romans*, 257.

245. "If we believe it to be true that God foreknows and predestines all things, that he can neither be mistaken in his foreknowledge nor hindered in his predestination, and that nothing takes place but as he wills it (as reason itself is forced to admit), then on the testimony of reason itself there cannot be any free choice in man or angel or any creature." Luther, *Career of the Reformer III*, 293.

246. Luther, *Word and Sacrament I*, 365.

sharp contrast, Luther evaluates the Epistle of James, which emphasizes the human role in Christian life, as "flatly against St. Paul and all the rest of Scripture in ascribing justification to works [2:24]."[247]

The whole. The dualistic view that Luther has of reality implies that the hierarchical understanding of the whole of medieval theology is still alive, although simplified when compared with, for example, Aquinas. Luther sees the temporal creation as something provisional, temporary, not as permanent. Creation goes in the direction of a spiritualized reality where time will finally disappear. "When these days of the earth come to an end, everything will come to an end, and there will follow days of heaven, that is, eternal [timeless] days."[248] In that new, timeless, and unchangeable reality, nobody will experience physical needs or will need to work. Social hierarchies, civil authorities, or institutions will disappear, including marriage and families.[249] "God will be 'everything to everyone,' that is, everybody will find all wants that are now satisfied by all things satisfied in God Himself."[250] In other words, "all that pertains to the essence of these temporal goods and is part of temporal life and works will cease to be."[251] All the elect will enjoy spiritual glorified or celestial bodies, made of a new essence or form.[252] "It will be a new mode of existence, free of all temporal necessities."[253] Humanity will experience God face-to-face and contemplating Him will be its only occupation.[254]

It seems that God is guiding the entire creation and the elect to where they will find their ultimate unity and wholeness in the timeless

---

247. Ibid., 396.

248. Luther, *Lectures on Genesis: Chapters 6-14*, 129.

249. Martin Luther, *LW*, vol. 54, *Table Talk*, ed. Theodore G. Tappert and Helmut T. Lehmann (Philadelphia, PA: Fortress, 1967), 291; Martin Luther, *LW*, vol. 28, *1 Corinthians 7, 1 Corinthians 15, Lectures on 1 Timothy*, ed. Hilton C. Oswald (Saint Louis, MO: Concordia, 1973), 182, 196.

250. Luther, *1 Corinthians 7, 1 Corinthians 15*, 141-142.

251. Ibid., 172.

252. Ibid., 194, 196, 198, 200. Luther describes these spiritual bodies as having different levels of brightness and glory, as well as possessing a high degree of strength and skill. Ibid., 184, 188. However, he insists, "It will be a completely spiritual existence, or life." Ibid., 190.

253. Ibid., 183. See also ibid., 184, 192.

254. Luther, *Table Talk*, 291; Jane E. Strohl, "Luther's Eschatology," in *The Oxford Handbook of Martin Luther's Theology*, ed. Robert Kolb, Irene Dingel, and L'ubomír Batka (Oxford, UK: Oxford University Press, 2014), 359-360.

realm of God. "All will be of one heavenly essence."²⁵⁵ Faith allows anticipating in time this timeless reality. However, history, time, and space are hindrances for the achievement of this goal. Flesh and blood cannot participate in the heavenly reality even if the Fall had never happened.²⁵⁶

John Calvin

Ontological and epistemological presuppositions. Like Luther, Calvin does not elaborate his ontological and epistemological presuppositions explicitly. However, they are still detectable in his writings, especially regarding his doctrine of God.²⁵⁷ He also distinguishes between temporality and eternity. Eternity is the realm of God and is equivalent to timelessness.²⁵⁸ Eternity or timelessness is the perspective from which Calvin interprets temporal reality. In the words of Barth, "Eternity is seen as the negation of all time and the position that underlies time, . . . its meaning, its transcendental content."²⁵⁹ Eternity is, therefore, the underlying reality, giving the real meaning, content, reference, and determination to the entire creation.

Calvin presents his epistemology mainly in terms of the knowledge about God. True wisdom consists fundamentally in knowing God and human beings. The sin and lowness of human condition lead to dissatisfaction. Only by knowing God, humans are able to know their real condition.²⁶⁰ Human beings have a natural instinct or awareness of the existence of God. There is a religious seed put by God in the human heart. This knowledge makes humans inexcusable for their sinfulness and ignorance of God.²⁶¹ That is why even philosophers have been able to grasp some discernment of God's nature although in a very vague way.²⁶² Knowledge about God is also present to some extent in nature. However, nature cannot provide a clear knowledge of God

---

255. Luther, *1 Corinthians 7, 1 Corinthians 15*, 184.
256. Strohl, "Luther's Eschatology," 360. See Luther, *1 Corinthians 7, 1 Corinthians 15*, 192-194.
257. See Charles B. Partee, *Calvin and Classical Philosophy* (Leiden, Netherlands: Brill, 1977), 27.
258. "In eternity there can be no room for first or last." Calvin *Institutes* 1.13.18.
259. Karl Barth, *The Theology of John Calvin*, trans. Geoffrey W. Bromiley (Grand Rapids, MI: Eerdmans, 1995), 155. Barth adds that in the temporal realm "everything is judged and determined by its relation to the eternal." Ibid.
260. Calvin *Institutes* 1.1.1-2.
261. Ibid., 1.3.1, 3; 1.4.1.
262. Ibid., 2.2.18.

either. Again, this knowledge only makes humans inexcusable for their condition.[263] The fundamental way to know God, then, is through Scripture. It is necessary to explore Calvin's interpretation of God's nature in Scripture, which also helps to understand his ontological and epistemological presuppositions better.

The interpretation of God. Calvin holds that knowing God in His essence is impossible.[264] Only God can know His own substance. Humans can know God only as He has revealed Himself in His Word but not as He really is.[265] Eternity is a synonym for timelessness and God is eternal rather than everlasting. Therefore, God's knowledge is timeless. He knows or foreknows everything as an eternal present. His knowledge of future events or things comes from His own mind where they are already real.[266]

God is also immutable. There is no change in His essence.[267] His immutability implies that He is unable to suffer or experience emotions such as anger.[268] In the same line, a timeless and immutable God cannot be spatial or material. The essence of God is spiritual in nature, which is in contrast to any corporeal matter.[269]

This interpretation of God's nature for Calvin is in harmony with the application of the *via negativa* in classical theology. According to Calvin, the Bible talks about God as nurses talk to little children, *accommodating* or adapting to their age.[270] The concrete hermeneutical consequence of the *via negativa* in Calvin's interpretation of God's na-

---

263. Ibid., 1.5.1, 12-15.
264. "His essence, indeed, is incomprehensible, utterly transcending all human thought." Ibid., 1.5.1.
265. Ibid., 1.13.21. See ibid., 1.6.1, 2.
266. "When we attribute prescience to God, we mean that all things always were, and ever continue, under his eye; that to his knowledge *there is no past or future*, but *all things are present*, and indeed so present, that it is not merely the idea of them that is before him (as those objects are which we retain in our memory), but that he truly sees and contemplates them as actually under his immediate inspection." Ibid., 3.21.5. Emphasis mine.
267. Ibid., 1.13.8; 1.11.2. Calvin affirms that God's essence is unknowable while at the same time affirms His timeless or eternal nature.
268. Ibid., 2.14.2; 2.16.2-3.
269. Ibid., 1.13.1; 1.11.2.
270. "Such modes of expression . . . do not so much express what kind of a being God is, as accommodate the knowledge of him to our feebleness. In doing so, he must, of course, stoop far below his proper height." Calvin *Institutes* 1.13.1.

ture in the biblical text is his *principle of accommodation*.²⁷¹ For example, the visible manifestations of God in the Old Testament, including those related to the earthly sanctuary, are hints "of his incomprehensible essence."²⁷² Calvin also admits that "God sometimes appeared in the form of a man, but this was in anticipation of the future revelation in Christ."²⁷³ Heavenly realities associated with God, such as His throne, are not literal either. "No place can be assigned to God."²⁷⁴ In practice, then, Calvin's "doctrine of accommodation . . . functions in roughly apophatic way [*via negativa*]."²⁷⁵

The interpretation of the world. According to Calvin, the world is a hierarchical structure, divided into two basic levels: temporality and eternity.²⁷⁶ The second is superior, the real one. Creation is designed to show the superiority of the timeless realm. The six-day narrative of Creation enables the believer to understand the contrast between the eter-

---

271. Regarding this principle of accommodation, see Ford L. Battles, "God Was Accommodating Himself to Human Capacity," in *Readings in Calvin's Theology*, ed. Donald K. McKim (Grand Rapids, MI: Baker, 1984), 21-42; Arnold Huijgen, *Divine Accommodation in John Calvin's Theology: Analysis and Assessment* (Göttingen, Germany: Vandenhoeck & Ruprecht, 2011). Huijgen explains that "accommodation as revelation, implies that God's essence lies behind God's revelation." Ibid., 388. See also Douglas Johnson, "The Word of Life: A Study of the Relationship Between the Doctrines of Revelation and Redemption, With Reference to the Theology of John Calvin and Contemporary Thought Concerning Speech and Action" (PhD thesis, Roehampton University, London, UK, 2013), 23-42; Timothy George, *Theology of the Reformers* (Nashville, TN: Broadman, 1988), 192-195.

272. Calvin *Institutes* 1.11.3. Emphasis mine.

273. Ibid. Commenting on Exod 33:20-21, Calvin does not consider Moses's description of God as literal. It may appear "puerile, but it is well adapted to our imperfection. . . . Moses was to see God only from behind. It is a similitude taken from men." John Calvin, *Commentaries on the Four Last Books of Moses, Arranged in the Form of a Harmony*, vol. 3, trans. Charles William Bingham (Edinburgh, Scotland: Calvin Translation Society, 1854), 382.

274. Calvin *Institutes* 3.20.40. "We must not ascribe to him any thing [sic] of a terrestrial or carnal nature." Ibid. See also John Calvin, *Commentaries on the Book of the Prophet Daniel*, vol. 2, trans. Thomas Myers (Edinburgh, Scotland: Calvin Translation Society, 1853), 33-34.

275. J. Todd Billings, *Calvin, Participation, and the Gift: The Activity of Believers in Union With Christ* (New York, NY: Oxford University Press, 2007), 78. See ibid., 163, n. 82; J. Todd Billings, *Union With Christ: Reframing Theology and Ministry for the Church* (Grand Rapids, MI: Baker, 2011), 70-75. "What patristic scholars call 'apophatic' thought with regard to the negative theology of the church fathers was certainly not foreign to Calvin." Ibid., 74-75.

276. See Richard A. Muller, *Christ and the Decree: Christology and Predestination in Reformed Theology From Calvin to Perkins* (Grand Rapids, MI: Baker, 1988), 38.

nity of God—His timeless transcendence—and the temporal creation.²⁷⁷

This contrast implies that "before" Creation there was no time. Time is a creation of God. The material creation works as a temporal mirror of the invisible timeless God.²⁷⁸ Creation, however, also involves the timeless or spiritual realm of heaven, akin to God, which is populated by angels and the souls of believers.²⁷⁹ Although angels can take human form, they possess a spiritual essence without bodily shape.²⁸⁰

The interpretation of the human being. Human beings are in an intermediate situation between the spiritual and the physical world. They have soul and body, although the soul is the superior and main part. Even in his original condition, Adam was a vessel of clay inhabited by an immortal spirit. The body is really a prison-house of the soul. The soul is able to know God because it is immortal, akin to the timeless heavenly world of God.²⁸¹ The image of God is present in the human soul rather than in the body.²⁸²

Despite his high regard for the human soul, Calvin believes that even before the Fall there was an unbridgeable gap between God and His creatures. "Had man remained free from all taint, he was of too humble a condition to penetrate to God without a Mediator."²⁸³ There is always a metaphysical abysm between God and His creatures.²⁸⁴ Calvin's hierarchical ontology²⁸⁵ requires a Mediator with temporal and timeless features.

---

277. The story of Creation is *"a means of giving a clearer manifestation of the eternity of God as contrasted with the birth of creation."* Calvin *Institutes* 1.14.1. Emphasis mine.

278. "That invisible God, whose wisdom, power, and justice, are incomprehensible, is set before us in the history of Moses as in a mirror, in which his living image is reflected." Ibid.

279. François Wendel, *Calvin: The Origins and Development of His Religious Thought*, trans. Philip Mairet (New York, NY: Harper & Row, 1963), 171-172; Calvin *Institutes* 1.14.9.

280. Calvin *Institutes* 1.14.9. "Scripture, in accommodation to us, describes them under the form of winged Cherubim and Seraphim." Ibid., 1.14.8.

281. Ibid., 1.15.1-2. See Wendel, *Calvin*, 173. Calvin explicitly describes the human soul using common Greek philosophical terms. Ibid., 1.15.6.

282. Calvin *Institutes* 1.15.3.

283. Ibid., 2.12.1. See González, *Historia*, 697. See also Calvin *Institutes* 2.6.4.

284. Barth considers that "no reformer was more strongly shaped than he [Calvin] was by the antithesis of time and eternity [timelessness]." Barth, *The Theology of John Calvin*, 125.

285. Huijgen uses this expression regarding Calvin's dualism. Huijgen, *Divine Accommodation*, 389.

Articulating agent and articulating action. Christ plays a fundamental role in Calvin's understanding of the principle of articulation. He is a Mediator between an inaccessible and inscrutable God and human sinners. Calvin holds that Christ mediates between God and His creation in general, including angels, in contrast to medieval theology that affirmed that Christ was a Mediator in connection with His incarnation. The entire creation has to be united to God through Christ, even though not all creatures or things are in need of reconciliation.[286] Calvin, however, understands Christ's mediation from a timeless viewpoint. Christ is God's divine Word and Wisdom, begotten by the Father from eternity as described in Prov 8, John 1, and other biblical texts.[287]

Christ is more than only God's creative Word. His mediation task before the Incarnation also manifests, after the Fall, in His revelation to the patriarchs and the prophets in the Old Testament and in His appearances as the Angel of the Lord.[288] Christ is the Mediator of the old covenant. In essence, for Calvin, there is only one eternal covenant encompassing the Old and the New Testament. This is a single spiritual covenant with essentially the same promises of eternal life and the same Mediator.[289]

In the context of the New Testament, Christ, as anointed of God, performs His mediation office as Prophet (He fulfills the Old Testament prophecies), King (He is the King of the church), and Priest (He is also the sacrifice for the elect's sins and the intercessor before the Father).[290] Through His sacrificial atonement and obedience, elects are

---

286. Stephen Edmondson, *Calvin's Christology* (New York, NY: Cambridge University Press, 2004), 24-32, 143. "He [Christ] is the Mediator in all of God's relating to what is not God." Ibid., 143. "The love of God rests on Christ in such a manner, as to diffuse itself from him to us all; and not to us only; but even to the angels themselves. Not that they need reconciliation . . . but even they become perfectly united to God, only by means of their *Head*. . . . Christ came 'to reconcile all things to himself, both those which are on earth, and those which are in heaven,' (Col. 1:20.)." John Calvin, *Commentary on a Harmony of the Evangelists Matthew, Mark, and Luke*, trans. William Pringle (Edinburgh, Scotland: Calvin Translation Society, 1845), 1:206. Emphasis in original. See also ibid., 2:314.

287. Calvin *Institutes* 1.13.7, 8, 10, 17, 18; 2.14.8. For Calvin, it would be "foolish to imagine any temporary command at a time when God was pleased to execute his fixed and eternal counsel, and something more still mysterious." Ibid., 1.13.7.

288. Ibid., 1.13.7, 10; 1.14.5, 9.

289. Ibid., 2.6.1-3; 2.10.1, 2, 8-9, 23.

290. Regarding the three offices of Christ, see ibid., 2.15.1-2, 3-4, 6. For an extensive discussion about these three offices in Christ, see Edmondson, *Calvin's Christology*, 89-181.

reconciled with the Father. Christ completes His work of Mediator through His resurrection, ascension, action through the Holy Spirit, dominion from heaven, and return to judgment.[291] After His incarnation, however, Christ's divinity, although manifested in time, is still immutable. Strictly, only His humanity suffers, not His divinity.[292] Thus, Christ is the supreme act of the revelation of God but only according to the principle of accommodation because Christ, regarding His divinity, is unknown. Christ preserves in Himself the abysm between God and humanity.[293]

Calvin understands Christ's mediation actions in the light of his view of providence and predestination. Providence is God's overruling government in the world, including intelligent creatures, inanimate objects, and events.[294] God's will determines every single event.[295] God's providence is immutable and timeless. God's timeless decisions involve past, present, and future in the temporal realm, without change in God's providential timeless law.[296] God never repents regarding His plans because that fact would imply that He has feelings and is changeable. Biblical expressions suggesting that God repented or changed His mind are just figurative speech accommodated to human understanding.[297] The providence of God is so overwhelming that even human disobedience to God is a result of His will.[298]

Calvin's understanding of providence involves predestination because, according to him, the believers and the church are the most important objects of divine providence.[299] The difference is that Calvin connects providence with creation in general (including angels and

---

291. Calvin *Institutes* 2.16.3, 5-7, 13-17.
292. Ibid., 1.13.7; 2.12.3.
293. See John Calvin, *Commentaries on the Catholic Epistles*, trans. John Owen (Edinburgh, Scotland: Calvin Translation Society, 1855), 53, 54. Regarding Christ as the supreme revelation of God, according to the principle of accommodation, see Battles, "God Was Accommodating Himself," 40-42.
294. Calvin *Institutes* 1.16.2, 3. "There is no random power, or agency, or motion in the creatures, who are so governed by the secret counsel of God, that nothing happens but what he has knowingly and willingly decreed." Ibid., 1.16.3.
295. Ibid., 1.16.4.
296. Ibid., 1.17.1, 2.
297. Ibid., 1.17.12-13.
298. "If we design anything contrary to his precept [of God], it is not obedience, but contumacy and transgression. But if he did not will it, we could not do it. *I admit this*." Ibid., 1.17.5. Emphasis mine.
299. Ibid., 1.17.6.

human beings) while predestination is a more specific term for divine decrees regarding the destiny of intelligent creatures.[300] Both are divine timeless simultaneous actions.[301] Calvin defines predestination as God's timeless decree by which He preordained the creation of some people for eternal salvation and others for eternal damnation.[302] Predestination is not based on divine foreknowledge but on divine will. God foreknows the future because He decrees that future.[303] If foreknowledge were the cause of predestination, it would mean that human will has some role in salvation. Then, human merits would be the cause of the election.[304] In contrast, the only cause of salvation is God's will. Justification is a manifestation of election/predestination.[305]

For Calvin predestination involves even the Fall, which is in harmony with God's will.[306] There is no right to claim that God is unjust because "the will of God is the supreme rule of righteousness."[307] In any case, there is no change in God's plans. Predestination and providence proceed from "one decision of the divine will, an eternal decision situated *outside time*."[308] Calvin's understanding of the relation between God and His creation implies a strong determinism. Nothing happens or exists that is not somehow already real or present in God's supreme and eternal will.

The providence-predestination pattern of relationship between God and His creation involves even Christ's mediatorial work. Calvin's doctrine of Christ and predestination "are intricately intertwined."[309]

---

300. Ibid., 3.23.4; 1.14.16. In connection with providence, predestination can also involve nations besides individuals. Ibid., 3.21.5-7.

301. Predestination does not have beginning according to Calvin. Ibid., 3.22.10. Regarding the connection between providence and predestination in Calvin, see Partee, *Calvin and Classical Philosophy*, 140-141. "Calvin does not make a sharp distinction between providence and predestination." Ibid., 140. Predestination is equivalent to the particular providence of God governing over the elect. See George, *Theology of the Reformers*, 210-211.

302. Calvin *Institutes* 3.21.5.

303. Ibid., 3.21.1; 3.21.5; 3.22.1; 3.23.6. Regarding predestination as the cause of prescience, see also ibid., 3.22.3-4, 8-9; 3.23.1, etc.

304. Ibid., 3.22.1.

305. Regarding election, justification is a "symbol of its manifestation." Ibid., 3.21.7.

306. "I admit that by the will of God all the sons of Adam fell into that state of wretchedness in which they are now involved." Ibid., 3.23.4. See also ibid., 3.23.5-8.

307. Ibid., 3.23.2. See also ibid., 3.22.4, 5, 7.

308. Wendel, *Calvin*, 267. Emphasis mine.

309. Edmondson, *Calvin's Christology*, 147.

As a member of the Trinity, Christ participates in the decree of predestination and is the One who applies it. Christ's work is understood in the light of providence and predestination.[310] God's eternal counsel decreed Christ's mediation and incarnation. "The decree was eternal and unchangeable, but must be carried into effect by *Christ Jesus our Lord*, because in him it was made."[311] Christ is, as Mediator, the supreme exemplification of predestination.[312] The ultimate cause of articulation and salvation, then, is not God in Christ but God's will through Christ, given that Christ implements God's providence-predestination.[313] Christ is at the same time the One who elects and mediates the election as eternal God. In the last sense, He is subordinated to the election.[314]

The whole. Christ as Mediator between God and the world-humanity has provided unity between heaven and earth. In one sense, Calvin understands that Christ has already achieved this unity through His work. "Formed into one body, we are united to God, and closely connected with each other. Without Christ, on the other hand, the whole world is a shapeless chaos and frightful confusion."[315] This unity includes humans and angels. Although angels were in harmony with God, because of their natural condition as creatures, they needed Christ's mediation, gathering them together (Eph 1:10) in order to make sure of their perfect commitment to God. Without Christ's work of mediation, angels could have changed and sinned, losing their eternal happiness and joy. Calvin implies that the level of the creatures in comparison with the Creator—even intelligent unfallen creatures such as angels—is so low that without a Mediator they would have been eventually lost, and wholeness, unity, and harmony would have been impossible.[316] A simplified version of the medieval hierarchy is still very

---

310. Wendel, *Calvin*, 274. See also Muller, *Christ and the Decree*, 35-38.

311. John Calvin, *Commentaries on the Epistles of Paul to the Galatians and Ephesians*, trans. William Pringle (Edinburgh, Scotland: Calvin Translation Society, 1854), 256 (commentary on Eph 3:11). Emphasis in original. See Calvin *Institutes* 2.12.4-5.

312. Calvin *Institutes* 2.17.1; Edmondson, *Calvin's Christology*, 148.

313. "We ascend to the ordination of God as the primary cause, because of his mere good pleasure he appointed a Mediator to purchase salvation for us." Calvin *Institutes* 2.17.1.

314. Ibid., 3.22.1, 7. See also Muller, *Christ and the Decree*, 37-38; Edmondson, *Calvin's Christology*, 143, 149. See also Calvin, *Galatians and Ephesians*, 197-201 (commentary on Eph 1:4-5).

315. Calvin, *Galatians and Ephesians*, 205 (commentary on Eph 1:10).

316. Ibid.

active in Calvin. The general harmony of the universe is only possible under the coercive implementation of God's timeless providence-predestination based on His will.

This harmony or unity seems to be not completely realized. The low concept that Calvin has regarding God's temporal creation—even before the effects of sin—points, as in Luther, toward a spiritualized eschatology where the elect will participate in God's glory. God will be one with His elect who will enjoy eternal blessing. Biblical prophets usually describe this incorporeal reality in corporeal terms because they were "unable to give a verbal description of that spiritual blessedness."[317]

Summary

The Protestant Reformation claimed to follow the *sola Scriptura* principle, but in practice, the reformers built their theology upon the typical classical distinction between timelessness and temporality. The reformers' assumed epistemology interprets God's reality in Scripture according to classical theology; namely, applying the *via negativa* and the principle of accommodation. God is timeless, immutable, impassible, simple, and spaceless. His knowledge of realities external to Himself comes from His own mind. He knows the future because His supreme will is the cause of everything that happens.

Luther and Calvin interpret the world as a creation of God. The physical world is in contrast to the spiritual one, which is superior. The creation of the physical world also involves the beginning of time. The timeless spiritual realm is the realm of God, angels, and the souls of the elect. The temporal world is transient. The interpretation of human nature is also dualistic. God created humanity but the problem of sin caused a total corruption of human nature. The human body became mortal but the soul is still immortal. There is no human free will. God's immutable will decides human destiny.

The articulating agent is Christ, who reveals the timeless, hidden God. All that Christ has done reflects God's timeless will and plan, which is the ultimate cause of salvation. Even Christ's intercession is timeless, performed in a timeless heaven. Christ is the Mediator between God and the entire world-humanity for Calvin. He is the instrument of God's creation and His way of revelation in the Old Testament as well as since His incarnation. This revelation, however, is always in

---

317. Calvin *Institutes* 3.40.10.

harmony with the *via negativa* and the principle of accommodation. The divine nature of Christ as such remains unknown.

Christ's articulating action implements God's providence-predestination in harmony with God's unchangeable will. Providence-predestination is so overwhelming that nothing in creation—including angels and human beings—escapes its control. Temporal events are only a mirror of God's will. Salvation, that produces reconciliation between God and humanity, is essentially the product of God's arbitrary predestination. There is no real human participation. Justification is a manifestation of predestination in the case of the elect. Justification (imputed righteousness, not imparted) is the essence of salvation. It is not a temporal action. It is essentially timeless and implies the forgiveness of past, present, and future sins. Ultimately, given their timeless character, providence, predestination, and justification-salvation are essentially only one timeless action manifested in time in particular events.

In Protestant theology, there is still a dualistic and hierarchical view of reality as a whole, although it is simpler than the medieval hierarchy. Temporal reality will finally disappear to give rise to a spiritualized reality, free of temporal needs. God will be everything in everyone. In the meantime, the believer can anticipate this reality through faith. In one sense, Christ has already united heaven and earth providing harmony and wholeness. But in the spiritualized eschatology of the reformers, the elect—angels and humans—will be fully one with God, sharing His glory in blessing and happiness.

The Principle of Articulation in Modern Theology

In general, classical theism claimed to defend an ontological distinction between God and His creation.[318] In classical theology, God's interventions in time or history did not compromise God's timelessness. That

---

318. This distinction, however, is sometimes blurred or fuzzy considering for example, the notion of participation of created particular things in the ideas in the mind of God. In Augustine or Aquinas, for example, particular things are already existent in God's mind. They are included in God's substance. Luther and Calvin also believe that God knows what He will do. God's knowledge and will are eternal as God. In consequence, particular things created by God are somehow already real in God's mind and essence. It seems to be that classical theism, therefore, has paved the way for the historical appearance of panentheism, discussed in this section. It is useful to remember here Aristotle's criticism of Plato's notion of participation. Plato was not able to explain change and multiplicity, virtually denying the reality of particular things. Only the ideas were actually real. See pp. 66-67 in this chapter.

was the case, for example, in God's creative activity, revelation, Christ's incarnation, or miracles. This interventionist understanding of God's activity in the world assumed that God, from time to time, violates or suspends natural "laws in order to bring about an extraordinary event. God makes something happen that would not have happened in the ordinary course of nature."[319] In other words, God's interventions in the world are punctiliar or instantaneous, without past or future, in contrast to a linear or temporal intervention (with duration) through history.

Kant, however, radically changed this general understanding of the relationship between God and the world. According to Kant's theoretical philosophy, God, the world, and the human soul were not really knowable as phenomena external to the mind; they were universal ideas but with only a mental reality. They were not empirical realities that could be the objects of science. In that context, God became only indispensable in the realm of morality.[320] It was not possible to know any cognitive revelation of God in the spatio-temporal realm or to develop a natural theology.

During the 19th century, liberal theology proposed an immanentist view of the divine activity in the world. Against classical theology, where God intervened in a supernatural way in His creation and in the cause-effect flow of history, liberal theology emphasized the universal immanent presence and activity of God in the world, enabling the interpretation of evolutionary and social progress as manifestations of God's designs and purposes. This immanentist perspective was compatible with the scientific view of the world as a closed temporal system ruled by natural cause-effect relationships.

Furthermore, it had the advantage of overcoming some problems of classical theology where apparently God had to correct His own timeless and unchangeable plans through interventions in the world, as well as resolving the obvious inconsistency implied in the fact that a timeless God was willing to violate His own natural laws.[321] What modern theology was proposing, then, is an absolute immanent understanding of God's actions in the world where the timeless purposes of God's activity did not require "temporal corrections." Schleiermacher

---

319. Nancey Murphy, *Beyond Liberalism and Fundamentalism: How Modern and Postmodern Philosophy Set the Theological Agenda* (Harrisburg, PA: Trinity Press International, 2007), 68.
320. Ibid., 56.
321. Ibid., 71.

(1768-1834) is a paradigmatic case for understanding liberal theology during the end of the 18th century and the beginning of the 19th.[322]

Friedrich Schleiermacher

Ontological and epistemological presuppositions. Modern theology maintained the ontological distinction between temporality and timelessness of classical theology. For Schleiermacher, timelessness is the realm of God, in contrast to time, which is "merely an adjunct to finite being."[323] Kant had already affirmed that a timeless God could not be the object of empirical knowledge. God was only a mental idea necessary for morality. How, then, was it possible to experience God? Schleiermacher proposes that the way is the *feeling* or "consciousness of being absolutely dependent or, which is the same thing, of being in relation with God."[324]

In Kant, God does not relate to feelings. God pertains to the realm of reason and morality, which requires the assumption of God's existence. Feelings are excluded from reason and morality. In Schleiermacher, in contrast, God is found in connection with the religious feeling. This feeling or consciousness is not knowledge (related to theology or sciences) or an action (related to ethics). It belongs to piety.[325] This feeling of absolute dependence is immediate. It is not the result of some kind of self-contemplation. It is a pre-theoretical or religious *a priori*, essential to human nature.[326] It relates to faith, which is the certainty about that feeling.[327]

If this feeling implies dependence on/relation with God, He must be the origin or the "Whence."[328] This feeling cannot come from the world or any part of it. The world is only the whole of the tempo-

---

322. Schleiermacher is usually considered the "father of modern theology." C. W. Christian, *Friedrich Schleiermacher* (Waco, TX: Word, 1979), 11.
323. Friedrich Schleiermacher, *The Christian Faith* (London, UK: T. & T. Clark, 1999), 206. Regarding the timelessness of God in Schleiermacher, see ibid., 203-205.
324. Ibid., 12.
325. Ibid., 5-10.
326. Ibid., 6, 26. See Robert R. Williams, *Schleiermacher: The Theologian; The Construction of the Doctrine of God* (Philadelphia, PA: Fortress, 1978), 4.
327. Schleiermacher, *The Christian Faith*, 68.
328. "The *Whence* of our receptive and active existence, as implied in this self-consciousness, is to be designated by the word 'God.'" Ibid., 16. Emphasis in original. Regarding the origin of the religious feeling, see Robert M. Adams, "Faith and Religious Knowledge," in *The Cambridge Companion to Friedrich Schleiermacher*, ed. Jacqueline Mariña (Cambridge, UK: Cambridge University Press, 2005), 37-39.

ral existence. Regarding the world, everybody has a feeling of freedom because it is possible to influence its individual parts, although in a limited way. This feeling of freedom is incompatible with a feeling of absolute dependence.[329] Absolute dependence is only compatible with God who does not depend on anything else.

How is a system of theology based on this religious feeling possible? What is the epistemological foundation for theology? Religious feeling is not knowledge in itself and it seems to be a very subjective experience to provide a basis for theology. Schleiermacher holds that Christian doctrines interpret or express in words the experience of religious feeling.[330] Doctrines build upon a *given* religious feeling and do not pertain to the sphere of reason. In their presentation, they should be coherent and rational but that rationality relates to the presentation, not to the religious experience in itself.[331] However, religious feeling or religious consciousness is not purely subjective. It is a universal experience, available for everybody in the same way.[332]

Schleiermacher believes that theology can use Scripture or confessions of faith as sources to the extent that they reflect the experience of religious consciousness of the community of faith. The development of this God-consciousness leads to the creation of communion.[333] In order to preserve the original purity of that experience in the context of a given community of faith, it is possible to appeal to those documents that testify about the original purity of the community. In the case of the evangelical or Protestant community, those documents are particularly the New Testament and Protestant confessions of faith.[334] Scriptural documents

---

329. Schleiermacher, *The Christian Faith*, 16-17.

330. "Doctrines, strictly speaking, are not knowledge, but rather systematically ordered expressions of piety." N. Murphy, *Beyond Liberalism and Fundamentalism*, 56-57. "Christian doctrines are accounts of the Christian religious affections set forth in speech." Schleiermacher, *The Christian Faith*, 76.

331. Schleiermacher, *The Christian Faith*, 67-68. "Religion is not knowledge and science, either of the world or of God. Without being knowledge, it recognizes knowledge and science." Friedrich Schleiermacher, *On Religion: Speeches to Its Cultured Despisers*, trans. John Oman (London, UK: K. Paul, Trench, Trubner, 1893), 36.

332. N. Murphy, *Beyond Liberalism and Fundamentalism*, 22; Schleiermacher, *The Christian Faith*, 133. This discussion allows understanding why, in Schleiermacher's theological system, the first doctrine is not God, as usual in classical theology, but the *self*. González, *Historia*, 867.

333. Schleiermacher, *The Christian Faith*, 26.

334. González, *Historia*, 865-866. See Schleiermacher, *The Christian Faith*, 112. Schleiermacher has a low concept of the Old Testament because it does not express

and confessions are at the same level as sources of theology. Scripture is not a cognitive revelation at all. A cognitive revelation would be contrary to the way in which God operates in the world as discussed below.[335]

The interpretation of God and the world. Schleiermacher understands God and His relation to the world in the light of his perspective of religion as an experience of the feeling of absolute dependence on God. Schleiermacher considers that "all attributes which we ascribe to God are to be taken as denoting not something special in God, but only something special in the manner in which the feeling of absolute dependence is to be related to Him."[336]

This understanding of God's attributes implies a particular application of the *via negativa* and *via eminentiae* that Schleiermacher explicitly admits.[337] Combining these ways with his dialectic method,[338] Schleiermacher affirms that the finite feeling of absolute dependence requires an eternal divine causality.[339] Eternity is equivalent to timelessness. The eternal divine causality conditions everything temporal and even time itself.[340] This timelessness involves unchangeability.[341]

---

very distinctively Christian religious emotions. Ibid., 62. Consequently, "the Old Testament appears simply a superfluous authority for Dogmatics." Ibid., 115.

335. Schleiermacher rejects the understanding of revelation as a cognitive content because "that would make the revelation to be originally and essentially *doctrine* [knowledge]." Schleiermacher, *The Christian Faith*, 50. Emphasis in original.

336. Ibid., 194.

337. "In considering the manifestations of the religious self-consciousness, if we find that everything which would destroy His presence in us must specially be denied of God, and everything which favours His presence in us specially be affirmed of Him, we can say in our own way that thus divine attributes are formulated by the methods of removal of limits [*via eminentiae*] and negation [*via negativa*]." Ibid., 200.

338. Regarding the dialectic method and the Neo-Platonism background of that method in Schleiermacher, see John W. Cooper, *Panentheism: The Other God of the Philosophers: From Plato to the Present* (Grand Rapids, MI: Baker, 2006), 81.

339. "The divine causality as opposed to the finite and natural is expressed in the term, the divine *eternity*." Schleiermacher, *The Christian Faith*, 201. Emphasis in original.

340. "By the Eternity of God we understand the absolutely timeless causality of God, which conditions not only all that is temporal, but time itself as well." Ibid., 203. Schleiermacher admits that some Bible passages teach the concept of eternity of God in terms of time without beginning or ending (Job 36:26; Ps 102:28), but he thinks that they are poetical passages. According to him, "the New Testament itself teaches us how for didactic purposes these [Old Testament passages] must be supplemented." Ibid., 205. Schleiermacher thinks there is support for a timeless understanding of the eternity of God in 2 Pet 3:8 (cf. Ps 90:4). Ibid.

341. According to Schleiermacher, the idea of unchangeability "is already contained in the idea of eternity." Ibid., 206.

In harmony with God's timelessness, God's omnipresence conditions everything spatial and space itself.[342] Schleiermacher understands this causality in absolute immanent terms. While he distinguishes God from the natural order, God is equated with the world in comprehension or scope.[343]

At the same time, in harmony with God's timelessness and spacelessness, God's omnipotence is the cause of everything that happens in time and space. Things cannot be or happen in another way than the way in which God's timeless will establishes.[344] Thus, God's omniscience refers to the knowledge of what God wills and produces. God's thought, will, omnipotence, and omniscience are all the same thing.[345]

Regarding God's personality, Schleiermacher prefers to see God as a living God. Personality seems to be incompatible with God's infinitude and impassibility. Schleiermacher wants to avoid in this way an anthropomorphic view of God.[346]

In his interpretation of the world, Schleiermacher holds that the traditional doctrines of creation and preservation are essentially one, because both, finally, derive from the idea of absolute dependence on God. This idea seems to be the real content of these doctrines. Creation does not refer to any temporal activity of God. Schleiermacher actually emphasizes more the idea of preservation rather than the idea of creation. The question of the origin in time of finite beings as a whole is not important in terms of religious feeling. It is not clear even if Schleiermacher can affirm a beginning, by contrast to the notion of an eternal world. He interprets the world as God's manifestation of His word. The feeling of absolute dependence on God does not necessarily require the affirmation of God as existing in a separate way from the

---

342. "By the Omnipresence of God we understand the absolutely spaceless causality of God, which conditions not only all that is spatial, but space itself as well." Ibid.

343. Ibid., 200.

344. Ibid., 211-218. "It is to be noticed that the one all-embracing divine will is identical with the eternal omnipotence." Ibid., 218.

345. "God knows all that is; and all that God knows is, and these two are not twofold but single; for His knowledge and His almighty will are one and the same." Ibid., 222.

346. "We have an idea of the Highest Being, not as personally thinking and willing but exalted above all personality, as the universal, productive, connecting necessity of all thought and existence." Schleiermacher, *On Religion*, 95. See ibid., 116.

world.³⁴⁷ Naturally, then, Schleiermacher rejects a literal interpretation of the biblical six-day story of Creation.³⁴⁸

Although Schleiermacher affirms God's freedom to create the world—as he interprets Creation—the world is in some way also necessary for God because as He is the absolute causality, the origination of the world pertains to His own nature and will. When God wills Himself, He also wills Himself as the Originator of the world.³⁴⁹ Schleiermacher, then proposes, "God is both opposite in kind and equal in scope to the world. . . . The world is not an alien, distorting medium through which God is apprehended, but is in some sense the self-manifestation of God."³⁵⁰ The absolute dependence on God, thus, is not only valid for humans but for everything finite. Moreover, there is a universal interdependence among particular beings in nature. Every individual depends on all the rest. In turn, as a whole, nature completely depends on God.³⁵¹

The interpretation of the human being. For Schleiermacher, the world's original perfection influences the human being stimulating God-consciousness. The world's original *perfection* refers to the totality of what constitutes the finite existence producing impressions on human beings as to stimulate their religious consciousness. *Original perfection* is the timeless ever-identical omnipotent causality that underlies the world and manifests in every temporal aspect of it. Original perfection ultimately refers to God Himself.³⁵² Human original perfection relates to the human predisposition toward God-consciousness, not to an original couple created to live for ever in a paradise. Sin, then, is human alienation or resistance regarding God-consciousness. Biblical stories about Eden are not historical but only ancient expressions of God-consciousness.³⁵³

---

347. Schleiermacher, *The Christian Faith*, 142-143, 145-150, 152, 155. See also Cooper, *Panentheism*, 85.
348. Schleiermacher, *The Christian Faith*, 151.
349. "If He [God] wills Himself, He wills Himself as Creator and Sustainer, so that in willing Himself, willing the world is already included; and if He wills the world, in it He wills His eternal and ever-present omnipotence, wherein willing Himself is included; that is to say, the necessary will is included in the free, and the free in the necessary." Ibid., 217. As John W. Cooper comments on, "Schleiermacher cannot affirm that creation is God's free choice. . . . God is both free and determined in that he is self-determining." Cooper, *Panentheism*, 85.
350. Williams, *Schleiermacher*, 85. See Schleiermacher, *The Christian Faith*, 174.
351. Schleiermacher, *The Christian Faith*, 173, 175.
352. Ibid., 233-238.
353. Ibid., 243-244, 252, 274; González, *Historia*, 868-869.

Schleiermacher completely reinterprets the doctrine of salvation from the perspective of God-consciousness. God-consciousness implies that He is the absolute causality. From this perspective, Schleiermacher holds that God is the cause of sin, which is necessary for redemption, and the cause of salvation through election and predestination without the real intervention of human will. Ultimately, however, the salvation of human beings does not differ in essence from God's immanent government of the world.[354] Schleiermacher's immanent understanding of God's operation in the world through natural causation does not allow him to believe in an afterlife. There is no immortality of the soul. Although he still holds a distinction between soul and body, he believes that the existence of the soul ceases after death. There is no resurrection of the dead either.[355] Redemption is, basically, the strengthening of God's consciousness.[356] If there is some kind of immortality, it takes place in the present temporal life, when human finitude becomes one and eternal with the Infinite in every moment.[357]

The articulating agent and the articulating action. As the absolute causality of the world and the religious feeling of absolute dependence, God is the articulating agent of the relationship between Himself and the world-humanity in a particular way. As said, Schleiermacher considers God's action in the world as absolutely immanent. He understands that God is the omnipotent cause of everything that happens in the world. Every mechanism of nature or the activities of apparently free causes are all traceable to God's ordination.[358] Schleiermacher does not accept the existence of supernatural events or special interventions of a timeless God in the temporal world separately from natural causation.[359] For him, the traditional understanding of miracle involves a suspension of the natural order and causality, an abrogation of nature, through which God operates in an immanent way in the

---

354. Schleiermacher, *The Christian Faith*, 326, 338, 536, 546, 551; Roger E. Olson, *The Journey of Modern Theology: From Reconstruction to Deconstruction* (Downers Grove, IL: InterVarsity, 2013), 141, 142.
355. Schleiermacher, *The Christian Faith*, 706, 709.
356. Walter E. Wyman Jr., "Sin and Redemption," in *The Cambridge Companion to Friedrich Schleiermacher*, ed. Jacqueline Mariña (Cambridge, UK: Cambridge University Press, 2005), 147.
357. Schleiermacher, *On Religion*, 101.
358. Schleiermacher, *The Christian Faith*, 189.
359. "We should abandon the idea of the absolutely supernatural." Ibid., 183.

world.³⁶⁰ Every particular event has an immediate relation to God and to nature. Thus, Schleiermacher defines miracle as an event seen from a religious perspective. Everything is miracle for him.³⁶¹

As God is the omnipotent cause of everything, He must also be the cause of evil. Due to the connection between sin and evil, if God is the cause of sin, He is also the cause of evil.³⁶² God is, thus, the absolute cause of everything through His encompassing immanent articulating action in the world, including the feeling of absolute dependence in human beings, which allows, in turn, positing God as the Whence of this feeling.

The whole. Although Schleiermacher makes a distinction between God and the world, God's action in the world is not distinguishable from the natural causation of the world itself. In other words, there is a partial identification of God with the world.³⁶³ If the world is a manifestation of God, and if the world is somehow necessary for God because when He wills Himself He wills the world, the interpretation of reality as a whole in Schleiermacher can be qualified as panentheism.³⁶⁴ Moreover, although Schleiermacher considers God as the absolute causality of the world or natural order, God equates the world in comprehensiveness.³⁶⁵ In this way, Schleiermacher becomes an antecedent of the bipolar view of God regarding the world that process theology developed since the 20th century.³⁶⁶

---

360. Ibid., 181-182, 192.
361. *"Miracle is simply the religious name for event."* Ibid., 88. Emphasis mine. For Schleiermacher, science will be able to explain every apparent supernatural event in terms of natural causation. Schleiermacher, *The Christian Faith*, 183-184.
362. Ibid., 338.
363. It is not surprising then that Schleiermacher looks with favor on Baruch Spinoza (1632-1677), considered as a pantheist philosopher. Schleiermacher, *On Religion*, 40, 41. He differentiates himself, however, from Spinozism. See ibid., 104-105.
364. Cooper, *Pantheism*, 88. "Schleiermacher holds that God and the world are asymmetrically but ontologically co-inherent." Ibid. See also Philip Clayton, "Systematizing Agency: Toward a Panentheistic-Participatory Theory of Agency," in *Schleiermacher and Whitehead: Open Systems in Dialogue*, ed. Christine Helmer (Berlin, Germany: Walter de Gruyter, 2004), 228.
365. As Roger E. Olson correctly evaluates, "Although it is not pantheism . . . his doctrine of God is panentheistic and thus, together with Hegel's concept of God as Absolute Spirit, a prototype of much later liberal theology." Olson, *The Journey of Modern Theology*, 144.
366. Robert R. Williams evaluates Schleiermacher's understanding of the relation between God and the world by saying that "God's equality in scope or immanence in the world is qualified by God's infinite qualitative difference from the

Process Theology

Modern theology, whereas still maintaining the immanent understanding of God in history, produced a main twist in the case of process theology. Schleiermacher understood that God's control of the world was absolute. The world does not produce change in God. During the 20th century, however, process theology assumed an explicit panentheistic understanding of the relationship between God and the world where the world produces change in God. Process theology has extensively developed its theological system upon the philosophical platform established by process philosopher Alfred North Whitehead (1861-1947) and the philosopher of religion Charles Hartshorne (1897-2000). Among process theologians, probably the most important contemporary expositor is John B. Cobb (born 1925).[367]

Ontological and epistemological presuppositions. According to process theology and philosophy, reality as a whole, including God and the world, is in constant process. Everything actual is in process. This view of reality would be in harmony with the Judeo-Christian tradition where God is active within history.[368]

The most basic entities constituting the entire reality are *actual occasions* or *occasions of experience*.[369] They succeed each other in such a way that perceiving them through the senses is impossible. They consist of momentary *events* that perish just after becoming or coming to be.[370] They are dipolar—or bipolar. They have a *physical* and a *mental pole*. The physical pole of every new occasion is able to *prehend*, *feel*, or grasp other past occasions, usually immediate past occasions. This *prehension* is an "appropriation" of some characteristics of prior oc-

---

world. God in relation to the world is but one polar aspect of God's bipolar being." Williams, *Schleiermacher*, 90.

367. See Olson, *The Journey of Modern Theology*, 404. See also Bruce G. Epperly, *Process Theology: A Guide for the Perplexed* (London, UK: T. & T. Clark, 2011), 15-16. The study follows mainly—although not exclusively—Cobb's exposition of process theology.

368. John B. Cobb Jr., *A Christian Natural Theology: Based on the Thought of Alfred North Whitehead* (Philadelphia, PA: Westminster, 1965), 40; John B. Cobb Jr. and David R. Griffin, *Process Theology: An Introductory Exposition* (Philadelphia, PA: Westminster, 1976), 14.

369. Cobb, *Natural Theology*, 40; Alfred North Whitehead, *Process and Reality: An Essay in Cosmology*, corrected ed. (London, UK: Free, 1978), 73 [113]. Bracketed pagination refers to the first American edition.

370. Cobb, *Natural Theology*, 29, 36; Cobb and Griffin, *Process Theology*, 14.

casions that perished.³⁷¹ The transition from one occasion to another constitutes temporality. The becoming of occasions is a process of *concrescence* or becoming concrete. But it is not a temporal process. Only the succession of occasions is temporal. Reality is a succession of timeless moments, where the succession in itself is temporal but every moment can be called a now.³⁷²

The new or becoming occasion does not reproduce exactly the same data of the previous occasions. The actual occasion introduces an element of originality or novelty through its mental pole.³⁷³ The actual occasion has some level of freedom to select which elements or characteristics of the previous occasions will include in its own process of becoming. Each actual occasion has a creative self-determination.³⁷⁴

According to Whitehead, actual occasions can also grasp or prehend with their mental pole *eternal objects*, similar to Platonic forms or ideas. However, they are not actual entities, like occasions, but abstract qualities, purely potential. God envisions all these eternal objects in His primordial nature—or timeless pole/side. The grasping of eternal objects means the introduction of novelty in the world; these objects introduce new possibilities or qualities not embodied yet by previous occasions.³⁷⁵

Additionally, every occasion prehends with its mental pole an *initial aim*, which is the purpose that governs the occasion. That initial aim derives from God and originates at the beginning of the new occasion. It is God's primordial vision for the occasion. This initial aim determines or influences the perspective from which the occasion prehends the past occasions and the eternal objects. The initial aim becomes the *subjective aim*, which is the unifying element that governs the interaction, linking physical and conceptual prehensions. The occasion, however, has some degree of freedom to determine to what extent the initial aim will be implemented.³⁷⁶

---

371. Cobb, *Natural Theology*, 30-31, 33; Whitehead, *Process and Reality*, 19 [28-29], 23 [35], 33 [49], 108 [165].

372. Cobb and Griffin, *Process Theology*, 15-16; Whitehead, *Process and Reality*, 23 [35].

373. Cobb, *Natural Theology*, 33.

374. Cobb and Griffin, *Process Theology*, 26-27.

375. Cobb, *Natural Theology*, 34, 42; Whitehead, *Process and Reality*, 22 [32], 23 [34], 31 [46], 44 [69-70].

376. Cobb, *Natural Theology*, 35, 96, 128, 150, 151; Cobb and Griffin, *Process Theology*, 26; Whitehead, *Process and Reality*, 85 [130]; 224 [342, 343]; 244-245 [373-

Although an occasion has some freedom to select the elements to be incorporated into its future, that freedom does not imply consciousness. Even in the case of a human occasion, the events in the human brain are not necessarily conscious. In the vast majority of cases, the occasions use their freedom just to reenact the past without significant changes. Modern physics, however, shows that even at the atomic level—for example in the behavior of electrons—there is an important spontaneous activity.[377]

In general, human experience is conscious of societies or groupings of occasions, not of individual occasions. These societies of occasions are highly interconnected. A basic example of this type of society is a molecule. Molecules are *enduring societies* of occasions, using Whitehead's language, because they are contiguous in time and successive. In objects such as molecules, an actual occasion reenacts past occasions with a low or trivial level of novelty, which provides stability to the world. In turn, enduring societies can group in *corpuscular societies* that involve several enduring societies. Examples are rocks or tables, gases, liquids, constituted by molecules.[378]

Process ontology has implications in terms of the interpretation of knowledge. Knowledge involves the experience of everything in the world to the extent that actual occasions include the experiences of the past—prehension of previous occasions—in their own becoming. In some way, everything in the world can know or have experience. Process theology holds a *panpsychism* or, more precisely, *panexperientialism*, which means that everything in the universe experiences everything else, although not necessarily in a conscious way.[379] The difference between subject and object is that the subject is in the present—an actual occasion—and the object is in the immediate past.[380]

Process thought's understanding of experience implies, in terms of human knowledge, the existence of a *prethematized* or *prereflective*

374]; Epperly, *Process Theology*, 29. In any case, every occasion is a synthesis—to some degree—of previous occasions, eternal objects, and the initial aim.

377. Cobb, *Natural Theology*, 35, 36-37, 39; Cobb and Griffin, *Process Theology*, 16-17; Whitehead, *Process and Reality*, 53 [83].

378. Whitehead, *Process and Reality*, 34-35 [51-52]; Cobb, *Natural Theology*, 40-43; Epperly, *Process Theology*, 23-24; Cobb and Griffin, *Process Theology*, 15; John B. Cobb Jr., *Whitehead Word Book: A Glossary With Alphabetical Index to Technical Terms in Process and Reality* (Claremont, CA: P. & F., 2008), 29-30.

379. Cooper, *Panentheism*, 168; Epperly, *Process Theology*, 23.

380. Cobb, *Natural Theology*, 44-45; Whitehead, *Process and Reality*, 56-57 [89].

level of knowledge or experience. This kind of knowledge is a preconscious apprehension of reality that can be in conflict with conscious beliefs. A little part of this knowledge becomes conscious, including particularly metaphysical and moral knowledge, as well as knowledge about God. Everybody has a preconscious knowledge of God, even those who claim to be atheists. This knowledge influences emotions and actions but is difficult to perceive it consciously. The emergence to consciousness of this preconscious knowledge in a particular case is possible through the stimulation produced by a verbal expression of this knowledge in the context of a religious tradition—not necessarily Christian—that manifests a similar universal experience. Usually, the founders of great religious traditions—Christ, Buddha, and others—are those who offer a *primary expression* to the intuition of the preconscious knowledge about God and the followers react through *responsive expressions* that originate different interpretative traditions.[381]

In the context of this epistemology, it is not surprising that Cobb defines theology in a broad sense as "any coherent statement about matters of ultimate concern that recognizes that the perspective by which it is governed is received from a community of faith."[382] This understanding of theology does not require as a starting point the use of sacred texts, creeds, or already organized theological systems. The only necessary starting point is the given perspective of *the community of faith*. This definition does not apply only to theology in the context of Christian community but also to any other statement regarding issues of ultimate concern in any other religious community, such as Buddhists or even communities that are not religious in the traditional sense, such as those united around political or philosophical ideologies.[383] This understanding of theology is congruent with the notion that revelation is universal, through the endowment of the initial aim that can stimulate "experiences of divine power and divine guidance."[384]

The interpretation of God and the world. Process theology reacts against classical theism by rejecting the view of God as unchangeable

---

381. Cobb and Griffin, *Process Theology*, 30-40. See Alfred North Whitehead, *Religion in the Making: Lowell Lectures 1926* (New York, NY: Macmillan, 1926; repr., New York, NY: Fordham University Press, 1996), 131-132.

382. Cobb, *Natural Theology*, 252. Cobb clarifies that he considers the expressions *ultimate concern* and *faith* as interchangeable, following Tillich. See ibid., 252, n. 1.

383. Ibid., 253, 256.

384. Epperly, *Process Theology*, 47-48.

and impassible, inherited from Greek philosophy. God is not an absolute, omnipotent controlling power.[385] However, process theology extensively bases its interpretation of God on Whitehead's ontology, which is not free of Greek influence. From Whitehead's perspective, God is the main exemplification of the ontological principles of his philosophy. God is an actual entity or occasion. As in the case of actual occasions, God is also dipolar. He possesses a primordial nature, which is timeless, and contains the eternal objects, possibilities, or potentialities. It is equivalent, to some degree, to Plato's world of ideas. God has also a consequent nature or physical pole that is everlasting and results or derives from God's prehensions of actual entities in the world in evolution. The world—every occasion—not only influences God but also completes His nature. The world is objectified in God introducing change and novelty in Him. This novelty involves the retention of positive values in an everlasting way, and the abstraction of evil experiences in the world.[386]

Hartshorne, explaining the two aspects of God in process theology, says that God is "finite *and* infinite, eternal *and* temporal, necessary *and* contingent, each in suitable and unique respects."[387] This double nature provides the base for the notion that "through this relative, temporal, material aspect deity includes the world."[388] Cobb also proposes that it is better to understand God as a living person rather than as an actual occasion.[389]

As said, in His relation to the world, God provides the initial aim to each occasion. This aim provides purpose and is unique or different for every occasion. God attracts the entities, or tries to persuade them, toward the realization or actualization of the best possibilities for them in their particular situation. The initial aim is the lure or attracting possibility that ultimately refers to God Himself as the desired object for every actuality and who is looking for the ideal realization for every occasion. At the same time, this aim works as a principle of limitation

---

385. Cobb and Griffin, *Process Theology*, 8-9.

386. Whitehead, *Process and Reality*, 343 [521], 18 [28-29], 46 [73], 88 [134], 345 [523-524]; Cobb, *Natural Theology*, 161, 163.

387. Charles Hartshorne, *A Natural Theology for Our Time* (La Salle, IL: Open Court, 1967), 128. Emphasis in original.

388. Charles Hartshorne and William L. Reese, *Philosophers Speak of God* (Chicago, IL: University of Chicago Press, 1953), 15.

389. Cobb, *Natural Theology*, 176, 188-192. Cobb follows Hartshorne regarding his interpretation of God as a person. See Cooper, *Panentheism*, 186.

for the possibilities of realization of every occasion. The ordering of potentialities or eternal objects in God's primordial nature involves the identification of ideal possibilities for every occasion.[390]

If God prehends the world in such a way that elements of the world become objectified in His consequent nature, and the world also prehends elements of God's consequent nature through the initial aim—and indirectly through the prehension of previous occasions—it means that there is a partial ontological identification between both. God and the world are mutually immanent. Actually, they create each other.[391]

It is necessary to notice that in process theology, God is not the supreme reality. The ultimate reality is creativity. Creativity is like the impulse for evolution and development involving the whole reality. It is not a characteristic subscribed to God in the absolute sense. He is not the absolute Creator of the world. Process theology believes that the world is, in some way, everlasting, and creativity has always existed in relation to every entity. God is like the administrator of this creativity, providing purpose and aim for it. Creativity never appears separately from entities in the universe. It always co-appears with God and every actual entity in the world. From the perspective of process theology, change and creativity are virtually the same.[392]

Process theology rejects *creatio ex nihilo* or out of nothing. That notion would imply that God is the Originator of the entire reality, as in classical theism. Creation, instead, is out of chaos. In this state of chaos, there are only simple actual occasions, not ordered as enduring societies or individuals. Creation implies the introduction of order but also novelty through the divine impulse, which results in the emergence of successive evolutionary stages: subatomic elements, atoms, molecules, and cells. Every evolutionary stage is the condition for the next.

---

390. Whitehead, *Process and Reality*, 85 [130], 224 [343], 244 [374], 344 [522]; Cobb and Griffin, *Process Theology*, 26, 53; Epperly, *Process Theology*, 29; Cobb, *Natural Theology*, 151, 155-156. Regarding the initial aim, see also Cobb, *Whitehead Word Book*, 72-73.

391. "It is as true to say that the World is immanent in God, as that God is immanent in the World." Whitehead, *Process and Reality*, 528. "It is as true to say that God creates the World, as that the World creates God." Ibid.

392. Whitehead, *Process and Reality*, 7 [11]; Cobb, *Natural Theology*, 210-211. Epperly, *Process Theology*, 29. Regarding the relation between God and creativity, Whitehead explains that the creativity exhibited in the universe is "impotent to achieve actuality apart from the completed ideal harmony, which is God." Whitehead, *Religion in the Making*, 119-120.

The appearance of living individuals implies an increment of the role of the mental pole, which is now able to introduce additional novel elements by itself. Plants and animals are, in turn, much more complex societies encompassing many cells. These complex-living individuals have, in the case of animals and human beings, *dominant* members—central nervous systems—leading the whole.[393]

Process theology holds that it is possible to interpret this evolutionary process in harmony with God's character and purpose. This affirmation raises the issue of the problem of evil in the world and the eventual responsibility of God for it, considering that evolution involves suffering and death. Process theology believes that God is responsible but not indictable by the problem of evil. Through the initial aim, God looks for the best possible realization or *enjoyment* for every entity in the world. The freedom that every occasion has to deviate from this original purpose introduces the possibility of evil. Every entity has an intrinsic capacity for good or evil. The increment of complexity in the world through evolution allows the existence of greater enjoyment but also greater suffering due to the correlative increment of self-determination in the world. This correlation does not depend on God's choice because it is inherent to the world, which is everlasting. The only way in which God could avoid evil is keeping the world in its initial state of chaos or lack of order. God is, though, an Adventurer that takes the risk of suffering in order to introduce the possibility of additional enjoyment in the world.[394]

The interpretation of the human being. Based on process ontology, the soul is interpreted as a society of occasions that constitutes the history of a human being or even an animal. The type of occasion that makes up the human or animal soul is the *dominant* occasion, only possessed by organisms with a central nervous system. They are the only ones that possess consciousness, situated in the brain. There is a close relation between dominant occasions and the organism that they preside. In the case of human beings, the occasions of the soul, as other occasions, prehend their immediate occasions—in this case, in the brain and the body—and ultimately, the whole world, but with a

---

393. Cobb and Griffin, *Process Theology*, 65-68; Cobb, *Natural Theology*, 143; Whitehead, *Process and Reality*, 102 [156]; 119 [182]; 343 [521]; Cobb, *Whitehead Word Book*, 30-31.

394. Cobb and Griffin, *Process Theology*, 68-75.

vast capacity for the synthesis of data and the introduction of novelty.[395]

The difference between human and animal souls is essentially in degree or in the level of complexity. There is no fundamental ontological difference. However, the difference is of such magnitude that it somehow becomes a quality difference. Humans have a potential for novelty that is beyond any animal. The same is valid for language, religion, and morality. In animals, the soul functions primarily to serve the body, while in humans, the soul has evolved to serve mainly its own enjoyment and purpose.[396] Human beings also have the capacity for self-determination, as actual occasions in general, within the limits determined by the influences of the previous occasions and the influence of the initial aim given by God. Humans, of course, have much more freedom than other entities to reject the actualization of the ideal possibilities that they face. Moreover, as conscious entities, their decisions have moral implications.[397]

Salvation, then, becomes the human "cooperation with God in actualizing the divine initial aim."[398] Process theology, however, is reluctant to affirm the existence of an afterlife. Process theologians highlight that the idea of an immortal soul or an afterlife is not necessarily incompatible with Whitehead's ontology but they perceive that there is no clear base to affirm its existence. What they can do is affirm its possibility in the best of cases.[399] This position is understandable considering that in Whitehead's ontology, every occasion perishes after becoming and achieving their realization of enjoyment. Salvation, therefore, is not a synonym for subjective or personal immortality but the actualization of God's initial aim.[400] What process theology affirms is an *objective immortality* that results in the prehension by God of the human occasion, immortalizing its *contribution* to the future. This kind of immortality is applicable to every other occasion, but in the case of human beings it "is relevant to our desire to have our experiences make a lasting difference and in fact to live on beyond themselves."[401]

---

395. Cobb, Natural Theology, 47-56, 82.
396. Ibid., 56-63; Cobb and Griffin, Process Theology, 84-88.
397. Cobb, Natural Theology, 92-97.
398. Olson, The Journey of Modern Theology, 412.
399. See the discussion in Cobb, Natural Theology, 63-71; Cobb and Griffin, Process Theology, 123-124.
400. Olson, The Journey of Modern Theology, 412.
401. Cobb and Griffin, Process Theology, 23. See a broader discussion about the issue of afterlife in Epperly, Process Theology, 135-154. This objective immortality is

The articulating agent and the articulating action. In process theology, God is not the omnipotent and all determining cause of the whole reality. God is sensitive and responsive to the influences of the world. Process theology believes that this view of God is consistent with the biblical understanding of God as love. As God is not omnipotent, His love is not purely creative—all determining—but creative and responsive at the same time. God is open to the input of the world and human beings that change His consequent nature. He is open to new knowledge because of His interaction with the world. In this sense, although He can know all that is knowable in a given moment of the history of the world—omniscience—He does not foresee the future. The future is open for Him as well as for human beings and all other actualities constantly making decisions. Consequently, God's immanent action in the world is *persuasive*, not coercive. God's persuasive love manifests in His provision of the best possibilities for every actual entity through His initial aim, but God cannot guarantee the best result. In contrast to classical theism, in process theology God articulates reality through *persuasion*, not coercion.[402]

The final goal of God's persuasion is to promote enjoyment throughout the entire evolutionary process. In connection with that goal, He provides order in the world but also novelty. Both are necessary in order to promote enjoyment and realization.[403]

As God's action in the world is purely immanent, there is no need for the concept of miracle or the supernatural, understood as an interruption of natural causality and laws as in classical theology. God acts in the world naturally, immanently, because, in the end, the world is somehow part of Him. God and the world are mutually interdependent.[404]

The whole. Occasions in the world are interdependent. Process thought proposes a view of reality based on Whitehead's philosophy

---

not *personal*, as in the case of the belief in the immortality of the soul. It refers to the human contribution to the future.

402. Cobb and Griffin, *Process Theology*, 29, 43-53. See also Epperly, *Process Theology*, 34, 38-40, 45-49.

403. Cobb and Griffin, *Process Theology*, 56-57, 59-60; Epperly, *Process Theology*, 45.

404. Olson, *The Journey of Modern Theology*, 413; David R. Griffin, "Process Theology and the Christian Good News: A Response to Classical Free Will Theism," in *Searching for an Adequate God: A Dialogue Between Process and Free Will Theists*, ed. John B. Cobb Jr. and Clark H. Pinnock (Grand Rapids, MI: Eerdmans, 2000), 5-6.

of organism, where everything in the world relates to everything, including God.[405] God's omnispatial standpoint encompasses the world. The world is part of God. The parts of the world, however, have some autonomy, some self-determination. The world is not separated from God, but there is not a total identification between both either. Cobb explains their relationship as a type of panentheism that synthesizes the concerns of classical theism and pantheism. God and the world are not the same, but God is not external to the world either.[406]

This view of the whole reality as organismic panentheism does not completely eliminate the hierarchical view of reality inherited from Greek philosophy. Whitehead considers European philosophical tradition—of which his philosophy and ontology are not an exception—as "a series of footnotes to Plato."[407] Although process theology does not believe in eternal objects or forms as actual in itself, it still postulates two realms of reality. One is the realm of actual occasions—temporal and transient. The other is the realm of abstract, eternal, or possible objects.[408] In turn, it seems that every occasion in itself involves in its composition these abstract or timeless elements in an actualized way. Somehow, then, the hierarchy is also present in the multiplicity of the very structure of reality.[409] This soft dualism, however, is more flexible than the previous ones because it is able to integrate human freedom, virtually denied by previous systems.

Summary

In spite of some important differences, the two cases of liberal theology just discussed have several elements in common. Both still maintain the ontological distinction between timelessness and temporality. Both believe that there is some *a priori* element in religious experience. Schleiermacher holds the existence of a feeling of absolute dependence on God, which is not knowledge, but the base for the interpretation of doctrines with a rational presentation. Process theology holds the existence of a prethematized level of knowledge, which is a preconscious apprehension of reality that can become only partially conscious. This

---

405. Whitehead, *Process and Reality*, 7 [10-11].
406. John B. Cobb Jr., *God and the World* (1998; repr., Eugene, OR: Wipf & Stock, 2000), 79-80.
407. Whitehead, *Process and Reality*, 39 [62].
408. See Cooper, *Panentheism*, 171-172.
409. See Whitehead, *Process and Reality*, 40 [63-64], 50-52 [80-82].

prethematized knowledge is explicable in the light of process ontology where the occasions—including human occasions—prehend the data of previous occasions as well as the ideal potentialities that God provides through the initial aim. From the perspective of modern theology, then, revelation becomes an immanent universal experience where the ultimate arbiter is the community of faith.

Regarding God and the world, Schleiermacher and process theology in general interpret God as having a timeless side or pole, and a temporal one related to His interaction with the temporal world. In the case of Schleiermacher, God's causality in the world is absolute, while in the case of process theology that causality is suggestive or persuasive, operating through the initial aim. Schleiermacher and process theology, moreover, are reluctant to admit a beginning for the world. The world seems to be everlasting; God creates or rather introduces novelty immanently, in harmony with the evolutionary process. The world is necessary for God and not only God for the world. There is also a total interdependence in the world.

Schleiermacher and process theology also agree in that they do not necessarily think in an afterlife in terms of personal or subjective immortality. There is no clear belief in resurrection either. The immanent action of God in the world leads them to understand salvation in terms of the strengthening of God's consciousness or the voluntary actualization of the initial aim originated in God.

Schleiermacher and process theology also find in God the articulating agent of the entire reality, but they differ in the understanding of the articulating action. In both cases, the articulating action is immanent in the world. There are no supernatural events. In the case of Schleiermacher, however, that immanent action refers to God's absolute and omnipotent causality, while in process theology, God's articulating action is persuasive. In Schleiermacher, the world cannot change God. In process theology, it does.

Both Schleiermacher and process theology see the whole reality in terms of panentheism. The world is a temporal manifestation of God. It is a part of God. Process theology is an organismic panentheism. The parts of the world have some degree of self-determination, a notion that is absent in Schleiermacher's view. Both versions of panentheism, however, maintain in some way a hierarchical view of reality but adapted to the mindset of modern science.

The Principle of Articulation Among the Adventist Pioneers

The Adventist sabbatarian pioneers emerged in the context of the Millerite movement. The Millerites were premillennialists. Premillennialism developed a high appreciation of time and space in the general context of the Protestant tradition. Puritans of Old and New England, for example, during the 17th century, are an example of this interest that led them to interpret the book of Revelation using a more historicist approach, trying to find a correlation between apocalyptic prophecies and historical events.[410] This positive interest in time and space was also evident during the 19th century. Historicist premillennialists interpreted apocalyptic prophetic periods in terms of the day-year principle and became absorbed by their interest in history. They saw a continuity of time and space between the present and future earth during the millennium.[411]

In general, this appreciation of time, space, and history was related to a literal-temporal interpretation of the Bible and the prophecies. The Millerites applied a more positive or literal approach to interpreting Scripture. Miller, for example, defended a literal-historical interpretation of the Bible in general and the prophecy in particular. Of course, Miller was aware that the Bible and the prophecies involved figurative language and symbols, but he also thought that those elements had a literal or temporal referent in reality.[412]

However, historicist premillennialists, in general, and the Millerites in particular, never applied this literal-historical hermeneutics to God and heavenly realities. They never abandoned the classical understanding of God as timeless, spaceless (incorporeal), and immutable.[413] As a

---

410. Joy Gilsdorf, *The Puritan Apocalypse: New England Eschatology in the Seventeenth Century*, Outstanding Studies in Early American History (New York, NY: Garland, 1989), 9. In contrast, Calvin avoided writing a commentary on the book of Revelation. Ibid.

411. Martin Spence, "The Renewal of Time and Space: The Missing Element of Discussions About Nineteenth Century Premillennialism," *The Journal of Ecclesiastical History* 63, no. 1 (2012): 85-87, 90-93.

412. Sylvester Bliss, *Memoirs of William Miller: Generally Known as a Lecturer on the Prophecies, and the Second Coming of Christ* (Boston, MA: Joshua V. Himes, 1853), 69-72; William Miller, *Evidence From Scripture and History of the Second Coming of Christ About the Year 1843: Exhibited in a Course of Lectures* (Boston, MA: Joshua V. Himes, 1842), 3-4.

413. See Spence, "Renewal of Time and Space," 87. For Millerites, "God's order

result, the Millerites could never situate God's literal sanctuary in heaven, as Adventists pioneers would later do. They interpreted the sanctuary of Dan 8:14 as a reference to the earth or the church.[414] The ontological dualism and the *via negativa* were still operative in Millerism. In virtue of their experience of the great disappointment in 1844 and the discovery of the reality of the heavenly sanctuary, the Adventist pioneers reacted against the classical theism of their days.

Ontological and Epistemological Presuppositions

The discovery of the heavenly sanctuary led the Adventist pioneers to change radically the ontological and epistemological assumptions underlying their interpretation of heavenly realities. This discovery involved an application of the literal hermeneutics of Millerism to heavenly realities.[415] In her first visions, for example, E. G. White referred to the New Jerusalem and the heavenly sanctuary as physical places.[416]

---

existed always, outside of time, as a single force. Change over time belonged only to human history; God was unchanging." Ruth Alden Doan, *The Miller Heresy, Millennialism, and American Culture* (Philadelphia, PA: Temple University Press, 1987), 55. Josiah Litch, for example, affirmed that God was "a pure spirit . . . without body or parts." Josiah Litch, *Prophetic Expositions; Or a Connected View of the Testimony of the Prophets Concerning the Kingdom of God and the Time of Its Establishment* (Boston, MA: Joshua V. Himes, 1842), 1:20.

414. William Miller, "Cleansing of the Sanctuary," *Signs of the Times*, April 6, 1842, 1. According to Litch the sanctuary of Dan 8:14 was "the church . . . of which Christ is the High Priest." Josiah Litch, *An Address to the Public, and Especially to Clergy, on the Near Approach of the Glorious, Everlasting Kingdom of God on Earth, as Indicated by the Word of God, the History of the World and Signs of the Present Times* (Boston, MA: Joshua V. Himes, 1841), 83.

415. In contrast, part of the Millerites after the great disappointment on October 22, 1844 went in the opposite hermeneutical direction by affirming that during that date, Christ "had come spiritually rather than physically (or literally) in the clouds of heaven. . . . Unfortunately, the tendency of this party to spiritualize Scripture spread across their belief system." George R. Knight, "The Rise of Sabbatarian Doctrines," in *1844 and the Rise of Sabbatarian Adventism*, ed. and comp. George R. Knight (Hagerstown, MD: Review & Herald, 1994), 143.

416. See Ellen G. Harmon, "Letter From Sister Harmon," *The Day-Star*, January 24, 1846, 31-32; Ellen G. Harmon, "Letter From Sister Harmon," *The Day-Star*, March 14, 1846, 7. These depictions "suggested the physical reality of a heavenly sanctuary." P. Gerard Damsteegt, "Among Sabbatarian Adventists (1845-1850)," in *Doctrine of the Sanctuary: A Historical Survey*, ed. Frank B. Holbrook (Silver Spring, MD: Biblical Research Institute, 1989), 25.

The pioneers realized that heaven was a physical-spatial place where change was possible.[417] The understanding of the 2,300 evenings and mornings of Dan 8:14 as starting on the earth and finishing on heaven with the purification of the heavenly sanctuary entailed that the heavenly and earthly realities were part of one and the same temporal-spatial creation and that reality did not involve any ontological dichotomy between timelessness and temporality.[418]

The application of the literal-temporal hermeneutics to heavenly realities involved a rejection of the classical *via negativa* to the interpretation of Scripture. The Adventist pioneers sought to interpret Scripture in the light of its own presuppositions by rejecting the philosophical ones.[419] They committed to a deeper application of the *sola Scriptura principle*, which they explicitly supported, while they also affirmed the Bible as the only standard to judge any other source of knowledge.[420]

The Interpretation of God

In harmony with their rejection of the *via negativa*, the Adventist pioneers also rejected any spiritualized vision of God. A literal, physical sanctuary in heaven implied a God who was able to experience time, space, and to interact with human history. Biblical physical depictions of God had to be taken seriously.[421] Uriah Smith, for example, clearly

---

417. Owen R. L. Crosier rejected the idea that heaven is "beyond change or improvement." Owen R. L. Crosier, "The Law of Moses," *The Day-Star Extra*, February 7, 1846, 42. James White opposed those who believed in a heaven, which "is immaterial in all its properties, and is therefore the negative of all riches and substances." James White, *Personality of God* (Battle Creek, MI: SDA Pub. Assn., [1861?]), 7.

418. Adventists believed the 2,300 days entailed a synchronization of temporal events in heaven and on the earth. See, for example, Uriah Smith, *Daniel and the Revelation: Thoughts, Critical and Practical, on the Book of Daniel and the Revelation; Being an Exposition, Text by Text, of These Important Portions of the Holy Scriptures* (Nashville, TN: Southern Pub. Assn., 1897), 195-237, 638-672; Ellen G. White, *The Great Controversy Between Christ and Satan* (Mountain View, CA: Pacific Press, 1950), 326-327, 421-436.

419. E. G. White states that "learned men . . . teach that *the Scriptures have a mystical, a secret, spiritual meaning not apparent in the language employed*. These men are false teachers. . . . The language of the Bible should be explained according to its obvious meaning." E. G. White, *The Great Controversy*, 598-599. Emphasis mine. See also ibid., 551.

420. Ibid., vii, 448, 595.

421. Even symbolic visions of heavenly realities refer to tangible realities. "Though the Revelation deals largely in *figures*, it does not deal in *fictions*. . . . Thus,

illustrates the Adventist reaction to the timeless and spaceless interpretation of the being of God. He describes the classical theism of his time as a system of theology that follows a mystical interpretation according to which "God is not a person, is without form, and has neither body nor parts."[422] Against this position Smith reminds, "Moses saw the God of Israel. Ex. 33: 21-23. An immaterial being . . . without body or parts, cannot be seen."[423]

Smith and other Adventist pioneers considered that the *via negativa* and its metaphorical understanding of the literal descriptions of God's person and actions virtually denied the revelatory value of Scripture and the capability of language to convey meaning.[424] Against this position, Smith argued that if Christ ascended to heaven with a physical body, "none can presume to deny him a local habitation."[425]

The pioneers perceived God as being able to intervene directly in history and human issues.[426] However, they understood that God was ontologically different from the world. God was a person, the Creator of the universe, and He did not depend on previous matter to create. God was also the Sustainer but without ontological "overlap" with His creation. Consequently, the pioneers rejected deistic or pantheistic interpretations of God's reality.[427]

---

in this vision [Rev 4-5] we know that the One upon the throne is God. He is really there. We know the Lamb symbolizes Christ. He too is really there. He ascended with a literal, tangible body; and who can say that he does not still retain it? If, then, our great High Priest is a literal being, he must have a literal place in which to minister." Smith, *Daniel and the Revelation*, 426. Emphasis in original.

422. Uriah Smith, *The State of the Dead and the Destiny of the Wicked* (Battle Creek, MI: Steam Press of the SDA Pub. Assn., 1873), 26-27. For the Adventist pioneers, *personality* implied the physical aspect.

423. Ibid., 28. Smith says that God is spirit (John 4:24) and the Bible also affirms the same regarding angels (Heb 1:7, 14), who have bodily forms or human shapes. Ibid., 27.

424. "He [God] told Moses that he would put his hand over him as he passed by, and then take it away, that he might see his back parts, but not his face. Has he hands? has he back parts? has he a face? If not, why try to convey ideas by means of language?" Ibid.

425. Ibid., 29. J. White described God as "possessing both body and parts." J. White, *Personality of God*, 7. E. G. White described God as having *form*, just as Christ had. Harmon, "Letter From Sister Harmon," March 14, 1846, 7. See Ellen G. White, *A Sketch of the Christian Experience and Views of Ellen G. White* (Saratoga Springs, NY: James White, 1851), 64.

426. See, for example, Ellen G. White, *Education* (Mountain View, CA: Pacific Press, 1952), 173.

427. See Ellen G. White, *Testimonies for the Church* (Mountain View, CA: Pa-

The Adventist pioneers believed that God was able to experience time and history because He was ontologically temporal. God's temporality was not the same as creation's time. God was temporal even before Creation. E. G. White described God's eternity in terms of everlastingness.[428] This temporality of God, however, was different from human or creation's temporality, not only because God is without beginning or end, but because He also was able to know the future exhaustively.[429] Apparently, E. G. White understood that God's experience of time is infinitely superior to the experience of time by His creatures. Still, God's temporality is compatible with the one of His creatures. Both, God and creatures, are temporal. At the same time, He transcends His creation in a way not totally revealed to human beings.[430]

In contrast to traditional theology, E. G. White also defined God's immutability in terms of the unchangeability of His character and purpose.[431] Consequently, she did not think of God as impassible. He does not only have emotions but He can also modify His course of action in order to accomplish His purposes when human beings change their relation to Him. In this sense, God can repent of some specific courses of action.[432]

---

cific Press, 1948), 8:258-259; E. G. White, *Education*, 131, 197-198; Ellen G. White, "The Revelation of God," *The Advent Review and Sabbath Herald*, November 8, 1898, 709-710; Ellen G. White, *Patriarchs and Prophets* (Washington, DC: Review & Herald, 1958), 114-115; Ellen G. White, *Counsels to Parents, Teachers, and Students* (Mountain View, CA: Pacific Press, 1943), 177.

428. E. G. White frequently used expressions such as the *times eternal* and *eternal ages* or *before the foundation of the world*, reflecting biblical vocabulary to talk about the time of God and the inner divine activity before Creation. See E. G. White, *Testimonies for the Church*, 8:270-271; Ellen G. White, *The Desire of Ages* (Mountain View, CA: Pacific Press, 1940), 22; Ellen G. White, "The Plan of Salvation," *Signs of the Times*, February 13, 1893, 230; Ellen G. White, "Surpassing Love Revealed in His Plan," *Signs of the Times*, December 15, 1914, 769.

429. "He [God] sees the most remote events of past history and the far distant future with as clear a vision as we do those things that are transpiring daily." Ellen G. White, *Manuscript Releases* (Silver Spring, MD: Ellen G. White Estate, 1990), 14:21.

430. E. G. White, *Testimonies for the Church*, 8:279. The Adventist pioneers understood God's transcendence in biblical terms, rather than in technical ones; for example, when the Bible describes the unsearchable greatness of God (Ps 145:3) or His infinite understanding (Ps 147:5). See ibid., 282, 283.

431. Ellen G. White, "The True Standard of Righteousness," *Adventist Review and Sabbath Herald*, August 25, 1895, 529; Ellen G. White, *Manuscript Releases* (Silver Spring, MD: Ellen G. White Estate, 1990), 19:182.

432. E. G. White, *Patriarchs and Prophets*, 630.

The Interpretation of the World

The Adventist pioneers and E. G. White in particular believed that God created the world in a recent six-day period. The story of Gen 1 was literal. E. G. White rejected evolution and the notion that the six days of Creation mean indefinite periods.[433]

E. G. White also affirmed that the world is ruled by natural laws established by God.[434] God's interventions in the world did not imply for her an interruption of those laws.[435] In addition, in nature, a law of service or obedient action[436] rules everything. Everything in nature attends to the needs of the life of the world and its own.

The Interpretation of the Human Being

For the Adventist pioneers, God created human beings in the image and likeness of God. This likeness involves the outward resemblance and character as a whole.[437] Based on their ontological assumptions, the Adventist pioneers could not accept the traditional view that the image of God lies essentially in the soul. They also dismissed the traditional body-soul dualism of classical theology as a pagan doctrine, along with the notion of a naturally immortal soul, and the belief in an eternal torment of the wicked. In contrast, they held a unitary view of the human being and the belief in the resurrection.[438]

E. G. White also believed that the same laws that are operative in the natural world are also operative in human beings. The law of ser-

---

433. See, for example, Ellen G. White, *Spiritual Gifts*, vol. 3 (Battle Creek, MI: SDA Pub. Assn., 1864), 90-93; E. G. White, *Patriarchs and Prophets*, 111-114; E. G. White, *Education*, 128-130.

434. E. G. White, *Patriarchs and Prophets*, 52.

435. "The Lord does not work through His laws to supersede the laws of nature. He does His work through the laws." Ellen G. White, *Testimonies for the Church* (Mountain View, CA: Pacific Press, 1948), 6:186.

436. Ellen G. White, *Life Sketches of Ellen G. White* (Mountain View, CA: Pacific Press, 1943), 87; E. G. White, *Education*, 103.

437. E. G. White, *Patriarchs and Prophets*, 45; E. G. White, *Education*, 20.

438. See, for example, James White, *Appeal on Immortality* (Battle Creek, MI: SDA Pub. Assn., n.d.); Uriah Smith, *Mortal or Immortal? Which? Or an Inquiry Into the Present Constitution and Future Condition of Man* (Battle Creek, MI: Steam Press of the Review & Herald Office, 1860); Uriah Smith, *Man's Nature and Destiny: Or the State of the Dead, the Reward of the Righteous and the End of the Wicked* (Oakland, CA: Pacific Press, 1884); Smith, *The State of the Dead*; E. G. White, *The Great Controversy*, 533-539, 545-550.

vice or obedient action is also applicable to human beings. Human happiness depends on obedience to God's laws.[439] Human beings, however, possess free will.[440] Thus, although God created Adam and Eve without a tendency to evil, they, as moral beings, had the opportunity to choose between good and evil. Thus, God's moral laws were also applicable to them.[441]

The problem of sin was a result of a voluntary human disobedience to God, instigated by Satan. Sin extended not only to every descendant of Adam and Eve but also to the rest of nature, introducing disharmony, suffering, and death. Human beings became separated from God, unable to solve the problem of sin by themselves. However, they still have the opportunity to choose to serve God in spite of their fallen condition.[442]

The Articulating Agent and the Articulating Action

Following William Miller's understanding of the Bible as "a system of revealed truths,"[443] the Adventist pioneers developed the Adventist theological set of beliefs in a systematic way. The Adventist leaders frequently referred to their theological system using expressions such as *system of truth* or *chain of truth*.[444] This system is present in the Bible, which "unfolds a simple and complete system of theology and philosophy."[445] The Bible contains a "harmonious chain of truth."[446]

---

439. E. G. White, *Education*, 99, 103, 196-197; E. G. White, *Life Sketches*, 87-88.

440. The will is "the governing power in the nature of man, the power of decision, or of choice." Ellen G. White, *Steps to Christ* (Mountain View, CA: Pacific Press, 1956), 47.

441. E. G. White, *Education*, 23; E. G. White, *Patriarchs and Prophets*, 48, 49, 52.

442. E. G. White, *Education*, 23-29; E. G. White, *Patriarchs and Prophets*, 53-60; E. G. White, *Steps to Christ*, 47-48.

443. William Miller, *William Miller's Apology and Defence* (Boston, MA: J. V. Himes, 1845), 6. See also William Miller, *Miller's Works*, vol. 1, *Views on the Prophecies and Prophetic Chronology* (Boston, MA: Joshua V. Himes, 1842), 11-12. See also ibid., 116.

444. E. G. White, *The Great Controversy*, 423. See also Uriah Smith and George I. Butler, *Replies to Elder Canright's Attacks on Seventh-day Adventists* (Battle Creek, MI: Review & Herald, 1895), 170; James White, "The Cause," *Advent Review, and Sabbath Herald*, October 29, 1861, 172; Uriah Smith, *An Appeal to the Youth* (Battle Creek, MI: Steam Press of the SDA Pub. Assn., 1864), 80.

445. Ellen G. White, *Christian Education* (Battle Creek, MI: International Tract Society, 1894), 106; Ellen G. White, *Fundamentals of Christian Education* (Nashville, TN: Southern Pub. Assn., 1923), 129.

446. E. G. White, *Life Sketches*, 215. E. G. White thought that the responsibility

E. G. White pointed out directly the person of Jesus Christ as the articulating agent of the system of truth. "*Christ is the complete system of truth.*"[447] Using a similar expression, she also said that "*Christ is the center of all true doctrine.* All true religion is found in His word and in nature."[448]

A more complex issue is the identification of Christ's articulating action. E. G. White, for example, identifies several actions of Christ regarding the articulation of the relationship between God and the world that are central for her. One important topic relates to Christ and His redemptive work.[449] As part of that work, E. G. White highlights Christ's crucifixion and resurrection[450] and Christ's work of atonement.[451]

Actually, E. G. White seems to connect the redemptive work of Christ with the broader issue of Christ as a Mediator. E. G. White exposes the role of Christ as Mediator in historical-temporal terms. Before the creation of the world, the Deity had already foreseen the introduction of the problem of sin and established a plan. The members of the Deity covenanted that Christ would become the Mediator between God and the fallen humanity. He would offer Himself as a substitutive sacrifice in order to provide the possibility of salvation.[452] Christ became the Mediator of this covenant known as the *everlasting covenant*.[453] After the Fall, this covenant was extended to Adam and

---

of the believers was "to gather up the scattered jewels of God's word into one perfect chain of truth." E. G. White, *Christian Education*, 85. Emphasis mine.

447. Ellen G. White, *The Ellen G. White 1888 Materials* (1987), Ellen G. White Writings Comprehensive Research Edition [CD ROM] (Silver Spring, MD: Ellen G. White Estate, 2008), 1273. Emphasis mine.

448. E. G. White, *Counsels to Parents*, 453. Emphasis mine.

449. "*Christ in His work* of redemption is seen to be *the great central truth of the system of truth.*" E. G. White, *Ellen G. White 1888 Materials*, 806. Emphasis mine. "*The central theme of the Bible*, the theme about which every other in the whole book clusters, *is the redemption plan.*" E. G. White, *Education*, 125. Emphasis mine.

450. "A crucified and risen Saviour is the great central theme of the Word of God." Ellen G. White, "Build on a Sure Foundation," *Advent Review and Sabbath Herald*, September 24, 1908, 7. See also E. G. White, *Ellen G. White 1888 Materials*, 806.

451. "The *atonement* of Christ is *the great central truth* around which cluster all the truths that pertain to the great work of redemption." Ellen G. White, *Manuscript Releases* (Silver Spring, MD: Ellen G. White Estate, 1990), 12:59. Emphasis mine.

452. E. G. White, *The Desire of Ages*, 834. Ellen G. White, *Manuscript Releases* (Silver Spring, MD: Ellen G. White Estate, 1990), 11:345.

453. Ellen G. White, "The Word Made Flesh," *The Advent Review and Sabbath Herald*, April 5, 1906, 8. "From eternal ages the covenant of grace (unmerited favor)

Eve in Eden, then to Noah, Abraham, and the people of Israel.[454] The intention of the successive covenants, which in essence were updates of the same everlasting covenant, was to promote the obedience to God's law.[455] Christ was the revelation of God and Mediator of each covenant, the link between heaven and earth.[456]

The everlasting covenant entailed Christ's incarnation. In that way, Christ could ratify that covenant made with Adam and Abraham through His sacrifice.[457] The incarnation of Christ also made possible a fuller revelation of God's character of love to the intelligences of the universe and the restoration of the broken relationship between God and humanity.[458] In E. G. White's view, all those who accept Christ and His substitutionary sacrifice by faith become part of the elect and are predestined to salvation.[459] In other words, predestination is God's plan to save humanity but in interaction with human will. Salvation is voluntary, not compulsive or coercive.

E. G. White understood that Christ's atoning work did not conclude with His atoning sacrifice on the cross. Atonement involves a process leading to the eradication of sin. The application of the merits of His sacrifice is also a work of mediation where Christ makes an atonement in heaven.[460] "The intercession of Christ in man's behalf in the sanctuary above *is as essential to the plan of salvation as was His death upon the cross.*"[461] For the Adventist pioneers, then, "the sanctuary was the key which unlocked the mystery of the disappointment of 1844. It opened to view a complete system of truth."[462] It provided the perspective from which they saw Christ's redemptive work in general.

---

existed in the mind of God. It is called the everlasting covenant." E. G. White, "The Plan of Salvation," 230.

454. E. G. White, *Patriarchs and Prophets*, 370-373; E. G. White, *Education*, 115; E. G. White, *Fundamentals of Christian Education*, 403.

455. E. G. White, *Patriarchs and Prophets*, 364, 371.

456. Ibid., 366-367.

457. Ibid., 370-371.

458. E. G. White, *The Desire of Ages*, 19-22, 25.

459. Ellen G. White, "Chosen in Christ," *Signs of the Times*, January 2, 1893, 134.

460. Christ "ascended up on high to make an atonement for our transgressions." Ellen G. White, *Faith and Works* (Nashville, TN: Southern Pub. Assn., 1979), 105.

461. E. G. White, *The Great Controversy*, 489. Emphasis mine.

462. Ibid., 423. "*The sanctuary in heaven is the very center of Christ's work* in behalf of men." Ibid., 488. Emphasis mine. The heavenly sanctuary is "the great central object in the plan of salvation through Jesus Christ." Uriah Smith, *Looking Unto Jesus: Or Christ in Type and Antitype* (Chicago, IL: Review & Herald, 1898), 56-57.

The Interpretation of the Whole

The entire reality that the Adventist pioneers tried to describe through their theological system was a reality in conflict. Christ's work of redemption entailed an opposition to the forces of evil. This conflict started in heaven with Satan's rebellion, followed on the earth with the sin of Adam and Eve, and it is still in process.[463] The great controversy involves every aspect of human life.[464]

E. G. White held that the great controversy is the grand central theme that the student of the Bible should know when he/she is trying to understand Scripture as a whole, in relation to its parts. That whole describes the entire reality as a cosmic conflict. It is possible to trace the temporal development of this conflict through historical and prophetic records from its beginning until its final consummation in the future.[465]

Changes in the Understanding of the Principle of Articulation

The 1888 GC session in Minneapolis is considered a key event in Adventist history. Several doctrinal topics were discussed in that session, including, especially, the identity of the ten horns in Dan 7, the law in Galatians and justification by faith.[466] The last one, however, is

---

463. Regarding the origin and development of the great controversy see, for example, E. G. White, *The Great Controversy*, 492-504, 531-535; E. G. White, *Patriarchs and Prophets*, 33-43, 52-61. E. G. White emphasized the wideness of this conflict through her conflict series: ibid.; Ellen G. White, *Prophets and Kings* (Mountain View, CA: Pacific Press, 1943); E. G. White, *The Desire of Ages*; Ellen G. White, *The Acts of the Apostles* (Mountain View, CA: Pacific Press, 1911); E. G. White, *The Great Controversy*.

464. E. G. White held that the student of the Bible "should see how this controversy enters into every phase of human experience; how in every act of life he himself reveals the one or the other of the two antagonistic motives; and how, whether he will or not, he is even now deciding upon which side of the controversy he will be found." E. G. White, *Education*, 190.

465. "The student should learn to view the word as a whole, and to see the relation of its parts. He should gain a knowledge of its grand central theme, of God's original purpose for the world, of the rise of the great controversy, and of the work of redemption. He should understand the nature of the two principles that are contending for supremacy, and should learn to trace their working through the records of history and prophecy, to the great consummation." Ibid.

466. George R. Knight, *A User-Friendly Guide to the 1888 Message* (Hagerstown, MD: Review & Herald, 1998), 19, 51-56.

probably the most important issue discussed there, particularly from the perspective of its theological impact.

The Adventist emphasis on the importance of the Ten Commandments and the Sabbath during the first four decades guided some Adventist leaders toward an interpretation of justification almost in legalistic terms. Smith and George I. Butler were expositors of that position, which paved the way for legalistic tendencies. Smith, for example, believed that justification involved the application of Christ's sacrificial merits that "cancel past sin, and gives us a new spiritual nature."[467] In the current Christian life, however, the righteousness of the law should "be fulfilled in us by our obedience to it."[468] Apparently, Smith and G. I. Butler "believed in justification for past sins, but emphasized the law and obedience for Christian living."[469]

In contrast to Smith and G. I. Butler, Ellet J. Waggoner, one of the main defenders of justification by faith in Minneapolis, believed that only the righteousness of Christ—obtained through faith—could provide righteousness for the Christian. This righteousness was more than a mere legal forgiveness; it involved a real change in the entire life of the believer.[470] Moreover, Waggoner remarked, the Gospel "is *present power* applied to the salvation of the one who has *present faith*. . . . The Gospel is the power of God to save men from sin. But it is present power, for *sin is ever present*."[471]

In general, E. G. White supported Waggoner and Alonzo T. Jones regarding their position about justification during 1888 session and even after, in spite of the fact that she had some differences with them.[472] She understood justification by faith from the general perspective of

---

467. [Uriah Smith], "Our Righteousness," *The Advent Review and Sabbath Herald*, June 11, 1889, 376.

468. Ibid. Smith held that "the law is spiritual, holy, just, and good, the divine standard of righteousness. Perfect obedience to it will develop perfect righteousness, and that is the only way any one can attain to righteousness." Ibid.

469. Knight, *Guide to the 1888 Message*, 90.

470. See, for example, Ellet J. Waggoner, *Christ and His Righteousness* (Oakland, CA: Pacific Press, 1890), 66. See also ibid., 51, 57.

471. [Ellet J. Waggoner], "A Present Salvation," *The Present Truth*, May 18, 1893, 146. Emphasis mine.

472. About E. G. White supporting Waggoner and Jones, see Ellen G. White to Ole A. Olsen, May 1, 1895, in Ellen G. White, *Manuscript Releases* (Silver Spring, MD: Ellen G. White Estate, 1990), 14:114-135. See especially pp. 128-129. Regarding differences between E. G. White and Waggoner and Jones, see Knight, *Guide to the 1888 Message*, 73-76.

the work of Christ in the sanctuary. Justification was not a punctiliar fact once and forever at the beginning of the Christian experience as in Luther. It involved the entire lifetime, requiring the continuous intercession of Christ in the heavenly sanctuary in favor of the believer.[473]

Moreover, justification was not something separate from sanctification. Obedience and sanctification were closely related to justification because "in order for man *to retain justification*, there must be *continual obedience*, through active, living faith that works by love and purifies the soul."[474] Obedience, though, did not have any meritorious value.[475]

The emphasis on justification, however, apparently led Waggoner to see the issue of justification by faith as the essential articulating action of Christ, the very center of Adventist theology. In 1891 he declared that Adventists tended to think that they had "the third angel's message, consisting of *a system of truth comprising such subjects as the law, the Sabbath, nature of man, advent*, etc., and that *to this we have superadded a little gospel, the idea of justification by faith*."[476] Waggoner, then, explained that righteousness by faith was not a doctrine among others in the context of the third angel's message. It was the very center of that message. "*Nothing can be added to the preaching of the righteousness of God by faith of Jesus Christ. . . . All of these doctrines are simply*

---

473. "The atoning sacrifice through a mediator is essential because of *the constant commission of sin*. Jesus *is officiating* in the presence of God, *offering up His shed blood*, as it had been a lamb slain. Jesus *presents the oblation offered for every offense and every shortcoming of the sinner.*" Ellen G. White, *Selected Messages*, vol. 1 (Washington, DC: Review & Herald, 1958), 344. Emphasis mine.

474. Ellen G. White, "The Way of Life," *Advent Review and Sabbath Herald*, November 4, 1890, 673. Emphasis mine. For E. G. White, "Justification is needed by believers all the way through their experience. Justification always runs parallel to or concurrently with sanctification." Woodrow W. Whidden II, *Ellen White on Salvation* (Hagerstown, MD: Review & Herald, 1995), 104. See also ibid., 151. "Unlike some of her twentieth-century interpreters, she did not define righteousness of Christ in a way that separated justification and sanctification." Knight, *Guide to the 1888 Message*, 94.

475. Ellen G. White, "The Grace of God Manifested in Good Works," *The Advent Review and Sabbath Herald*, January 29, 1895, 65. It is "Christ, the atoning sacrifice, who is able to impart his righteousness to the sinner, and *make his efforts acceptable before God*. When we take Christ for our Saviour, we are enabled to become obedient children, keeping all the commandments of God." Ellen G. White, "The Gospel for Both Jews and Gentiles," *The Signs of the Times*, August 5, 1889, 466. Emphasis mine.

476. Ellet J. Waggoner, "Bible Study: Letter to the Romans—No. 1," *General Conference Daily Bulletin*, March 8, 1891, 33. Emphasis mine.

divisions, lines depending upon that one thing,—all summed up in the doctrine of righteousness by faith. We can preach nothing else."[477] His own emphasis on justification by faith pushed Waggoner to see the articulation of Adventist message from a soteriological view, with all the other doctrines turning around it. Remarkably, he did not mention the sanctuary in his enumeration of doctrines.[478]

A second major attempt to change Adventist's understanding of the principle of articulation relates to the so-called pantheism crisis. Some denominational leaders began to promote what is usually considered as pantheistic ideas, including especially Dr. John H. Kellogg and Waggoner. This crisis came to a peak during the period between 1901 and 1903, particularly stimulated by the publication of Kellogg's book *The Living Temple*.[479] In the original version of that book, Kellogg strongly suggested an immanent understanding of God's operation in nature.[480] The living things of nature such as trees, shrubs, insects, or even human beings were creators. The process of Creation is continuous, never finished.[481] It is clear that, at least partially, Kellogg identified God and the world as in modern theology when he said, *"Nature is simply a philosophical name for God,* who is the active force in nature—the 'all in all.'"[482]

For Kellogg, every manifestation of God's power implied the presence of God. He was the "All-Energy, the infinite Power, and all-per-

---

477. Ibid. Emphasis mine.

478. The time would demonstrate that this change would have an enormous potential to reorient Adventist theology. See Chapter 4 in this study. Waggoner's germinal change was accompanied by a subtle change in the understanding of God's ontology. As early as 1891, he explained that God's eternity is an eternal now or timeless present. "What is eternity?—It is something that has neither beginning nor ending. . . . Past, present, and future are all present with God. He lives in an ETERNAL NOW." Ellet J. Waggoner, "Bible Study: Letter to the Romans—No. 13," *General Conference Daily Bulletin*, March 22, 1891, 203. Capital letters in original. Apparently, Waggoner also held that God's knowledge was unchangeable. "God has not changed a hair's breadth from the plan which He knew before the world began." Ibid., 202.

479. George R. Knight, *A Brief History of Seventh-day Adventists* (Hagerstown, MD: Review & Herald, 1999), 116. Richard W. Schwarz, *Light Bearers to the Remnant* (Mountain View, CA: Pacific Press, 1979), 288.

480. "God is the explanation of nature,—not a God outside of nature, but in nature, manifesting himself through and in all the objects, movements, and varied phenomena of the universe." John H. Kellogg, *The Living Temple* (Battle Creek, MI: Good Health, 1903), 28.

481. Ibid., 29, 41, 53-54.

482. Ibid., 483. Emphasis mine.

vading Presence."[483] Apparently, Kellogg did not want to deny God's personality. God was more than nature, but the physical descriptions of God in the Bible were not literal for him. They were only necessary because of the impossibility of human mind to worship something that is not concrete.[484] In an implicit application of the *via negativa*, Kellogg considered that God cannot be understood through anthropomorphic representations but through the observation of Him in nature. Nature bears testimony of God as a presence, an Intelligent Being, who is "beyond our comprehension as are the bounds of *space and time*."[485]

Technically speaking, Kellogg was a panentheist, rather than a pantheist.[486] As in modern theology, he believed that God was more than a purely immanent being because He had a personality, although immaterial. At the same time, He had an immanent *side* in nature. E. G. White saw the clear theological consequences of Kellogg's theory: "There is in it [Kellogg's understanding of God] the beginning of theories which, carried to their logical conclusion, would destroy faith in the sanctuary question and in the atonement."[487] E. G. White qualified Kellogg's ideas as *mysticism* and as the *alpha* of a kind of apostasy that would reappear later. This mysticism would remove the pillars of Adventist faith.[488]

---

483. Ibid., 29. "Where God's Spirit is at work, where God's power is manifested, God himself is actually and truly present." Ibid., 28.

484. "We naturally desire to form a definite, clearly defined conception of the being whom we worship. The Bible supplies this human need." Ibid., 31.

485. Ibid., 33. Emphasis mine. According to Kellogg, "the concept of a personal God was essentially a conceptual construct for the benefit of ordinary minds who needed such an ultimately nonfactual *accommodation* to their intellectual limitations. The implication was that real intellectuals like himself could perceive the spiritual reality beyond the anthropomorphic accommodation." Woodrow Whidden, Jerry Moon, and John W. Reeve, *The Trinity: Understanding God's Love, His Plan of Salvation, and Christian Relationships* (Hagerstown, MD: Review & Herald, 2002), 213. Emphasis mine.

486. See Jerry Moon, "The Quest for a Biblical Trinity: Ellen White's 'Heavenly Trio' Compared to the Traditional Doctrine," *JATS* 17, no. 1 (2006): 151. See also Norman Young, "The Alpha and the Omega Heresy: Kellogg and the Cross," *Adventist Heritage* 12, no. 1 (1987): 38.

487. Ellen G. White, *Manuscript Releases* (Silver Spring, MD: Ellen G. White Estate, 1987), 2:243. E. G. White frequently referred to Kellogg's theory as *pantheism*. The more technical term *panentheism* was not popular during her days. Even though the term was coined before the times of E. G. White by Karl Krause (1781-1832), it became popular during the 20th century because of process theology, particularly by Hartshorne (mid-20th century). See Cooper, *Panentheism*, 26.

488. E. G. White, *Selected Messages*, vol. 1, 201-205.

She also emphasized that the personality of God involved a physical aspect; namely, that God was a spatio-temporal being.[489] Personality and the spatiality-temporality of God were inseparable for E. G. White. The denial of God's spatiality was a denial of His personality according to the pioneer's ontology of God.[490]

Kellogg was clearly aware that he was in line with the modern theology of his time that tried to harmonize religion and evolutionary science. He used to quote authors such as Herbert Spencer—philosopher and evolutionary scientist—and was acquainted with several other liberal theologians of his time.[491] Actually, his immanent theology "brought him closer to the liberal theological mainstream in America."[492] Under that influence, Kellogg tried to reformulate the principle of articulation in Adventist theology virtually in every aspect, changing the interpretation of God, the world, and the human being in terms of his panentheistic view. The articulating agent was not Christ but an incorporeal all-pervading God, whose articulating action was purely immanent. Everything in nature is a *miracle* and God is "all in all" (1 Cor 12:6).[493]

Conclusion

The review of the main interpretations of the principle of articulation in Christian tradition shows that this principle has not been inter-

---

489. "The new theories in regard to God and Christ, as brought out in 'The Living Temple', are not in harmony with the teaching of Christ. The Lord Jesus came to this world to represent the Father. He did not represent God as an essence pervading nature, but as a personal being." Ellen G. White to the Teachers in Emmanuel Missionary College, September 23, 1903, in *Spalding and Magan Collection* (1985), 324, Ellen G. White Writings Comprehensive Research Edition [CD ROM] (Silver Spring, MD: Ellen G. White Estate, 2008).

490. In the context of the crisis occasioned by Kellogg, E. G. White sharply rejected any spiritualized interpretation of the being of God. Regarding God the Father, she affirmed, "The Father is all the fulness [sic] of the Godhead *bodily*, and is invisible to mortal sight." Ellen G. White, *Testimonies for the Church Containing Messages of Warning and Instruction to Seventh-day Adventists: Regarding Dangers Connected With the Medical Missionary Work*, Series B no. 7 (n.p.: Published for the author [1906]), 62. Emphasis mine. Regarding the Son, she said, "The Son is all the fulness [sic] of the Godhead *manifested*." Ibid., 63. Emphasis mine.

491. Brian C. Wilson, *Dr. John Harvey Kellogg and the Religion of Biologic Living* (Bloomington, IN: Indiana University Press, 2014), 95-102.

492. Ibid., 102.

493. Kellogg, *The Living Temple*, 28, 49, 483, 484-485.

preted in the light of the *sola Scriptura* principle. The main representatives of the hierarchical model—Augustine and Aquinas—assumed that it was possible to interpret Christian theology and its principle of articulation in the light of the Greek philosophical background. In the case of the panentheistic model of modern theology—Schleiermacher and process theology—the situation is similar. There is a modification of the philosophical background in terms of the influence of modern philosophy but there is no attempt or claim to interpret the principle of articulation by applying the *sola Scriptura* principle. Moreover, the hierarchy timeless-temporality was modified but not eliminated.

The soteriological model of the Protestant Reformation—Luther and Calvin—affirmed the *sola Scriptura* principle. An analysis of this model, however, shows that in practice the basic ontological and epistemological presuppositions inherited from Greek philosophy—through the influence of medieval theologians such as Augustine—strongly determined the interpretation of the principle of articulation in non-biblical terms. Once again, the hierarchy of medieval theology was simplified but it was still clearly present.

The Adventist pioneers, in contrast, represent a radical departure from Christian tradition. They rejected the ontological and epistemological presuppositions implicit in the interpretation of the principle of articulation in Christian theology, which paved the way for an interpretation of that principle in the light of the Bible itself. During the end of the 19th century and the beginning of the 20th, however, history shows that Adventist theology was vulnerable to the influence of the soteriological and modern models.

CHAPTER FOUR

The Principle of Articulation in Current Adventist Theology

Introduction

The purpose of this chapter is to analyze and evaluate the interpretations of the principle of articulation in current Adventist theology. The first section discusses the evangelical Adventist model[1] of interpretation of the principle of articulation. The main representative of this model is D. Ford, although the discussion also includes other exponents. In a similar way, the second section examines the modern Adventist model of interpretation, where the chosen representative is Guy, but also other authors complement the discussion. The third section considers the Adventist theodicy model of interpretation of the principle of articulation with Gulley as the main representative, though other theologians in a similar line supplement the exposition.

As in Chapter 3, first, it is necessary to explore each model briefly in terms of its ontological and epistemological presuppositions. Second, each section analyzes the interpretations of the principle of articulation in its basic components in the three models, based on the outline provided by the phenomenological analysis of the principle of articulation in Chapter 2. Finally, an evaluation of each model in the light of the *sola Scriptura* principle follows. This evaluation entails the clarification of the provenance of the presuppositions involved in each model as well as their effect on the interpretation of the princi-

---

1. There is an explanation about this model and the others mentioned in this introduction at the beginning of every section in this chapter, before analyzing and evaluating them.

ple of articulation in Adventist theology. The discussion regarding the interpretation of the principle of articulation in Christian tradition in general—Chapter 3—provides the necessary background to clarify the origin of the interpretations of that principle in current Adventist theology and to evaluate them.

Evangelical Adventist Model

Evangelical Adventism[2] considers that the evangelical emphasis on the Gospel is more in harmony with the purpose that Adventism has historically had regarding the preparation of the world for the second coming of Christ. They usually interpret the "everlasting gospel" of Rev 14:6 in terms of the evangelical understanding of the Gospel. From this perspective, Gospel is virtually equivalent to justification, redemption, forgiveness, and salvation.[3]

Evangelical Adventists perceive themselves as being in line with the emphasis on justification by faith that goes back to the 1888 Minneapolis GC session. They also identify themselves with the evangelical emphasis on the Gospel and justification by faith as presented by Adventist Church leaders such as Arthur G. Daniells,[4] and evidenced in relevant events and church documents during the 20th century. Particularly important is the 1952 Bible Conference, with the publication of the two volumes of *Our Firm Foundation*,[5] and the publication of the key book *Seventh-day Adventist Answer Questions on Doctrine* (1957),[6] which has LeRoy E. Froom as one of its main

---

2. Regarding the expressions *evangelical Adventism* or *evangelical Adventists*, see Larry Christoffel, "Evangelical Adventism—*Questions on Doctrine*'s Legacy," paper presented at the Question on Doctrine 50th Anniversary Conference, Andrews University, Berrien Springs, MI, October 24-27, 2007; Larry Christoffel, "'I, if I Be Lifted Up'—A Response," *Ministry*, December 1992, 12-13.

3. Michelle Rader, David VanDenburgh, and Larry Christoffel, "Evangelical Adventism: Clinging to the Old Rugged Cross," *Adventism Today*, January-February 1994, 6-8. See also LeRoy E. Froom, *Movement of Destiny* (Washington, DC: Review & Herald, 1971), 33, 34.

4. Rader, VanDenburgh, and Christoffel, "Evangelical Adventism," 7. See Daniells, *Christ Our Righteousness*, 71-73. Daniells enumerates almost all the Adventist doctrines as embraced by the doctrine of righteousness by faith.

5. Rader, VanDenburgh, and Christoffel, "Evangelical Adventism," 7. See *Our Firm Foundation: A Report of the Seventh-day Adventist Bible Conference Held September 1-13, 1952, in the Sligo Seventh-day Adventist Church Takoma Park, Maryland*, 2 vols. (Washington, DC: Review & Herald, 1953).

6. "Evangelical Adventists consider the positions taken in *Questions on Doctrine*

contributors and disseminators.⁷

From a broader perspective, evangelical Adventists also consider that Adventists are—or they should be—in continuity with evangelicals and the Protestant Reformation in their understanding of the centrality of the Gospel and justification by faith.⁸ Adventists would be essentially evangelicals.⁹ Adventist distinctive doctrines, then, should never

---

to be an expression of both authentic and evangelical Adventism." Rader, VanDenburgh, and Christoffel, "Evangelical Adventism," 7. Emphasis in original. See Leaders, Bible Teachers, and Editors, *Seventh-day Adventist Answer Questions on Doctrine* (Washington, DC: Review & Herald, 1957). For Larry Christoffel, evangelical Adventism is a legacy of *Questions on Doctrine*. See Christoffel, "Evangelical Adventism."

7. George R. Knight, *A Search for Identity: The Development of Seventh-day Adventist Beliefs* (Hagerstown, MD: Review & Herald, 2000), 166. In turn, Froom points out Daniells as his mentor and William W. Prescott as the denominational leader that influenced Daniells with his emphasis on the topic of righteousness by faith. See Froom, *Movement of Destiny*, 377, 380-381, 398, 400. See also William W. Prescott, *The Doctrine of Christ: A Series of Bible Studies for Use in Colleges and Seminaries* (Washington, DC: Review & Herald, 1920).

8. Rader, VanDenburgh, and Christoffel, "Evangelical Adventism," 7; Christoffel, "Evangelical Adventism," 14. Daniel Heinz, a German Adventist historian specialized in Adventist Church in Europe, holds that "Adventists sense a continuity with the history and the teachings of the sixteenth-century Reformation, as do other Protestant Churches. This emphasis on salvation by faith strongly influenced Adventist believers." Daniel Heinz, "Introduction: Seventh-day Adventists in Europe; Heirs of the Reformation," in *Heirs of the Reformation: The Story of Seventh-day Adventists in Europe*, ed. Hugh Dunton et al. (Grantham, England: Stanborough, 1997), 11. Heinz considers that there is a "theological continuity between the Reformation and Adventism." Ibid., 12. This continuity includes the soteriological aspect. Ibid. See also Geoffrey J. Paxton, *The Shaking of Adventism* (Wilmington, DE: Zenith, 1977), 17-29.

9. In the same line, for example, Arthur N. Patrick affirms that "Ellen White, Adventism's most notable author and one of its key founders, was clearly an Evangelical." Arthur N. Patrick, "Are Adventists Evangelicals?" *Ministry*, February 1995, 17. This idea is also implicit in Froom, *Movement of Destiny*. See, for example, ibid., 74, 75. A similar conviction seems to be behind the "Joint Statement of the World Evangelical Alliance and the Seventh-day Adventist Church" where Adventist participants agree that "Adventists can subscribe to the WEA [World Evangelical Alliance] Statement of Faith." "Joint Statement of the World Evangelical Alliance and the Seventh-day Adventist Church," 1, accessed June 17, 2016, http://www.worldevangelicals.org/news/WEAAdventistDialogue20070809d.pdf. In a statement that suggests at least a partial acceptance of the idea that Adventists are evangelicals, George R. Knight states that Adventism should uplift "its specifically Adventist insights and integrates them with those of *evangelical Christianity*. And in that combination we find the message that God commanded in Revelation 14 to be preached to all the world before the Advent." Emphasis mine. George R. Knight, *The Apocalyptic Vision and the Neutering of Adventism: Are We Erasing Our Relevancy?* (Hagerstown, MD: Review & Herald, 2008),

eclipse the Gospel or be the focus of Adventist faith. "By insisting on maintaining the cross as the central truth of Adventist doctrine and evangelism, evangelical Adventism guards against the temptation to make distinctive Adventist doctrine into the gospel."[10]

Evangelical Adventists defend the *sola Scriptura* principle. They see themselves in line with the tradition of the reformers by insisting "upon letting Scripture interpret itself (*sola scriptura*) as the only basic rule of faith and practice for the Christian and the church. They have arrived at their understanding of the Gospel and its implications through consistent application of this principle."[11]

According to evangelical Adventists, Adventist evangelists and theologians such as Harold M. S. Richards, Edward Heppenstall, and D. Ford facilitated the emergence of the movement.[12] The most paradigmatic representative, however, is D. Ford—the crystallizer of evangelical Adventism.[13] He, as nobody else, has emphasized the centrality of the Gospel in harmony with the evangelical or Protestant view.[14] His writings deserve a closer examination regarding the way in which he interprets the principle of articulation in Adventist theology. Other names, though, will complement the discussion.

Ontological and Epistemological Presuppositions

The ontological and epistemological presuppositions underlying D. Ford's understanding of the principle of articulation are not explicit

---

106. See also Robert S. Folkenberg, "Will the Real Evangelical Adventist Please Stand Up," *Adventist Review*, April 1996, 16-19.

10. Rader, VanDenburgh, and Christoffel, "Evangelical Adventism," 8. See ibid., 6.

11. Ibid., 8. "Evangelical Adventism is committed to making the gospel of Jesus Christ and the authority of Scripture central in Seventh-day Adventist doctrine and evangelism. It does not see itself as a 'new theology' but rather as the continuation of a gospel-centered emphasis that began in Adventism over 100 years ago.... Evangelical Adventists believe that this emphasis does not reject the importance of distinctive Adventist doctrine, but rather gives it a firm foundation." Ibid. See also Christoffel, "Evangelical Adventism," 12, 17.

12. Alan Crandall, "Whither Evangelical Adventism?" *Evangelica*, May 1982 [n.p.], quoted in Larry Christoffel, "Evangelical Adventism—*Questions on Doctrine*'s Legacy," paper presented at the Question on Doctrine 50th Anniversary Conference, Andrews University, Berrien Springs, MI, October 24-27, 2007, 11.

13. See ibid.

14. Geoffrey J. Paxton affirms that an examination of D. Ford's teaching has shown "a praiseworthy consistency in Reformation theology." Paxton, *The Shaking of Adventism*, 116.

in his writings. He does not discuss them on purpose. D. Ford, however, implicitly understands that reality involves timelessness/spacelessness and temporality/spatiality. The first realm is the one of God and His timeless actions. The second realm is the one of God's creation.[15]

D. Ford also makes an explicit separation between spiritual or theological knowledge and scientific or historical knowledge. God does not intend to communicate in Scripture real factual scientific or historical information but spiritual one.[16] Consequently, there is no need to harmonize science with a literal reading of Scripture. The interpreter understands the unchangeable truth of Scripture through faith, not through science, because the latter is related to a changeable world.[17] Scientists who are believers, in turn, require the application of a methodological naturalism that enquires about the *how* and the *when*, not about the *why* and the *who* of things in the natural world. This methodological naturalism is in contrast to the philosophical naturalism, followed by non-believer scientists.[18]

This separation between spiritual-theological knowledge and scientific knowledge allows D. Ford to interpret biblical texts that can contradict common scientific ideas in a non-literal way. D. Ford quotes Lawrence T. Geraty who qualifies the *universal* flood story as a *supra-*

---

15. See Desmond Ford, *Genesis Versus Darwinism: The Case for God in a Scientific World* (n.p.: A&S, 2014), 22. In these references, D. Ford quotes Lee Strobel, an evangelical writer. See Lee Strobel, *The Case for a Creator: A Journalist Investigates Scientific Evidence That Points Toward God* (Grand Rapids, MI: Zondervan, 2004), 284-285. See also D. Ford, *Genesis Versus Darwinism: The Case*, 28. In this reference, D. Ford quotes James G. Murphy but the original reference is not provided. See however James G. Murphy, *A Critical and Exegetical Commentary on the Book of Genesis* (Andover, MA: Warren F. Draper, 1866), 28. See the discussion about D. Ford's interpretation of God below, p. 151ff.

16. D. Ford, *Genesis Versus Darwinism: The Case*, 102, 76, 110, 111, 148.

17. Ibid., 109. In this reference, D. Ford quotes J. R. van de Fliert, a Reformed geologist. See J. R. van de Fliert, "Fundamentalism and the Fundamentals of Geology," *Journal of the American Scientific Affiliation* 21 (1969): 69-81. See also D. Ford, *Genesis Versus Darwinism: The Case*, 155.

18. D. Ford, *Genesis Versus Darwinism: The Case*, 184, n. 1. Although D. Ford does not describe in detail his understanding of methodological and philosophical naturalism, the idea is that methodological naturalism explains natural phenomena in terms of natural cause-effect relationships but does not deny the existence of God. God can be an immanent cause using natural laws to introduce changes in the natural world. Philosophical naturalism, instead, denies the existence of God. All that exists is the natural world. For this distinction, see James P. Moreland and William L. Craig, *Philosophical Foundations for a Christian Worldview* (Downers Grove, IL: InterVarsity, 2003), 354, 358.

historical event rather than a historical one.[19] D. Ford admits that the biblical text clearly refers to a real universal flood, but still he does not consider this story as literal but as parabolic.[20] Something similar occurs with the six-day story of Creation that D. Ford interprets in a parabolic or metaphorical, non-literal sense.[21] This story is essentially language adapted to the first readers.[22] Both stories refer to spiritual truth that transcends time and space.

D. Ford seems to assume that the timeless realm is the reference for understanding the temporal one. The realm of temporality finds its meaning in the sphere of what is timeless. The parabolic language that God uses in His revelation seeks to teach abstract truth, related to the Gospel. As the Gospel is spiritual truth, the biblical stories about Creation and the universal flood that use parabolic language intend to teach about "redemption and how to live by the gospel."[23]

D. Ford believes in the inspiration of Scripture and its infallibility.[24] He also explicitly supports the *sola Scriptura* principle.[25] Given the spiritual meaning of Scripture, he thinks, the interpreter does not need to "be troubled by any apparent lack of conformity to our modern views of history and science."[26]

---

19. D. Ford, *Genesis Versus Darwinism: The Case*, 110. D. Ford takes this expression from Lawrence T. Geraty, "Archaeology of the Flood," in *Understanding Genesis: Contemporary Adventist Perspectives*, ed. Brian Bull, Fritz Guy, and Ervin Taylor (Riverside, CA: Adventist Today, 2009), 192.

20. D. Ford, *Genesis Versus Darwinism: The Case*, 98, 110.

21. Ibid., 112. "It is clear that the six days of Genesis 1 constitute a parabolic week for all the time involved in God's origination of the entire universe." Ibid., 139.

22. Ibid., 160-161, 165.

23. D. Ford, *Genesis Versus Darwinism: The Case*, 102.

24. See ibid., 97. "We believe in the infallibility of Scripture, but not the infallibility of interpreters." Ibid., 179. D. Ford, however, does not offer a clear explanation of his understanding of infallibility.

25. In the context of his discussion about E. G. White and the investigative judgment, D. Ford declares, "As for me, I must make Scripture the sole basis of doctrine." Desmond Ford, "Daniel 8:14, the Day of Atonement, and the Investigative Judgment," paper presented at the Sanctuary Review Committee, Glacier View, CO, August 10-15, 1980, 641. "Believing in the priesthood of all believers as well as Sola Scriptura I will remember that . . . no ecclesiastical creedal statement shall move me one whit if obviously contrary to the plain testimony of the Word of God." Ibid. Underlined in original. In a similar context, D. Ford affirms, "We have always claimed to base our doctrine on Scripture alone." Ibid., 627. See ibid., 605. See also Desmond Ford and Gillian Ford, *The Adventist Crisis of Spiritual Identity* (Newcastle, CA: Desmond Ford, 1982), 246.

26. D. Ford, *Genesis Versus Darwinism: The Case*, 89.

Further insight regarding D. Ford's ontological and epistemological presuppositions—based on which he interprets the principle of articulation in Adventist theology—requires additional exploration of his view about God and His actions regarding the world and the human being. This exploration includes D. Ford's understanding of the Adventist historical doctrine of the heavenly sanctuary—God's dwelling place.

The Interpretation of God

According to D. Ford, God is timeless and immaterial.[27] God is beyond and *before* time and space.[28] He is not *tied up* by time.[29] D. Ford also seems to believe that He does not change His mind as a result of His interaction with His creatures.[30] God is passionless.[31] D. Ford also interprets God's actions from a timeless perspective. God's actions regarding the temporal world, for example, are instantaneous, with an impact on the sequence of past-present-future of the temporal world. D. Ford explains that "time for God is not the same as time for us. The Bible distinguishes between *kairos* time and *chronos* time. The former usually alludes to some high point in God's plan, whereas the second only has to do with the duration of days and months and years as we know it."[32] D. Ford, then, affirms that "we must not bind God up with

---

27. Ibid., 22. D. Ford here quotes Strobel that in turn quotes Ps 90:2 as supporting God's timelessness and John 4:24 as supporting God's immateriality. Strobel, *The Case for a Creator*, 284-285. For a similar interpretation of 2 Pet 3:8 (that quotes Ps 90) in Luther and Schleiermacher, see footnotes 191 and 340 in Chapter 3.

28. Genesis 1 presumes that God is "beyond all limits of time and place; as he [God] is before all time and place." D. Ford, *Genesis Versus Darwinism: The Case*, 28. In this reference, D. Ford is affirmatively quoting J. G. Murphy but the original reference is not provided. See however J. G. Murphy, *A Critical and Exegetical Commentary*, 28.

29. D. Ford quotes in his support the evangelical theologian and philosopher William A. Dembski who explicitly says that "throughout Scripture God is portrayed as unbound by time." William A. Dembski, *The End of Christianity: Finding a Good God in an Evil World* (Nashville, TN: B & H, 2009), 51. See D. Ford, *Genesis Versus Darwinism: The Case*, 130. Dembski also describes God as "transtemporal." Dembski, *The End of Christianity*, 50.

30. "We cannot change God's mind, because he knows reality." Desmond Ford, *Right With God Right Now: How God Saves People as Shown in the Bible's Book of Romans* (Newcastle, CA: Desmond Ford, 1999), 134.

31. D. Ford says that God's wrath "is not an emotion with God. It is an attitude that is opposed to anything that is destructive of what God has made." Ibid., 44.

32. D. Ford, *Genesis Versus Darwinism: The Case*, 130. Emphasis in original.

the chains that the calendar and clock put upon us."[33] He also suggests that God does not change His plans. Prayers, for example, do not change God's line of action. They are relevant only because God already foreknows them, not because there is change in God.[34]

Just as D. Ford interprets God as timeless, he also interprets God as spaceless and without any physical appearance. In contrast to the position of the Adventist pioneers that rejected a view of God without body or parts,[35] D. Ford affirms it. In relation to Gen 1-3, D. Ford declares that God did not use vocal cords and perform any physical activity as described in those chapters. He does not have physical parts either. Spatial depictions of God are expressions of an anthropomorphic language.[36]

In the context of the understanding of the nature of God's actions, D. Ford proposes interpreting biblical language to talk about God as analogical language. Commenting on Exod 20:8-11, D. Ford quotes Gordon J. Wenham favorably in order to suggest that the six days of Creation and God's rest on Sabbath are analogical language. Actually, "all language about God is analogical."[37] As a result, it is not possible to interpret God's actions in Scripture that look similar to human actions in a literal way.[38]

D. Ford's understanding of the analogical language about God constrains him to interpret biblical expressions about God that speak of His repentance (Gen 6:7; 1 Sam 15:11; Jonah 4:2), breathing (Gen 2:7), resting (Gen 2:2-3; Exod 20:11), or making tunics (Gen 3:21) as anthro-

---

33. Ibid.

34. Ibid. Regarding this argument, D. Ford depends on Clive S. Lewis, although D. Ford does not provide specific bibliographical reference. See, however, Clive S. Lewis, *Mere Christianity*, rev. ed. (New York, NY: Macmillan, 1952), 130-133.

35. See pp. 131-132 in Chapter 3.

36. "We have never known an omnipotent God, who is an omnipresent Spirit, to use vocal cords and condescend to the activities of a surgeon, a gardener, a walker, and a seamstress. But all these are to be found in Genesis chapters 1-3. God is a spirit according to John 4:24. . . . Therefore he has no vocal cords or physical parts such as we know—hands, feet, buttocks, etc." D. Ford, *Genesis Versus Darwinism: The Case*, 146, 294, 387.

37. Gordon J. Wenham, *Genesis 1-15*, Word Biblical Commentary (WBC) 1 (Waco, TX: Word, 1987), 40. See D. Ford, *Genesis Versus Darwinism: The Case*, 386.

38. "By speaking of six days of work followed by one day's rest, Genesis 1 draws attention to the correspondence between God's work and man's and God's rest as a model for the Sabbath, but that does not necessarily imply that the six days of creation are the same as human days." Wenham, *Genesis 1-15*, 40. See D. Ford, *Genesis Versus Darwinism: The Case*, 386.

pomorphisms.³⁹ D. Ford, however, does not always apply the analogical interpretation to God's actions described in Scripture. He interprets *literally* those passages that he thinks do not contradict his timeless assumption regarding the nature of God. The Bible is speaking about God literally (not analogically) in John 5:17 when it "denies that God ever rests."⁴⁰ In a similar way, "the New Testament is clear when it tells us that God is spirit and one who is changeless (John 4:24; Heb. 13:8)."⁴¹

D. Ford also faces the issue of God's transcendence and immanence. Particularly, D. Ford wants to explain God's immanent action in the world. He quotes Jürgen Moltmann (a panentheist theologian) and Langdon Gilkey (a liberal theologian) for that purpose.⁴² Although D. Ford does not accept Moltmann's perspective of God,⁴³ he wants to emphasize the permanent dependence of the world on God's constant creative activity and sustenance. God's power is immanently active in everything. "God is in all things, either creatively to sustain, or permissively to allow decay and death. Every breath is his gift, as is every moment of existence."⁴⁴

At the same time, D. Ford explains the *mechanism* through which God acts immanently in the world in terms of an assumed changelessness of God. He understands God's omnipresence, omniscience, and omnipotence, in terms of His absolute immutability. In order to produce something, God only needs to will it. What God thinks or wills in His timeless realm is what happens in the temporal one. The affirmation that God creates in six literal days is just baby talk, not a valid description of what God has really made in the timeless realm.⁴⁵

---

39. See D. Ford, *Genesis Versus Darwinism: The Case*, 386.
40. Ibid., 387.
41. Ibid., 386. In consequence, God's resting in Exod 20:11 is not literal according to D. Ford.
42. See ibid., 292. See Jürgen Moltmann, *God in Creation: An Ecological Doctrine of Creation; The Gifford Lectures 1984-1985*, trans. Margaret Kohl (London, UK: SCM, 1985), 98; Langdon Gilkey, *Maker of Heaven and Earth: A Study of the Christian Doctrine of Creation* (New York, NY: Anchor, 1965), 106-109.
43. See D. Ford, *Genesis Versus Darwinism: The Case*, 292.
44. Ibid., 293.
45. "Genesis uses anthropomorphic terms when speaking of divine actions. . . . But the Bible's revelation of God as omnipresent, omniscient, and omnipotent teaches us that God needs only to will a thing and it is. He does not need to speak or to fashion. The Genesis picture of the Almighty taking six days to create the universe is similar to the picture of a very tall man bending down to lisp to a tiny child." Ibid., 294. The notion that what God thinks or wills in His timeless realm is what happens

The basic timeless presupposition underlying the interpretation of the nature of God leads D. Ford, to some extent, to interpret the dwelling place of God in a spiritualized way. Somehow, D. Ford applies his analogical interpretation to heavenly realities. A timeless and spaceless God cannot dwell in a temporal material sanctuary. In notorious contrast to the interpretation of the Adventist pioneers, D. Ford holds that the heavenly sanctuary is a reference to heaven itself, not a building. The sanctuary is *real* but not *literal*. Scripture and E. G. White use the language of the types to talk about heavenly realities but that literal language does not require a literal correspondence in heavenly antitypes. In a perfect realm, there is no need for literal buildings protecting heavenly beings. Such depictions are appropriate only to describe the fallen conditions of the human realm.[46]

D. Ford holds that he is not alone in his interpretation of heavenly realities. He finds evidence of a similar interpretation, for example, in some Adventist documents or authors that suggest that the heavenly sanctuary is not a tangible or concrete reality.[47] Actually, other

---

in the temporal world is not unique of D. Ford. Erickson, a contemporary evangelical classical theologian, articulates this idea better. "If God is metaphysically outside of space-time, how does he influence what happens within it? It would appear that the direct working of God is simply by his thinking or willing something to be. In other words, his actions are in some sense acts of creation. If God in his mind thinks something to be the case, it is. This does not require him to exert physical influence on the physical universe. In this sense, his activity influencing the physical world is parallel to his nonperceptual knowledge of the creation." Millard J. Erickson, *God the Father Almighty: A Contemporary Exploration of the Divine Attributes* (Grand Rapids, MI: Baker, 1998), 276.

46. "The heavenly sanctuary, being 'heaven itself' and 'not made with hands' is not a building. 'Real' and 'literal' should never be equated. A building suggests limitations, but to reject a building does not mean to reject the reality of the heavenly sanctuary. Buildings are what they are because of the imperfect conditions which characterize sin-cursed existence. We have walls and doors and a roof to keep out inclement weather, fierce animals, and untrustworthy people. Heaven is not threatened by any of these. . . . The fact that EGW [E. G. White] speaks of the heavenly sanctuary as the abode of the great God and all His angels makes this matter plain. As with other prophets, EGW frequently used the language of the type, leaving it to the reader to make the transition." D. Ford, "Daniel 8:14," 31. "Our pioneers applied the details of the sanctuary type . . . in a way their spiritual descendants could never do." Ibid., 590, 626.

47. See the references provided in ibid., 116-119. D. Ford points out the fact that several Adventist documents do not mention the two *apartments* of the heavenly sanctuary (the Holy and the Most Holy Places) as it was usual during the time of the Adventist pioneers, and they only talk about the first and second *phases* of Christ's

contemporary Adventist authors also distrust the belief in a literal heavenly sanctuary where God dwells. Roy Adams, for example, feels uncomfortable with the pioneers' *conceptualization* of the heavenly sanctuary in literal, physical terms. He explains the pioneers' literal view by saying that the "Adventist pioneers were dealing with an audience accustomed to thinking in concrete terms and not much given to abstract, philosophical reasoning or speculation."[48] In contrast, R. Adams feels that contemporary "Adventists today may wish to de-emphasize the notion of a physical movement from one compartment

---

ministry in heaven. Regarding the use of apartment terminology in Adventist pioneers, see [Uriah Smith], *A Declaration of the Fundamental Principles Taught and Practiced by the Seventh-day Adventists* (Battle Creek, MI: Steam Press of the SDA Pub. Assn, 1872), 8. Examples of the phase language quoted by D. Ford are the following: (1) The *Fundamental Belief of the Seventh-day Adventists* published in 1931 in GC of SDAs, *Yearbook of the Seventh-day Adventist Denomination: The Official Directories* (Washington, DC: Review & Herald, 1931), 378. (2) The "Additional Note on Chapter 10," in the comment on Hebrews, in Francis D. Nichol, ed., *Seventh-day Adventist Bible Commentary*, rev. ed. (Washington, DC: Review & Herald, 1957), 7:468. See "An Open Door" [Rev 3:8], *Seventh-day Adventist Bible Commentary*, 7:758. (3) The following statement by Arthur W. Spalding, "We speak of all this [the antitypical Day of Atonement] in the language of men. . . . The holy place and the most holy—[are] not rooms as we conceive them but the ineffable abode of the great God and His ministering spirits." Arthur W. Spalding, *Captains of the Host: First Volume of a History of Seventh-day Adventists Covering the Years 1945-1900* (Washington, DC: Review & Herald, 1949), 103. (4) Leaders, Bible Teachers, and Editors, Questions on Doctrine, 389. However, it is fair to recognize that Questions on Doctrine still supports the existence of a literal sanctuary in heaven, something that D. Ford does not mention. See ibid., 365-368. Other documents that D. Ford does not mention but that also follow the same phases terminology are: (1) The 1980 statement of "Fundamental Beliefs of Seventh-day Adventist," according to which "in 1844, at the end of the prophetic period of 2300 days, He [Christ] entered the *second and last phase* of His atoning ministry." GC of SDAs, *Seventh-day Adventist Church Manual* (Silver Spring, MD: GC of SDAs, 1981), 43. Emphasis mine. (2) The Consensus Document "Christ in the Heavenly Sanctuary," elaborated by the Sanctuary Review Committee at Glacier View. See Sanctuary Review Committee, "Christ in the Heavenly Sanctuary," Consensus Document, Glacier View Ranch, CO, August 10-15, 1980, *Ministry*, October 1980, 16-19. The omission of any language that suggests a literal interpretation of heavenly realities seems to be significant. Richard Hammill has highlighted that "for 50 [in 1980] years the church has not tried to make a statement . . . about *geographical divisions in the heavenly sanctuary*." "Fourteenth Business Meeting: Fifty-Third General Conference Session; April 25, 1980, 9:30 A.M.," *Adventist Review*, May 21, 1980, 17. Emphasis mine.

48. Roy Adams, *The Sanctuary Doctrine: Three Approaches in the Seventh-Day Adventist Church*, AUSDDS 1 (Berrien Springs, MI: Andrews University Press, 1981), 263.

of the heavenly sanctuary to the other."⁴⁹ Instead of a physical movement, he prefers to conceptualize this action in terms of a change of phase that avoids the *crude* literal interpretation of the heavenly sanctuary by the Adventist pioneers.⁵⁰

Although R. Adams's interpretation of the movement in the heavenly sanctuary seems to be only a modification of terminology, he substantiates his position by appealing to Aulén, the Lutheran theologian. Based on him, R. Adams suggests that the crude terminology used to express the doctrine of the sanctuary actually is just external imaginary to hide a deeper theological truth.⁵¹ In other words, R. Adams implicitly agrees with the distinction between real and literal that is present in D. Ford. As heavenly realities are not really knowable as they are in themselves through biblical descriptions, R. Adams proposes a *functional* or *theological* interpretation of the heavenly sanctuary.⁵² R.

---

49. Ibid.

50. Ibid. Regarding *crude* literalism, see the following footnote.

51. Ibid., 263-264. R. Adams quotes Aulén's statement which affirms that *"it must be admitted that it is not surprising that many features in the patristic teaching should awaken disgust, such as its mythological dress, its naïve simplicity, its grotesque realism. . . .* It should be evident that the historical study of dogma is wasting its time in pure superficiality if it does not endeavour to penetrate to that which lies below the outward dress, and look for the religious values which lie concealed underneath." Gustaf Aulén, *Christus Victor: An Historical Study of the Three Main Types of the Idea of the Atonement*, trans. Arthur G. Hebert (New York, NY: Macmillan, 1969), 47. Emphasis mine. See R. Adams, *The Sanctuary Doctrine*, 263, where R. Adams omits the italicized part. R. Adams also quotes Aulén (paraphrasing Luther) when he declares that "always the doctrine of Divine things is set forth in crude outward images." Aulén, *Christus Victor*, 109. See R. Adams, *The Sanctuary Doctrine*, 264. However, Aulén makes it clear that Luther "distinguishes the [theological] idea itself and the imagery in which it is clothed." Aulén, *Christus Victor*, 109. Aulén means that for Luther, the imagery used to describe theological truths is not real.

52. Roy Adams, *The Sanctuary: Understanding the Heart of Adventist Theology* (Hagerstown, MD: Review & Herald, 1993), 48. "It would seem that the safer approach [to the interpretation of the heavenly sanctuary] is to concentrate on the *theological signification*, rather than on the *structural specification*." Ibid., 55. Emphasis in original. In theory, R. Adams is rejecting an *extreme literalism* that interprets the relationship between the earthy and the heavenly sanctuary in "a one-on-one correspondence." Ibid., 43. For practical purposes, however, R. Adams rejects almost any literal interpretation of the heavenly sanctuary and physical correspondence between both sanctuaries. His reaction against the literal interpretation entails an implicit change in the ontological and epistemological presuppositions involved in his interpretation of heavenly realities.

Adams suggests that the correspondence between the earthly and the heavenly sanctuary "ought to be seen primarily in terms of 'functional correspondence,' providing us with 'conceptual tools and vocabulary.' In other words, the earthly form puts words ('vocabulary') in our mouths, allowing us to speak about the unspeakable, to comprehend the incomprehensible, however dimly."[53] The correspondence between the earthly and the heavenly, therefore, is *spiritual* or *theological*, but not physical.[54] There is no such thing "as a building that God erected on some vacant lot in heaven (to put it crassly)."[55]

In this context, R. Adams seems to be aware of the potential accusation of spiritualism against his interpretation of heavenly realities. In theory, then, he rejects "the belief system that tends to dematerialize heavenly things after the manner of the ancient Greek philosophers, especially Plato,"[56] and he affirms that "to say something is figurative or nonliteral is not to deny that there is palpable reality behind it."[57] In practice, however, R. Adams reduces the palpable reality of the heavenly sanctuary to God's dwelling place and government seat. The sanctuary becomes essentially Christ (the High Priest) and the angels in the presence of God's throne, whatever is the form of that throne.[58]

---

53. Ibid., 64. R. Adams is borrowing here the concept of functional correspondence from Dulles. See Dulles, *Models of the Church*, 23. R. Adams is aware that Revelation and Hebrews mention furniture and parts of the heavenly sanctuary. For him, however, the biblical language to describe the heavenly sanctuary is "an attempt to capture the sublime in human language. It is a call to contemplation, not rationalization." R. Adams, *The Sanctuary: Understanding*, 70. Phrases such as *first-apartment ministry* or *second-apartment ministry* do not relate to a change of position in the heavenly sanctuary but only to a change of function. Ibid., 113.

54. See the examples R. Adams provides in R. Adams, *The Sanctuary: Understanding*, 65-67.

55. Ibid., 70.

56. Ibid., 71. R. Adams thinks that what he is "proposing *is far removed from that* [spiritualism] *as possible*." Ibid. Emphasis in original.

57. Ibid., 67.

58. Ibid., 71. The tendency to see the heavenly realities where God dwells in non-literal terms, in contrast to the pioneers' perspective about them, is a commonplace interpretation in Adventist evangelical theology. Norman H. Young, for example, expresses in controversy with Richard M. Davidson that "the theological concerns of Hebrews should not be debased into crassly spatial terms no matter to what part of the sanctuary one relates the author's language." Norman H. Young, "'Where Jesus Has Gone as a Forerunner on Our Behalf' (Hebrews 6:20)," *AUSS* 39, no. 2 (2001): 173. Emphasis mine. Young also reveals his own hermeneutical perspective in contrast to Davidson's interpretation of the types in Hebrews in other sharp state-

The Interpretation of the World

D. Ford tries to explain the origin of the world in a way that allows him to conciliate the biblical story of Creation with the claim of science, geology, and paleontology, according to which the universe, the earth, and particularly life in general—as the geological column apparently would reflect—have existed through billions of years. D. Ford does not believe in a literal six-day creation process performed just a few thousand years ago as the biblical text describes.[59] According to D. Ford, it is not right to use the Bible to establish how old the universe or the earth is. In contrast, D. Ford relies on scientific methods that claim that the earth and the universe are 4.5 billion and 13.6 billion years old, respectively.[60]

The world is a temporal reality and Gen 1 holds "a linear view of time rather than a cyclical one."[61] D. Ford seems to endorse the idea that time is a creation of God. He quotes Gilkey (who in turn is following Augustine in this point) when he affirms, "God, who is eternal [timeless], has created time with a beginning and an end. . . . Time is, moreover, 'going somewhere': from its beginning in creation it moves toward its end or goal, and its moments are meaningful because they lead to this eternal [timeless] goal."[62] It is not very clear, however, to

---

ments. For example, he suggests that Davidson "treats Hebrews as though it were a literalistic commentary on the O[ld] T[estament] types." Norman H. Young, "The Day of Dedication or the Day of Atonement? The Old Testament Background to Hebrews 6:19-20 Revisited," *AUSS* 40, no. 1 (2002): 68. Emphasis mine. Young also affirms that Davidson "perceives the mobility of the enthroned Jesus within the heavenly sanctuary in more materialistic terms than I do." Ibid., 62, n. 5. Emphasis mine. Compare with Richard M. Davidson, "Inauguration or Day of Atonement? A Response to Norman Young's 'Old Testament Background to Hebrews 6:19-20 Revisited,'" *AUSS* 40, no. 1 (2002): 69-88. Young also adds, in the context of his interpretation of Heb 6:19-20, that "we must emphasize that Hebrews is using Day of Atonement language to achieve a theological idea and not to give a spatial description of the heavenly sanctuary." Young, "The Day of Dedication," 68, n. 25. Emphasis mine. Young even suggests that the author of Hebrews can be reflecting some Alexandrian insight. See Norman H. Young, "The Gospel According to Hebrews 9," *New Testament Studies* 27, no. 2 (1981): 201. For additional examples of the tendency to de-emphasize a literal interpretation of the sanctuary, see Marvin Moore, *The Case for the Investigative Judgment: Its Biblical Foundation* (Nampa, ID: Pacific Press, 2010), 282; Florin G. Lăiu, "The Sanctuary Doctrine: A Critical-Apologetic Approach," paper presented at the Biblical Research Committee, Cernica-Bucharest, Romania, November 16, 2011.

59. See, for example, D. Ford, *Genesis Versus Darwinism: The Case*, 112, 139, 294.
60. Ibid., 114, 120, 122, 139.
61. Ibid., 150, 12, 13.
62. Gilkey, *Maker of Heaven and Earth*, 302. See D. Ford, *Genesis Versus Dar-*

what extent D. Ford supports the notion that time will arrive at an end given that he seems to believe in a literal or temporal millennium and in a spatio-temporal new earth.[63]

D. Ford is aware that the acceptance of the notion that life has existed through millions of years on the earth—as the standard interpretation of the geological column affirms—involves a potential theological problem: the existence of death and suffering during all that time. According to Rom 5:12, death was a result of the Fall, not a necessary factor in the process of Creation. D. Ford argues, however, that Rom 5:12 refers only to human beings, not to the life on the earth in general. Genesis 1 and 2 actually show that fruits and vegetables were food for humans and animals. Consequently, "death" existed even before the Fall.[64] Death is even necessary to avoid excessive multiplication of life forms.[65]

D. Ford's viewpoint apparently implies that God is responsible for natural death and suffering in the world before the Fall. D. Ford combines ideas coming from evangelical authors such as Lewis, Dembski, and the progressive Adventist theologian Jack Provonsha in order to suggest that Satan could cause the problem of evil before the Fall.[66] Christ's sacrifice benefits those who have lived before the cross as well as those who have lived after. The cross has a retroactive effect that provided salvation for the saints who died before that event. "Similarly, the Fall *casts its shadow backwards*, and this when joined with the activity of the great adversary . . . should explain for us the problem about suffering and death before the arrival of *Homo sapiens*."[67]

Although D. Ford believes that life has existed during billions of years on earth, he rejects Darwinism and chance as the mechanism to

---

winism: The Case, 465. D. Ford does not provide comments on this quotation beyond his obvious general support. However, the idea that time is God's creation is common among evangelical defenders of progressive creationism. See, for example, Hugh Ross, *The Creator and the Cosmos: How the Greatest Scientific Discoveries of the Century Reveal God*, 2nd ed. (Colorado Springs, CO: NavPress, 1995), 77.

63. Desmond Ford, *Crisis! A Commentary on the Book of Revelation* (Newcastle, CA: Desmond Ford, 1982), 2:712-721, 736-737; Desmond Ford, *The Time Is at Hand! An Introduction to the Book of Revelation* (Bloomington, IN: iUniverse, 2009), 36-37, 41-42.

64. See D. Ford, *Genesis Versus Darwinism: The Case*, 124, 307-308.

65. D. Ford suggests that such multiplication would produce, as a consequence, a total collapse of the natural environment. See ibid., 133, 136.

66. See the discussion in ibid., 129-131.

67. Ibid., 130. Emphasis in original.

explain the development of life. Chance is equivalent to atheism. It implies total physical causation and (natural) determinism. Darwinism is a typical case of philosophical naturalism.[68]

Moreover, Darwinism—including its neo-Darwinian version—is unable to explain macroevolution or the appearance of life by chance.[69] A fundamental problem with the standard evolutionary theory, D. Ford thinks, is the fact that there are no transitional species in the geological column. The geological column does not evidence any gradual development of life. They appear abruptly and remain without significant change, including more complex forms of life. Even neo-Darwinism, which admits the sudden appearance of new species in the geological column, does not offer a good explanation for that phenomenon with its theory of genetic mutations.[70]

D. Ford proposes that the solution to the dilemma of the lack of transitional species is the theory of progressive creationism. Regarding this theory, D. Ford does not claim originality. In essence, he is following and adapting ideas from evangelical scholars such as Bernard Ramm, Hugh Ross, Alan Hayward, and Robert Newman.[71] According to D. Ford, progressive creation means that God is the Creator of the new kinds of species that suddenly appear in the different stages of the geological column.[72] Although D. Ford is not so explicit, it seems to be that between one creative divine intervention and another, there is only a limited possibility of variation within each kind. Only God is able to introduce new kinds with major changes and a higher level of complexity regarding the previous kinds. D. Ford is really persuaded that progressive creationism resolves the tension between science and Scripture.[73]

---

68. See ibid., 184, n. 1, 185, 192, 194.

69. D. Ford frequently appeals to this argument against Darwinism or neo-Darwinism. See ibid., 203, 234, 252.

70. Ibid., 208, 212, 220, 225, 234.

71. Ibid., 283. Actually, D. Ford mentions *Richard* Newman but apparently, it is a mistake as a comparison with his bibliographical references suggests. See also ibid., 502.

72. Ibid., 297.

73. "Progressive Creationism solves the problems of geology, archaeology, and accepted science. It teaches that God is the author of all life and that he has willed into existence successive kinds and ultimately our first parents." Ibid., 302. "Belief in progressive creation enables us to acknowledge the assured facts about both inspired records of Scripture and the facts of science. We know that this world is four and a half billion years old. We know that God first created single-celled creatures and then progressively brought on the scene more complex forms of life and finally man. We know that Genesis

Although D. Ford has defended progressive creationism in recent publications,[74] it is not clear that he has always adhered to this theory. In his book *Answers on the Way*, he affirms, following Francis D. Nichol, that "Seventh-day Adventists do not agree that the deposition of the different [geological] strata took many millions of years."[75] Regarding the existence of life on the earth, he also says that, in spite of the fact that the age of the earth is not precisely known, "the theory of eons during which life accidentally evolved is far removed from the biblical teaching of a special creation in historical time."[76] This is possibly the belief of many evangelical Adventists yet.

The Interpretation of the Human Being

According to D. Ford, Adam and Eve were the climax of God's progressive creation of the successive forms of life. They probably appeared around 100,000 or 200,000 BC. The Fall occurred just after their appearance.

However, there is a temporal gap between chapters 3 and 4. In Gen 1-3, Adam is not a proper name. It is only used as such in chapter 4 onward. Moreover, chapter 4 seems to describe the so-called Neolithic world—around 10,000 BC—because it mentions cities, agriculture, and domestic animals and plants.[77] D. Ford's idea of the gap between Gen 3 and 4 allows him to affirm that "the early chapters of the Bible can support the modern scientific idea that the earth is very, very ancient with mankind being older than we thought."[78]

In harmony with his theory of progressive creationism, D. Ford holds that the appearance of Adam and Eve, then, was the result of a special creative divine intervention. Previous hominids are not ances-

---

is inspired but also that it is God's way of speaking, not ours." Ibid., 307.

74. See D. Ford, *Genesis Versus Darwinism: The Case* and Desmond Ford, *Genesis Versus Darwinism: Abridged for Adventists* (n.p.: Desmond Ford, 2015). This second book is essentially a summary of the first one with the addition of some articles at the end, particularly oriented for Adventists.

75. Desmond Ford, *Answers on the Way: Scriptural Answers to Your Questions* (Mountain View, CA: Pacific Press, 1977), 21. According to Nichol, the creationist position does not necessarily deny that there is a clear order in the geological column. Francis D. Nichol, "Scientific Ideas Are Not Infallible," *Review & Herald*, January 7, 1965, 7. See D. Ford, *Answers on the Way*, 20-21.

76. D. Ford, *Answers on the Way*, 133.

77. See D. Ford, *Genesis Versus Darwinism: The Case*, 139-140, 286.

78. Ibid., 288.

tors of human beings.[79] "*Homo sapiens* had no preceding intermediates. He appeared abruptly as the climax of God's creative work."[80] The Neanderthals or the Cro-Magnons are Adam's descendants, completely humans, who lived during the gap time between Gen 3 and 4.[81]

Moreover, the Adam and Eve of Gen 4 are not the same than those of Gen 3. They have the same name but they are different persons. D. Ford highlights that Adam can mean simply *man*. Although in Gen 1-3 Adam can be a proper name, Adam is mainly a generic term to refer to humanity in general.[82] Between the Adam of Gen 3 and the Adam of Gen 4, there "is a vast period of time, which God deliberately leaves undiscussed because it is of no value to his people until modern times."[83] In this way, D. Ford is making an effort to conciliate the interpretation of Genesis regarding the world, with the scientific interpretation that requires long periods for the appearance of the different species, including human beings.[84]

D. Ford differentiates progressive creationism—his own conviction—from theistic evolution. He is very respectful of those Christians who believe in that position.[85] Many theistic evolutionists, nonetheless, do not believe in the real existence of Adam and Eve, something that denies the testimony of biblical texts such as Luke 3, Rom 5, and 1 Cor 15. D. Ford is aware that denying the real existence of Adam and Eve involves the denial of a real historical Fall.[86] D. Ford concludes, therefore, "If there was no Fall there is no need of redemption and, therefore, no need of Christ and his Cross."[87]

D. Ford also discusses the issue of original sin. He seems to understand that human beings were seminally present in Adam when he

---

79. According to D. Ford, there is no evidence that fossil hominids where humans. Ibid., 234.
80. Ibid., 264. Emphasis in original. See also ibid., 282-283.
81. Ibid., 280.
82. See the discussion in ibid., 280-281, 290.
83. Ibid., 281.
84. "The only way we can preserve the theological teaching of Genesis is to recognize that the inspired writer has not said anything about the long period when humans existed after the original Adam (man) of Genesis 1-3. Moses knew nothing about these and God did not tell him. Between Genesis 3 and 4 lie many thousands of years of human existence." Ibid., 282.
85. "It is a great mistake to speak slightingly of those committed to this faith." Ibid., 305.
86. Ibid., 306.
87. Ibid. See also ibid., 507.

sinned. In some way, then, every human sinned when Adam sinned.[88] He emphasizes the impact of original sin on human nature. He describes the consequences of original sin in terms of separation from God, disorder in the whole human nature, corruption of the imagination, perversion of the faculties, and selfishness that involves thoughts and actions.[89] D. Ford, however, does not believe in an absolute depravity of human nature. There is a human total depravity but in the sense that "we are weak in every part."[90] Actually, human beings still reflect God's image and likeness, but after the Fall they became self-centered and lustful. Even conversion does not eliminate the old evil desires[91] or "residual depravity."[92]

Human beings, then, still preserve their free will.[93] However, since human beings are not naturally inclined to follow God, He has to help them to change their will but preserving their freedom. "God does that for everybody he converts. God changes our will, then our wants. God changes all of that."[94]

D. Ford supports the historical Adventist position regarding the state of the dead and the resurrection. He holds that those who died are sleeping, to use the biblical expression. They are unaware of anything.[95] D. Ford also believes in a literal resurrection of the dead at the beginning of the millennium for those who will be saved, and a literal resurrection at the end of that period for those who will be lost.[96] There is no eternal torment or hell.[97]

---

88. "We were all in Adam and Eve when they sinned. Seminally, we were there. Thus, by the sin of one, condemnation came on all of us." D. Ford, *Right With God Right Now*, 87.

89. See D. Ford, *Genesis Versus Darwinism: The Case*, 52, 202, 360.

90. D. Ford, *Right With God Right Now*, 199.

91. Ibid., 200.

92. Desmond Ford, *Physicians of the Soul: God's Prophets Through the Ages* (Nashville, TN: Southern Pub. Assn., 1980), 86.

93. "God does not make us automatons, he does not make us puppets. God never takes away our freedom at any point." D. Ford, *Right With God Right Now*, 202.

94. Ibid., 201. D. Ford states this point in partial reaction to the Calvinist notion of irresistible grace.

95. Ibid., 135.

96. D. Ford, *Crisis!* 2:717-719; D. Ford, *The Time Is at Hand!* 37-40.

97. D. Ford, *Right With God Right Now*, 228, 229.

The Interpretation of the Articulating Agent

Given the importance of the Gospel in evangelical Adventist theology, it is not surprising that D. Ford emphasizes the centrality of Christ as the One who performs the essential articulating action in the relationship between God and humanity. D. Ford describes Jesus, in virtually poetic terms, as "the mediator between God and men; he is the Daysman from on high. . . . Jesus is ever central, between the Father and the Spirit, between time and eternity, between law and grace, between us and condemnation and earth."[98]

From a systematic theological perspective, D. Ford also considers that all the divisions of theology, theology proper, Christology, pneumatology, anthropology, soteriology, ecclesiology, and eschatology "have to do with Christ and His work."[99] In harmony with the evangelical Adventist emphasis on the centrality of the Gospel, he also suggests that although eschatology is the area of theology unfolding nowadays because of the proximity of the last days, soteriology is even more important.[100] "Soteriology . . . comprehends within it elements of Christology, pneumatology, anthropology, and the other divisions as well."[101] Christ and His soteriological action—as D. Ford interprets them—are the core of D. Ford's theology, providing articulation to his thought.

The Interpretation of the Articulating Action

If soteriology is central to D. Ford's theological system, justification is the most important issue in soteriology. While the study of soteriology also involves sanctification and glorification, "justification is the most important of the three areas of soteriology."[102] Justification is, therefore, the essential action that God performs to articulate the relationship between God Himself and humanity. In D. Ford's words, justification is the Gospel's "chief metaphor"[103] and "the heart of the gospel."[104]

D. Ford sees justification in strictly forensic or imputed terms.[105]

---

98. D. Ford, *Genesis Versus Darwinism: Abridged*, 201.
99. D. Ford, *Answers on the Way*, 71. See ibid., 70-71.
100. Ibid., 71.
101. Ibid.
102. Desmond Ford, *The Coming Worldwide Calvary: Christ Versus Antichrist* (Bloomington, IN: iUniverse, 2009), 75, 74.
103. Ibid., 97.
104. D. Ford, "Daniel 8:14," 580.
105. D. Ford, *The Coming Worldwide Calvary*, 84, 107, 108; D. Ford, "Daniel 8:14,"

"Justification means a declaring righteous, never making righteous. . . . God declares me not subjectively righteous but forensically so. Justification has to do with my standing, not my state."[106] For D. Ford, this declaring righteous means essentially that justification is once and forever. In that sense, justification is not a process but a punctiliar fact. "Justification is both *instantaneous and one hundred per cent*."[107] Justification is not only God's forgiveness applicable to past sins.[108] It covers, in fact, the whole life of the believer. "The justification that I have received covers my past, present, and future."[109] D. Ford compares justification to an umbrella that constantly covers the sins of the believer before God.[110]

As justification is an instantaneous decision once and forever, according to D. Ford, it is incompatible with the notion of a judicial process or investigative judgment at the time of the end. In one sense, justification is already the judgment of the believer. "Justification is God's ultimate verdict for all who abide in Christ."[111] Consequently, D. Ford also sees the judgment as a punctiliar fact. There is no real temporal judicial process with heavenly registers of human actions. "The books are the memory of God, and the *decision instantaneous* according to whether a genuine trust in the merits of Christ."[112]

D. Ford contrasts his understanding of justification and judgment with that of the Adventist pioneers who thought that justification and

---

A182; D. Ford, *Answers on the Way*, 79, 152; D. Ford, *Right With God Right Now*, 37.

106. D. Ford, "Daniel 8:14," A182; D. Ford, *The Coming Worldwide Calvary*, 76.

107. D. Ford, "Daniel 8:14," A182. Emphasis mine. For similar statements, see also D. Ford, *Physicians of the Soul*, 86; D. Ford, *Right With God Right Now*, 21, 127, 156; D. Ford, *Genesis Versus Darwinism: The Case*, 311.

108. "We have often erred by reducing justification to merely an initial blessing of forgiveness of past sins." D. Ford, "Daniel 8:14," 583.

109. D. Ford, *The Coming Worldwide Calvary*, 77. D. Ford also quotes William H. Griffith Thomas favorably who declares, "Forgiveness is an act, and a succession of acts from time to time. Justification is an act, which results in a permanent attitude or position in the sight of God. Forgiveness is repeated throughout our life. *Justification is complete and never repeated. And since it refers to our spiritual position before God, it covers the whole of our life, past, present, and future.*" William H. Griffith Thomas, *The Catholic Faith: A Manual of Instruction for Members of the Church of England*, new ed. (London, UK: Longmans, 1920), 84. Emphasis mine. See D. Ford, *The Coming Worldwide Calvary*, 123. See also D. Ford, *Right With God Right Now*, 20, 21, 58, 127.

110. D. Ford, *Physicians of the Soul*, 110. "Justification . . . arches over you, and covers you, all the time." D. Ford, *Right With God Right Now*, 21.

111. D. Ford, "Daniel 8:14," 583.

112. Ibid., 626. Emphasis mine.

the investigative judgment were two different things. He considers that E. G. White had a "linear rather than punctiliar view of the pre-Advent judgment—a view natural enough when the infant movement was trying to understand the mystery of the delayed Advent after 1844."[113] In other words, according to the Adventist pioneers, the investigative judgment is a temporal process, while according to D. Ford it is just an instant—punctiliar view. Moreover, D. Ford holds that the inspired descriptions of the judgment—whether biblical or from E. G. White—are necessarily metaphorical "because the judgment itself, belonging to *things supernal*, is *ineffable*."[114]

D. Ford also affirms that justification is an anticipation of the judgment that seals the believer's destiny. But this judgment occurs during the life of the believer and concludes at the end or close of the personal probationary time, namely, when the believer dies.[115] As justification is 100 percent, covering past, present, and future sins, there is no tension between justification and the result of the judgment at the end of the probationary time. The former is an anticipation of the latter. In the words of D. Ford, justification is "a continued status up to and through judgment day."[116]

From a more general perspective, the judgment includes the final destiny of believers and unbelievers. D. Ford assimilates the judgment in general to Christ's priestly ministry. There is no investigative judgment of professed believers since 1844 or a judgment of the wicked during the millennium. Human beings are judged according to their attitude to the cross as the result of which they are either covered by

---

113. Ibid.

114. Ibid. Emphasis mine. In a similar statement, D. Ford points out that "because the public judgment at Christ's advent belongs to the *supernal realm* all descriptions of it by inspired messengers are necessarily *parabolic or metaphorical*." Ibid., A185. Emphasis mine. Regarding E. G. White's description of the investigative judgment, D. Ford says, "Ellen G. White in her investigative judgment chapter [of *The Great Controversy*] is speaking *truly but not literally* when she refers to heaven's careful survey of every thought, word, and deed, as well as the prompting motives." Ibid., 626. Emphasis mine. See also ibid., 624-626.

115. Ibid., A183, A185, A186. This is the only real "investigative judgment" according to D. Ford. "The investigative judgment is and always has been Christ's scrutiny of His own, summing up day by day their progress in well doing as evidence of their trust in His merits. This judgment for individuals terminates with the close of their probation by death or at the last test." Ibid., A186.

116. D. Ford, "Daniel 8:14," 583. "Justification is over us all the time, until we die, until Jesus comes." D. Ford, *Right With God Right Now*, 156.

Christ's intercession or condemned at the close of every personal probationary time when they die.[117]

D. Ford also believes in an eschatological judgment in the future in relation to the second coming of Christ—for the believers—and at the end of the millennium before the great white throne—for the wicked. However, this judgment is only a manifestation of what has been already decided at the end of the probationary time of every human life and anticipated by justification in the case of the believers.[118] The judgment announced by Rev 14:7 is a manifestation of a decision already made, not the beginning of a temporal judgment process.[119] The same is valid for the judgment of the wicked at the end of the millennium, where their destiny has been already decided.[120] The judgment is a public manifestation in time—through reward or punishment—of God's previous instantaneous decision.

Even though D. Ford considers that justification occurs when God declares the believer as righteous based on his/her attitude of faith toward Christ's sacrifice, justification is also something that already happened on the cross itself.[121] Christ's death "for me, that is justification."[122] Actually, salvation was already a reality on the cross.[123] While D. Ford thinks that in Adam everybody has sinned, he also affirms that the "Calvary covers all our sins, past, present, and future."[124] In the same way, in Christ everybody died and paid for his/her sins.[125] The world became legally justified at the cross.[126] The believer only needs to appropriate of a justification already done.[127]

---

117. D. Ford, "Daniel 8:14," A183, A185.
118. Ibid., A183, A184.
119. "'The hour of His Judgment has come' (or 'is come' KJV) points to *the manifestation of what is already decided*." Ibid., A184. Emphasis mine.
120. Ibid., A185.
121. "The gospel is about what God did for me. That brings justification. The gospel is about Christ's finished work on the cross." D. Ford, *Right With God Right Now*, 22.
122. Ibid., 98.
123. "We were saved 2,000 years ago by Christ's work at Calvary." Ibid., 84. See also ibid., 81.
124. D. Ford, *The Coming Worldwide Calvary*, 81.
125. "Not only did Christ die for us as our Substitute, but we died with him who was our representative. At Calvary, legally all of us paid for our sins of yesterday, today, and tomorrow." D. Ford, *Right With God Right Now*, xii, 271.
126. Ibid. "Because of the cross, the whole world now stood legally justified." Ibid., 66, 70.
127. "All men and women are legally free, legally justified [at the cross], all that

D. Ford also holds that legally speaking, God's judgment was already performed on the cross.[128] The Gospel, therefore, is essentially justification, and justification (and judgment) is performed in essence in Christ's atonement on the cross. D. Ford sees Christ's sacrifice on the cross as the final atonement. "Calvary was the only place of complete atonement."[129]

D. Ford states that justification and righteousness are equivalent expressions in the New Testament. Righteousness by faith is the same as justification and never involves sanctification.[130] As justification has to do with the believer's standing before God and covers past, present, and future sins, justification "is the one [righteousness] that save."[131] In other words, justification is the gift of salvation itself. When God declares a person justified, the person is already saved.[132]

Sanctification, therefore, is not part of salvation in itself but a consequence or fruit that appears spontaneously and inevitably.[133] Salvation becomes essentially a punctiliar event, not a process. Justification is perfect, instantaneous, and complete. Sanctification, in contrast, is always a process, the work of Christ *in* the believer. By its temporal nature, it is always unfinished, incomplete, and imperfect.[134] Human actions after justification do not modify God's salvation.[135] D. Ford's

---

remains is for each individual to accept the gift." Ibid., 66.

128. D. Ford, "Daniel 8:14," A183. "Legally, the world's judgment day was Calvary. There sin was atoned for, and transgressions and iniquity legally removed from the human race for all who would choose to accept the gift." D. Ford, *Genesis Versus Darwinism: Abridged*, 203.

129. D. Ford, *Right With God Right Now*, 55.

130. Ibid., 37, 40-41, 245-246, 367-368.

131. Ibid., 246. D. Ford emphasizes that justification is a status or position, in contrast to sanctification that is an inner condition or state. Ibid., 21.

132. "We are saved by an objective gospel, something that happened outside us; we just lay hold of it." Ibid., 117. D. Ford admits that there is no salvation without sanctification. But this connection is due to the fact God always sanctifies the one that He justifies. Ibid. See also ibid., 161.

133. "Sanctification is the fruit of justification. . . . Sanctification is a derivative of justification." Ibid., 14, 37, 38, 40. Regarding the spontaneity of sanctification, D. Ford claims to paraphrase Paul in Rom 7 by saying, "The fruit of holiness appears spontaneously. It can't be otherwise." Ibid., 118. "Sanctification is the *inevitable result* of justification." D. Ford, *Answers on the Way*, 137. Emphasis mine. See also D. Ford, *The Coming Worldwide Calvary*, 80.

134. D. Ford, *Right With God Right Now*, 21-22, 37, 38, 247; See D. Ford, *Genesis Versus Darwinism: The Case*, 311.

135. "Every minute of your standing before God does not depend on how **you** are doing, but on how Christ has done." D. Ford, *Right With God Right Now*, 20. Bold

view of justification entails that the believer remains essentially a sinner even after being justified. "In essence, as Luther said, 'The Christian is always a sinner, always a penitent, and always right with God.'"[136]

D. Ford's view of justification virtually implies that the believer cannot become lost. Given his Adventist background, however, D. Ford believes in human free will and then he rejects the Calvinist view of predestination.[137] The predestined are those who accept God's call and are chosen for salvation.[138] D. Ford, therefore, admits that *in theory*, it is possible to reject Christ after accepting His salvation.[139] At the same time, however, D. Ford feels sympathy for the Calvinistic doctrine of perseverance, according to which those who are elect will inevitably persevere in Christian life until obtaining salvation. He suggests that the "perseverance of the saints is a very appealing doctrine. In my opinion, it is very close to the truth, because looking to Jesus, you cannot be lost."[140] Only a deliberate sin can produce a separation between the believer and Christ.[141] In any case, he finally needs to recognize that there is no support in the New Testament for the teaching that "once saved, always saved."[142]

D. Ford ascribes to justification by faith the central role in the articulation of the Adventist theological system. "The 'righteousness of faith' (which, according to Luther, is the article of a standing or falling church) is justification by faith."[143] Moreover, in tune with Luther, D. Ford believes that the Epistle to the Romans is the most important book of Scripture.[144]

---

type in original. "Even when I fail as a Christian, I am justified by **faith**." Ibid. Bold type in original. See also D. Ford, *The Coming Worldwide Calvary*, 81.

136. D. Ford, *The Coming Worldwide Calvary*, 78. See also D. Ford, *Right With God Right Now*, 255.

137. See, for example, D. Ford, *Answers on the Way*, 100-102; D. Ford, *Right With God Right Now*, 201, 215-218, 335-338.

138. D. Ford, *Right With God Right Now*, 223-224.

139. Ibid., 202.

140. Ibid. D. Ford has some similar affirmations. "I think *the usual rule in Christian life is that a person soundly converted rarely pulls away from Christ*.'" Ibid., 309. Emphasis mine. "It is rare for a person to apostatize who has become a true Christian." Ibid. See ibid., 233.

141. "Despite continuous failures, the believer's sins are not reckoned against him or her. See Romans 4:8. While a course of premeditated willful sin can separate the believer from Christ, a million shortcomings cannot." D. Ford, *The Coming Worldwide Calvary*, 81.

142. D. Ford, *Right With God Right Now*, 309.

143. Ibid., 40.

144. "Luther said Romans is 'the chief part of the New Testament and the purest gospel.'" Ibid., 8. See also ibid., 139.

D. Ford is not alone in his understanding of justification by faith as the central articulating action of the Adventist theological system. Other Adventist theologians and authors ascribe to justification a similar role that leads to a reinterpretation of Adventist doctrines such as the sanctuary and the investigative judgment.[145] In this sense, R. Adams comments that some Adventist leaders have strong misgivings regarding the doctrine of an investigative judgment being performed in the heavenly sanctuary because "the concept of an investigative judgment flies in the face of righteousness by faith and Christian assurance."[146]

Arnold V. Wallenkampf represents the typical discomfort of some Adventists regarding the possibility that the investigative judgment could imply a threat to the assurance of salvation. Reacting against the evangelical accusation that the investigative judgment determines the destiny of those judged there, Wallenkampf suggests, "Possibly the term investigative judgment is infelicitous since it may connote that decisions as to a person's destiny are being made during it. But such is not the case."[147] Inadvertently echoing D. Ford's view of the judgment as just a manifestation of God's previous decisions, Wallenkampf proposes, "Probably it might more correctly be called an audit. . . . *No decisions are made in an audit*. The audit is just confirmatory. *The investigative judgment might therefore more appropriately be called the pre-advent heavenly audit*."[148]

---

145. Although this reinterpretation does not go so far as the one of D. Ford, the systematic effect of justification by faith as the articulating action upon Adventist doctrines is observable, as the examples in the following two paragraphs illustrate.

146. R. Adams, *The Sanctuary*, 117. It seems that R. Adams himself is reinterpreting the reality of the heavenly sanctuary and the investigative judgment in the light of his understanding of righteousness by faith. In the case of the investigative judgment, although he does not deny its reality and its evaluative role—that he refers to as *unnerving* but essential—he prefers to emphasize the judgment as vindication of God's people. Ibid., 128. Regarding R. Adams's reinterpretation of the reality of the heavenly sanctuary, see in this chapter pp. 155-157.

147. Arnold V. Wallenkampf, "A Brief Review of Some of the Internal and External Challengers to the Seventh-day Adventist Teachings on the Sanctuary and the Atonement," in *The Sanctuary and the Atonement: Biblical, Historical, and Theological Studies*, ed. Arnold V. Wallenkampf and Richard Lesher (Washington, DC: Review & Herald, 1981), 597.

148. Ibid. Emphasis mine. Wallenkampf does not consider himself as an evangelical Adventist. Here, however, he is reacting against Anthony H. Hoekema's accusation that the investigative judgment determines who is going to be saved and who is not, by denying any real decision-making process in the investigative judgment. Interestingly, the Adventist pioneers considered that kind of process as a main pur-

Marvin Moore is another Adventist contemporary author that suggests that justification by faith is God's articulating action in the light of which it is necessary to evaluate any other doctrine. "The righteousness by faith that provides Christians with the assurance of acceptance by Christ *now* is one of those foundational teachings of Scripture against which every other teaching must be judged."[149] Moore clearly explains the articulating effect that this articulating action should perform in Adventist theological system: "Any doctrine that contradicts the gospel [namely, justification by faith] has to be a false doctrine. We must either revise our understanding of that doctrine so that it comes into harmony with the gospel, or we must reject it as error."[150]

While some contemporary Adventist authors may not be completely aware that they could be adopting an evangelical interpretation of the articulating action,[151] others explicitly hold that Adventist and evangelical interpretations of justification are essentially the same and, in both cases, justification is the articulating center. A report of bilateral conversations between Lutherans and Adventists affirms, "The doctrine of justification by grace through faith alone is *central to both Lutherans and Adventists*. A discussion of this central tenet seems a good place to begin theological reflection."[152] The document considers

---

pose of that judgment. "This work of examination of character, of determining who are prepared for the kingdom of God, is that of the investigative judgment, the closing of work in the sanctuary above." E. G. White, *The Great Controversy*, 428. For E. G. White, judgment involves examination and decision. "Every name is mentioned, every case closely investigated. Names are accepted, names rejected." Ibid., 483. Wallenkampf's reaction toward evangelicals is more of a concession than a clarification.

149. Moore, *Case for the Investigative Judgment*, 27-28. Emphasis in original.

150. Ibid., 28. It is interesting to notice that Moore also expresses his concerns about the reality of the heavenly sanctuary. For him, the sanctuary is probably a structure with basically one room but he prevents additional speculation about the structure of the sanctuary by saying "that in explaining it to us, God is limited to using language and images that are familiar to us. Thus, I think it's a mistake for us to argue overly much about heavenly architecture." Ibid., 282.

151. The mentioned Adventist authors (R. Adams, Moore, etc.) do not necessarily identify themselves as evangelical Adventists. To a greater or lesser extent, however, they exemplify the impact of the evangelical interpretation of the principle of articulation on Adventist theology.

152. GC of SDAs and the Lutheran World Federation, "Adventists and Lutherans in Conversation: 1994-1998; Report of the Bilateral Conversations Between the Lutheran World Federation and the Seventh-day Adventist Church," in *Lutherans & Adventists in Conversation: Report and Papers Presented: 1994-1998* (Silver Spring, MD: GC of SDAs, 2000), 6. Emphasis mine.

that Lutherans and Adventists have a *"shared understanding of justification by faith* [that] gives us today the possibility to say that *both churches teach salvation in an essentially congruent manner."*[153] The same document also recognizes differences between Lutherans and Adventists in matters of salvation but only in emphasis. The Lutherans' understanding of justification by faith is correct and it is the heart of Adventist teaching, too.[154]

The Interpretation of the Whole

D. Ford does not offer an explicit interpretation of the whole. However, there is an implicit interpretation of it in his theology. Given the importance of his interpretation of the Gospel, justification, and the cross, as constituting the essential articulating action of God, his interpretation of the whole must have a relation to those issues.[155]

D. Ford interprets that the cross is a microcosm. The cross event involves the whole humanity, represented by those around this event that participated in it, such as the Jewish authorities, common people, and soldiers. In some way, the whole world is there, including every human being.[156] The Trinity was also there in the person of Christ reconciling God and humanity.[157] The cross, then, becomes the event that produces legal justification and the reunion or reconciliation between God and His creatures.[158] The cross undid the consequences of the Fall and "the **whole world** was acquitted at Calvary."[159] The cross, thus, is so central for D. Ford's interpretation of the whole reality that everything is ultimately reduced to the cross event. The cross provides reconciliation and wholeness to the universe.[160] In Christ, particularly on the cross, God achieves the unity of the whole reality, temporal and timeless.

---

153. Ibid., 8. Emphasis mine.
154. Ibid.
155. As D. Ford expresses, justification is the issue around which "the whole of true religion revolves." D. Ford, *Right With God Right Now*, 19.
156. "The cross event is a microcosm. The whole world is present in its representatives.... There is a whole world there, and we are there." Ibid., 31. See ibid., 30-31.
157. Ibid., 38.
158. Ibid., 66, 333. See also D. Ford, *The Coming Worldwide Calvary*, 75-76.
159. D. Ford, *Right With God Right Now*, 116. Bold type in original. See also ibid., 88.
160. Ibid., 70, 333.

Critical Evaluation

D. Ford's ontological and epistemological assumptions are in line with the Protestant interpretation of those presuppositions.[161] He implicitly assumes that reality is essentially a duality, timelessness-temporality. Timelessness is the realm of God, while temporality is the realm of creation.

Moreover, D. Ford's distinction between spiritual or theological knowledge and scientific or historical knowledge also conceals an ontological dualism that leads to an epistemological dualism. This interpretation of knowledge implies that creation and its knowledge are temporal, but it preserves timelessness as the realm of God and theological knowledge, which provides the perspective from where to interpret temporal reality. In this way, D. Ford reenacts in the context of Adventist theology an adapted version of the traditional hierarchy, which is characteristic of the theology of the Protestant reformers, and he reinterprets Adventist theology in the light of this dualism.

Regarding D. Ford's epistemological assumptions and his interpretation of God, it is clear that he is applying the classical *via negativa*—although D. Ford never uses this expression—in his interpretation of the biblical texts. In general, D. Ford is in line with medieval and Protestant theology in this matter. The knowledge about God and His actions requires a metaphorical or parabolic interpretation of biblical depictions of God that show that He has a physical appearance or acts in the spatio-temporal realm. Those depictions are anthropomorphisms, according to D. Ford.

In this sense, although D. Ford claims to support the *sola Scriptura* principle, in fact, his understanding of God's being and the use of the *via negativa* that is applied to the interpretation of God are not traceable to Scripture itself but to Protestant theology, which in turn adopted those ideas from Catholic medieval theology. Ultimately then, D. Ford's ontological and epistemological presuppositions go back to Greek philosophy itself.

As D. Ford situates God and His actions in the realm of timelessness, he naturally interprets God's plans and knowledge as unchangeable or immutable. D. Ford's justification for the need of prayer, for example, illustrates this point.[162] Prayers are relevant because God fore-

---

161. See pp. 90, 100-101 in Chapter 3
162. Regarding D. Ford's justification for prayer, see p. 152 in this chapter.

knows them, not because He changes His plans based on those prayers. Prayers are not a cause of God's (fore)knowledge because that would imply a change in God's mind. The same applies to the form in which D. Ford understands the relationship between God and the world. God does not interact directly with the world in general. What He timelessly thinks or wills is what happens in the world.[163]

The problem with this view of God's knowledge and His relationship to the world is that it assumes that God cannot know anything external to Himself and the world does not produce change in God. He is impassible. As God is timeless, there is no novelty or change in His knowledge or will. If the external things of the world are not the cause of God's knowledge of those things and the world cannot produce change in God, only the opposite can be true. God's knowledge is the cause of everything, whether things, events, and human actions (such as prayers) in the world. Here, D. Ford is implicitly aligning himself with the Thomistic understanding of God's knowledge and interaction with the world where God is ultimately the cause of everything.[164]

D. Ford seems to be unaware of the implication of the notion that there is no change in God's knowledge. Taken to its logical consequences, this notion entails that God's knowledge and will predetermine everything that He knows, including human destiny. This position, however, is inconsistent with D. Ford's rejection of the Calvinist view of predestination.[165] D. Ford does not make any clear conscious effort

---

163. See p. 153 in this chapter.

164. See the discussion regarding God's causal knowledge in Augustine and Aquinas in pp. 75-76, 84 in Chapter 3. Peckham explains how a timeless view of God conveys a causative understanding of God's knowledge regarding His relation to the world. "As timeless, God can only act upon a temporal world by timeless predestination of particular effects within time. In order for God to timelessly determine all of his own 'actions' that will take effect in time, he must know (timelessly) all the actions of any others. Yet, if God's knowledge (omniscience) is absolutely independent from anything other than himself . . . then how could God know the actions of others unless they are determined by his will or his nature? The supposition that such a timeless, absolutely self-sufficient, immutable, and unqualifiedly impassible God 'acts' upon the world seems to presuppose determinism." John C. Peckham, "Divine Passibility, Analogical Temporality, and Theo-Ontology: Implications of a Canonical Approach," in *Scripture and Philosophy: Essays Honoring the Work and Vision of Fernando Luis Canale*, ed. Tiago Arrais, Kenneth Bergland, and Michael F. Younker (Berrien Springs, MI: Adventist Theological Society, 2016), 46.

165. Regarding D. Ford's rejection of the Calvinist view of predestination, see in this chapter, pp. 163, 169.

to conciliate his view of God's foreknowledge and His relation to the world with his belief in human free will, showing in this way a serious lack of inner coherence in his thinking.

Regarding the analogical language to interpret God in Scripture, D. Ford is ultimately following a similar view to the one of Aquinas. The analogy between human and divine actions builds upon the timeless understanding of God, which is the result of the implicit application of the *via negativa*. According to D. Ford, human beings and actions are temporal while God, His being, and His actions are analogical to the ones of His creatures, but timeless. Consequently, the *analogy* between both includes, actually, a very strong equivocal component: the contrast between temporality and timelessness, where the element of similarity is seriously diminished.[166]

D. Ford's application of the *via negativa* is also observable regarding his interpretation of the dwelling place of God in heaven or the heavenly sanctuary. The distinction made by D. Ford, R. Adams, and others—implicitly or explicitly—between real and literal is another way to say that heavenly realities are real but not spatio-temporal. That is the reason why they prefer to talk about a functional correspondence between earthly and heavenly realities. While the earthly sanctuary was a real, concrete spatial place, evangelical Adventism tends to interpret the heavenly sanctuary in a much less material or physical form. Interesting enough, this view of the sanctuary is not consistent with the belief in a literal temporal millennium in heaven as D. Ford holds, along with Adventism in general.[167]

Evangelical Adventist interpretation of the heavenly sanctuary represents, in the end, an implicit systematic accommodation to the understanding of God as timeless and spaceless—although the supporters of this interpretation may not always be aware of that fact. The notion of a spaceless God is systematically inconsistent with a material dwelling place for Him. In summary, then, the ontological and epistemological presuppositions of the evangelical Adventist model affect the interpretation of the nature of God, His actions, and His dwelling place in heaven.

D. Ford's interpretation of the world, particularly its origin, also presupposes God's timeless being and actions. That God creates through instantaneous or punctiliar events implies that D. Ford follows

---

166. This strong equivocal component is already present in Aquinas's understanding of analogical language. See pp. 79-80 in Chapter 3.
167. See pp. 158-159 in this chapter.

the interventionist understanding of God's actions according to which He acts in the world by interrupting normal natural processes. The theory of progressive creationism suggests that God abruptly intervenes in the natural cause-effect becoming of the world by creating new kinds of species and then *disappears* until the following intervention. With these punctiliar interventions, God does not compromise His timelessness, while He is still able to intervene in time.[168] D. Ford's progressive creationism is in line with the position of many evangelical scholars—that he frequently quotes in his support—and it is a good illustration of the potential systematic theological consequences that derive from his interpretation of the principle of articulation.

The fact that D. Ford proposes a retroactive application of the effects of the Fall also reinforces the notion that, according to him, God intervenes in a timeless way in the world. The consequences of the Fall that God establishes are applicable to the past because, from the perspective of a timeless God, the distinction between past, present, and future does not exist.[169] Moreover, although D. Ford does not deny that the first chapters of Genesis describe a Creation in six literal days and a universal flood, he still interprets those events in a non-literal or parabolic way for the sake of his application of the *via negativa* to God's interventions in the world.

In this way, D. Ford dismisses the literal meaning of the biblical text although he does not ignore it.[170] D. Ford also overlooks biblical

---

168. Regarding the interventionist understanding of the relationship between God and the world in classical theology, see pp. 109-110 in Chapter 3. A punctiliar intervention does not have past or future, as a point does not have continuity as a line or line segment. It is not clear how D. Ford is able to reconcile his interventionist understanding of progressive creationism—that implies and interruption of natural causality—and the application of a methodological naturalism that only studies nature from the perspective of natural causality.

169. Actually, D. Ford seems to use a Dembski's quotation to suggest that this retroactive application of the effects of the Fall is possible because God is essentially timeless and past and future are the same for Him. See D. Ford, *Genesis Versus Darwinism: The Case*, 130-131. D. Ford quotes here Dembski, *The End of Christianity*, 50-51.

170. Regarding a literal interpretation of Gen 1, see Gerhard F. Hasel, "The 'Days' of Creation in Genesis 1: Literal 'Days' or Figurative 'Periods/Epochs' of Time?" in *Creation, Catastrophe, and Calvary*, ed. John T. Baldwin (Hagerstown, MD: Review & Herald, 2000), 40-68. Regarding the biblical evidence for a literal universal flood, see Richard M. Davidson, "Biblical Evidence for the Universality of the Genesis Flood," in *Creation, Catastrophe, and Calvary*, ed. John T. Baldwin (Hagerstown, MD: Review & Herald, 2000), 79-92. See also Randall W. Younker, "How Can We Interpret the First Chapters of Genesis?" in *Understanding Creation:*

evidence that potentially contradict progressive creationism. An example is the explicit biblical information that connects suffering in nature with human suffering in Rom 8:18-23.[171] If suffering in nature is the result of the Fall, death in nature cannot be preexistent to the Fall as D. Ford claims. Ultimately, D. Ford seems unaware that his interpretation of the biblical texts operates upon presuppositions that are external to the text itself and that he does not follow the *sola Scriptura* principle.[172]

D. Ford's interpretation of the human being also reveals the influence of the evangelical ontological and epistemological presuppositions. D. Ford again goes beyond the biblical evidence. In order to harmonize his understanding of the origin of the human being with progressive creationism—which assumes God's timelessness—he is willing to interpret Adam in Gen 1-3 as a synonym for humanity, although this Adam has only one wife called Eve in chapters 1-3. D. Ford

---

Answers to Questions on Faith and Science, ed. L. James Gibson and Humberto M. Rasi (Nampa, ID: Pacific Press, 2011), 69-77.

171. In D. Ford's commentary on Romans (*Right With God Right Now*), for example, he completely avoids commenting on Rom 8:18-23, a text that connects suffering in nature with human suffering, as Marco T. Terreros notices. "That the creation has been 'subjected' [Rom 8:20] is a reference to an event in time which indicates that the creation was not originally born in that bondage." Marco T. Terreros, "Death Before the Sin of Adam: A Fundamental Concept in Theistic Evolution and Its Implications for Evangelical Theology" (PhD diss., Andrews University, Berrien Springs, MI, 1994), 193. Several texts connect suffering and death in nature with human sin and fall and the end of death and suffering in nature with the end of human sin. See Gen 3:17-19; Isa 11:6; 65:24; Rom 5:12; Rev 21:4. Terreros mentions that in Rom 5:12, the *world* (*kosmos*) refers to the entire creation, not only to humanity. Ibid., 168. For extensive references and discussion of pertinent biblical texts, see ibid., 150-201.

172. By affirming the existence of suffering and death in nature before the Fall, evangelical theologians are mainly motivated by the influence of science. As Terreros concludes, after an extensive review of the related literature, "Evangelicals justify the affirmation of death before the Fall mostly through arguments drawn from sources other than Scriptures." Terreros, "Death Before the Sin," 147. Erickson, who believes in the authority of the Bible as supreme in theology but also supports progressive creationism, honestly admits that the exegetical considerations in Gen 1 are not really the ones that control the interpretation of the six-day story of Creation. "We should note that historically the nonbiblical disciplines have in fact contributed to our theological knowledge—sometimes despite the reluctance of biblical exegetes and theologians. It was not primarily exegetical considerations that moved theologians to observe that, of the various possible meanings of the Hebrew word יוֹם (*yom*), 'a period of time' might, in the case of interpreting the creation account, be preferable to the more literal and common 'twenty-four-hour day.'" Erickson, *Christian Theology*, 59. See also ibid., 21-22 on the role of the Bible in theology according to Erickson.

also introduces an artificial distinction between the Adam of Gen 3 and the one of Gen 4 against all obvious evidence.[173]

In a similar way, an ontological dualism seems to be implicitly present in D. Ford's view of original sin. In the context of his discussion about Rom 5:12-19, D. Ford affirms that in Adam, everybody sinned because all were there, seminally present in him.[174] Taken seriously, this idea places D. Ford at the edge of traducianism that involves an anthropological dualism.[175] D. Ford does not see the potential inconsistency between his view of original sin and the Adventist historical understanding regarding the human being that he in theory subscribes.[176]

Ultimately, however, the influence of the evangelical or Protestant ontological and epistemological presuppositions comes through the adoption of the evangelical interpretation of the articulating action in evangelical Adventist theology. As in the case of Luther, D. Ford under-

---

173. Clifford Goldstein persuasively argues that D. Ford's position about the two Adams does not have real textual support. As Goldstein rightly points out, in order to sustain his position, D. Ford highlights that the Adam of Gen 1-3 is distinguished from the Adam of Gen 4 using the definite article *hā* in the first case. "However, Genesis 3:24-4:1, the two verses where the transition between the two Adams supposedly took place, demolishes his argument. The word *ha-adam*, ('the man') supposedly referring to the Adam of Genesis 1-3 only, also appears in Genesis 4:1, in reference to Ford's other Adam, too. Hence, the linguistic distinction between his two Adams falls apart in the first instance it was supposed to have been revealed." Clifford Goldstein, "Two Adams, Two Eves?" *Adventist Review*, February 3, 2016, para. 5, accessed July 21, 2016, http://www.adventistreview.org/two-adams,-two-eves.

174. See D. Ford, *Right With God Right Now*, 87.

175. As Erickson explains, according to traducianism, "we receive our souls by transmission from our parents, just as we do our physical natures. So we were present in germinal or seminal form in our ancestors; in a very real sense, we were there in Adam. His action was not merely that of one isolated individual, but of the entire human race. Although we were not there individually, we were nonetheless there. The human race sinned as a whole and became guilty." Erickson, *Christian Theology*, 578.

176. Moreover, D. Ford ignores the biblical evidence according to which, *"there is no reference here* [in Rom 5:12] *to the imputation of the sin of Adam to 'all'*. There is clearly an element of solidarity with him, but it is a solidarity *in result* not in the act and that was possible only because Adam represented the human race. What he did had an impact on his descendants. The fact that there is no reference to the imputation of sin may explain why Paul avoids using in this passage the phrase 'in Adam.' Nowhere do we find Paul saying 'in Adam all sinned;' although he says 'in Adam all die' (1 Cor 15:22)." Ángel Manuel Rodríguez, "Justification and the Cross," paper for the Biblical Research Institute, 2002, 2, accessed July 22, 2016, https://www.adventistbiblicalresearch.org/sites/default/files/pdf/Rom%205_12-21_0.pdf. Emphasis in original.

stands justification as instantaneous. It is a punctiliar fact, once and forever, involving past, present, and future. However, if justification covers the whole life of the believer, it seems that he/she is unavoidably predestined to be saved. In other words, this notion of justification makes sense from the perspective of a timeless view of predestination and God's actions, where the election of the believer is an unchangeable fact.[177]

Nonetheless, D. Ford rejects Calvinistic predestination. Consequently, he has to admit that the believer needs to voluntarily accept the gift of justification. The notion that the believer has a probationary time until he dies also implies that the status of the believer can change as a result of his/her own decision, in the use of his/her free will.

This inconsistency between his view of justification and his rejection of Calvinist predestination pushes D. Ford to make ambiguous statements. He says, for example, "Those who are justified by faith alone *have already the verdict of the last judgment*—it is theirs for as long *as they truly believe.*"[178] However, if justification is the verdict of the last judgment, it cannot be conditional to the hesitation of the believer's faith or his/her eventual posterior unbelief.[179] In a similar way, D. Ford also states that "if you are looking to Jesus [believing in Jesus], justification is never repeated in the sense of a **new** justification."[180] Nonetheless, he also recognizes that "because we are weak and in the flesh, because of the plurality of things that tempt us in this world, *there is not one of us who always looks to Jesus all the time.*"[181]

Does the believer need justification again in that case? D. Ford's answer is negative. The impact of the Protestant view of justification leads D. Ford to affirm categorically, "Don't ever think that when you make a mistake you have suddenly slipped out of justification."[182] In practice, D. Ford's understanding of justification has the tendency to make God's forgiveness almost irrelevant. Confession of sins is just a way for the believer to get relief from his/her guilt. But the believ-

---

177. See, for example, the discussion about justification in Luther and Calvin in Chapter 3, pp. 97, 106, 109.
178. D. Ford and G. Ford, *The Adventist Crisis*, 79. Emphasis mine.
179. After all, "justification is a continuous, uninterrupted blessing all your days in all your ways, so that your standing before heaven is always 100 percent." D. Ford, *Right With God Right Now*, 156.
180. Ibid., 21. Bold type in original. Obviously, the conditional *if* at the beginning of the sentence implies that it is possible to stop looking to Jesus.
181. Ibid., 158. Emphasis mine.
182. Ibid.

er does not lose justification.[183] D. Ford virtually reduces salvation to justification, as in the case of the Protestant Reformation. Sanctification is only a quasi-automatic consequence of justification[184] and an external manifestation of a justification already consummated.[185] In summary, then, although D. Ford denies Calvinistic predestination, his understanding of justification by faith still assumes that timeless view of predestination.

---

183. "You are covered by Christ's merits. The idea of confession of sin is to relieve the burden of guilt. That's all. *We do not confess in order to be forgiven.* You have already been forgiven by the cross of Christ. You are just laying hold of it to allay the feeling of guilt." Ibid., 316. Emphasis mine. "God is not waiting for your memory to work so that you can pray about all your sins, receive forgiveness, and so be right with God again. No! Long before you ask for forgiveness, God gives it to you." Ibid., 158. D. Ford makes a distinction between justification and forgiveness. See ibid., 39-40, 142-143.

184. As in the case of justification, D. Ford is also ambiguous regarding the issue of the spontaneity and inevitability of sanctification. On the one hand, he affirms that "because of the Holy Spirit, good things happen *automatically.*" Ibid., 164. Emphasis mine. He also says that "sanctification is an *inevitable* and essential part of Christian experience." Ibid., 72. Emphasis mine. See also ibid., 114. On the other hand, D. Ford admits that sanctification is not passive, it requires effort, and although it "is the fruit of salvation, . . . it doesn't come automatically." Ibid., 303. D. Ford's ambiguity in this aspect is the result of the fact that he understands sanctification only as virtually an automatic fruit of an instantaneous justification, but at the same time, he is confronted with the biblical evidence in relation to the personal efforts that sanctification requires. See ibid., 249-250, 303.

185. "The evidence to the world and to the universe that you have been justified—though not to God because he knows your heart already—is whether you are sanctified." Ibid., 161. D. Ford finds support for his view of legal justification on the cross in Rom 5:18-19, among other texts. Ibid., 66. See D. Ford, *The Coming Worldwide Calvary*, 76. However, Rodríguez, commenting on Rom 5:18, clarifies that there is no support for legal justification in that passage. "Some have tried to avoid the trap of universalism, while still emphasizing the parallel between Adam and Christ, arguing that all were legally justified in Christ independent of any faith-commitment but that one could reject that legal status through a personal decision against Christ. This suggestion actually breaks the parallel between Adam and Christ and destroys the internal logical consistency of the argument. Let me explain. The actual result of the sin of Adam, namely condemnation, was not something that we could reject, avoid or even accept. It was simply ours. Pressing the parallel between Adam and Christ would mean that the 'righteousness of life' that Christ brought 'to all men' was also unavoidable and permanent. By introducing the idea of a legal universal justification that could be rejected the parallel between Adam and Christ, on which the argument rests, is broken. Consequently, Rom 5:18 should not be used to support the theory of legal universal salvation." Rodríguez, "Justification and the Cross," 10.

A last aspect in relation to D. Ford's interpretation of justification is his tendency to reduce God's salvific activity to only one action, the cross. The judgment of believers is reduced to justification, and justification is reduced to a legal justification, taking place on the cross. Although D. Ford says that every individual has to accept that justification, justification is already real on the cross.[186] In the end, D. Ford's tendency to reduce God's articulating action to only one punctiliar event correlates with the fact that from a classical theological perspective, God's timeless actions are essentially one. From this perspective, "God does not decide at a particular point in time to redeem the world. The judgment and the redemption are already decided at the moment of Creation, which of course, from God's point of view, is the very same moment as the moment of the end of time—and as every other moment in between."[187] God's salvific actions in history are, in fact, temporal manifestations of what is only one action from God's timeless perspective.

In conclusion, D. Ford's timeless view of the Gospel operates as a reductive or abstractive suprahistorical, beyond-time *filter* that eliminates or transforms in parabolic language everything in Scripture that does not match his understanding of justification by faith, such as the heavenly sanctuary or the investigative judgment.[188] The same abstract view of the Gospel—justification—allows D. Ford to interpret the biblical story of Creation and the universal flood as parabolic teachings regarding the Gospel itself.[189] In this way, D. Ford opens the door for the scientific interpretation of origins at the expense of a more literal or affirmative interpretation of the biblical narrative. Moreover, with his reinterpretation of the principle of articulation, D. Ford reintroduces in Adventist theology the classical hierarchy timelessness-temporality

---

186. "The New Testament refers in places to the legal justification of the whole world *quite apart from what happens to individuals* when they lay hold of that legal accomplishment." D. Ford, *Right With God Right Now*, 333. Emphasis mine.

187. Keith Ward, *God: A Guide for the Perplexed* (London, UK: Oneworld, 2002), 143.

188. Malcolm Bull and Keith Lockhart explain this fact plainly, regarding the doctrine of the sanctuary, when they say, "Ford's conception of salvation made the doctrine of the sanctuary redundant." Malcolm Bull and Keith Lockhart, *Seeking a Sanctuary: Seventh-day Adventism and the American Dream*, 2nd ed. (Bloomington, IN: Indiana University Press, 2007), 88.

189. In a suggestive way, D. Ford affirms, "We only read Genesis properly when we find Jesus there." D. Ford, *Genesis Versus Darwinism: The Case*, 69. Of course, D. Ford is referring to his particular interpretation of Christ and His actions.

where timelessness is the element that underlies the rest of reality and provides meaning to temporal creation.

Modern Adventist Model

The modern model involves what is usually considered liberal or progressive Adventist theology. *Progressive Adventism* is the favorite self-denomination of the advocates of this theological trend. They claim to hold a non-fundamentalist vision of Adventism—in contrast to the alleged fundamentalist perspective of traditional Adventism—that promotes open dialogue through free press and academic freedom for Adventist theologians and scientists.[190]

Progressive Adventists recognize that they have also been called *liberal* Adventists. Although they do not necessarily reject the term, they admit that it has a negative connotation that they prefer to avoid. In the general context of liberal Christian theology, it involves the rejection of Christ's divinity and resurrection.[191]

Progressive Adventism was *institutionalized* during the 1960s. The first issue of *Spectrum*, a journal supported by the Association of Adventist Forums in California, was published in 1969.[192] Some of its main contributors are Ronald Graybill, Gary Land, Raymond F. Cottrell, Charles Scriven, Jonathan Butler, Ervin Taylor, Richard Rice, Brian Bull, David R. Larson, and Guy. During the last years, the magazine has also published articles or *posts* online, not only in English but also in Spanish. Another periodical publication supporting progressive Adventism is the magazine *Adventist Today*. Its first issue was published in 1993 and its first editor was Cottrell.[193] The magazine is supported by the Adventist Today Foundation, based in California.

Progressive Adventism represents a radical re-approach to Adven-

---

190. Ervin Taylor, "Progressive Adventism: A Nonfundamentalist Vision," *Adventist Today*, September-October 2001, 14. Taylor, for example, considers that the settled beliefs of the Adventist Theological Society are a typical example of Adventist fundamentalism. Ibid. For additional general characterization of progressive Adventism from a more pastoral perspective, see also Steve Daily, "What Is Progressive Adventism?" *Adventist Today*, May-June 2002, 16-17.

191. Ron Corson, "Progressive and Traditional Adventists Examined," *Adventist Today*, November-December, 2002, 18; Daily, "What Is Progressive Adventism?" 16.

192. See the introduction to the first issue. Alvin L. Kwiram, "Introduction," *Spectrum* 1, no. 1 (1969): 4-5.

193. See Raymond F. Cottrell, "Welcome to *Adventist Today*," *Adventist Today*, May-June 1993, 2.

tist theology. It frequently implies a questioning or rejection of historical Adventist doctrines such as the sanctuary and the investigative judgment.[194] It also involves an inclusive view of the remnant—as an entity that includes Christians from different creeds—and a rejection of an eschatological role for the Sabbath.[195] The representatives of this perspective maintain that historical doctrinal positions require revision in the light of the current times, and pluralistic interpretations are all welcome. The Bible itself reflects different views about God that are not reconcilable. Revelation is progressive.[196] Consequently, science has an important role. "Science is not derived from the Bible, but it does illuminate our perspectives, both spiritual and physical. The progressive Adventist has a healthy respect for science and research."[197]

Probably, the most significant spokesperson and promoter of modern Adventist theology is Guy. He has been part of *Spectrum*'s editorial staff from the beginning and an active collaborator as a writer or member of the editorial board. Beyond his theological trends, he has been considered as one of the most important Adventist systematic theologians.[198] Guy, along with other authors in a similar vein, will be the focus of the discussion in this section.

Ontological and Epistemological Presuppositions

The modern Adventist model assumes what seems, in first instance, a temporal ontology of reality as a whole. Guy considers, for example, that a classical view of time is probably impossible in the context of modern theology. The notion that what is "really real" is timeless, unchangeable, and immutable (as assumed in Greek philosophy, medieval Christianity, or early rationalism) is not acceptable anymore in the context of modern thought.[199]

---

194. Madelynn Jones-Haldeman, "Progressive Adventism: Dragging the Church Forward," *Adventist Today*, January-February, 1994, 9; Corson, "Progressive and Traditional Adventists," 18.

195. Corson, "Progressive and Traditional Adventists," 18.

196. Jones-Haldeman, "Progressive Adventism," 9, 10, 11.

197. Ibid., 11.

198. Gary Chartier, "From La Sierra to Cambridge: Growing Up Theologically," *Spectrum* 20, no. 2 (1989): 5.

199. Fritz Guy, "Man and His Time: Three Contemporary Theological Interpretations" (PhD diss., University of Chicago, IL, 1971), 404. See also Guy, *Thinking Theologically*, 176.

Consequently, time is not the negative counterpart of a timeless positive eternity. It is not a threat or enemy, nor is space. Time and space are not responsible for decay, disintegration, and death. Temporality is not a passing from being into non-being, a limitation or deficiency of being.[200] At the same time, in the modern context, it is probably impossible "to view all the events that occur in the temporal process as the unfolding of a predetermined teleological program (as suggested by Aristotle and, in a different way, by Augustine) or of an ineluctable evolutionary progression (as envisioned by Bergson, Alexander, and Teilhard)."[201]

In contrast to the classical view, Guy thinks that a modern view of time must derive from a philosophy of becoming and must recognize that time is an ontological relationship. Time or temporality is a relationship among existing entities. It is a succession of events, duration. It is not an entity in itself. It does not have an absolute status separated from things in general. Ontologically, time is secondary to things or events. It is not like a "big box," receptacle, or container, encompassing the entities or events of reality. The world, including human beings, has a history. Every finite being has a past, present, and future.[202]

Guy also holds that contemporary culture assumes some presuppositions or underlying intuitions in connection with the nature of reality that "may offer support for the reasonableness of our faith and credibility of our theology."[203] He considers these underlying intuitions as elements that are—or should be—relevant for Adventist theology.[204] Among these underlying intuitions or presuppositions that Guy identifies, there are two related to the nature of reality: (1) the modern view of the integrity of nature and (2) the view of reality as having a dynamic character. Regarding the first one, Guy means that reality is ontologically interrelated.[205] This interrelatedness of reality implies

---

200. Guy, "Man and His Time," 404, 439.

201. Ibid., 404.

202. Ibid., 405, 437, 438, 440, 442; Fritz Guy, "God's Time: Infinite Temporality and the Ultimate Reality of Becoming," *Spectrum* 29, no. 1 (2001): 19, 20. There is no "real time apart from the world and existing objects." Guy, "Man and His Time," 438. Guy highlights that the idea that time has some kind of independent existence from things is Newtonian. See ibid., 405, 438, 438, n. 1.

203. Guy, *Thinking Theologically*, 160, 170.

204. Ibid., 159-160.

205. "The nature of reality presupposes the ontological interrelatedness and conceptual coherence of the natural universe." Ibid., 173.

that everything participates in an infinite cause-effect sequence. Although this intuition seems to be in contradiction with the traditional Christian understanding of Creation as the beginning of the world—without an infinite past—Guy thinks that it is also possible to interpret Creation as the world's ontological dependence on God instead of a temporal beginning.[206] Guy points out that this interrelatedness of everything existing has been observed by process philosophy and the current chaos theory.[207]

The second underlying intuition of modern culture—dynamic reality—implies that reality is in constant becoming. Reality is more than entities or existence. It consists of events and change. Guy thinks that this cultural intuition constitutes the possibility of Whitehead's process ontology and Hegelian idealism.[208] Guy also believes that these cultural intuitions—the interrelatedness of reality and its dynamic character—exhibit an important level of continuity with a biblical worldview and may be considered as a consequence or offspring of the Christian religion.[209]

Regarding the epistemological assumptions involved in the modern Adventist model, Guy is aware that knowledge entails interpretation. The knower always carries a personal background that conditions the knowledge of any object. This fact is also the case in theological knowledge, including the interpretation of the biblical text and the interpretation of faith. "Just as it is common knowledge in science that there are no uninterpreted data of nature, so it should be common knowledge in theology that there are no uninterpreted texts of Scripture. To read a text is to interpret it."[210] Moreover, "knowledge has no *a priori* limits; it is as boundless as time and space."[211]

---

206. "One might argue that the fundamental theological significance of creation is the ontological dependence of the world rather than its temporal finitude." Ibid., 174.

207. Ibid.

208. Ibid., 175-176. "Reality is not simply 'being' but also 'becoming'; it consists not only of entities and existence, but also of events and change. Indeed, events are ontologically prior to entities: matter turns out to be, in its most fundamental form, a sort of jiggle in space." Ibid., 175-176.

209. Ibid., 179-180.

210. Fritz Guy, "Interpreting Genesis One in the Twenty-First Century," *Spectrum* 31, no. 2 (2003): 7. See also Guy, *Thinking Theologically*, 46-47, 155-157, 159.

211. Guy, *Thinking Theologically*, 171. Emphasis in original. Guy considers that the notion of *open-ended knowledge* is another underlying intuition of modern culture. A result and confirmation of this intuition is the progress of natural and human sciences. Ibid., 170, 172.

Theological knowledge, therefore, is also open-ended, "in the process of becoming, in transit and transition."[212] The human understanding of theological truth is always partial, unfinished, changing, inadequate, incomplete, and distorted. Truth is always an approximation, although it is important for spiritual experience and theological reflection.[213] Guy explicitly subscribes to a critical realist epistemology. He considers critical realism as the prevalent perspective among theologians and scientists. From this view, theological assertions refer to real things outside of the mind, such as the word *God*. This correspondence does not mean that it is possible to describe God adequately or accurately, but it is still possible to say something meaningful about Him.[214] For Guy, then, while there is a correspondence between theological assertions (God, His actions, doctrines) and the objects that they refer to, that correspondence is not literal.[215]

However, the epistemological presuppositions of the modern Adventist model usually become clearer in the context of the discussion about the relationship between science and theology, as well as in relation to the sources of theology. In spite of the fact that Guy affirms a non-dualistic temporal ontology, he introduces a sharp separation between theological or religious knowledge and scientific knowledge, which ultimately reintroduces an ontological dualism. According to Guy—and other modern Adventists—Scripture has a spiritual and theological purpose and function, facilitating "an awareness and experience of *ultimacy*—ultimate reality, meaning, value, and destiny."[216] The bib-

---

212. Ibid., 65.
213. Ibid., 60, 67, 75, 107, 250. Guy asserts that Adventist epistemology agrees with postmodernity in the rejection of Enlightenment's foundationalism "according to which absolute certainty can be attained on either a rationalist or empiricist basis." Ibid., 195, n. 25.
214. Ibid., 61, n. 34, 184, 185, n. 6.
215. Guy affirms that he employs "an informal 'correspondence theory' of truth compatible with my critical realist epistemology. . . . Provided that the word 'correspondence' is not taken in a literal, representational sense." Ibid., 249, n. 53. Guy agrees that "the Christian gospel claims to be 'truth.' That is, it claims to be grounded in reality, in the way things actually are." Ibid., 249. However, he is reluctant to accept a literal correspondence between theological assertions of the Christian gospel (truth) and the things as "they are" because Guy and modern Adventist theologians frequently hold a symbolic or metaphorical view of doctrines and the language to talk about God. See below the discussion in pp.191, 196-197 in this chapter.
216. Fritz Guy, "The Purpose and Function of Scripture: Preface to a Theology of Creation," in *Understanding Genesis: Contemporary Adventist Perspective*, ed.

lical text communicates "eternal, supernatural truth"[217] through temporal resources as those found in biblical stories. These stories, such as the universal flood, communicate *supra-historical* events.[218]

The purpose of Scripture, then, is not to communicate temporal-historical or scientific truths but the timeless nature of God. Theology addresses questions related to the *who* and the *why* of reality but is not involved in the *how* or the *when*. These last two questions are the concern of science, which studies the physical phenomena and natural processes through observation and experimentation.[219] In contrast, "theology is our interpretation and best understanding of our experience of God, whom we encounter through Scripture, prayer, hymns, preaching, meditation, and so forth."[220] In consonance, the biblical text requires a serious interpretation but not necessarily a literal one.[221]

This understanding of the relationship between science and theology considers that these disciplines are complementary but they have different foci. The first one focuses on the physical-temporal truth. The other one, in the eternal, supernatural, or supra-historical truth of Scripture. However, the relationship between these disciplines is not entirely reciprocal because there is no Christian science. On the other hand, "good theology is never scientifically illiterate, because theology is concerned not only with God but also with the relations between God and everything else, including the physical universe."[222]

As Scripture and theology cannot ignore science, the interpretation of Scripture should follow the scientific standards of high criticism.[223]

Brian Bull, Fritz Guy, and Ervin Taylor (Riverside, CA: Adventist Today, 2009), 86. Emphasis in original.

217. Brian Bull and Fritz Guy, "Then a Miracle Occurs," in *Understanding Genesis: Contemporary Adventist Perspective*, ed. Brian Bull, Fritz Guy, and Ervin Taylor (Riverside, CA: Adventist Today, 2009), 66.

218. Geraty, "Archaeology of the Flood," 192.

219. Fritz Guy, "Change, Scripture, and Science: Good News for Adventist Thinking in the Twenty-First Century," *Spectrum* 39, no. 3 (2009): 54.

220. Ibid.

221. Fritz Guy, "Negotiating the Creation-Evolution Wars," *Spectrum* 20, no. 1 (1989): 45. See also Ervin Taylor, "Death Before Sin?—Yes," *Adventist Today*, Fall 2010, 12.

222. Fritz Guy, "Change, Scripture, and Science," 54. See ibid., 53-54.

223. "The 'historical-critical' method of Bible study, used properly, can be a valid and powerful tool for Seventh-day Adventists." Larry G. Herr, "Genesis One in Historical-Critical Perspective," *Spectrum* 13, no. 2 (1982): 51. See also Jerry Glad-

It is necessary to read the Bible as a culturally conditioned book. Even the assumptions of Jesus Christ regarding the real existence of Adam, Eve, and Noah should be understood in terms of "the human cultural perspectives and assumptions of his time and place."[224]

Another important aspect regarding the epistemological assumptions of modern Adventist thought is the fact that theology involves more than the Bible as the source for theology. Guy considers that "the Reformation motto *Sola scriptura*, 'By scripture alone,' popularly interpreted as 'the Bible and the Bible only,' has always been a polemical exaggeration."[225] In contrast, he prefers *prima Scriptura*, where Scripture is first but not alone. He affirms something similar to the Wesleyan quadrilateral that includes Scripture, secular or scientific knowledge (reason), religious experience, and, with some qualifications, theological tradition.[226]

Regarding the role of Scripture as a source of theology, Guy considers—in harmony with his strong separation between theological and scientific knowledge—that Scripture is intended to answer religious rather than scientific questions. Religious questions are related to the *meaning* of the factual events rather than the cause of those events.[227] Scripture has a complementary role in relation to factual-research disciplines (sciences), instead of a judging, correcting, or controlling role. This role also applies to the relationship between Scripture and other human disciplines, particularly creative-artistic disciplines (art in general) and theoretical-constructive disciplines (such as philosophical projects).[228]

---

son, "Taming Historical Criticism: Adventist Biblical Scholarship in the Land of the Giants," *Spectrum* 18, no. 4 (1988): 31; Robert M. Johnston, "The Case for a Balanced Hermeneutic," *Ministry*, March 1999, 12. See also Richard Rice, *Reason and the Contours of Faith* (Riverside, CA: La Sierra University Press, 1991), 84-85.

224. Taylor, "Death Before Sin?—Yes," 13.

225. Guy, *Thinking Theologically*, 137. Emphasis in original.

226. Ibid., 137, 98-99. Rice prefers the motto *sola Scriptura* but he understands it in a way that actually is better described as *prima Scriptura*. "People sometimes think of this [*sola Scriptura*] as a call to eliminate everything but the Bible from theological consideration. This is not only impossible . . . but it is not faithful to the activity of the great Reformers. . . . For the Reformers themselves, the Bible was by no means the only object of theological reflection." Rice, *Reason and the Contours*, 93. *Sola Scriptura* means that Scripture is a higher authority in theology but not the only one. Ibid.

227. Guy, *Thinking Theologically*, 139-141.

228. Ibid., 142-147. Scripture does not "judge, correct, or control the knowledge that results from these disciplines." Ibid., 144.

Given this role of Scripture, its significance is essentially theological rather than historical or factual. "Scripture does not dispute the facts of the natural and human sciences; it provides an understanding of humanity, nature, and God in which all knowledge has its ultimate significance."[229] Thus, although Scripture is considered a historical revelation, what is really important is the theological meaning of the events that it narrates.[230]

Regarding the role of the other sources, tradition, reason, and experience, Guy considers them as *ingredients* of Adventist theological thinking. The first one is referred to as the *historical-theological* ingredient. There is no need or even possibility of avoiding the theological inheritance of the past. In the particular case of Adventists, they read Scripture and theological history through Adventist eyes.[231] The *secular-cultural ingredients* constitute the second source. These ingredients involve not only sciences, as already mentioned, but also arts and theoretical disciplines such as philosophy. Guy emphasizes the importance of producing theology that is relevant in the modern socio-cultural and scientific era.[232] The last source refers to the *personal-experiential*

---

229. Ibid., 146.

230. Ibid., 147. See also Guy, "Change, Scripture, and Science," 53.

231. Guy, *Thinking Theologically*, 151-152. Guy explains that theological traditions have frequently been notoriously ambiguous as to be a "reliable 'ground' for, or justification of, a particular interpretation of faith." Ibid., 99. However, Guy believes that this ambiguity or distorting effect is also present to some extent in the other sources, but as they are always present in theological thinking, it is preferable to acknowledge and identify them in order to avoid the pernicious effect resulting from ignoring or denying them. Ibid., 138-139. Regarding tradition, "it is just not possible to obliterate this historical conditioning and read scripture absolutely *de novo*." Emphasis in original. Ibid., 152. Rice also considers that avoiding tradition in the interpretation of the Bible is a futile attempt. Rice, *Reason and the Contours*, 92. He actually strongly endorses the role of tradition and experience in Christian theology. See ibid., 88-93. He also suggests that "what a group of Christians believe is probably influenced more directly by the tradition of their community than it is by the contents of the Bible." Ibid., 91.

232. Guy, *Thinking Theologically*, 153-155. "The challenge for Adventists, therefore, is to articulate a theological understanding that is authentically Christian, identifiably Adventist, and culturally meaningful." Ibid., 155. By defending the use of natural theology, Rice also considers that "in its effort to communicate the claims of faith, . . . Christian theology can never avoid the specific form of unbelief confronting it. And to meet this challenge it must find public or rational evidence to support these claims." Rice, *Reason and the Contours*, 193. Regarding Rice's endorsement of natural theology, see particularly ibid., chapters 4-6.

ingredients. They include personal background, religious experience, personality, and intellectual abilities. In a more general way, "the shared experience of the community is a significant ingredient in its collective understanding of faith."[233]

These ingredients, in practice, are more than mere resources to take into consideration at the time of doing theology. Their inevitability, according to modern Adventist theology, transforms them in real sources for the theological task. They can produce, then, significant changes in Adventist theology.[234] Moreover, the general understanding of the sources of theology in modern Adventism seems to imply that God's revelation is not limited to Scripture or nature. God's revelation involves science and culture. They have a virtually revelatory value that transforms them into fundamental sources of theology.[235] Something similar occurs with the community of believers, whose lives, actions, and thoughts also have a revelatory value.[236]

A result of this understanding of the sources of theology in the context of modern Adventist theology is that theology is not the systematic study of Scripture, or the study of reality (God, world, human being, and their relationship) from the perspective of Scripture. Instead, theology is the study of "the Bible as understood and interpreted by the community of faith."[237] In this view, the object of theological reflection is the Christian doctrine or Christian belief. In other words, there is a priority of what the church (or the community of faith) be-

---

233. Guy, *Thinking Theologically*, 156. See the discussion in ibid., 155-157. In a similar vein, Rice affirms that doctrines do not arise "from the Bible alone, but from the dynamic interplay between the Bible and the living experience of the church." Rice, *Reason and the Contours*, 90.

234. "It is the dynamic interaction of personal-experiential ingredients with the secular-cultural, the historical-theological, and the biblical-scriptural ingredients that make an interpretation of faith what it is, and that make theological thinking endlessly fascinating." Ibid., 157.

235. "The best evidence we now have about how God created the world has been revealed to us in the great advances in science inspired by God, which has occurred over the last 500 years. In addition, God has graciously allowed us to obtain much better understandings of how the divine presence communicates to the human family in all cultures in ways they can best appreciate and understand at the time that the communication occurred." Taylor, "Death Before Sin?—Yes," 13.

236. "Revelation . . . is, first of all, a divine disclosure that creates a community in which life expresses this revelation in symbols of action, imagination and thought under the guidance of prophets." Herold Weiss, "Revelation and the Bible: Beyond Verbal Inspiration," *Spectrum* 7, no. 3 (1976): 52.

237. Rice, *Reason and the Contours*, 89.

lieves in connection with its tradition and experience, over the biblical interpretation.[238]

In this understanding of theology, doctrines are not so much accurate descriptions of ultimate realities—God or the world, for example. They are rather symbolic expressions that arise from the underlying religious experience that can be expressed in different ways or through different doctrinal formulations.[239] Thus, the veracity of the doctrinal beliefs—or the reality of what they describe—in relation to their biblical foundation is not necessarily denied, but it is a secondary issue. What is important is the meaning of doctrines as symbolic manifestations of the experience of believers. In this view, "systematic theology explores the inner vitality of the various symbols and ideas [doctrines] with which a religious community expresses its faith and seeks to integrate these contents within a coherent, cohesive framework of thought."[240]

A last corollary of the epistemological presuppositions in modern Adventist theology is the claim that the methodology of Adventist theology is not particularly distinctive. Adventist theology has distinctive beliefs but not a distinctive theological methodology. His distinctiveness relates to its particular tradition and community but its methodology is not unique.[241]

---

238. Ibid., 89-92. Similarly, Guy defines theology as *interpretation of faith* or thinking about its meaning. Guy, *Thinking Theologically*, 4. It involves thinking about "the content, basis, and implications of one's own religious life, including experience (or 'spirituality') and practice as well as belief." Ibid.

239. Rice seems to suggest this view of doctrines in Rice, *Reason and the Contours*, 93-94, 205.

240. Richard Rice, "The Relevance of the Investigative Judgment," *Spectrum* 14, no. 1 (1993): 38, n. 1. "The truth of faith cannot be uttered in any other way than in symbol and metaphor. The language of the Bible is the language of metaphors: The People, The Covenant, The Tree, The Crown, The Bread, The Wind, The Vine, The Way, Reconciliation, Justification, Sanctification, Redemption." Weiss, "Revelation and the Bible," 54.

241. "Adventist theological thinking has, to be sure, its distinctive content, because it develops within a particular religious tradition and community of faith; and it includes some subjects that Christians have generally ignored (such as Sabbath time and the Biblical symbolism of the sanctuary in heaven) or only recently addressed (such as the multidimensional wholeness of human personhood). But Adventist theology is not methodologically unique among Christian theologies. . . . It does not have its own separate way of thinking theologically." Guy, *Thinking Theologically*, viii-ix.

The Interpretation of God

According to Guy, if nature is temporal, so it is appropriate and probably necessary to consider God as temporal instead of timeless. Actually, if human experience is a valid indicator of the basic character of reality, God and nature should be considered as temporal. That God is temporal—not temporary—implies that He experiences and knows the sequence past-present-future in a temporal way.[242] Guy is aware that Philo and classical theologians such as Augustine, Boethius, and Aquinas—under the philosophical influence of Parmenides and Plato—have affirmed God's timelessness. Although some biblical materials refer to God's unchangeability (Mal 3:6; Ps 102:27; Jas 1:17), they actually describe God's character, rather than God's being.[243]

Guy considers that a timeless God would be unable to relate to the world, as in the case of Christ's incarnation. He could not hear petitions either. Even more, the very idea of God as personal would be virtually meaningless. In order to make possible the interaction between God and the world, including humanity, God needs to be temporal.[244]

God's temporality, however, is unique. It is an infinite temporality, different from the temporality of the world-humanity. God is omnitemporal because He coexists with every temporal being and is prior to everything else. God is the permanent source of creativity and the ground of stability. God's infinite temporality also "perfectly retains the positive meaning and consequences of all events in all time. God makes the past present in ever new ways, so that nothing good is ever lost."[245]

Guy understands God's relationship to the past and the future in a way that involves some analogy to human reality. Humans are able to know and retain something of the past conceptually. God is also able to this retention but in His case, that conceptual retention is complete, perfect. All the past is present to God in spite of the continuous additions of new events. In relation to the future, human beings have a finite freedom. The future for them is open only in terms of intention. In the case of God, the future is open in terms of intention but also in terms of purpose. This divine purpose "cannot be subverted or prevented from ultimate achievement by any temporal contingency or development."[246]

---

242. Guy, "God's Time," 21, 26-27.
243. Ibid., 22-24.
244. Ibid., 24-26; Guy, "Man and His Time," 475.
245. Guy, "God's Time," 26. See also Guy, "Man and His Time," 477.
246. Guy, "Man and His Time," 478.

God does not control all the events, however, but He can creatively respond to the new events that He incorporates in the fulfillment of His intention or purpose for His creatures.[247]

In any case, the future is still open for God. Namely, God does not have an exhaustive knowledge of the future—like humans—except in terms of the knowledge of His own actions. Guy, then, supports the view of the openness of God. He evaluates that Rice is the one who has better conceptualized this idea in Adventist thought.[248]

This view, however, does not imply an absolute rejection of God's timelessness. Rice, the main proponent of the open view of God in Adventism, also rejects the timeless classical view of God. According to him, if God were absolutely timeless and unchangeable, then His knowledge and experience would also be timeless. God would know past, present, and future in a simultaneous timeless perception. He would comprehend the entire reality from His eternal present. That absolutely timeless perspective of God would imply that the future is also unchangeable.[249]

Rice points out that the timeless understanding of divine foreknowledge is incompatible with human free will. If the future is closed—already determined by God's foreknowledge—human free will is not real.[250] In contrast, he proposes an "open view of God."[251] He thinks that "God's experience of temporal reality is progressive, developmental, and thus open."[252]

Rice, however, does not believe that God is completely temporal. His conception of God explicitly shares with process theism the notion of dipolar theism. It also "conceives God as both absolute and relative, necessary and contingent, eternal and temporal, changeless and changing. It attributes one element in each pair of contrasts to the appropriate aspect of God's being—the essential divine character or the concrete divine experience."[253] In other words, God has a timeless "pole" and a temporal one. The timeless pole or "side" refers to His existence, as

---

247. Ibid.
248. Guy, "God's Time," 25.
249. Richard Rice, *God's Foreknowledge and Man's Free Will* (Minneapolis, MN: Bethany, 1985), 15-16.
250. See the discussion in ibid., 17-19, 21.
251. Ibid., 25.
252. Ibid., 26. In other words, "the future retains its essential indefiniteness from God's perspective as well as from ours." Ibid.
253. Ibid., 33.

well as His character. Both are unaffected by the world.²⁵⁴ The temporal pole refers to "his experience of the world."²⁵⁵ In this way, Rice does not hold an idea of God as completely open but only partially open. He is partially open and partially closed. Therefore, "this openness involves only one aspect of God, namely, His experience."²⁵⁶

While Rice admits his intellectual indebtedness to process theology, he also considers that his position is not the same as process theology view of God's dipolarity. One of the main reasons is that he denies that God depends ontologically on the world or that God and the world are mutually dependent.²⁵⁷ However, he has contributed to open the way for a more radical (modern) interpretation of God's relation to the world in Adventist theology.²⁵⁸

Larson, Rice's colleague, a former president of the Association of Adventist Forums and a specialist in Whitehead's process philosophy, suggests "that Rice didn't go far enough."²⁵⁹ According to Larson, Adventism has many elements in common with process theology. "We reject dualism, affirm freedom, and make God's love first, middle, and

---

254. Ibid., 27. "What makes God God (that which distinguishes Him essentially from all other forms of reality) is thus absolutely unchangeable. Correctly, the classical view of God has always insisted on this." Ibid.

255. Ibid., 30.

256. Ibid., 26. Rice is very explicit at this point. "I don't reject divine timelessness, I reject only the idea that God is entirely timeless. God is both temporal and eternal, both relative and absolute, etc." Richard Rice, Professor of Theology at Loma Linda University, interview by Laurent B. Kassay, Silang, Cavite, Philippines, July 4, 2001, in Laurent B. Kassay, "Richard Rice's Anticipatory Theory of Divine Foreknowledge: A Critical Evaluation" (PhD diss., Adventist International Institute of Advanced Studies, Silang, Cavite, Philippines, 2001), 278. Regarding this dipolarity in God, see also Richard Rice, "Process Theism and the Open View of God: The Crucial Difference," in *Searching for an Adequate God: A Dialogue Between Process and Free Will Theists*, ed. John B. Cobb Jr. and Clark H. Pinnock (Grand Rapids, MI: Eerdmans, 2000), 163-200. Rice also essentially supports this dipolar understanding of God in his systematic theology, although in a less technical way. See Rice, *Reign of God*, 98.

257. Richard Rice, "Biblical Support for a New Perspective," in *The Openness of God: A Biblical Challenge to the Traditional Understanding of God* (Downers Grove, IL: InterVarsity, 1994), 33. See Richard Rice, "Why I Am a Seventh-day Adventist," *Spectrum* 24, no. 1 (1994): 38. See also Rice, interview, 278, where he admits his indebtedness to process thought.

258. Rice's open theism represents a position of compromise between modern theology—particularly its version of process theology—and traditional classical theism. George L. Goodwin, "The Openness of God: A Compromised Position?" *Spectrum* 12, no. 1 (1981): 62-63.

259. David R. Larson, "On Openness of God," *Spectrum* 12, no. 3 (1982): 61.

last, for example."²⁶⁰ Larson is the modern Adventist theologian that most explicitly affirms a panentheistic view of God based on process thought, but with some modifications.

Larson proposes that panentheism²⁶¹—in its process theology variety—is congruent with Adventist thought in several aspects. He mentions six aspects in particular. Panentheism rejects pantheism, deism, contra-naturalism (the interventionist model according to which God does not break natural laws when produces a miracle), body-soul dualism, determinism, and radical individualism. In positive terms, this means that (1) God is closely related to the world, but is more than the world; (2) He interactively participates in human life; (3) His interaction does not violate natural laws but He uses them; (4) human beings are physical and spiritual unities; (5) human beings have free will that they can use to interact with God and to improve their lives; and (6) relationships make up who one is.²⁶²

Larson correctly explains that according to process theology, the world is necessary and essential to God. Larson thinks, however, that the world is essential to God but not necessary. Although the world is not logically necessary for God, God is what He wills or He decides to be. As God has decided to create and to be with the universe, "God's relationship to a universe of some sort is constitutive of God, as process philosophy holds. . . . This suggests to me . . . that God has never been and never will be 'home alone' but is everlastingly related to a universe of some type that nevertheless depends upon God for its sheer actuality."²⁶³

---

260. David R. Larson, "Process Theology and Me," *Spectrum*, February 25, 2008, para. 11, accessed August 18, 2016, http://spectrummagazine.org/article/column/2008/02/25/process-theology-and-me.

261. Larson defines *panentheism* as "the idea that everything is 'in' God and that God is 'in' everything." David R. Larson, "'Panentheism' Is Not a Four-Letter Word!" *Spectrum*, July 30, 2010, para. 1, accessed August 18, 2016, http://spectrummagazine.org/article/column/2010/07/30/%E2%80%9Cpanentheism%E2%80%9D-not-four-letter-word. Larson quotes Acts 17:28 in support of this understanding of panentheism.

262. Larson, "Panentheism," para. 5-8.

263. David R. Larson, "Traditional Free Will Theism and the Ten Core Doctrines of Process Philosophy," David R. Larson, July 14, 2010, para. 9, accessed August 18, 2016, https://www.davidrlarson.com/2010/07/traditional-free-will-theism-and---the-ten-core-doctrines-of-process-philosophy--by-david-r-larson----how-much-difference-pe.html. For Larson's distinction between the world as essential but not necessary for God, see also Larson, "Panentheism," para. 19; David R. Larson, "Necessarily, Essentially, Neither or Both: How Does God Love the Universe?" paper

In other words, in God's decision about to be is included His decision of not to be alone.²⁶⁴

In harmony with this panentheistic view of God, Larson argues that God is not omnipotent. His power has limitations, including ontological limitations. These ontological limitations involve the fact that, although God is the Supreme Being, the power of other beings limits God's power, even if the power of these beings is God's gift. "The divine realm includes many guests. God's power is limited by their presence and by their power."²⁶⁵

Regarding the interpretation of God in modern Adventist theology, a last important issue is the language to talk about God. Guy highlights that theology involves—whether directly or indirectly—a language to talk about God. All this language is, in some way or another, metaphorical, symbolic, mythical, or analogical. In other words, nothing is literal language. Expressions such as Father, King, or Creator, are also anthropomorphic metaphors to talk about God using literal terms.²⁶⁶ In a more technical way, "because of the ontological difference between our reality and God's—that is, between finitude and infinity—our language cannot be applied directly to God."²⁶⁷

This metaphorical language is also applicable to God's character, attitudes, or actions, including biblical expressions referring to God's jealousy, anger, or vindictiveness, as well as to any statement affirming that God loves human beings and takes care of them.²⁶⁸ Guy also considers the language used by the Bible to talk about heavenly realities as symbolic. Biblical descriptions of heaven have the purpose of communicating through symbols an understanding of God, His attitudes, and actions, regarding the created universe. Guy admits that the difference between the transcendent reality of heaven and the earthly realities cannot be absolute because, in that case, it would be impossible to understand anything about heaven. However, he still affirms, "We are almost

---

presented at the Annual Meeting of the American Academy of Religion, San Antonio, TX, November 20-23, 2004, 1.

264. Larson, "Necessarily, Essentially, Neither or Both," 1.

265. David R. Larson, "The Omnipotence Fallacy and Beyond," *Spectrum* 23, no. 3 (1993): 41.

266. Guy, *Thinking Theologically*, 185-186, 187. "The more concrete our language about God is, the more metaphorical it is: if we can talk non-metaphorically (that is, literally) about God at all, it is only at a very high level of abstraction." Ibid., 186.

267. Ibid., 187.

268. Ibid., 187-189.

wholly ignorant of the nature of heaven; all we know about it is that it is the transcendent reality where the presence of God is 'centered' or 'most readily perceived.'"[269] It is possible to talk about heaven in spiritual terms—as for example, in order to suggest that there is a *spiritual* proximity between heaven and earth—but "we cannot talk meaningfully about heaven in spatio-temporal terms."[270]

The Interpretation of the World

In agreement with the historical-critical method of exegesis, and the symbolic understanding of doctrines, Guy and other modern Adventist theologians consider that the biblical narrative of Creation in Genesis does not describe this event in literal terms. From this perspective, Gen 1 is a theological, metaphorical, or symbolic explanation of origins, not a factual one. The purpose of Scripture is clearly spiritual, theological, and salvific, not scientific. Genesis uses an ancient cosmology to transmit a theological message.[271]

That message has to do with the relationship between God and the world. God is the supreme Creator and source of everything that exists. The universe and human life then, have a purpose, meaning, and value. In Guy's words, the accounts of Creation are "an invitation to experience the ultimate trustworthiness of reality."[272]

Guy considers Creation as a temporal divine activity, in consonance with the contemporary cultural understanding of reality as temporal and dynamic.[273] This temporal understanding of Creation, however, is not necessarily the biblical one. In connection with the rejection

---

269. Fritz Guy, "Confidence in Salvation: The Meaning of the Sanctuary," *Spectrum* 11, no. 2 (1980): 45.

270. Guy, *Thinking Theologically*, 244.

271. Guy, "Interpreting Genesis One," 11-12; Guy, "Purpose and Function of Scripture," 96-99; Dalton D. Baldwin, "Creation and Time: A Biblical Reflection," in *Understanding Genesis: Contemporary Adventist Perspectives*, ed. Brian Bull, Fritz Guy, and Ervin Taylor (Riverside, CA: Adventist Today, 2009), 35-51; Herr, "Genesis One," 61. See also Raymond F. Cottrell, "Extend of the Genesis Flood," in *Creation Reconsidered: Scientific, Biblical, and Theological Perspectives*, ed. James L. Hayward (Roseville, CA: Association of Adventist Forums, 2000), 275.

272. Guy, "Purpose and Function of Scripture," 98-99. See also Guy, "Interpreting Genesis One," 12.

273. Guy, *Thinking Theologically*, 179. In this context, Guy suggests that "the notion of 'nontemporal action' has no discernible meaning. This logical fact identifies a decisive defect in all notions of a 'timeless' God." Ibid., 179, n. 46.

of the literal interpretation of the biblical account of Creation, modern Adventist theology accepts that God has created the world through a process of evolution, not in six literal days, a few millennia ago. They do not believe in a universal flood either.[274] This interpretation of the world is built upon certain presuppositions regarding the nature of the world and its relationship to God.

Guy believes that "God gives to created reality an ontological identity and dignity of its own; granting it freedom to be itself, God respects it for what it is, what it does, and what it becomes, even when the outcome is not a fulfillment of God's creative intention."[275] When Guy and other modern Adventist theologians refer to created reality as gifted with freedom, they are not only thinking about intelligent creatures such as human beings. They are also thinking about the world in general. Within some limits, the material substance has some kind of free choice that allows matter to "create" or change its own reality. As Brian Bull points out, this natural freedom to choose has a cost. "The price that God and humans pay is that earthquakes happen, mountains are built, and much that is beautiful follows."[276]

These evils are not the result of wrong moral decisions or ethical violations. The destructive power of natural elements exists mostly because "all beings, and not merely those relatively few who enjoy moral freedom, have at least some ability, however slight, to pursue

---

274. Two fundamental books supporting a creation through evolution written by modern Adventists are James L. Hayward, ed., *Creation Reconsidered: Scientific, Biblical, and Theological Perspectives* (Roseville, CA: Association of Adventist Forums, 2000); Brian Bull, Fritz Guy, and Ervin Taylor, eds., *Understanding Genesis: Contemporary Adventist Perspectives* (Riverside, CA: Adventist Today, 2009). These books are collections of articles written mostly by scientists and theologians that, in general, consider that it is necessarily a radical reinterpretation of the historical Adventist position of origins, more in harmony with the evolutionary theory. The first volume includes a chapter by Whitehead. See Alfred North Whitehead, "Religion and Science," in *Creation Reconsidered: Scientific, Biblical, and Theological Perspectives*, ed. James L. Hayward (Roseville, CA: Association of Adventist Forums, 2000), 337-343. Moreover, the volume also suggests that the acceptance of process thought is part of a Christian mature faith. See Graeme Sharrock, "Faith Development in a Scientific Culture," in *Creation Reconsidered: Scientific, Biblical, and Theological Perspectives*, ed. James L. Hayward (Roseville, CA: Association of Adventist Forums, 2000), 331, 333.

275. Guy, *Thinking Theologically*, 144.

276. Brian Bull, "Living in Incommensurate Worlds," *Spectrum* 31, no. 2 (2003): 21. "Earthquakes, tidal waves, fires, and floods may be an inescapable part of a world that exercises its own version of freedom." Ibid., 22.

their own perceived goods to the detriment of the whole of which they are a part."[277] This natural destruction does not represent God's will, but is not sinful because it is not conscious or deliberate.[278] It is simply the result of God's freedom given to natural entities. Guy formulates this point by saying, "This fact that God has, in effect, put the universe on a very long leash, goes a long way toward explaining the presence of evil in the world-not only moral evil, *but natural evil as well.*"[279]

The freedom of the world in general is the reason why God creates through evolution. God gave the world freedom from the beginning to be itself within some limits determined by natural laws. This freedom implies that, to some extent, the world participates in the process of Creation. In this process, God cannot be coercive because, in that case, He would annul the world's freedom. This way to create the world necessarily takes a long time. Evolution, then, is the only option to create. At the same time, the world by itself would not be able to achieve the outcomes that God wants to reach through Creation; for example, the creation of humans in the image of God.[280] Therefore, this process involves God's guidance and providence.[281]

It is not necessarily clear if, for modern Adventist thinkers, the process of Creation is already complete (through evolution). However, despite of the tendency to understand God in panentheistic terms, they affirm a *creatio ex nihilo*.[282] As God's love for His creation is essential to Him but not necessary,[283] it is still required an explanation about the way in which that creation originated. Guy proposes a kenotic interpretation of Creation. It is necessary "to understand creation as divine

---

277. Larson, "The Omnipotence Fallacy," 41.
278. Ibid., 41-42.
279. Guy, *Thinking Theologically*, 144-145. Emphasis mine.
280. Bull, "Living in Incommensurate Worlds," 22; Larson, "Traditional Free Will Theism," para. 41, 42.
281. The "guiding process, which ensures that God's outcomes will be achieved, I understand to be Providence." Bull, "Living in Incommensurate Worlds," 22.
282. Although Guy has said that the doctrine of creation can be interpreted as referring to the world's ontological dependence on God and not as a reference to the temporal finitude of the world, he still seems to believe—along with other modern Adventist theologians—that the world has a beginning, as the following discussion suggests. See p. 185 in this chapter.
283. Larson, "Necessarily, Essentially, Neither or Both," 1. Larson clarifies the meaning of *essential*: "When we say that some feature of a thing is 'essential,' we mean that it is a defining characteristic of the item in question." Ibid., 4.

self-limitation expressed in the Christological idea of 'self-emptying.'"[284]

From this perspective, God's self-emptying manifested in the Incarnation and the cross—where God became flesh and suffered—is the model for understanding Creation. God's self-emptying does not manifest only in relation to the Incarnation and the cross but also in relation to human life and the whole cosmos. "In the light of the cross of Christ we see everything else: our own lives, human history, and the whole cosmos. God is not only the Great Designer and Immanent Sustainer, but also the Constant Participant and Suffering Redeemer."[285] This self-emptying or participation is more than just a sympathetic fellowship or interaction of a loving personal ultimate reality with created reality. "The *ultimate reality is self-invested in created reality*, committed to its flourishing and fulfillment."[286] In other words, in Incarnation, God invests Himself in humanity; in Creation, God invests Himself in created reality in general.

The Interpretation of the Human Being

Guy affirms that human beings are temporal creatures who are aware of their temporality. They have a capacity for abstraction related to their linguistic abilities and rationality, which is the base for their freedom and moral choices. Their awareness of the past and the anticipation of the future is what allows them to see their time as a unity, and provides them with identity and individuality. In one sense, every human being is his/her own past (by his/her memories), and his/her future (by anticipation). Human freedom consists in the capacity to influence the future, although it is a finite, limited capacity. The present constitutes the occasion when freedom is experienced.[287] Human beings cannot change the past but can change the meaning of the past through repentance and forgiveness. The Gospel offers the opportunity for the individual to orient his/her life regarding an open future, rather than in connection with the past. Death is not the end of everything in the sense that there is a hope beyond death.[288]

Guy believes that human beings were created in the image of God.[289]

---

284. Guy, "Interpreting Genesis One," 12.
285. Ibid.
286. Guy, *Thinking Theologically*, 145. Emphasis mine.
287. Guy, "Man and His Time," 441, 442, 444, 445, 446, 447, 449.
288. Ibid., 455-457, 460, 463, 466-468.
289. Ibid., 450. The image of God involves the use of intelligence and rational-

However, Guy and other modern Adventist theologians hold that God created human beings through a process of evolution. The long evolutionary process guided by God produced as a result sentient human beings who were free to choose to love God and to serve Him.[290] Against this background, Guy tries to explain the meaning of the human fall in Gen 2-3. He proposes that a theological interpretation of these chapters implies that God took a serious risk by creating human beings. Sin is not ontologically necessary. According to Gen 2-3, sin is a perversion, not an essential part of creation. It appeared after Creation as a result of the wrong use of human freedom. Humans did not want to live as God's image, according to God's creative purpose. Guy quotes the panentheist theologian Keith Ward who defines sin as "to claim autonomy, knowledge and power . . . without love and without responsibility, in the name of selfish desire."[291]

From Guy's perspective, death was a reality millions of years before the appearance of human beings. Consequently, death is only "the wages of sin" (Rom 6:23) in the sense that sin implies "a radical break between human spirit and God; it is estrangement and guilt, existence without God, the perception of God as an enemy from whom to hide."[292] In other words, Guy seems to interpret death as separation from God. Biological death—including the death of human beings—was already a reality before the Fall. But after the Fall, sin produced "a loss of a sense of transcendence, and hence slavery . . . to death without hope, death as oblivion. It is a distortion of human existence into a downward spiral of radical insecurity and more sin—selfishness and greed, hostility and violence, gender disorder, and sexual exploitation."[293]

According to Guy, human vocation is the fulfillment and actualization of the values that are the characteristic of the relation between

---

ity. Guy, *Thinking Theologically*, 57, 95. For a broader discussion about the understanding of the image of God, see Rice, *Reign of God*, 129-133. According to Rice, the image of God involves functions such as dominion over creation and stewardship but also characteristics such as reason, symbolization, and self-determination or self-creativity.

290. Guy, "Interpreting Genesis One," 12; Bull, "Living in Incommensurate Worlds," 22.

291. Keith Ward, *God, Faith and the New Millennium: Christian Belief in an Age of Science* (Oxford, UK: Oneworld, 1998), 49. See Guy, "Interpreting Genesis One," 13.

292. Guy, "Interpreting Genesis One," 13.

293. Ibid.

God and His creation: love, creativity, enjoyment. These values are the foundation for human morality. Guy also thinks that Scripture identifies human destiny "as an everlasting personal future of flourishing and fulfillment in the presence of God; this is the ground of human hope."[294]

Guy and modern Adventist theologians hold the Adventist historical position of the state of the dead. However, they do not emphasize death as a consequence of sin. They usually emphasize human nature in terms of the wholeness and unity of human existence as a multidimensional unity.[295]

The Interpretation of the Articulating Agent

Guy highlights the centrality of Christ in Scripture. Christ is the center of Scripture, not from an exegetical perspective but as a theological principle. This is what he refers to as theological Christocentricity.[296] In consonance, although Guy thinks that Adventist theological thinking involves the three interdependent poles of Christian Gospel, cultural context, and Adventist heritage, the most important one is the Christian Gospel. According to Guy, the integrity of the three poles is important but the Gospel takes some priority, in the same way that Jesus's stories in Scripture have a reciprocal relationship with the rest of Scripture but not completely symmetrical.[297]

However, Guy seems to understand Christ's centrality in terms of a wider central issue. Christ is the center because He is the supreme and central revelation of God's character that provides meaning to the entire Scripture.[298] The Gospel ultimately refers to the wider central issue of God's character of love. "As the center of Christian faith and life, the fact that God is everlasting, universal, and comprehensive love, should govern our thinking about everything else."[299] The Gospel is a basic criterion and motivation for Adventist theology and experience

---

294. Guy, *Thinking Theologically*, 145.

295. Ibid., viii, 11, 62, 92, 123, 245-249; Rice, *Reign of God*, 120-121, 151. Rice barely mentions human death as a consequence of sin in his discussion about sin. See ibid., 146.

296. Guy, *Thinking Theologically*, 132-133.

297. Ibid., 228. The idea is that Jesus's stories are central to understanding the rest of the Bible.

298. "The theological meaning of the whole scripture is centered in Jesus the Messiah, the definitive revelation of the character of God; and the meaning of each part of scripture is understood in relation to this central revelation." Ibid., 132.

299. Ibid., 229.

because it impels the believers "to respond to God's love theologically as well as experientially."[300]

Given the centrality of God, or more specifically of God's love, distinctive beliefs, insights, or practices should not be the center of Adventist theology. Any distinctive element as the center of Adventist theology would lead to theological eccentricity regarding the center of Christian theology. In other words, the center of Adventist theology cannot be different from the center of Christian theology in general.[301] If God should be the center in terms of His essential attribute of love, it is necessary to explore the way in which modern Adventist theology understands God's love in operative terms.

The Interpretation of the Articulating Action

In modern Adventist theology, God's actions in the world are essentially immanent in the sense that they are not usually distinguishable of natural causation. God uses evolution as the natural mechanism through which He performs His creative activity. This mechanism is consistent with God's character of unconditional love because, during the evolutionary process, He suffers with those who suffer in that process.[302] "An infinite vulnerability to suffering is part of the truth that 'God [the Creator] is love' (1 John 4:8, 16)."[303]

The understanding of God's actions in the world in modern Adventist theology often becomes clearer in connection with its understanding of miracles. According to Guy and Bull, biblical authors have a tendency to understand unexplained natural phenomena in terms of divine causation. They always presuppose that there is a direct divine intervention behind these phenomena. There is a tendency to find supernatural explanations, to see miracles everywhere. In contrast, in recent times, there is a tendency to explain every natural phenomenon in terms of natural causation. Today, there is a better understanding of the infrastructure of nature, including natural law or regularity, as well as a knowledge of the randomness in nature in connection with

---

300. Ibid., 230. As the following discussion makes clear, Guy has in mind an understanding of God's love that is close to the one of process theology.

301. Ibid., 251. "Our distinctiveness is not the proper center of our theology or our spirituality." Ibid., 10.

302. Guy, "Interpreting Genesis One," 12; Bull, "Living in Incommensurate Worlds," 21.

303. Guy, "Interpreting Genesis One," 12. Bracketed in original.

quantum indeterminacy.[304] Although this situation does not completely deny the possibility of supernatural interventions—such as God's creation or Christ's miracles and resurrection—a claim that a supernatural intervention happened "puts the burden of proof on the claim of a supernatural occurrence."[305]

Modern Adventist thinkers would agree with E. G. White that miracles do not imply an interruption of the operation of natural laws.[306] Guy and Bull, for example, define *miracle* as an event, which is inexplicable based on the actual knowledge of nature.[307] At the same time, however, it seems that a miracle is something linked to the perspective of the observer.[308] It is better to pay attention to the revelatory significance of miracles described in the Bible such as those related to the Exodus and Christ's miracles. Consequently, "divine involvement is most comprehensible not as intervention from the outside, but rather as, first, the active presence of God in and with all created reality and, second, the moral and religious impact of historical events and developments such as peace, freedom, and justice."[309] The exception, according to Guy, is Jesus's resurrection, because "it represents a truly extraordinary event, happening in history but not simply an outcome of the dynamics of history."[310]

In general, however, miracles are usually natural events interpreted as such for the observer. God usually does not act in an extraordinary way distinguishable from the natural causation. Thus, prayers do not change God's mind or induce Him to answer with miraculous interventions. Prayer allows the believers to understand their circumstances, see the alternatives, perceive God's will, and live with the consequences, accepting restrictions and opportunities graciously.[311]

---

304. Guy and Bull, "Then a Miracle Occurs," 55.
305. Ibid. See ibid., 64-65.
306. David R. Larson, "Think Less of God Intervening, Think More of God Participating," *Spectrum*, September 1, 2008, para. 13, accessed August 28, 2016, http://spectrummagazine.org/article/column/2008/09/01/think-less-god-intervening-think-more-god-participating. Compare with E. G. White, *Patriarchs and Prophets*, 194-195.
307. Guy and Bull, "Then a Miracle Occurs," 64, 67, n. 3. Larson defines "miracles as events that defy the laws of nature as we presently formulate them." David R. Larson, "The Moral Danger of Miracles," *Spectrum* 18, no. 4 (1988): 13. See also David R. Larson, "Was Spinoza Right About Miracles?" *Spectrum* 32, no. 2 (2004): 47-51.
308. Larson, "Was Spinoza Right About Miracles?" 48.
309. Guy, *Thinking Theologically*, 149.
310. Ibid.
311. Larson, "The Moral Danger of Miracles," 18; Larson, "The Omnipotence

In consequence, it is better to understand God's articulating action in the world in terms of participation rather than in terms of intervention. God does not completely determine the events in the world. He only partially determines them through His participation.[312] This participation should be understood in the light of the fact that God's character is love. God's articulating action in the world is not coercing, judging, or controlling. He is not an omnipotent sovereign. He articulates the relationship between Himself and the world-humanity through His persuasive and attractive power.[313] Guy considers that God's comprehensive love should be the center of Adventist theology. "The idea that God is universal love—self-giving and vulnerable, persuasive rather than coercive, always *with us*, and all created reality as supportive presence and encouraging assistance toward our highest possibilities—does function successfully as a theological and spiritual center."[314]

God relates to creation in terms of His character of love and thus, His relation to sinful humans implies forgiveness.[315] This forgiveness is eternal or timeless as God's character of love. It is a fact in God's being as an attitude, but it is enacted in history in Christ's life and death. In this way, human beings can acknowledge, respond, and experience divine forgiveness in their lives.[316] God will finally win the controversy between good and evil by the attractiveness of His love.[317]

Although the notion that God's power is persuasive love rather than coercive seems to diminish God's power, Larson affirms, in connection with process theology, that the opposite is true. Persuasion requires be-

---

Fallacy," 43. "In these ways, prayer enables one to combine the joys and sorrows of one's life into a work of art whose brilliance and shadows coalesce as a joyful response to divine love." Larson, "The Moral Danger of Miracles," 18-19.

312. See Larson, "Think Less of God Intervening," para. 2.

313. "Because the character of God really is love—love that is always and everywhere actively involved in enhancing the experience of created reality—God is best understood not as omnipotent Sovereign but as infinite Lover, not as a disinterested Judge pronouncing sentence on a culprit but as a passionately concerned Parent welcoming a child home. God's power is not coercive and controlling, but attractive and persuasive; and God's justice is not the exercise of a supreme will, but the actualization of a universal love." Guy, *Thinking Theologically*, 227.

314. Ibid., 103. Emphasis in original.

315. Fritz Guy, "The Ultimate Triumph of Love," *Southern Asia Tidings*, February 1989, 4.

316. Fritz Guy, "Divine Forgiveness as Experienced Event," *AUSS* 5, no. 2 (1967): 88, 89, 91, 93, 94, 100.

317. Guy, "The Ultimate Triumph of Love," 4.

ing stronger than what coercion requires. "Let us be clear: process theology holds that a God who is persuasive is stronger, not weaker, than is a God who is coercive."[318]

Modern Adventist theologians are aware that the idea that God persuades His creation through His universal, comprehensive, and unconditional love—without coercion or control—is difficult to conciliate with some biblical materials. This is the case, for example, of biblical narratives where God commands to exterminate Canaanites or the apocalyptic imaginary of judgment in the book of Revelation.[319] Guy admits that not all the content of Scripture is easy to relate to his understanding of God's unconditional love. He suggests "not to be obsessed with the biblical imagery of warfare."[320] Larson more explicitly assesses that massive extermination does not reflect God's will—no matter what the Israelites believed—because simply it "is not compatible with the character of God as embodied in Jesus Christ."[321]

The Interpretation of the Whole

Although modern Adventist thinkers have not necessarily explicitly expressed their understanding of reality as a whole in terms of a panentheistic perspective, it appears that the main representatives—such as Guy and Bull—see the relationship between God and the world in that way. Guy, in particular, does not ignore Whiteheadian philosophy and process theology. He has criticized Cobb—the process theologian— because he has not sufficiently tried to adapt Whitehead's process philosophy for the use of Christian theology as Augustine and Aquinas have done with other philosophical systems in the past.[322] Guy points out

---

318. David R. Larson, "Coercive or Persuasive Power: Which Is Stronger?" David R. Larson, July 21, 2007, para. 13, accessed August 29, 2016, http://www.davidrlarson.com/2007/07/coercive-or-per.html. "God's approach functions the other way. Instead of increasing coercive power until it becomes persuasive, it increases persuasive power until it becomes coercive in a different sense. God's power is limited. But because it can convince without crushing, no force in the entire universe is more powerful than the divine ability to persuade." Larson, "The Omnipotence Fallacy," 43.

319. Guy, *Thinking Theologically*, 103; Guy, "The Ultimate Triumph of Love," 4; David R. Larson, "Jesus and Genocide: Another Alternative," *Spectrum* 34, no. 3 (2006): 66-69.

320. Guy, *Thinking Theologically*, 103; Guy, "The Ultimate Triumph of Love," 4.
321. Larson, "Jesus and Genocide," 68.
322. Fritz Guy, "Comments on a Recent Whiteheadian Doctrine of God," *AUSS* 4, no. 2 (1966): 126-128. Stuart R. Sprague has noticed this critique. Stuart R. Sprague,

some aspects of Cobb's Whiteheadian doctrine of God that he believes deserve revision in order to be acceptable in the context of a Christian theology. He considers Whitehead's philosophical rationalization of God and the ontological subordination of God to the entire process of reality as problematic.[323]

However, Guy finds some elements in process thought that can be useful in order to formulate a doctrine of God. "Certainly the idea of primordial and consequent natures . . . is a suggestive way of understanding the relationship of God's transcendence, absoluteness, and eternity on the one hand and his relatedness and responsiveness to history on the other."[324] From this perspective, the world is important for God and He "is in some way experientially conditioned by it."[325] Furthermore, according to Guy, the notion of *initial aim* could be a way to explain providence and the activity of the Holy Spirit.[326]

The acceptance of the dipolar view of God implies that in Adventist modern theology, the hierarchy timeless-temporality still persists. It never disappeared. Moreover, the radical immanentist view of God's action in the world, where God's operation in the world is indistinguishable from natural causation, points to the direction of some type of panentheistic ontology. The claims that all creation (not only intelligent creatures) has some kind of freedom to choose and that the future is open for all even for God (in the sense of undetermined) go on the same path. As Larson explicitly present it, "This is why panentheism, the view that God includes but surpasses the universe . . . increasingly is our preferred doctrine of God."[327]

Critical Evaluation

From the perspective of its ontological assumptions, modern Adventist theology emphasizes, in contrast to classical theology, the basic

---

"Shaping a Process Theology: The Theological Method of John B. Cobb, Jr." (PhD diss., Southern Baptist Theological Seminary, Louisville, KY, 1975), 47-48.
323. Guy, "Recent Whiteheadian Doctrine of God," 128-132.
324. Ibid., 133.
325. Ibid. "It seems to make less difficult—though of course not more true—the simultaneous affirmations that God is ontologically unconditioned and that what he experiences is in a certain sense dependent on human response, so that how human beings use their creaturely freedom does make a difference to him." Ibid.
326. Ibid., 133-134.
327. Larson, "Was Spinoza Right About Miracles?" 49.

temporality of reality as well as its integrity and dynamic character. This emphasis, however, does not represent an attempt to be in line with biblical temporal ontology[328] but an adjustment to modern theological perspectives and an adaptation to cultural intuitions, as Guy clearly explains.[329] Actually, modern Adventist thinkers' sympathy for a view of reality as constant becoming seems to bring them closer to a process ontology of becoming, rather than to a biblical ontology.

At the same time, modern Adventist epistemological assumptions reveal an implicit ontological dualism, which is inconsistent with the proclaimed temporal ontology. Guy, for example, affirms a critical realistic epistemology, in a similar vein with John Polkinghorne.[330] This understanding of critical realism is common among those theologians and scientists who have an interest in the relationship between science and religion, many of them supporting some version of panentheistic ontology.[331] Polkinghorne holds that it is possible to know the physical world, although scientific knowledge or affirmations are imperfect and always under constant correction and expansion.[332] He believes that

---

328. Guy affirms that "the notion that temporality is an imperfection is an inheritance from classical thought and is contradicted by the consistent evidence of Scripture." Guy, *Thinking Theologically*, 115. However, it is clear that the basic source of his ontological assumptions is not Scripture but the philosophical-theological and cultural convictions and intuitions.

329. See pp. 183-185 in this chapter.

330. Guy actually refers to Polkinghorne in relation to critical realism. See Guy, *Thinking Theologically*, 61, n. 34, 185, n. 6. Guy affirms that critical realism is the prevalent understanding of knowledge among scientists and theologians. Ibid.

331. See John Polkinghorne, *Belief in God in an Age of Science* (New Haven, CT: Yale University Press, 1998), 123. Among these authors, Polkinghorne mentions Ian G. Barbour, Arthur R. Peacocke, and Polkinghorne himself. Ibid., 48, n. 1. Regarding the panentheistic view of these scientists and theologians, see Cooper, *Panentheism*, 302-304, 307-310, 315-317. Polkinghorne in particular defends an eschatological panentheism, but he considers that panentheism is not yet a present reality. However, he still supports a dipolar theism and his perspective about the relationship between God and the world are similar to those of Peacocke, Clayton, and Moltmann, all of them panentheists. Although he tries to differentiate from them, in practice, "the difference appears to be more terminological than substantive." Cooper, *Panentheism*, 316.

332. "Like most scientists, I believe that the advance of science is concerned not just with our ability to manipulate the physical world, but with our capacity to gain knowledge of its actual nature. In a word, I am a realist. Of course, such knowledge is to a degree partial and corrigible. Our attainment is verisimilitude, not absolute truth. Our method is the creative interpretation of experience, not rigorous deduction from it. Thus, I am a critical realist." Polkinghorne, *Belief in God*, 104. Regarding Polkinghorne's critical realism, see also John Polkinghorne, *Beyond Science: The*

critical realism is also applicable to theological knowledge.

Polkinghorne considers, however, that as God is beyond the scope of physical experimentation, it is necessary to appeal to apophaticism—the *via negativa*—in order to obtain some knowledge about the Deity.[333] From this perspective, theology cannot expect the same degree of success as physical sciences. Theological language will "be the *allusive* and open language of *symbol* rather than the precise language of mathematics that is so effective in science. To a significant degree in theology, prosaic clarity has to give way to something more like *poetic discourse*."[334]

This is also the way in which Guy understands critical realism in the context of theology. The fact that he denies that theological assertions have a literal—although not necessarily exhaustive—correspondence with the objects that they describe, involves an implicit use of the traditional *via negativa*.[335] That is why, according to Guy and modern Adventist thinkers, Scripture and theological assertions have only a spiritual, metaphorical, and theological significance. They refer to eternal or supernatural truth, not to historical or empirical facts.

Due to the application of the *via negativa*, modern Adventist thinkers follow an understanding of the relationship between science and theology (or theological knowledge) according to which both disciplines are valid parallel sources of knowledge. Thus, they are not really complementary as Guy claims. They should work separately. In practice, science and religion can work only partially together in

---

Wider Human Context (Cambridge, UK: Cambridge University Press, 1996), 18-19.

333. "There is a tradition in theology, called apophaticism, which warns against the hubris of claiming exact knowledge of deity." John Polkinghorne, *Science and Religion in Quest of Truth* (New Haven, CT: Yale University Press, 2011), 12, 20.

334. Ibid..12. Emphasis mine.

335. Critical realism, particularly in theology, does not necessarily involve the *via negativa*. Osborne, for example, explains that critical realism, in the context of theology, holds that theological assertions are, to some extent, valid representations of what they describe, but they cannot be completely precise depictions of theological truth. Critical realism is open to other possible interpretations of theological truth (doctrines, biblical texts) because it involves an awareness that the knower always has presuppositions that conditions his/her knowledge. Osborne, *The Hermeneutical Spiral*, 398, 417. See also John C. Peckham, "The Analogy of Scripture Revisited: A Final Form Canonical Approach to Systematic Theology," *Mid-America Journal of Theology* 22 (2011): 51; Peckham, *Canonical Theology*, 212; John C. Peckham, "The Concept of Divine Love in the Context of the God-World Relationship" (PhD diss., Andrews University, Berrien Springs, MI, 2012), 15.

the sense that science can inform religion but religion cannot inform science. In order to avoid a conflict between science and religion, this approach requires an interpretation of the Bible—including the first chapters of Genesis—that is serious but not literal. The Bible contains spiritual insights, metaphors about divine reality; it is not literal language.[336] Supporters of this position are Barbour, Peacocke, and Polkinghorne, who are all defenders of some variety of panentheistic theology.[337]

As modern theology and the variety of panentheistic ontologies have affirmed that God has a primordial timeless pole or side, it is not surprising to find that modern Adventist theology—that sympathizes with these theological perspectives—also applies the *via negativa* in the interpretation of doctrines in general and of God in particular. Although Guy emphasizes temporality as a basic characteristic of reality, and in his interpretation of God he highlights God's temporality, it is clear that he implicitly believes that God is, in some aspect, timeless. This belief is more explicit in Rice and Larson, but it is also implicitly pointed out by Guy's view of doctrines as symbols.

The modern Adventist understanding of doctrines parallels Tillich's understanding of doctrines as symbols.[338] Tillich believes that "everything we say about God is symbolic."[339] Religious symbols—doctrines or beliefs—should not be interpreted in a literal way. They are symbols of the faith of a religious community, symbolic expressions of the ultimate concern of their members. These religious symbols are assertions about God that involve a negation—*via negativa*.[340] God is something completely hidden to human knowledge because nothing concrete or literal can be said about Him and His actions. Consequently, as Lewis

---

336. Leonard R. Brand, "A Biblical Perspective on the Philosophy of Science," *Origins* 59 (2006): 12-13, 15-18. See pp. 186-188, 188-189 in this chapter. See also Guy, "Purpose and Function of Scripture," 91-96; Guy, "Interpreting Genesis One," 12.

337. See Brand, "A Biblical Perspective," 15. See footnote 331 in this chapter.

338. Guy actually refers to Tillich in this regard among other theologians. Guy, *Thinking Theologically*, 185, n. 7. See also Fritz Guy, "The Presence of Ultimacy," *Spectrum* 9, no. 1 (1977): 48, 53, n. 1, 54, n. 4. Regarding the understanding of theology as symbolic, see also Macquarrie, *Christian Theology*, 175-370.

339. Tillich, *Systematic Theology*, 2:9. "Everything religion has to say about God, including his qualities, actions, and manifestations, has a symbolic character and that the meaning of 'God' is completely missed if one takes the symbolic language literally." Ibid. See also ibid., 1:238-241. See also Paul Tillich, *Dynamics of Faith* (New York, NY: Harper, 1957), 51.

340. See Tillich, *Systematic Theology*, 1:239-240; Tillich, *Dynamics of Faith*, 117.

S. Ford says, "Tillich's *via symbolica* becomes a *via negativa*."[341]

This evaluation is also valid regarding Guy and modern Adventist theology. Guy, in particular, is not consistent when he affirms God's temporality while at the same time he applies the *via symbolica* or *via negativa* to the interpretation of God and doctrines in general. He cannot reasonably affirm that God is temporal without qualifications, while at the same time he denies that it is possible to talk about heavenly realities using spatio-temporal terms because they have to be interpreted applying a "negative argument."[342]

Process thought has conditioned the modern Adventist understanding of the nature of God, His actions, and His relation to the world-humanity in several other aspects. First, although modern Adventist theologians hold that God is timeless in one aspect, they situate God's knowledge and experience in relation to the world in the realm of divine temporality, His temporal pole. As process thought interprets God's temporal knowledge of the future in a virtually univocal way, similar to the human knowledge of the future, Guy and other modern Adventist theologians do the same. God does not have any exhaustive knowledge of the future.

Moreover, God is not omnipotent in modern Adventist theology, in line with process theology. This is the case because not only does God limit His power regarding the power of His creatures—including non-intelligent creatures—but also because His response to the world's events is limited to His creative reactions to them once they already happened. This response tries to incorporate those events in the fulfillment of God's intention. However, God is not completely sovereign in terms of His possibilities to response to the world's events because He does not know events still in the future.

As these convictions do not stem from Scripture but from philosophical presuppositions underlying modern theology, modern Adventist theology is unable to explain the phenomenon of biblical apocalyptic prophecy. Prophecies of books such as Daniel and Revelation involve

---

341. Lewis S. Ford, "Tillich and Thomas: The Analogy of Being," *The Journal of Religion* 46, no. 2 (1966): 244. Emphasis in original.

342. Guy seems to use this expression as virtually a synonym for *negative way*. He applies this negative argument to heavenly realities and the heavenly sanctuary. Guy, "Confidence in Salvation," 45. Regarding Guy's depiction of heavenly realities as not describable through spatio-temporal terms, see Guy, *Thinking Theologically*, 244. See also the discussion in pp. 186, 197 in this chapter.

complex and detailed anticipations of interactions between God and the world-humanity, where God acts as the sovereign of history. Guy, Rice, and Larson avoid commenting on these prophecies that assume that God is able to know not only the past and the present, but also the future (Dan 2:28; Rev 1:19).[343]

Another conditioning of process thought on modern Adventist theology is the affirmation of the freedom of the world in general—and created things in particular—to choose or contribute to the creation of its own reality. The parallel with the freedom of the occasions—in process ontology—to determine to what extent they will follow the initial aim provided by God is not difficult to see. As in process thought, the world is free to "decide" to produce natural evil. Guy and Bull follow, regarding this issue, Polkinghorne's explanation about what he denominates as *free-process defense*.[344] This concept derives from process philosophy (Whitehead, Hartshorne). It is an expansion of the concept of *free-will defense*, according to which the evil in the world is the result of wrong moral decisions by moral creatures. Free-process defense involves the entire physical world, which is gifted with freedom because of God's love.[345]

While Guy affirms that evil is not ontologically necessary, it is difficult to see how natural evil—manifested in the process of evolution that resulted in the emergence of human beings—did not favor the appearance of moral evil too. After all, as Polkinghorne points out, the gift of freedom, which is a gift of love, allows the creatures to be themselves according to their proper character. Snow produces destructive

---

343. This avoidance is particularly striking in the case of Rice who has a section dedicated to eschatology in his *Reign of God*. The same happens in his writings dedicated to explicate biblical prophecy in general in the context of his open view of God. See Rice, *Reign of God*, 319-332; Rice, *God's Foreknowledge*, 75-81; Rice, "Biblical Support," 50-53. See also Kassay, "Richard Rice's Anticipatory Theory," 239.

344. See Guy, *Thinking Theologically*, 145, n. 26; Bull, "Living in Incommensurate Worlds," 23, n. 7.

345. John Polkinghorne, *Science and Providence: God's Interaction With the World* (Philadelphia, PA: Templeton Foundation, 2005), 77; Thomas J. Oord, "Free Process Defense," *Encyclopedia of Science and Religion*, ed. J. Wentzel V. van Huyssteen (New York, NY: Macmillan, 2003), 339. "That world is endowed in its fundamental constitution with an anthropic potentiality which makes it capable of fruitful evolution. The exploration and realization of that potentiality is achieved by the universe through the continual interplay of chance and necessity within its unfolding process. The cosmos is given the opportunity to be itself." Polkinghorne, *Science and Providence*, 77.

avalanches, lions attack their prey, cells mutate to produce new life or cancer, and "it is the nature of humankind that sometimes people will act with selfless generosity but sometimes with murderous selfishness."[346] Polkinghorne concludes that these things "are the necessary cost of a creation given by its Creator the freedom to be itself. Not all that happens is in accordance with God's will because God has stood back, making metaphysical room for creaturely action."[347]

Modern Adventist theology goes in the direction of what can be called as an "Adventist" version of kenotic Trinitarian panentheism.[348] In this version of panentheism, the world is essential to God, although not necessary. This position implies that the world is not eternal or ontologically necessary for God, as in process thought, but it is still essential to demonstrate God's nature of love beyond the boundaries of the Godhead.[349]

God limits Himself in order to provide "space" for His creatures. In this sense, God created the world *ex nihilo* through a process that follows a kenotic Christological pattern by which God self-emptied and invested Himself in the world in a demonstration of supreme love and infinite vulnerability that allowed the world to be itself. Every creature, including unanimated ones, has some power for self-determination in a way that does not necessarily harmonize with God's will.[350]

---

346. Polkinghorne, *Belief in God*, 13.

347. Ibid.

348. Regarding the notion of kenotic Trinitarian panentheism, see Philip Clayton, "Kenotic Trinitarian Panentheism," *Dialog: A Journal of Theology* 44, no. 3 (2005): 250-255. Clayton understands his own position as an intermediate between open theism and process theology. He combines *creatio ex nihilo* with a Trinitarian panentheism. In the following paragraphs, the language describing the modern Adventist understanding of the relationship between God and the world deliberately uses his own vocabulary and concepts already introduced during the previous discussion of the modern Adventist interpretation of the principle of articulation.

349. Clayton expresses a similar idea in ibid., 251. See also Larson's explanation about the world as essential but not ontologically necessary for God in pp. 195-196 of this chapter. The distinction between *essential* and *necessary* is problematic. If the world is essential to God by His own decision, as Larson suggests, then, it means that there was a moment in the past when the world was not essential to God because He had not yet decided that the world would be essential for Him. On the other hand, it could be argued that this "decision" pertains to the timeless pole of God, and therefore, there is not a "moment" in temporal terms in which He made that decision. In that case, however, the decision would be unchangeable, unavoidable. Can something essential to God's nature also be unnecessary?

350. These concepts are virtually all present in Guy. See pp. 199-200 in this

Consequently, God's only option to create is through a providentially guided evolution. Otherwise, the results of Creation would be God's arbitrary imposition. Natural evil is the consequence of intrinsic possibilities—the existence of free process—already present in the world from the beginning, which unfolded through the evolutionary process. Moral evil is the result of human decisions but it is not completely separate from natural evil because humans are outcomes of an evolutionary process that involves natural evil. In this process, God is committed to promoting flourishing, fulfillment, creativity, and enjoyment based on His timeless character of love.

As God is love, He can lead His creation and articulate the whole reality only in terms of persuasion. God is not an omnipotent overwhelming power that judges, forces, or controls His creatures. God articulates reality through a persuasive providential action that is radically immanent in the world and it is not usually distinguishable from natural causality itself. Miracles are mainly in the eyes of the observer. God suffers with the world and tries to attract or lure it with His love. Christ's sacrifice would be a way to demonstrate God's love. God's persuasive love is stronger than coercion and is the way by which God finally will defeat the evil in the universe.

The previous landscape suggests that the ontology of becoming and the panentheistic view of God, common in modern theology, have a strong influence on the interpretation of the principle of articulation in modern Adventist theology.[351] In turn, this interpretation of the principle of articulation implies a substantive reinterpretation of several

---

chapter. The connection with Polkinghorne and Moltmann is evident. Both are quoted in Guy, "Interpreting Genesis One," 16, n. 46; Guy, *Thinking Theologically*, 145, n. 26, 145, no. 27. Regarding the similarities to Polkinghorne see, for example, John Polkinghorne, *Science and the Trinity: The Christian Encounter With Reality* (New Haven, CT: Yale University Press, 2004), 96-97. Regarding the similarities to Moltmann, see Jürgen Moltmann, *The Trinity and the Kingdom: The Doctrine of God*, trans. Margaret Kohl (Minneapolis, MN: Fortress, 1993), 109, 118. According to Moltmann, "The divine kenosis which begins with the creation of the world reaches its perfected and completed form in the incarnation of the Son." Ibid., 118. See also Clayton, "Kenotic Trinitarian Panentheism," 252 and the references there; Holmes Rolston III, "Does Nature Need to Be Redeemed?" *Zygon* 29, no. 2 (1994): 218-221.

351. As Guy points out, the notion that everything is in becoming is a leading cultural intuition present in Western thought "since the eighteenth century. Thus even post-Barthian theology, which can hardly be accused of being dominated by Whiteheadian philosophy, can declare that God's being is in becoming." Guy, *Thinking Theologically*, 176. The same conclusion is valid for modern Adventist theology, too.

Adventist doctrines. The ontological dualism still underlying the dipolar view of God as well as the symbolic interpretation of doctrines, involves radical changes regarding the doctrines of the sanctuary and the judgment, to mention two prominent illustrations. Guy does not deny those doctrines but he reinterprets them in the light of the *via negativa*. The sanctuary becomes a revelatory *symbol* of God's continuous redemptive activity. The correspondence between the earthly and the heavenly sanctuary is functional, not literal.[352]

In the same line, the judgment and books of heaven symbolize that God considers every person as well as individual decisions and actions seriously.[353] The judgment refers to the transcendent moral order that governs the created order. It also represents that sin is not a permanent reality but an irregularity of that order.[354] The biblical language about the sanctuary and the judgment is not a literal depiction of a heavenly temple or of God's actions. They are real transcendent realities but not literal. "Meaning is not limited to literal signification."[355] No literal decisions are made in heaven.[356]

Guy does not admit the centrality of any Adventist distinctive doctrine in the Adventist theological system. He believes only in the possibility of a distinctive totality or whole.[357] The distinctiveness of this totality, however, is barely prominent considering not only the peripheral role that he ascribes to Adventist distinctive beliefs, but also its radical reinterpretation, as in the case of the sanctuary and the investigative judgment.

---

352. "The point of this *symbolic language* is to indicate that, although the exact nature of this reality is not known (or knowable) by human beings, the fact of its reality and its *revelatory function* are indeed known, and therefore that it is meaningful to us." Guy, "Confidence in Salvation," 45. Emphasis mine.

353. Ibid., 45, 48. "The correspondence between earthly and heavenly reality is best understood in terms of eternal principles, ultimate values and interpersonal relationships." Ibid., 45.

354. Ibid., 49.

355. Ibid., 45. Regarding the biblical language of the sanctuary as symbolic, see also Guy, *Thinking Theologically*, viii, 135.

356. "To my knowledge, no current Adventist interpretation maintains that an examination of records is necessary for 'determining who are prepared for the kingdom of God' and will therefore be saved for eternity." Guy, *Thinking Theologically*, 91. Guy is quoting E. G. White, *The Great Controversy*, 428. Furthermore, it is not clear that 1844 has a literal meaning for Guy considering his symbolic interpretation of the sanctuary and the judgment.

357. Guy, *Thinking Theologically*, 251.

In practice, the possibility of a distinctive totality seems to be doubtful considering that from a methodological perspective, Guy and modern Adventist theology reject *sola Scriptura* and consequently, any possible distinctive theological method that builds upon biblical ontological and epistemological assumptions. It is clear that in modern Adventist theology the role of the multiple sources—particularly secular science and contemporary philosophy as well as theological traditions—is highly determinant of a theological system and the interpretation of its principle of articulation.

Adventist Theodicy Model

In contrast to the evangelical Adventist model (usually simply identified as evangelical Adventism) and the modern Adventist model (usually identified as progressive Adventism), the Adventist theodicy model remains unidentified as such in Adventist literature. It is possible to consider the Adventist theodicy model as equivalent to the so-called *mainstream Adventism*.[358] That identification is possible on the condition that the mainstream be considered with a certain flexibility.[359]

The fundamental characteristic shared by the representatives of this model is that they hold the *great controversy* as the binding theme of Adventist theology.[360] Usually, the proponents of Adventist theodicy model

---

358. For this designation, see Kenneth H. Wood, "The Mother of Us All: Mainstream Adventism," *Adventist Today*, January-February 1994, 4-5.

359. See ibid., 5. For example, some representatives of this model believe that Christ took an unfallen human nature while others believe that Christ took a fallen human nature and both groups are part of this model. See, for example, Benjamin Rand, "What Human Nature Did Jesus Take? Unfallen," *Ministry*, June 1985, 8, 10-21; Kenneth Gage, "What Human Nature Did Jesus Take? Fallen," *Ministry*, June 1985, 9-21. Benjamin Rand and Kenneth Gage are actually pseudonyms for Gulley and Herbert E. Douglass. For the purpose of this discussion, both authors can be considered as representatives of the Adventist theodicy model even if they have some theological differences between them. It should be reminded that models are explanatory patterns of complex realities. "There are no pure types [models] in any realm of life." Tillich, *Dynamics of Faith*, 55.

360. For the Adventist theodicy model, the great controversy motif works as the background for all other doctrines. "Against the background of the cosmic controversy between Christ and Satan, it [mainstream Adventists] sees itself as the remnant church, which keeps 'the commandments of God,' and has 'the testimony of Jesus Christ'—defined by the Revelator as 'the spirit of prophecy.' Its mission is to take the three angels' messages to 'every nation, and kindred, and tongue, and people.' The basis for this self-perception and mission is found in Revelation 14:6-12; 12:17;

highlight the essential role of E. G. White in the promotion of the great controversy theme in Adventist theology.[361] Woodrow W. Whidden, for example, considers the great controversy as an optimistic theological theodicy that constitutes E. G. White's central organizing theme.[362] According to Douglass, the great controversy theme is E. G. White's unifying or organizing principle, the conceptual key of her writings.[363]

In recent times, Joseph Battistone was probably the first to highlight the centrality of this theme in E. G. White's writings.[364] Even more recently, the topic of the great controversy as the center of Adventist theology has received significant attention by Adventist authors, at least partially motivated by the publication of a book about the warfare worldview in 1997 by Gregory A. Boyd, an evangelical theologian, advocator of open theism and theistic evolution.[365] After that year, many Adventist publications emphasizing the centrality of the great contro-

---

19:10." Wood, "The Mother of Us All," 4. Significantly, Wood does not mention the doctrine of the sanctuary in his article as part of the convictions of the mainstream Adventism. Several Adventist theologians refer to the cosmic controversy as central or fundamental for Adventist theology. Douglass affirms that the great controversy theme "is the core concept that brings coherence to all biblical subjects. . . . Herein lies the uniqueness of Adventism." Herbert E. Douglass, "The Great Controversy Theme: What It Means to Adventists," *Ministry*, December 2000, 5. According to Cindy Tutsch, the conflict between Christ and Satan is an interpretative lens. Cindy Tutsch, "Ellen White on Eschatology and the End of Evil," in *The Great Controversy and the End of Evil: Biblical and Theological Studies in Honor of Ángel Manuel Rodríguez in Celebration of His Seventieth Birthday*, ed. Gerhard Pfandl (Silver Spring, MD: Review & Herald, 2015), 285.

361. Probably, from a historical perspective, a crucial event in the development of the great controversy theme by E. G. White was her vision about the topic in 1858. See Michael W. Campbell, "Great Controversy Vision," *The Ellen G. White Encyclopedia*, ed. Denis Fortin and Jerry Moon, 2nd ed. (Hagerstown, MD: Review & Herald, 2013), 853-854.

362. Woodrow W. Whidden II, "The Triumph of God's Love: The Optimistic, Theological Theodicy of Ellen G. White," *AUSS* 53, no. 1 (2015): 197-214.

363. Douglass, *Messenger of the Lord*, 22. See E. G. White, *Education*, 125, 190. See also p. 138 in Chapter 3. Douglass also refers to this theme in E. G. White writings as "the heartbeat of Adventism." See the title of Herbert E. Douglass, comp. *The Heartbeat of Adventism: The Great Controversy Theme in the Writings of Ellen G. White* (Nampa, ID: Pacific Press, 2010).

364. See Joseph Battistone, *The Great Controversy Theme in E. G. White Writings* (Berrien Springs, MI: Andrews University Press, 1978). See also Douglass, *Messenger of the Lord*, 264, n. 5.

365. Gregory A. Boyd, *God at War: The Bible and Spiritual Conflict* (Downers Grove, IL: InterVarsity, 1997). See also Gregory A. Boyd, *Satan and the Problem of Evil* (Downers Grove, IL: InterVarsity, 2001).

versy, or commenting on its role in Adventist theology, quote or discuss Boyd's publications on the topic.[366]

However, the most important work in terms of the articulation of Adventist theology in the light of the great controversy theme is the one developed by Gulley in his *Systematic Theology*. This work has four volumes.[367] The discussion in this section is mainly based on that work, although complemented by other Adventist authors such as Davidson, who has written about this topic from a more biblical methodological perspective.

Ontological and Epistemological Presuppositions

Gulley reveals his ontological and epistemological presuppositions mainly in connection with his theological interest. He is aware that theological tradition in general has built upon the ontological assumption of the timelessness of being which is traceable to Parmenides, Plato, and Aristotle. Christian theological tradition assumed the Greek understanding of being as unchangeable, motionless, and

---

366. See, for example, Frank B. Holbrook, "The Great Controversy," in *Handbook of Seventh-day Adventist Theology*, ed. Raoul Dederen (Hagerstown, MD: Review & Herald, 2000), 1000; Whidden II, "The Triumph of God's Love," 197, n. 2; Richard M. Davidson, "Cosmic Metanarrative for the Coming Millennium," *JATS* 11, nos. 1-2 (2000): 102-119, who extensively quotes Boyd; Richard M. Davidson, "Ezekiel 28:11-19 and the Rise of the Cosmic Conflict," *The Great Controversy and the End of Evil: Biblical and Theological Studies in Honor of Ángel Manuel Rodríguez in Celebration of His Seventieth Birthday*, ed. Gerhard Pfandl (Silver Spring, MD: Review & Herald, 2015), 58; Tutsch, "Ellen White on Eschatology," 286. Usually these sources quote Boyd in positive terms because, as Gulley states, "Boyd can be applauded for calling attention to the cosmic controversy." Gulley, *Prolegomena*, 413. However, some publications also have reacted to Boyd showing the differences between his understanding of the biblical warfare worldview and the one of E. G. White and Adventists about the great controversy. See Gulley's discussion of Boyd's interpretation of the biblical worldview in Gulley, *Prolegomena*, 407-414. See also Martha O. Duah, "A Study of Warfare Theodicy in the Writings of Ellen G. White and Gregory A. Boyd" (PhD diss., Andrews University, Berrien Springs, MI, 2012).

367. Gulley, *Prolegomena* (vol. 1); Norman R. Gulley, *Systematic Theology*, vol. 2, *God as Trinity* (Berrien Springs, MI: Andrews University Press, 2011); Gulley, *Creation, Christ, Salvation* (vol. 3); Norman R. Gulley, *Systematic Theology*, vol. 4, *The Church and the Last Things* (Berrien Springs, MI: Andrews University Press, 2016). See also Norman R. Gulley, "The Cosmic Controversy: World View for Theology and Life," *JATS* 7, no. 2 (1996): 82-124.

timeless and ascribed these characteristics to God.[368]

Gulley also considers that Heidegger is the philosopher who in recent times overcame the traditional view of being as timeless and interpreted it as temporal, although he did it from the perspective of human existence. He thinks, however, that it is also necessary to interpret "God as temporal in His relation with human existence in the historical-temporal flux of divine-human relationship."[369] Gulley, then, recognizes that change and becoming are basic characteristics of reality although not necessarily in the way that process thought understands them.[370]

Gulley holds that no one lives without presuppositions. Knowledge is never completely objective as empiricism or positivism seems to claim.[371] Consequently, the knower cannot know exhaustively the reality that he/she seeks to understand, although a progression in knowledge is possible.[372] At the same time, Gulley rejects the Kantian reductionist understanding of knowledge as only empirical knowledge that led in theology to see revelation in a non-cognitive way. Following Canale, he highlights that philosophy traditionally assumed a timeless view of reason while he holds that theology should hold an interpretation of reason as temporal, in harmony with the temporal nature of the cognitive self-revelation of God in Scripture.[373]

As the epistemological foundation of theology, Gulley and Davidson propose following the *sola Scriptura* principle.[374] Gulley, thus,

---

368. Gulley, *Prolegomena*, 4-8.
369. Ibid., 9-10. Gulley considers that "this [interpretation] was accomplished by Fernando Canale." Ibid., 10.
370. Ibid., 86. The difference between Gulley and process thought regarding the understanding of becoming is clearer in the discussion about Gulley's interpretation of God and the world. See in this chapter pp. 221-229.
371. Ibid., 22, 69. "There is no fully objective observation of reality, for the observer always brings to the process his or her culture, training, and, therefore, presuppositions, assumptions, and premises. The mind is never a *tabula rasa* (empty). To some degree . . . we do filter reality through the contours of our mind." Ibid., 162. Emphasis in original.
372. Ibid., 36. Gulley is aware that epistemological foundationalism has been under questioning in recent times. Although the title of Chapter 3 in his *Prolegomena* is "Foundationalism," apparently, he understands the term in the context of his discussion about the sources of theology, where he defends the idea of Scripture as the only valid foundation for theology (Eph 2:20). Ibid., 95, 97-98.
373. Ibid., 29, 373-374.
374. See, for example, ibid., 166-168, 372-373, 421, 694-695. Gulley's intention is to base his theological system on the *sola Scriptura* principle. Ibid., xxii. See also Gulley, *Church and the Last Things*, 18, 487; Davidson, "Biblical Interpretation," 60.

cannot agree with Guy's *prima Scriptura* (Wesleyan quadrilateral)[375] or with the notion—also common in modern Adventist theology—that the experience of the community of believers is a valid source for theology.[376] While philosophy can help theology to provide methodological precision, it does not have any foundational role in theology.[377] Science should not intimidate theology either.[378] Scripture is above tradition as well. "The only way to check whether reason, tradition, or experience is authentic is by Scripture."[379] Gulley and Davidson not only hold the *sola Scriptura* principle but, in consonance, they also believe that as a source of theology Scripture is sufficient, reliable, clear, and internally consistent. Thus, Scripture is the interpreter of Scripture itself. Moreover, Scripture as a whole—not only some parts—is the standard for testing theology.[380]

As Gulley understands that knowledge involves presuppositions, he also believes that the reader of the Bible always approaches the text with presuppositions that can aid or hinder a better comprehension. Those presuppositions can include denominational beliefs and personal convictions. In order to preclude the reading of one's theology in the text, it is necessary to be open to the interpretation of that text through history.[381] Faith is a condition for a better understanding of Scripture but it is also a result of a reading with faith.[382] The student has to allow the text to inform and correct presuppositions.[383]

---

375. Gulley, *Prolegomena*, 112. See also 557-559. Regarding Guy's understanding of the sources of theology, see in this chapter pp. 186-191.

376. Gulley, from his *sola Scriptura* perspective, criticizes Rice's position in that sense. "Rice adds the dynamic experience of the Christian community as a source and criterion of Christian beliefs to Scripture's role in the same. . . . If Christian beliefs are found in Scripture, does this not unwittingly place Christian experience as a source and criterion over Scripture?" Gulley, *Prolegomena*, 372. Regarding Rice's position, see pp. 190-191 in this chapter. This disagreement seems to imply a different understanding of the object of theology: For Gulley it is Scripture, while for modern Adventist theology it is the beliefs and experiences of the religious community.

377. Gulley, *Prolegomena*, 43, 92-93.

378. Ibid., 154-157. "Theological science is independent, as are all other sciences that remain true to their own given objects." Ibid., 155.

379. Ibid., 709.

380. Gulley, *Prolegomena*, 661-668, 674-677; Davidson, "Biblical Interpretation," 61-66.

381. Gulley, *Prolegomena*, 657, 655.

382. Ibid., 73-74. See also Davidson, "Biblical Interpretation," 66-68.

383. Ibid., 152. In a similar vein, Davidson suggests, "Interpreters must make a decision that their preunderstandings will derive from and be under the control of

Gulley holds that the understanding of Scripture is progressive. The text has one meaning if it is seen from the Holy Spirit's intention as the Author, but from the reader's perspective, the meaning is always changing because there is always the possibility of a better understanding as the result of successive readings. Gulley identifies this process as a *hermeneutical circle* in a way that is reminiscent of Gadamer's circle of understanding. Apparently, Gulley considers that there is no clear limit to this progression in biblical knowledge.[384] There is always the possibility to go deeper into this process. The successive change in the reader is the result of the *hermeneutical spiral*.[385] In consonance, Gulley sees theology as an open-ended discipline.[386]

The Interpretation of God

Gulley rejects the traditional understanding of God as timeless, which is the result of the adoption by Christian tradition of the Greek philosophical ontology.[387] He alerts that the influence of Parmenidean ontology "has been enormous. The idea of God's timelessness is a foundational idea that has affected much of Christian theology."[388] Gulley

---

the Bible, constantly open to modification and enlargement of their ideas on the basis of Scripture. They must consciously reject any external keys or systems to impose on Scripture from without." Davidson, "Biblical Interpretation," 67.

384. Gulley, *Prolegomena*, 653. In this sense, Gulley's negative evaluation of Gadamer as assuming an essentially subjective hermeneutics seems to be a misunderstanding. See ibid., 589. Gadamer does believe in the possibility of arriving at a unity of meaning in the interpretation of the text by comparing rival interpretations. See pp. 28-29 and footnote 32 in Chapter 2.

385. Gulley, *Prolegomena*, 654, 653. Gulley takes the concept of hermeneutical spiral from Osborne, *The Hermeneutical Spiral*. "With growth in the knowledge of the Word, the reader brings a growing knowledge to the subsequent study of the Word. . . . So the life and situation of the reader is not just his or her cultural context but his or her biblical knowledge context." Gulley, *Prolegomena*, 653. Regarding the hermeneutical spiral, see also Davidson, "Biblical Interpretation," 66.

386. Gulley, *Prolegomena*, 151.

387. See, for example, ibid., xxiii, 1, 42.

388. Ibid., 6. For a discussion of philosophers and theologians who have contributed to promote the view of God as timeless, see Gulley, *God as Trinity*, 179-182; 184-193; Gulley, *Church and the Last Things*, 385. In his discussion Gulley includes Parmenides, Plato, Aristotle, Augustine, Aquinas, Francis Turretin, Schleiermacher, and more recent evangelical theologians, Augustus H. Strong, Louis Berkhof, Wayne Grudem, Norman L. Geisler, and Carl F. H. Henry. See also Gulley's evaluation of other theologians such as Herman Bavinck, Barth, or Erickson. Gulley, *God as Trinity*, 193-198. He considers that they admit some kind of temporality in God—at least

admits that there is some justification for process theology's rejection of the Thomistic interpretation of God as unchangeable.[389] Gulley, however, is aware that process theology "was intended to replace the classical God but it was merely a nonbiblical view of God attempting to replace a nonbiblical view of God."[390] Gulley also rejects the version of process ontology that Guy follows as a modern Adventist.[391]

Gulley proposes an understanding of God as relational Trinity. This view of the Trinity implies that the Father, Son, and Holy Spirit "experience an eternal, divine, reciprocal love among themselves, which necessitates a temporal experience in the give-and-take exchange in their nature as God of love."[392] The mutual loving and dynamic relationship among the members of the Godhead necessarily involves the fact that God is temporal and that He has always been so. As God is love, His love does not appear after the creation of the world. He manifests toward His creation the love that already pre-exists in the context of the Godhead.[393]

Gulley sees God's nature in terms of love. Before the Fall and the introduction of the problem of sin, the best way to describe God's nature is simply *love*. During the existence of sin, though, Gulley prefers to describe God's nature as *holy love* because, in this context, God manifests His anger against sin and He has to act as a judge. Even here, however, God's punishment upon the impenitent is not a negation of God's love but rather a demonstration of His love for those who fol-

---

partially. His evaluation is probably debatable. The same happens with his suggestion that Tillich and Pannenberg holds a temporal view of God. See ibid., 206-207. This fact, however, does not preclude appreciating in general Gulley's valuable argumentation in order to demonstrate that the view of God as timeless has a philosophical origin.

389. Gulley, *Prolegomena*, 77. See also Gulley, *God as Trinity*, 219.

390. Gulley, *God as Trinity*, 240. Gulley adds that process theology, in relation to classical theology, constitutes "merely an exchange of one set of problems (immutable/impassible) for another set of problems (dependent on world for body/dependent on human decisions to know the future)." Ibid. See Gulley's discussion and evaluation regarding process theology and open theism in ibid., 231-272. See also Gulley, *Prolegomena*, 76-88.

391. Gulley, *Prolegomena*, 115. Gulley identifies Guy's understanding of reality as becoming, as a "process ontology [that] goes back to the philosophy of A. N. Whitehead." Ibid.

392. Gulley, *God as Trinity*, 3. See also ibid., 20, 22-32, 45, 121, 176. "The Trinitarian interrelationship is temporal, not timeless. For any true relationship requires a temporal give-and-take among the three Persons." Ibid., 168.

393. See ibid., 4, 50, 130.

lowed Him. Rightly understood, all God's acts are in harmony with His nature of love. The supreme demonstration of God's holy love takes place on the cross. The cross meets justice and mercy. At the end of the cosmic controversy, though, God's nature is again better described as simply love because holy love is not necessary any more.[394]

According to Gulley, then, love is "the very nature of God, and not merely one of His attributes."[395] The persons of the Godhead, although transcendent in relation to creation, have a relationship of love among them, which is immanent in the Deity. This love is never holy love, which is only necessary because of the relationship with sinful creatures. Thus, even during the cosmic controversy, the immanent love of the members of the Deity remains the same.[396]

Gulley, following Barth to some extent, opposes the scholastic dualistic separation between God as He is in Himself (God's being) and His attributes and acts. Attributes are just a manifestation of God's being. All attributes of God are in harmony with God's love or His holy love and they reveal His love. Gulley then classifies the attributes in two classes: incommunicable and communicable. The first class includes those attributes that describe God as He is independent of His creation (in Himself), and the second class includes those attributes that describe God in relation to creation. Ultimately, however, all attributes pertain to God's being or nature. The first group explains what is unique regarding God, while the second group explains what He shares with His creatures.[397]

Gulley, though, admits that this classification has some limitations. For example, omniscience, on the one hand, could be a part of the incommunicable attributes if it is considered in absolute terms. On the other hand, it can also be communicable to the extent that intelligent creatures have the possibility of knowing at least a small part of God's unlimited knowledge. Gulley warns, then, that there is no attribute of God that is absolutely communicable while at the same time there is no divine attribute absolutely incommunicable. He thinks that no classifi-

---

394. See Gulley's discussion about love and holy love in ibid., 45-50.
395. Ibid., 53. This statement is Gulley's conclusion after the discussion of biblical evidence in ibid., 51-53, 44.
396. Ibid., 49-50.
397. Ibid., 61-63. See also ibid., 66-67. Gulley evaluates that the sum of God's revealed attributes is the hermeneutical context for understanding any particular attribute. Ibid., 62.

cation does justice to the attributes of God.[398]

Gulley also admits that the classification of attributes is just human. Scripture does not provide a classification. Gulley, nevertheless, wants to highlight the biblical distinction between God and His creatures, between His transcendence and immanence. He seems to consider that His attributes are communicable to a lesser or higher degree rather than strictly incommunicable or communicable. In any case, the attributes are real, revealed in God's Word. There is no way to discover them through human reason or feelings.[399]

Gulley, then, describes the attributes based on his classification. On the one hand, the incommunicable attributes comprehend God's independence (self-existence), omnipresence (God is present everywhere and even beyond all space), eternity (in the sense of everlastingness), omnipotence, omniscience (including foreknowledge), and constancy (unchanging character and purpose). There is a total identity between God's character of love and His attributes.[400] On the other hand, communicable attributes refer to God's self-impartation. Gulley includes here the fruit of the Spirit mentioned in Gal 5:22-23 and the gifts of the Spirit mentioned in Rom 12, 1 Cor 12, and Eph 4. Gulley highlights that the fruit of the Spirit is essentially one: love (see 1 Cor 13). At the same time, he underlines that the gift of prophecy is the only one that appears in all the list of gifts in the New Testament and it is probably the most important (1 Cor 14:1, 39) because it relates to God's self-revelation during the cosmic controversy.[401]

Gulley does not consider, in his description of God's attributes, the traditional notions of immutability and impassibility. They assume God's timelessness and the application of the *via negativa*. If God is unchangeable and unable to experience feelings because of something external to Him, He cannot be the relational God of love.[402]

Gulley deeply believes that the interrelationship and the unity of the triune God has to be understood in terms of a historical reciprocal love. The three members of the Trinity are equal, self-existent, al-

---

398. Ibid., 63, 64.
399. See Gulley's discussion and qualification regarding this classification in ibid., 64-67.
400. See Gulley's discussion of incommunicable attributes in ibid., 67-73.
401. See Gulley's discussion of communicable attributes in ibid., 73-77.
402. Ibid., 217-220, 223, 224. Gulley documents the Greek origin of this classical view of God as immutable and impassible in ibid., 219-225.

though with different functions in the context of the plan of salvation. There is no eternal or timeless generation of the Son and no timeless procession of the Holy Spirit as traditional theology affirmed. Gulley rejects the traditional view of the relations between the members of the Trinity as relations of timeless origin. This mistaken formulation of the relation between the members of the Trinity plagues the theologies of the East and the West.[403]

Gulley finds then that his view of God as relational Trinity with an everlasting history of reciprocal love is incompatible with the timeless view of God and the classical understanding of God's transcendence and immanence. He finds biblical evidence for his temporal interpretation of God in the fact that Scripture understands God's eternity as a synonym for everlastingness.[404] There are also biblical texts showing God's temporality or temporal activities even before Creation (Mic 5:2; Prov 8:23; Eph 1:4-5).[405]

Gulley concludes that God's temporality is quantitatively and qualitatively different from the time of His creation. God's time is *infinite time*, in contrast to the *finite time* of creation. God is infinite, without beginning or ending. However, infinite and finite times are both sequential, making God's temporality *compatible* with creation's temporality. "God's transcendence is not different from His immanence, for it is the transcendent/immanent God who is fully present at both levels of His presence. God's transcendent presence in infinite time is not different from His immanence in finite time."[406] Gulley's understanding of God's infinite time allows him to affirm that "*God is transcendent in His immanence.*"[407]

Another issue regarding Gulley's interpretation of God relates to his view of anthropomorphisms to talk about God in the Bible. In spite of his interpretation of God as temporal, Gulley hesitates to interpret biblical descriptions of God as having a physical aspect in literal terms. He admits that according to Christ, God has a *form* (John 5:37). Gulley, then, enumerates an extensive list of God's physical char-

---

403. Ibid., 121, 130, 134, 135.
404. Gulley quotes, for example, 1 Chr 16:36; 29:10; Pss 41:13; 92:2; 103:17; 106:48, etc. See ibid., 174, 175.
405. Gulley actually includes in his discussion several other texts. See ibid., 175, 176.
406. Ibid., 205, 210.
407. Ibid., 216. Emphasis in original.

acteristics taken from Bavinck, a Reformed theologian, that includes, for example, voice (John 5:37), face (Exod 33:20, 23), back (Jer 18:17), arm (Exod 15:16), and bosom (Ps 74:11).[408]

Gulley considers, following Bavinck,[409] that these expressions are anthropomorphisms by which Scripture accommodates to human finite intellect. The reader should take into account that God is spirit (John 4:24) and omnipresent (Jer 23:24). Gulley warns against speculation regarding God's physical characteristics. At the same time, he is aware that according to Scripture, God created humans in His own image (Gen 1:26-27) with His own hands (Gen 2:7, 21-22) and there are other biblical descriptions of God as having physical characteristics (Gen 3:8; 18:1-33; Isa 6:1, etc.).[410] Gulley highlights, however, that all these references depict God before Christ's incarnation.[411] Gulley admits, nonetheless, that the Bible presents God as having a location (Dan 7:9-10), although He is omnipresent.[412] It seems that Gulley understands God's physical appearance in connection with Christ's incarnation, and not necessarily as a real or literal characteristic of God.[413]

Something similar happens with biblical depictions of God's emotions. Feelings such as joy (Isa 62:5; 65:19), sorrow (Ps 78:40; Isa 63:10), or wrath represents accommodation language. According to Gulley—and in line with Bavinck—they are actually descriptions of God in terms of human emotions in order "to accommodate our finite human understanding of God who is infinite."[414]

A last consideration regarding Gulley's interpretation of God is that, in harmony with his view of God as temporal, he also considers heaven—the dwelling place of God—as spatio-temporal. He holds, for example, that the biblical descriptions of the heavenly sanctuary are literal.[415] In more technical terms, Gulley suggests that "the original

---

408. Ibid., 57. See Herman Bavinck, *Reformed Dogmatics*, vol. 2, *God and Creation*, trans. John Vriend (Grand Rapids, MI: Baker, 2004), 100.

409. Gulley quotes Bavinck in positive terms when he affirms, "Scripture does not just contain a few scattered anthropomorphisms but is anthropomorphic through and through.... God stoops down to his creatures, speaking and appearing to them in human fashion." Bavinck, *God and Creation*, 99-100. See Gulley, *God as Trinity*, 57.

410. Gulley, *God as Trinity*, 57-58.

411. Ibid., 58.

412. Ibid. See also ibid., 213; Gulley, *Creation, Christ, Salvation*, 668.

413. See Gulley, *God as Trinity*, 58, 212.

414. Ibid., 58. See also Gulley, *Prolegomena*, 82.

415. Gulley, *God as Trinity*, 446. Gulley believes that there is a heavenly sanctu-

sanctuary (in heaven) is just as ontologically real in function and furniture as is the typical sanctuary (on earth, see Heb. 9)."[416]

Interpretation of the World

The proponents of the theodicy model in general believe in a recent six-day creation of the world in line with the description of Creation in Gen 1-2. Gulley is a typical representative of this position, along with Davidson.[417] In harmony with his view of God as relational Trinity, Gulley understands Creation as a temporal action of God.[418] The fact that God is a relational and loving God implies that God cannot use an unloving and evil way to create the world, as it is the case with evolution, where suffering and death are part of the creative process.[419]

---

ary with two rooms, where God has His throne, in typological correspondence with the earthly sanctuary. The spatial location of God in His physical dwelling place or heavenly sanctuary is not incompatible with God's omnipresence, as Christ's presence in the Most Holy Place of the earthly sanctuary before His incarnation was not incompatible with His omnipresence. Gulley, *Creation, Christ, Salvation*, 668. "One should not be concerned that heaven's sanctuary has two rooms, any more than we should be concerned by Christ's words, 'In my Father's house are many rooms.' . . . Of course, the magnitude of these rooms is beyond our grasp, but that doesn't question their reality." Ibid., 668, n. 16. See also ibid., 493, n. 29. For Gulley, between the heavenly and the earthly sanctuary, "there is a spatiotemporal correspondence." Gulley, *Church and the Last Things*, 23.

416. Gulley, *God as Trinity*, 458. See ibid., 453. In a similar vein, Davidson affirms, "According to the Scripture God is not essentially incompatible with space and time; He is the very God who has dwelt 'from the beginning' (Jer 17:12) in a heavenly palace or temple; who truly dwelt in the sanctuary in the wilderness and in the Jerusalem Temple; who, in the ongoing work of redemption, is now engaged in a real, historical-temporal activity in a real spatiotemporal heavenly sanctuary." Richard M. Davidson, "Sanctuary Typology," in *Symposium on Revelation*, vol. 1, *Introductory and Exegetical Studies*, ed. Frank B. Holbrook (Silver Spring, MD: Biblical Research Institute, GC of SDAs, 1992), 105. See also Davidson, "Inauguration or Day of Atonement?" 86-87.

417. Regarding Davidson's understanding of Creation, see Richard M. Davidson, "The Genesis Account of Origins," in *The Genesis Creation Account and Its Reverberations in the Old Testament*, ed. Gerald A. Klingbeil (Berrien Springs, MI: Andrews University Press, 2015), 59-129; Richard M. Davidson, "Understanding the 'When' of Creation in Genesis 1-2," in *In the Beginning: Science and Scripture Confirm Creation*, ed. Bryan W. Ball (Nampa, ID: Pacific Press, 2012), 97-113.

418. Gulley, *Creation, Christ, Salvation*, xxi.

419. Ibid., 12, 14. Gulley believes that the timeless view of God facilitates understanding Creation in terms of evolution because a timeless God cannot participate in a temporal creation and still remain timeless. Ibid., 10. Gulley thinks that Augustine

Gulley also rejects the notion of the eternity of the world as incompatible with the biblical understanding of Creation. There is an absolute beginning of the world. God is omnipotent. He does not depend on the world as process theology holds, nor does He need an evolutionary process to create it. A creation through a process of evolution is inconsistent with an instantaneous final resurrection and re-creation of the world.[420]

Gulley holds that the creation of angels precedes the Creation week of Gen 1, as well as the rebellion of angels in heaven. There is no need to postulate a creation of angels at the beginning or during the Creation week as many Greek and Latin Church Fathers affirmed. They usually believed that time appeared during the Creation week. A creation of angels before that week seemed to be impossible. However, if God is temporal, God has a history, which is prior to the history of the earth. Time, then, did not appear with the Creation week.[421] Evidently, Gulley believes in a prior creation including—or consisting in—the creation of angels before the creation of the earth.[422]

Gulley believes, however, that Gen 1:1 refers to a creation *ex nihilo* (see Rom 4:17; Heb 11:3) in the sense of a creation that does not depend on something that existed before—although angels already existed at the moment to start the Creation week. There is no eternal

---

prepared the way for this perspective of Creation because he held that God created the world but without compromising His unchangeability. Ibid. For Augustine's interpretation of the world and Creation, see pp. 73-74 in Chapter 3.

420. Gulley, *Creation, Christ, Salvation*, 10-12. See also ibid., 74, 83-84.

421. "Time is not located in the first creative act of God, but in the Creator Himself, in His inner-Trinitarian history from eternity. For such a God, the creation of angels before humans is not a problem, for history is not confined to planet earth. History is embedded in the eternal divine relationship of the Trinity." Gulley, *God as Trinity*, 278.

422. Gulley, however, evaluates the possibility of a passive gap between Gen 1:1 and 1:3 negatively. According to this view, Gen 1:1 refers to the creation of heaven and earth in general (the universe) while Gen 1:3 onward refers to the organization of the earth and the creation of life on the planet. See Gulley's discussion on this interpretation in Gulley, *Creation, Christ, Salvation*, 26-30, and his evaluation of this theory in ibid., 30-31. Gulley's evaluation follows—at least partially—Marco T. Terreros, "What Is an Adventist? Someone Who Upholds Creation," *JATS* 7, no. 2 (1996): 147-149. Davidson, on the other hand, supports the possibility of a passive gap. See, for example, Davidson, "The Genesis Account of Origins," 87-102. Nevertheless, beyond the differences in the exegesis of Gen 1:1-3, Gulley and Davidson agree that there is a creation prior to the Creation week of Gen 1, which is in harmony with the general Adventist historical understanding of the origin of the great controversy. See ibid., 49-50.

matter. Everything exists because God has sustained it from the beginning and He has a purpose for His creation.[423]

Gulley rejects a non-literal interpretation of the Genesis account of Creation. The narrative has a theological purpose—that involves the introduction of the Sabbath—but is not disconnected from the literal meaning of the narrative. Creation was not instantaneous, as Augustine believed. The Creation days do not represent long periods or ages either. They are twenty-four-hour days.[424]

Gulley and Davidson also support the historicity of the biblical flood. They reject the possibility of a local flood and appeal to the biblical evidence for a global flood.[425] Gulley is aware of the challenge that represents the standard scientific interpretation of the geological column but he also suggests that scientists, as researches in general, have a bias in the interpretation of the evidence based on their philosophical convictions.[426] As in the case of the account of Creation, it is clear that the theological significance of the biblical story about the universal flood is inseparable from its historicity.[427]

The Interpretation of the Human Being

In harmony with his understanding of Creation, Gulley believes that the first human beings are not the product of evolution—or theistic evolution—but God's direct hands-on creation.[428] They were created in the image of God. Gulley seems to suggest that the image and likeness involve a similarity with God's form, although Gulley reminds that God is spirit and omnipresent, and thus, He is not limited to a body. The exception is Christ because He became human. Gulley, then, rejects that the affirmation that God has a form is anthropomorphic. God, moreover, takes physical form as in Christ's manifestations in the form of an angel or a human in the Old Testament. The image of

---

423. Gulley, *Creation, Christ, Salvation*, 33-38. Based on Job 38:7, Gulley affirms that "God's angels were [there], showing that the creation of planet earth was after the creation of angels." Ibid., 38.

424. See ibid., 38-42, 43-51, 53-56.

425. Ibid., 366-377; Richard M. Davidson, "The Genesis Flood Narrative: Crucial Issues in the Current Debate," *AUSS* 42, no. 1 (2004): 49-77; Davidson, "Biblical Evidence for the Universality."

426. Gulley, *Creation, Christ, Salvation*, 377-378, 384.

427. Davidson, "The Genesis Flood Narrative," 76.

428. Gulley, *Creation, Christ, Salvation*, 82-83, 85.

God, therefore, involves the physical aspect.[429] "The fact is God cannot be understood in His transcendency, but that must not interfere with the fact that God takes real form. Humans minds cannot comprehend how God can be omnipresent and yet localized in a specific form at the same time."[430]

The image of God, therefore, involves the whole human being. It is not confined to some aspect of the human person as the soul. It is what human beings are.[431] The image of God actually includes several aspects. First, human beings were created as male and female (Gen 1:27). The first couple had to reflect the Trinitarian interrelationship of love as equals—without subordination from one another—but with different functions, as the different functions of the members of the Trinity in the context of Creation.[432] Second, the image of God involves the dominion or rulership of man and woman over the other creatures, reflecting God's loving nature as protective stewards (Gen 1:26). Dominion is related to the ability to fructify and increase in number (Gen 1:28). Third, the image of God includes character—mental and spiritual attributes—and the possibility of reflecting God's communicable attributes. Human beings can enter in communion with God and worship Him. Finally, God's image implies the moral freedom to choose between good and evil (Gen 2:16-17).[433] Gulley evaluates its significance by saying that "without the freedom of choice, the other gifts . . . would be meaningless."[434]

Gulley believes that even after the Fall, God's image remains (Gen 9:6; 1 Cor 11:7; Jas 3:9). Humans are still unique in comparison with animals. The image was damaged but it was not destroyed. Human beings still have some moral autonomy. Thus, God does not need to

---

429. Ibid., 85, 90. See Gulley, *God as Trinity*, 279-280.
430. Gulley, *Creation, Christ, Salvation*, 85.
431. Ibid., 86, 109.
432. Ibid., 87-88, 95. Regarding the subordination debate in connection with the debate about eternal subordination in the Trinity, see ibid., 95-97.
433. Ibid., 87-89, 91-92, 103.
434. Ibid., 92. Davidson also supports a wholistic understanding of the image of God. Richard M. Davidson, "The Nature of the Human Being From the Beginning: Genesis 1-11," in *"What Are Human Beings That You Remember Them?" Proceedings of the Third International Bible Conference, Nof Ginosar and Jerusalem; June 11-21, 2012*, ed. Clinton Wahlen (Silver Spring, MD: Biblical Research Institute, 2015), 22. Emphasis in original. See ibid., 12-22.

predestine them—or some of them—in order to save them.⁴³⁵

Gulley—as Adventists in general—rejects any dualistic interpretation of the human being that supposes the existence of an immortal soul separable from the body. Human beings are a whole. A soul is not something that human possess. It is what they are. The notion of the immortality of the soul is an inheritance from the Greek thought. From a biblical perspective, there is no immortal life after death except through the participation in the resurrection that take place at the Second Coming where the believers will receive immortality (1 Cor 15:51-54; 1 Thess 4:16-17). The so-called intermediate state is a time of unconscious resting, according to the biblical depiction (John 11:11-14; 1 Cor 15:51; 1 Thess 4:13-14). Heaven will be a corporate experience, not an individual one.⁴³⁶ Gulley also rejects the existence of an actual hell as well as a purgatory. The wicked are destroyed in the second death at the end of the millennium.⁴³⁷

Gulley sees the problem of sin in the context of the cosmic conflict between God and Satan. The problem of sin actually started in heaven. Lucifer, a cherub who became Satan, rebelled against God, wanting to usurp His place. He fought against Christ and was casted out from heaven with a third of the angels who followed him (see Isa 14; Ezek 28; Rev 12). The conflict moved to the earth where the serpent or Satan (Rev 12:9) tempted Adam and Eve to distrust God and eat the fruit of the forbidden tree in order to be like God. Gulley believes in the historicity of the narrative of the Fall.⁴³⁸

The most obvious result of sin was the broken relationship between God and humanity, the broken relationship between humans, the curse of the ground, and the introduction of pain and death (Gen 3). Sin is more than an act of disobedience (1 John 3:4). It is also a spiritual—rather than genetic—tendency to sin inherited from Adam (Ps 51:5). Because of sin, the image of God in humanity was damaged. Through human sin, the whole nature suffered pain and death

---

435. Gulley, *Creation, Christ, Salvation*, 93-94, 109.

436. Ibid., 109-122, 125-126; Gulley, *Church and the Last Things*, 32, 235-236. See Davidson, "Nature of the Human Being," 22-25, 30-32, 40-41. See also Norman R. Gulley, *Christ Is Coming! A Christ-Centered Approach to Last-Day Events* (Hagerstown, MD: Review & Herald, 1998), 259-266, 277-298.

437. Gulley, *Church and the Last Things*, 245-247, 650-651, 692-695, 718-726; Gulley, *Christ Is Coming*, 268-275, 305-324; Gulley, *God as Trinity*, 299-304.

438. Gulley, *Creation, Christ, Salvation*, 136-142. Regarding the description of the beginning of the cosmic controversy in Gulley, see also Gulley, *Prolegomena*, 433-438.

and it was affected by the controversy (Rom 8:18-23). Satan also took Adam's place as the ruler of the world (Job 1). The only hope for humanity became God's promise of salvation (Gen 3:15).[439]

Gulley appeals to the concept of *total depravity* to explain the effect of sin regarding the image of God. He does not understand the concept in a Calvinistic way. Gulley believes that free will was not lost after the Fall but humans need the power of God in order to enable them to choose Him willingly. Total depravity implies that humanity became under Satan's control, although humanity does not share Adam's guilt as Augustine held. The effect of total depravity, however, involves the freedom to choose to the point that fallen humans, controlled by the power of sin, are unable to decide to follow God by their own choice. When God enables a person through the power of the Spirit, then the person is in condition to respond to God's initiative.[440] Apparently, Gulley sees himself in line with Arminian theology when he affirms that "theologians have called this approach of God to fallen people *prevenient grace*."[441] God operates through human conscience and nature to attract people and lead them to an experience of new birth.[442]

The Interpretation of the Articulating Agent

Gulley is aware that a system of theology requires inner coherence among its doctrines. He evidently thinks that Scripture has an implicit internal coherence. He also believes that the element that allows seeing the coherence or the articulation of Scripture is the biblical worldview.[443] The biblical worldview works as a hermeneutical indicator, framework, or guide that allows a consistent interpretation of the set of biblical doctrines and corrects them when they do not fit in that worldview.[444] This worldview makes a systematic theology possible because it influences the entire system. "It is the context within which the system is devel-

---

439. Gulley, *Creation, Christ, Salvation*, 104, 142-145, 156-158, 160. See also Davidson, "Nature of the Human Being," 32-38.
440. Gulley, *Creation, Christ, Salvation*, 146-149.
441. Ibid., 148. Emphasis in original. Gulley holds that Gentiles or non-Christians also respond to Christ although they do not know Him. He finds some support for this idea in John 1:9 that says that Christ enlightens everyone. Ibid., 149.
442. Ibid., 149-152.
443. Gulley, *Prolegomena*, xxvi.
444. Ibid., 140. According to Gulley, it is the task of systematic theology to penetrate Scripture in order to discover this worldview. Ibid.

oped. The worldview limits the boundaries of the system. To be true to Scripture, a system must accept the biblical worldview."[445]

Gulley also holds—in the context of his discussion of the postmodern opposition to the notion of system and worldviews—that "worldviews have a center."[446] At the same time, Gulley holds that "[theological] systems have a central focus around which each loci revolves.... There is a movement in the system when it has a *central focus or theme*."[447] Both, then, worldviews and theological systems have a moving center or central theme.

Gulley thinks that several theological systems in the past have developed their worldview based on cultural, philosophical, or scientific ideas, rather than on biblical materials. In contrast, he proposes developing his Adventist systematic theology from the perspective provided by the worldview of the *cosmic controversy* metanarrative.[448] Gulley considers that his proposal of the cosmic controversy as the worldview of Scripture—and of his theological system—is wider than a soteriological worldview.[449]

Since for Gulley the cosmic controversy is the biblical worldview, he describes this issue as "a theme in the system."[450] The central issue in the cosmic controversy is the question of the justice of God.[451] "*God as just* is the ultimate truth standing *at the center* of the cosmic controversy. A systematic theology must look at all the major loci from the vantage point of the cosmic controversy and examine them through the light of God's justice."[452] He considers that a theological system, in or-

---

445. Ibid., 142. For examples of non-biblical worldviews in Gulley, see ibid., 142, 390-392.

446. Ibid., 482.

447. Ibid., 145. Emphasis mine.

448. Ibid. "The cosmic controversy metanarrative provides the worldview within which the inner coherence of all doctrines is seen by their placement with the unfolding drama. To this degree I concur with coherentist philosophers who rejects knowledge as a collection of isolated facts, for beliefs form a system.... I find in Scripture and its cosmic controversy worldview the basis for a system form of knowledge." Ibid., xxvi, xxiii.

449. Ibid., 430. Apparently, Gulley has in mind here the Protestant or evangelical soteriological principle of articulation.

450. Ibid., 447. Actually, Gulley dedicates the entire Chapter 10 of his *Prolegomena* to the cosmic controversy as the biblical worldview. Ibid., 387ff. See also *God as Trinity*, 286-288.

451. Gulley, *Prolegomena*, 447, xxv.

452. Ibid. First emphasis in original. Second emphasis mine. "God's justice is

der to be biblical, should have the same center as Scripture.[453] Although Gulley is not so explicit, it seems that for him the cosmic controversy worldview is the implicit system of Scripture.[454]

Gulley, however, also proposes that in his "theological system, Christ is both the *center and the context*."[455] He explains that he chooses Christ as a center because "He is the center of the cosmic controversy throughout the Scripture."[456] In consonance, Gulley attaches great importance to the role of Christ as Mediator. He considers that God installed Christ as a Mediator between Himself and the unfallen angels. He is Michael, the archangel mentioned in Dan 10 and 12, Jude 9, and Rev 12. He is also the Angel of the Lord of the Old Testament.[457] Gulley finds biblical evidence for Christ's installation as Mediator in Prov 8:22-23, following Davidson to some extent.[458] Gulley concludes that "Michael [Christ] became a mediator between the transcendent God and angels."[459]

Although Christ was appointed from everlasting (Prov 8:23), He was concretely installed with the creation of angels, before the creation of human beings. Gulley suggests that God could make the decision to install Christ as Mediator between angels and God under the appearance of an angel—Michael the archangel—in view of His foreknowledge of the future rise of the cosmic controversy. Christ condescended to assume that angelic role and mingled among angels in order to avoid excuses for the forthcoming conflict. In this way, Gulley understands Christ's mediatorial role, even before the Fall, essentially in relation to the cosmic controversy, rather than in connection with a general role of mediation between God and creation.[460]

According to Gulley, then, Christ is the center and the context of the Adventist theological system. At the same time, he also refers to the

---

central in the metanarrative of the cosmic controversy, and all doctrines of systematic theology must be understood in relation to this issue." Ibid., 442.

453. Ibid., 146.

454. This fact implies that a worldview is essentially a system—although not necessarily an explicit one. Gulley, however, does not offer a specific definition of these notions.

455. Gulley, *Prolegomena*, 148. Emphasis mine. See Gulley, *Church and the Last Things*, 275-276.

456. Gulley, *Prolegomena*, 148, 446.

457. Gulley, *God as Trinity*, 281. See Richard M. Davidson, "Proverbs 8 and the Place of Christ in the Trinity," *JATS* 17, no. 1 (2006): 52.

458. Gulley, *God as Trinity*, 282-283. See Davidson, "Proverbs 8," 48-50, 53.

459. Gulley, *God as Trinity*, 283.

460. Ibid. See also ibid., 298-299.

cosmic controversy in similar terms. Namely, the cosmic controversy is the central focus/theme of the system and is also the context in which the system is developed.[461] In parallel, Gulley suggests that the center of the cosmic controversy is the justice of God.[462] In spite of these different approaches, it is clear that Gulley sees the cosmic controversy worldview as an organizing central focus or general theme. The cosmic controversy theme is "its organizing and theologically orientating center."[463]

Davidson also elaborates a proposal regarding the theological center in connection with the cosmic controversy. Davidson develops a sevenfold center of Scripture that he finds summarized in Gen 1-3. Each element is in some way included in Gen 1-3, the canonical introduction to the Bible. In Gen 1-2, Davidson finds the first two aspects of this multiple center: Creation and character of God. The second one would be evident from the mention of God's two names, *Elohim*, which emphasizes the transcendence of God, and *Yahweh*, which is the personal and covenantal name of God. The character of God as Creator is important in order to understand what happens in Gen 3.[464]

The third aspect or facet of this center is the emergence of the moral conflict around the issue of God's character that is announced in Gen 3:15. In the same verse, it is possible to find the fourth, fifth, and sixth facets of Davidson's proposed theological center. The fourth one is the

---

461. Gulley proposes that all Adventist doctrines should be arranged around Christ as the center and cosmic conflict as the context. This proposal requires, according to him, listing the cosmic controversy as the first fundamental belief. Gulley, "The Cosmic Controversy," 87-93. It is interesting to notice that Gulley suggests that this arrangement of doctrines around Christ as center would facilitate the acceptance of Adventism by other evangelicals. Ibid., 88-89.

462. Gulley grants centrality to other issues as well. He affirms, for instance, that "the atonement is the very heart of theology. It is the center around which all other theological truths orbit." Gulley, *Creation, Christ, Salvation*, 601. In a similar way declares that "the theme of this system is that by definition the Persons of the relational Trinity have an inner history of reciprocal love for one another—a love that overflows into creation." Gulley, *God as Trinity*, 4.

463. Russell Staples, review of *Systematic Theology*, vol. 1, *Prolegomena* by Norman R. Gulley, *AUSS* 43, no. 2 (2005): 351. Again, according to Staples, the cosmic controversy "constitutes the central organizing theme of Gulley's theology." Ibid., 350.

464. Richard M. Davidson, "Back to the Beginning: Genesis 1-3 and the Theological Center of Scripture," in *Christ, Salvation, and the Eschaton: Essays in Honor of Hans K. LaRondelle*, ed. Daniel Heinz, Jiří Moskala, and Peter M. van Bemmelen (Berrien Springs, MI: Old Testament Department, SDA Theological Seminary, Andrews University, 2009), 11-13.

covenantal promise of the Gospel regarding a solution for the conflict centered in Christ, the Messianic Seed. The fifth relates to the substitutionary atonement. Christ, the Seed, dies in favor of the fallen human beings. The sixth facet is the prediction of the end of the controversy, when the serpent is defeated.[465]

The seventh facet relates to the identification of Eden as the first sanctuary of God on earth.[466] Against this background, Davidson concludes, "The sanctuary is the setting of the rise of the great controversy on earth, just as it was the setting for its prior inception in heaven, as described in Isa 14 and Ezek 28. The sanctuary is the battleground of the moral conflict, and the seventh facet of the multi-faceted theological center of Scripture."[467]

In integrating this multi-faceted center,[468] Davidson sees the great controversy as the overarching theme, encompassing all the rest. At the same time, the issue of God's character underlies the entire controversy. The Creation reflects the original plan or design of God for this earth. The substitutionary atonement of Christ on the cross is the central fact of this conflict that Davidson visualizes as the first of a set of concentric circles where the following circle is the work of Christ (including His life and death) and the next one is the entire plan of redemption. These concentric circles are *tridimensional* because they reflect the ongoing process developed during the great controversy.[469] In this multi-faceted-center, the sanctuary is "the setting for the outworking of the Great

---

465. Ibid., 13-16.
466. Davidson sees several elements in common between the Eden and the earthly sanctuaries, whether intertextual relationships or structural parallels. Some of them include the eastward orientation of both the Eden and the earthly sanctuaries and the threefold division of the Eden and the sanctuaries (earth, garden, and the midst of the garden as parallel to court, the Holy, and the Most Holy Place). There are also several textual parallels between the account of Creation in six days and the construction of the tabernacle in six sections. After the Fall, the Garden also has cherubim that are "placed" (or "dwelling," cf. Exod 25:8) at the entrance. Ibid., 16-18. For a broader explanation of the Eden as the first sanctuary on the earth, see Davidson, "Cosmic Metanarrative," 108-111; Richard M. Davidson, "Earth's First Sanctuary: Genesis 1-3 and Parallel Creation Accounts," *AUSS* 53, no. 1 (2015): 65-80. Regarding the sanctuary as a battleground or setting of the great controversy, see Davidson, "Cosmic Metanarrative," 111-116.
467. Davidson, "Back to the Beginning," 18.
468. Davidson also finds these multi-faceted center present in the book of Job and in Rev 20-22. Ibid., 19-24.
469. Ibid., 26-28.

Controversy, . . . the window into the entire biblical system of truth."[470] Thus, while Davidson admits the importance of the sanctuary as the setting, window, or battleground of the great controversy, Davidson's multi-faceted center sees the issue of the great controversy as, ultimately, the encompassing concept of the center.[471]

The Interpretation of the Articulating Action

In consonance with the interpretation of the articulating agent of the Adventist theological system in terms of the cosmic controversy or great controversy theme, the theodicy model tends to emphasize the vindication of God's character as the articulating action that explains all other God's actions. The cosmic controversy involves a questioning of God's love and justice. Consequently, Gulley considers that his "system needs to unfold God's self-revelation to answer this accusation, and each doctrine should make a contribution to this end."[472] Gulley thinks that other non-biblical worldviews do not allow answering the questions raised by theodicy. The influence of the Parmenidean-Platonic-Aristotelian view of God as timeless, for example, implies that God determines human destiny (as in Augustine and Calvin), a fact that distorts God's character of love. In contrast, the cosmic controversy, that assumes God's temporality, allows God to demonstrate or reveal His justice before the universe (stemming from His nature of love) at the same time allows exposing Satan's injustice (stemming from His loveless nature).[473]

The Adventist theodicy model, then, emphasizes that God's activities through history such as God's covenants, the activity in the earthly sanctuary, the life and the supreme sacrifice of Jesus Christ at Calvary, and His ministry in the heavenly sanctuary, seek the vindication of God's character.[474] "Throughout Scripture the controversy against God unfolds and the vindication of God unfolds, so that in the end all intel-

---

470. Ibid., 27.
471. Davidson concludes that his proposal of a multi-faceted center should operate as an orientation point—rather than an organizing principle—allowing making sense of the whole Scripture. His distinction between orientation point and organizing principle, however, wants to avoid the impression that the suggested center is an imposition upon the text. See ibid., 28-29.
472. Gulley, *God as Trinity*, 284.
473. Gulley, *Prolegomena*, 452.
474. Gulley, *God as Trinity*, xix, 6.

ligent created beings will conclude that God was not what the enemy made Him out to be, and so they acknowledge God as He is."[475] In this context, the Adventist theodicy model usually focuses on God's eschatological judgment, particularly the investigative judgment. The representatives of the model do not see this judgment as a decision-making process that determines the destiny of those who have professed Christianity.[476] Rather they see the investigative judgment as essentially a culminating instance in the process of God's vindication before the universe. It is an exhibition of evidence.[477]

Gulley, for example, explains that God does not need a judgment because He is omniscience. The judgment seeks to demonstrate God's justice to His creatures. Genuine Christians are not really under judgment. God just reveals their loyalty in order to demonstrate the justice of His decision.[478] The end-time judgment is an implementation of the double verdict of the judgment that took place at the cross, which is effective when individuals accept or reject

> what Christ has done for them when He was judged in their place at the cross (John 12:31). . . . No subsequent judgment calls into question the judgment of Calvary; it neither differs from nor adds to Calvary but only reveals and applies what was completed then. In other words, judgment day primarily took place at Calvary.[479]

In the same vein, Davidson holds that it is possible to see the investigative judgment as a *final audit* when the year ends. The auditors

---

475. Ibid., xx.
476. The decision-making view of judgment was common among the Adventist pioneers. See footnote 148 in this chapter. See also E. G. White, *The Great Controversy*, 480-491.
477. The Adventist pioneers were also aware of the vindicatory aspect of the judgment but still they considered that the judgment was a decision-making process determining who were in condition to receive eternal life. Smith is an example in this sense. "God has not seen fit to decide by his own omniscience who are worthy of immortality, but has left the determination of that question to the investigation and decision of the Judgment, that an intelligent universe may be able to understand for themselves the righteousness of his doings." U[riah] S[mith], "The Judgment of Rev. 14:7," *The Advent Review and Herald of the Sabbath*, January 13, 1874, 36.
478. Gulley, *Creation, Christ, Salvation*, 500-502. See also Richard M. Davidson, "The Good News of Yom Kippur," *JATS* 2, no. 2 (1991): 21.
479. Gulley, *Church and the Last Things*, 649. "The pre-advent judgment implements the double verdict of Calvary. This is actualized in two stages: (1) at the second coming of Christ and (2) after the Millennium." Ibid., 650. See ibid., 226.

confirm that the accounts are accurate and vindicate the accountant.[480] William H. Shea also conclusively affirms, regarding the investigative judgment, that it "doesn't change any of the decisions that Christ has made about individuals through the course of time."[481] Consequently, the judgment is described as demonstrative, revelatory, vindicatory, affirmative, or confirmatory of God's justice or fairness. The decision regarding who will be saved has been already made before.[482]

The Interpretation of the Whole

Gulley and Davidson describe the cosmic controversy or great controversy as not only the center of Adventist theology, but also the context, boundary, metanarrative, and general overarching theme of the system.[483] Considering these characteristics, the great controversy becomes a better description of the system as a whole in the context of sin. In this sense, Gulley, Davidson, and those representatives of this model remain close to the interpretation of the whole among the Adventist pioneers.[484]

Reality as a whole involves a conflict between good and evil. More specifically, it involves a conflict between Christ and His followers, and Satan and his followers. However, the strong emphasis on this view of the whole does not allow perceiving easily how the system interconnects its diverse elements. Gulley, for example, suggests that the sanc-

---

480. Davidson, "The Good News," 27, n. 60. Davidson concludes his comparison by saying, "At the end of history, God opens the books, as it were, for a public audit His business practices. The auditors testify to His impeccable integrity." Ibid.

481. William H. Shea, Foreword to *The Case for the Investigative Judgment: Its Biblical Foundation* by Marvin Moore (Nampa, ID: Pacific Press, 2010), 7-8.

482. Jiří Moskala, "Toward a Biblical Theology of God's Judgment: A Celebration of the Cross in Seven Phases of Divine Universal Judgment (An Overview of a Theocentric-Christocentric Approach)," *JATS* 15, no. 1 (2004): 153, 154; Roy Gane, *Who's Afraid of the Judgment? The Good News About Christ's Work in the Heavenly Sanctuary* (Nampa, ID: Pacific Press, 2006), 21-22; Ivan T. Blazen, "Justification and Judgment," in *70 Weeks, Leviticus, and the Nature of Prophecy*, ed. Frank B. Holbrook (Washington, DC: Biblical Research Institute, GC of SDAs, 1986), 382-383; Clifford Goldstein, "Investigating the Investigative Judgment," *Ministry*, February 1992, 8. See Edward Heppenstall, "The Pre-Advent Judgment," *Ministry*, December 1981, 15; Edward Heppenstall, *Our High Priest: Jesus Christ in the Heavenly Sanctuary* (Washington, DC: Review & Herald, 1972), 124.

483. See the interpretation of the articulating agent of this model in pp. 232-237 in this chapter.

484. See the interpretation of the whole in the Adventist pioneers in p. 138.

tuary is God's teaching device that constitutes a system in Scripture, which is necessary to explore in order to guide the understanding of the most important aspects of theology.[485] In practice, however, it seems that Gulley, tries to use the concept of the cosmic controversy with that purpose, not the sanctuary. In general, the proponents of the theodicy model would concur with Douglass when he affirms that the uniqueness of Adventism "is not some particular element of its theology, such as its sanctuary doctrine. Rather, the distinctiveness of Adventism rests in *its overall understanding* of the central message of the Bible that is governed by its seminal, governing principle—the Great Controversy Theme."[486]

Critical Evaluation

The Adventist theodicy model represents a serious effort to build an Adventist theology based on biblical ontological and epistemological presuppositions. The model explicitly rejects the timeless understanding of being and knowledge—including the *via negativa*—so frequently assumed in Christian tradition. The model, then, involves a genuine effort to elaborate theology applying the *sola Scriptura* principle, not only at the doctrinal level but also at the level of those basic presuppositions.

In its interpretation of God, therefore, this model rejects the view of God as timeless and unchangeable while at the same time avoids the temporal-timeless view of God of process theology. Gulley correctly considers that God's nature of love necessarily implies that God is temporal but His time is qualitatively and quantitatively different from creation's time. Moreover, his understanding of God's holy love clearly implies that His justice is not in contradiction with His love, as the modern Adventist model seems to believe, following the lead of process ontology. As Peckham explains, divine love does not exclude or nullify divine justice. Divine love includes justice.[487]

Few remarks, however, are in order regarding Gulley's interpreta-

---

485. Gulley, *God as Trinity*, 459-460. See also ibid., xix, 412, 463; Gulley, *Creation, Christ, Salvation*, 670; See also Norman R. Gulley, "Why the Sanctuary Is So Important," *Ministry*, August 2014, 23.

486. Douglass, "The Great Controversy Theme," 5. Emphasis mine.

487. Peckham, "The Concept of Divine Love," 616, 619. "If God loves everyone (cf. John 3:16) his concern for all requires that he mete out justice and finally eradicate evil. . . . Thus, the benefits of God's love have a limit." Ibid., 620.

tion of God. Gulley's classification of God's attributes in incommunicable and communicable goes back to Turretin (1623-1687), a Reformed theologian. It is common even today among those following the Calvinist tradition. Turretin's intention was to use this classification in order to defend the traditional notion of God's simplicity—which involves God's timelessness—protecting God's transcendence by contrasting Him with His creatures.[488] This fact can explain why Gulley needs to take several precautions before applying the distinction. If, as Gulley suggests, classifications of attributes are only human and there are no absolutely incommunicable or communicable attributes, it would be better to avoid classifications. In fact, traditional classifications tend to emphasize the distinction between transcendence and immanence with transcendence being understood in terms of God's timelessness and immutability.[489] Gulley clearly disagrees with this view of God's transcendence. The adoption of this classification, therefore, seems to be inconsistent with his temporal understanding of God's transcendence.[490]

A second remark regarding Gulley's interpretation of God relates to his view of His physical characteristics and emotions as anthropomorphisms. It is clear that Gulley is under the influence of classical theology at this point. He explicitly follows Bavinck in this sense. Bavinck, as a Calvinist theologian, applies the principle of accommodation language and the *via negativa* in his interpretation of God's nature. In discussing that topic, Bavinck actually says, "Eternity cannot be defined except as a negation of time."[491] Gulley, therefore, is not consistent

---

488. Andy Snider, "Story and System: Why We Should Not Categorize the Attributes of God," paper presented at the 64th Annual Meeting of the Evangelical Theological Society, Milwaukee, WI, November 14-16, 2012, 3-4. Turretin apparently developed this distinction in reaction to Socinianism. See ibid.

489. Andy Snider seems to imply this understanding of transcendence in terms of timelessness in the usual classifications of God's attributes in ibid., 13, 15, 16.

490. The reason why Gulley discusses the fruit of the Spirit and the gifts of the Spirit in connection with the doctrine of God—as communicable attributes—and not in connection with soteriology, ecclesiology, and the mission of the church is not clear. The identification of the fruit of the Spirit and the gifts of the Spirit as God's attributes seems to be a by-product of the classification chosen by Gulley that simply requires locating some elements in the category of the communicable attributes.

491. Bavinck, *God and Creation*, 100. Bavinck is very explicit in his use of the *via negativa*. "Even the so-called incommunicable attributes of God, such as immutability, independence, simplicity, eternity, and omnipresence, are presented in Scripture in forms and expressions derived from the finite world and are *therefore stated negatively*. . . . Scripture never even attempts to describe these perfections of God

when he affirms that God is temporal, has a form and a spatial location, while at the same time, he interprets biblical depictions of God's physical appearance and emotions as anthropomorphisms.

Actually, Gulley's interpretation of God's nature in Scripture is inconsistent with his own interpretation of the human being because he holds that the image of God involves the whole human being, including the physical aspect. Although these problems in Gulley's interpretation of God are not too prominent in the context of the entire system that Gulley has developed, they illustrate in a practical way the risk involved in the development of a biblical Adventist theology that uncritically borrows materials from Christian tradition. This borrowing—as it is illustrated in the prior discussions of the evangelical and modern Adventist models—has the potential to introduce significant changes in Adventist theology, considering the systematic nature of theological knowledge and knowledge in general.[492]

Gulley and Davidson rightly interpret the world in harmony with the *sola Scriptura* principle. The world is a creation of God with a temporal beginning—against Schleiermacher or process theology. Creation is interpreted in a literal biblical way rather than in harmony with the negative way or theistic evolutionary theories.[493] The world is also a unitary—non-dualistic—reality, in contrast to Christian tradition.

Something similar occurs with the interpretation of the human being as a unitary entity. It is clear that for Gulley, the sinful human condition is not the result of an ontological abyss or distance between God and His human creatures. Sin is a historical reality that started in heaven and continued on earth as a result of a voluntary rupture of the relationship with God.

---

positively in terms of their own essence and apart from any relation to the finite." Ibid. Emphasis mine.

492. The difficulty with Gulley's classification of God's attributes, as well as the inconsistency in his interpretation of God's nature, is probably explicable because of the massive nature of his work, where there is an extensive interaction with secondary sources and the dependence on them is important and difficult to avoid. These problems (particularly the second one) do not have a significant impact on Gulley's system because he does not necessarily take the ideas that he quotes to their logical hermeneutical consequences. An example in this sense is the fact that Gulley still interprets heavenly realities as spatio-temporal, particularly the heavenly sanctuary. See pp. 226-227 in this chapter.

493. Actually, Gulley extensively discusses and questions theistic evolution, evolutionary theory, and their implications for theology. See Gulley, *Creation, Christ, Salvation*, 170-390. See also Chapters 31 to 33 in Gulley, *Christ Is Coming*, 375-409.

The only difficulty concerning Gulley's interpretation of the human being relates to his understanding of human depravity and prevenient grace that seems to be at least potentially in tension with his view of the image of God as involving free will even after the Fall. Gulley affirms that humans, controlled by sin, are unable to make right spiritual decisions. Apparently, the Fall almost overruled or canceled free will. Prevenient grace, then, has to equip humans with the freedom to choose. In that case, however, one can wonder if human freedom was really preserved after the Fall. It would be probably clearer and more coherent with Gulley's own view of the image of God after the Fall simply to affirm that God takes the initiative in personal salvation in interaction with a very weak human will. This conceptualization of God's initiative can avoid the common Arminian idea that prevenient grace is some kind of infusion of grace that enables a canceled will.[494]

It is not so easy to perceive Gulley's interpretation of the articulating agent and the articulating action, in connection with his interpretation of the whole. The Adventist theodicy model emphasizes the importance of the cosmic controversy worldview[495] as the central theme or

---

494. Apparently, Gulley unintentionally lacks some precision in his understanding of prevenient grace. It seems that he wants to suggest that human free will is very weak, rather than strictly canceled, and needs God's initiative in order to respond affirmatively. Gulley himself seems to understand prevenient grace in terms of God's initiative, to some extent, but he sounds ambiguous in explaining the role of human free will after the Fall. He says that "freedom to choose was not lost in the Fall, although humans now need God's enabling power in order to willingly choose God." Gulley, *Creation, Christ, Salvation*, 146. See also ibid., 672, 673, 674, 702, n. 64. At the same time, he affirms that total depravity really involves human freedom to choose. Ibid., 147. Thus, God needs to "equip them [humans] (prevenient grace) with freedom of choice to respond to His invitation to be saved." Gulley, *God as Trinity*, 530, n. 283. See ibid., 581. It may be useful to remind that Arminius did not necessarily modify Calvinist anthropology. See Roger E. Olson, *Arminian Theology: Myths and Realities* (Downers Grove, IL: InterVarsity, 2006), 32-33. As Olson explains, "Arminianism regards original sin primarily as a moral depravity that results from *deprivation of the image of God*." Ibid. Emphasis mine. Consequently, in order to affirm the existence of free will after the Fall it was necessary to postulate prevenient grace as a "special *infusion* of God's grace." Ibid., 33. Emphasis mine. Gulley himself is aware that in the Protestant context, the notion of infusion frequently entails that God acts upon human beings based on His absolute sovereignty, ignoring human freedom. Gulley, *Creation, Christ, Salvation*, 673.

495. Ronald H. Nash defines worldview as "a conceptual scheme by which we consciously or unconsciously place or fit everything we believe and by which we interpret and judge reality." Ronald H. Nash, *Faith and Reason: Searching for a Rational Faith* (Grand Rapids, MI: Zondervan, 1988), 24. Nash understands a worldview "as

focus on the system. Gulley actually organizes his systematic theology around this central topic. However, as discussed in Chapter 2, a center is not necessarily an articulating agent. In theological systems in particular, an articulating agent or real epistemological center always refers to God.[496] This is not the case with the cosmic controversy motif. Although the cosmic controversy in the Adventist theodicy model involves God, it is also clear that the cosmic controversy involves several other beings such as angels (fallen and unfallen), human beings, and the world (nature, universe). The cosmic controversy also includes the actions of those beings—particularly the actions of intelligent creatures. As such, then, it is better to identify the cosmic controversy as a way to name the system as a whole rather than as a center.[497]

Moreover, the cosmic controversy does not describe the way in which God articulates the relationship between Himself and the world. Actually, it describes the opposite. The cosmic controversy points out the ontological reality about how sin resulted in the disarticulation of the relationship between God and His creation.[498]

The theodicy model seeks to use the great controversy as a central them that is actually a better description of the whole in the context of the problem of sin. This is probably the reason why Gulley—as well as Davidson—feels compelled to suggest that the cosmic controversy has a more "concrete" center. This center—that for Gulley is also the center of the system—is identified either as Christ or as God's justice

---

a conceptual system." Ibid., 25. Gulley does not offer a clear explanation regarding his understanding of worldview. Based on the discussion of his interpretation of the articulating agent, it seems that for him it refers to a view of reality as a whole (metanarrative) that is systematic in nature, it has a center or central agglutinating element, and it works as a context for his system. For practical purposes however, in Gulley, the cosmic controversy theme frequently operates as a central motif that he uses to structure his system.

496. This fact is valid also for a biblical theological system that claims to operate based on the *sola Scriptura* principle, where God's final authorship is assumed. If there is ultimately only one author, then Scripture is necessarily a system, regardless of the particular way in which the text is organized as a whole. See pp. 56-57 in Chapter 2.

497. See the discussion of the interpretation of the whole in Adventist theodicy model in pp. 239-240 in this chapter.

498. Gulley himself underlines this point by saying that "God is holy. He hates the *cosmic controversy and its sin* because it broke the relationship of love between intelligent created beings (both angelic and human) and Himself." Gulley, *God as Trinity*, 5. Emphasis in original.

(character).⁴⁹⁹ Davidson actually proposes a multifaceted center that includes the sanctuary, which he considers as the battleground of the cosmic controversy. However, if the great controversy is the overarching theme—and reality— encompassing all the rest (the whole), it would be more natural to say that the great controversy is the battleground, context, or whole in which the sanctuary develops its activities.⁵⁰⁰ Ultimately, however, the Adventist theodicy model still uses the cosmic controversy as a conceptual center in a way that resembles the notion of *ordo disciplinae*, although its intention goes beyond that function.

The cosmic controversy works, thus, as an imprecise center. The selection of the vindication of God's character as the articulating action may involve the risk of reducing Adventist theology to theodicy, neglecting the realities that existed before the beginning of sin and that will exist after the end of it. The representatives of the theodicy model, for example, do not deny that God's judgment is a process, as evangelical Adventism does. However, they have the tendency to see the judgment in almost exclusively vindicatory terms, neglecting its soteriological dimension and virtually identifying the decision-making aspect of the judgment with God's foreknowledge or—more probably—with a decision made by God about the destiny of every individual during his/her life in relation to his/her acceptance or rejection of Christ's sacrifice.⁵⁰¹ It is not difficult to see here a resemblance to the evangelical Adventist understanding of the judgment that, in the case of believers, reduces the judgment to justification. While Adventist theodicy is essential for Adventist theology, particularly in the context of the belief in a real ongoing pre-advent investigative judgment, Adventist theology should not be limited to theodicy.

---

499. See other suggestions made by Gulley in footnote 462 in this chapter.

500. Gulley actually says that the sanctuary "is God's control center against the cosmic controversy." Gulley, *God as Trinity*, 453. However, he emphasizes that "the contribution of the sanctuary as system to systematic theology is the visual aids it provides about redemption and resolution of the comic controversy." Ibid., 457.

501. The argument in this sense is presented usually in this way: God foreknows who will be saved and who will be lost. Moreover, God already justified the believers (or condemned the unbelievers) during their lives. Therefore, He does not need a judgment to determine the destiny of human beings. That decision is already made (in connection with God's foreknowledge or with the acceptance or rejection of Christ's sacrifice). Thus, the judgment is only a demonstration of evidence for the universe that God is just. See pp. 238-239 and the references in footnote 482 in this chapter.

Conclusion

This chapter analyzed and evaluated the three main models of interpretation of the principle of articulation in current Adventist theology. The chapter allows concluding that the evangelical Adventist model tries to adapt Adventist theology to the interpretation of the principle of articulation in the soteriological model of Protestant theology. The modern Adventist model, in turn, searches to adapt Adventist theology to the interpretation of the principle of articulation in the panentheistic model of modern theology. The Adventist theodicy model, in contrast, avoids a general adaptation of Adventist theology to some of the models in Christian tradition. It focuses on the topic of the great controversy as a cognitive or conceptual center that tends to see the articulating action of the system mainly in terms of the vindication of God's character. As a result, the investigative judgment becomes essentially an exhibition of evidence or audit where God has already decided the final destiny of believers and unbelievers in a way that recalls the evangelical Adventist understanding of judgment and its reduction of the judgment of believers to justification.

From the perspective of the *sola Scriptura* principle, on the one hand, it is important to notice that although the evangelical Adventist model affirms this principle in theory, it does not follow it in practice. This model does not operate based on biblical ontological and epistemological assumptions and consequently, its interpretation of the principle of articulation is inconsistent with the *sola Scriptura* principle. On the other hand, the modern Adventist model does not claim to follow the *sola Scriptura* principle. On the contrary, it explicitly supports the use of several sources for theology, which implies the use of non-biblical ontological and epistemological presuppositions and results in a non-biblical interpretation of the principle of articulation. This fact does not mean that it is impossible to "redeem" some elements from these models. Any redeemable element, however, should be in harmony with the *sola Scriptura* principle.

The Adventist theodicy model, instead, represents a more conscious and substantial effort to base the interpretation of the principle of articulation on biblical ontological and epistemological presuppositions, in harmony with the *sola Scriptura* principle. Some inconsistencies remain, for example, in connection with the interpretation of God's ontology. The main problem with this model, however, lies in the imprecise articulation of the system. The identification of the articulating agent and the articulating action results particularly vague. This fact can facilitate a certain lack of inner consistency as the discussion of the model exemplifies.

CHAPTER FIVE

The Principle of Articulation: Toward a Scriptural Interpretation

Introduction

The purpose of this chapter is to outline a biblical[1] systematic interpretation of the principle of articulation based on the *sola Scriptura* principle. The first section briefly discusses the ontological and epistemological presuppositions. The rest of the sections of the chapter follows the structure resulting from the phenomenological analysis of the principle of articulation in theology. First, there is a discussion about the interpretation of God, the world, and the human being. Second, the chapter proposes a biblical interpretation of the articulating agent and the articulating action. Finally, the chapter considers the interpretation of the whole.

It is necessary to remember that the discussion of this proposed interpretation of the principle of articulation is, as established in Chapter 1, more like a general outline that can provide the base for additional discussion, construction, and expansion. It is beyond the scope of this chapter to develop an exhaustive treatment of the interpretation of the principle of articulation from a biblical perspective. The general approach, then, is not exegetical or analytical, but rather synthetic and systematic. The discussion, however, takes advantage of prior research in the field of biblical studies that can provide support for a scriptural interpretation of the principle of articulation, as well as some developments in systematic theology and the study of the presuppositions of theology. At the same time, the chapter takes

---

1. Regarding the meaning of the word *biblical* here, see Chapter 1, footnote 35.

into consideration the discussion carried out in prior chapters, often interacting—sometimes implicitly—with the analyzed models and interpretations in Christian tradition in general and in Adventism in particular.

Ontological and Epistemological Presuppositions

The discussion of the prior two chapters suggests that in Christian tradition and, to some extent, in recent Adventist theology, the ontological presuppositions coming from philosophy—whether Greek or modern philosophy—have strongly determined the understanding of being in general and of the being of God in particular. In contrast, several theologians have highlighted the fact that in order to understand the biblical interpretation of being in general, it is necessary to understand first the biblical interpretation of God.[2] As the Originator or Creator of all other reality that is not God, Scripture requires discovering the biblical interpretation of God's being before understanding the biblical interpretation of being in general. In this sense, a radical separation between the biblical interpretation of God and being in general is ultimately not possible.[3] As already discussed

---

2. In a more technical way, Canale affirms that the Bible does not follow an onto-theo-logical order but a theo-onto-logical order to understand being in general. In other words, it is necessary to understand first the biblical interpretation of the being of God in order to understand the biblical interpretation of being in general. Canale, *A Criticism of Theological Reason*, 347, 352, 384. See also Canale, "Deconstrucción y teología," 20. Canale's terminology is echoing in a creative way Heidegger's terminology. See Martin Heidegger, "The Onto-theo-logical Constitution of Metaphysics," in *Identity and Difference*, trans. Joan Stambaugh (New York, NY: Harper & Row, 1969), 42-74. Canale is not the only one who sees the theo-onto-logical understanding of being in the Bible. According to King L. She, "Biblical ontology is theo-onto-logical." King L. She, *The Use of Exodus in Hebrews*, Studies in Biblical Literature 142 (New York, NY: Peter Lang, 2011), 60. See his complete discussion in ibid., 53-60. Kevin J. Vanhoozer has also highlighted the necessity of following a theo-onto-logical approach in the interpretation of Scripture. Kevin J. Vanhoozer, *Remythologizing Theology: Divine Action, Passion, and Authorship* (New York, NY: Cambridge University Press, 2010), xv, 43, 183, 222. For a discussion about onto-theo-logy and its impact on biblical hermeneutics, see Merold Westphal, "Onto-theology," *Dictionary for Theological Interpretation of the Bible* (*DTIB*), ed. Kevin J. Vanhoozer (Grand Rapids, MI: Baker, 2005), 546-549.

3. See Kerbs, *El problema de la identidad*, 217, 225.

in Chapter 2, there are two basic interpretations of being: timeless and temporal. The same is valid for the interpretation of God.[4] The discussion in Chapter 3 has presented evidence that the interpretation of God as timeless does not come from Scripture but from non-biblical philosophy.

There is no trace of a timeless God in Scripture. Exodus 3:14, for example, the *locus classicus*[5] used to prove that God is timeless and lives in an eternal present, actually reveals the opposite. God reveals Himself to Moses not as a temporal manifestation of His timeless being but as God Himself, His very presence. When God mentions His name, He reveals Himself as a temporal being. He has a *past* as the God of the Fathers (Abraham, Isaac, and Jacob) with whom He had a covenantal relationship (see Exod 3:3, 13, 15, 16). He has a *present* in which He reveals Himself as the one who *is* with His oppressed people (3:14). God also has a *future* because His name will be a memorial for future generations to whom God will reveal His covenantal name YHWH (3:15).[6]

God is also personally present and speaking in time and space in several other biblical passages in direct and intimate communion with human beings.[7] Indeed, any action of God regarding the world includ-

---

4. See Chapter 2, pp. 48-51.

5. For Exod 3:14, 15 as a *locus classicus* to discuss the understanding of being and the being of God in the Bible, see Canale, *A Criticism of Theological Reason*, 292, 392; Stanley J. Grenz, *The Named God and the Question of Being: A Trinitarian Theo-Ontology* (Louisville, KY: Westminster John Knox, 2005), 133-134. Aquinas interprets Exod 3:14 ("I AM THAT I AM") as referring to the eternal present of God; namely, as a reference to God's timelessness. Aquinas *ST* I, q. 13, a. 11, resp. Aquinas actually explicitly finds support for his interpretation in Augustine, according to which God's "existence knows not past or future, as Augustine says (De Trin. v)." Ibid. For Augustine's interpretation of this passage, see Chapter 3, p. 72.

6. Canale, *A Criticism of Theological Reason*, 342-346. Wolterstorff also argues that God is temporal based on Exod 3-4. The text shows that God has a history. He responds to human situations, performs successive actions (including speaking), and answers Moses's successive protests. Nicholas Wolterstorff, "Unqualified Divine Temporality," in *God & Time: Four Views*, ed. Gregory E. Ganssle (Downers Grove, IL: InterVarsity, 2001), 187-188, 203-204, 207. Wolterstorff summarizes his point by saying that in Scripture, "God has a history, and in this history there are changes in God's actions, responses and knowledge." Ibid., 188.

7. Some examples of God's presence in time and space mentioned in Scripture in narrative contexts are Gen 18; 32:24-30; Exod 24:9-11; 33:7-11, 18-23; Num 12:8; Deut 5:4, etc. Of course, the temporal interpretation of God's being in these passages is possible only by eliminating the extra-biblical *via negativa*. Scripture "portrays God as having

ing Creation, the Exodus, Christ's incarnation, and others reveal that God is temporal and experiences time in a sequential way.[8] Moreover, if God is love (1 John 4:8) and God's reciprocal intra-Trinitarian love and fellowship is real, as Gulley holds,[9] God's temporality is the necessary assumption to explain the fellowship among the members of the Godhead.[10]

In Scripture, then, there is no notion of a timeless eternity that would convey that reality is a dualism between timelessness and temporality. As Cullmann explains, "Between everlastingly continuing time and limited time, the New Testament makes absolutely no difference in terminology. Eternity is the endless succession of the ages."[11] On the other hand, "the idea that time in which human beings live is not eternity [Heb. '*ôlām*], or that eternity is the time in which God distinc-

---

fellowship with and interacting with human beings at various times in their lives. How is this possible for a God who has no sequence in his mental life?" John S. Feinberg, *No One Like Him: The Doctrine of God* (Wheaton, IL: Crossway, 2001), 430.

8. "Not only is it preferable to adopt a temporal notion of divine eternity because it is hard to make sense of atemporal eternity, but many of the arguments used against atemporalism are also quite compelling. In particular, arguments about God as a person, God's action, the biblical portrait of God's interactions with the world, the problem of divine simultaneity with events in time, and some of the issues raised about divine omniscience are difficult to handle with atemporalism." Ibid., 431. The fact that God experiences time sequentially is evident in biblical depictions of God's actions that show that He changes. "For example, a God who changes his relationship with a repentant sinner incorporates a sequence in his handling of that person, but that sequence necessitates time and so rules out atemporalism." Ibid., 432.

9. See Chapter 4, p. 222.

10. "If all members of the Trinity are equally omniscient (and they are), and there is no possibility of sequence in what any of them consciously thinks, then all three always have the same thought they have always been thinking and always think exactly what the other two members are thinking. But, then, how is fellowship possible? . . . They can't at one point feel no emotion toward what they know and then at another moment rejoice with one another. Anticipating anything new is impossible. In such circumstances, it is hard to make sense of how the members of the Godhead could fellowship with one another." Feinberg, *No One Like Him*, 430.

11. Cullmann, *Christ and Time*, 62. As Wolterstorff notices, James Barr has questioned Cullmann's argumentation regarding God's temporality (although not necessarily his conclusions) because of his lexicographical approach to the issue of time in the New Testament. Wolterstorff, however, also concludes that God is temporal in Scripture "by seeing that God's temporality is presupposed by the biblical presentation of God as redeemer. . . . The lexicographical and philosophical cases coincide in their results." Wolterstorff, *Inquiring About God*, 156. The danger of a pure lexicographical approach is that it can potentially ignore the ontological presuppositions assumed by the text and superimpose on it the presuppositions of the interpreter.

tively lives, does not appear to correspond with the O[ld] T[estament] conception."[12] Thus, reality as a whole, from a biblical perspective, is temporal.

The modern Adventist model and the Adventist theodicy model agree with this perspective of reality as temporal. Modern Adventism, however, holds this position based on cultural intuitions and philosophical reasons rather than biblical ones. Moreover, it is not systematically consistent with its explicit affirmations in this sense. Nevertheless, Guy has correctly pointed out that time is not like a "box" or container.[13] This perspective of time would imply that "outside" of the box there is no time, which would reintroduce the ontological dualism between timeless and temporality. If all particular beings are temporal—God and the world—it is better to think about time as not having an independent ontological status but as secondary to the things itself.[14] Said in another way, "time never appears or is given to us as a 'thing,' but co-appears with all things as a basic characteristic of their being."[15]

A temporal understanding of being requires a temporal understanding of knowledge. As mentioned in Exod 3, God reveals His own presence or being as temporal. In the same way, in Exod 6:3, 4, God's temporal self-revelation is the cause by which God made Himself known to Abraham, Isaac, and Jacob with whom He established His covenant in the past and to whom He promised the inheritance of

---

12. Moisés Silva, ed., *"aiōn, aiōnios," New International Dictionary of New Testament Theology and Exegesis*, rev. ed. (Grand Rapids, MI: Zondervan, 2014), 1:195.

13. See p. 184 in Chapter 4. See also Canale, *Basic Elements of Christian Theology*, 73-74; Canale, *Cognitive Principle of Christian Theology*, 250-252.

14. The fact that Scripture presents God as being everlasting and as having a temporal existence, even before Creation, supports this view of time. As Ps 90:2 affirms, "God existed *before* creation, indeed from everlasting to everlasting. How could God exist *before* creation and yet be timeless?" Wolterstorff, "Unqualified Divine Temporality," 190. Emphasis in original. If God is temporal, and so is the world that He created, there is no exception to the fact that particular beings are temporal. Time is an inherent characteristic of every temporal real entity. In this sense, William L. Craig's proposal is questionable: "God is simply timeless without creation and temporal subsequent to creation." William L. Craig, *Time and Eternity: Exploring God's Relationship to Time* (Wheaton, IL: Crossway, 2001), 235. The problem here is that if God can *change* from timeless to temporality—if He can experience this succession—then He is not really unchangeable. It is difficult then to see how He can be timeless, considering the systematic relation between unchangeability (immutability) and timelessness. See Peckham, "Divine Passibility," 34.

15. Canale, *Basic Elements of Christian Theology*, 73.

Canaan. In Exod 6:5, God makes Himself known as the one who evaluates Israel's situation of bondage in view of His prior covenant and promise. In Exod 6:6, 7, God will be known in the future as Deliverer in fulfillment of His prior covenant and promise. In other words, God is known based on His temporal presence (I Am) and actions through a temporal extension that involves past, present, and future.[16]

Theological knowledge in Scripture is then a temporal knowledge. It refers to God's presence and acts that are inseparable. It involves a cognitive "gathering" of the extended presence-acts of God through time.[17] As a result, there is no application in Scripture of any *via negativa* or *via symbolica* that refers to God's reality and actions in metaphorical terms. Doctrines are not symbols or metaphors of spiritual realities.

Moreover, it is not possible to conceive the knowledge of the temporal world in general—or anything in the world in particular—in terms of timelessness either. The temporal knowledge of God in Scripture requires a temporal epistemology. In consequence, the relationship between the knower and the object of knowledge is necessarily temporal and involves the personal history of the knower.[18]

---

16. See Canale, *A Criticism of Theological Reason*, 369, 373, 375-378. See also Kerbs, *El problema de la identidad*, 248-250. This linking between God's temporal presence or acts and the knowledge about Him is actually frequent in Scripture. In connection with the ten plagues of Egypt, for example, see Exod 7:5, 17; 8:10, 22; 9:14, 29; 10:2. In connection with the crossing of the Red Sea, see Exod 14:4, 18. In connection with the provision of manna, see Exod 16:12. See also Isa 49:23, 26; 60:16. These references are mentioned in John M. Frame, *The Doctrine of the Knowledge of God* (Phillipsburg, NJ: Presbyterian & Reformed, 1987), 2. There is also a connection between the dwelling of God in the tabernacle and Israel's knowledge of God in Exod 29:46: "And they shall know that I am the LORD their God, that brought them forth out of the land of Egypt, that I may dwell among them: I am the LORD their God" (KJV). A key text is also Exod 33:14-15, where God promises that His presence (literally "face") will be with Israel and that presence is related to the knowledge about God. In the context, God and Moses speak each other face to face (v. 11) and God shows Moses His presence and glory (vv. 18-23; see also 34:4-9).

17. Canale, *A Criticism of Theological Reason*, 378-379. See Kerbs, *El problema de la identidad*, 250-251.

18. It is interesting to notice in this context that in Scripture, parallel registers of the same stories, events, or people are common. A typical example is the four Gospels. Although each one has the same object of knowledge—Christ's life and ministry—it is clear that the writers of the Gospels have different backgrounds and interests that result in diverse theological emphasis and objectives when they write. In spite of that, it is still possible to perceive a basic harmony and unity of meaning among them—echo-

At the same time, the fact that the knowledge of God depends on God's self-revelation implies that any legitimate theological endeavor should be grounded in Scripture alone (*sola Scriptura* principle), because only Scripture is God's inspired record of the revelation of His own temporal presence and actions, which offers an inspired interpretation of that revelation. Other historical sources of theology—such as tradition, science, reason, philosophy, and experience—usually do not operate based on biblical ontological and epistemological presuppositions and lead to divergent interpretations of the principle of articulation in theology. In turn, these divergent interpretations result in divergent systems of theology, as Chapters 3 and 4 illustrate.[19]

Since it is temporal and historical, theological knowledge—as well as knowledge in general—is always progressive, open, and never completely accomplished (Hos 6:3). Moreover, a complete knowledge of God is impossible not only because of the sinful condition of human beings (1 Cor 13:12) but also because there is no way to get an exhaustive knowledge of an infinite God. In His transcendence, He is ultimately unsearchable (Ps 145:3; Isa 40:28). What human beings can progressively know is God in His immanence, which means that the

---

ing Gadamer. Speaking about biblical writers, E. G. White also points, "The Creator of all ideas may impress different minds with the same thought, but each may express it in a different way, *yet without contradiction*. . . . It is seldom that two persons will view and express truth in the very same way. Each dwells on particular points which his constitution and education have fitted him to appreciate. The sunlight falling upon the different objects gives those objects a different hue." E. G. White, *Selected Messages*, vol. 1, 22. Emphasis mine.

19. Scripture recognizes nature as a general way of revelation with an individual salvific purpose (see Pss 8:3; 19:1-4; Rom 1:19-20; 2:14-15). However, it is not possible to develop a theology from nature because natural revelation does not involve a language based on which a knower can elaborate a cognitive system. From the perspective of the *sola Scriptura* principle, it is possible to develop a theology *about* nature from a biblical viewpoint rather than a natural theology. For useful discussions about natural revelation and natural theology from an Adventist perspective, see Gulley, *Prolegomena*, 190-225; Peter M. van Bemmelen, "Revelation and Inspiration," in *Handbook of Seventh-day Adventist Theology*, ed. Raoul Dederen (Hagerstown, MD: Review & Herald, 2000), 27-29; Kerbs, *El problema de la identidad*, 260-262; Canale, *Cognitive Principle of Christian Theology*, 28-40. For a favorable view of natural theology, see Alister E. McGrath, *A Scientific Theology*, vol. 1, *Nature* (Grand Rapids, MI: Eerdmans, 2001), 241-305. Erickson defends the position that there is a general revelation, but "it cannot be used to construct a natural theology." Erickson, *Christian Theology*, 137. See Erickson's discussion regarding general revelation and natural theology in ibid., 121-142.

infinite and uncreated God adapts Himself to the finite and created possibilities of knowledge of His intelligent creatures.[20]

The Interpretation of God

The fact that God is temporal does not mean that He experiences time necessarily in the same way as His creatures do. God is similar to His creation in some aspects, but He is also different in other aspects. God experiences time, for example, in a way that is beyond the possibilities of His creatures. His experience of time does not have beginning or end because He is God from everlasting to everlasting (Ps 90:2). Thus, a long period for transient humans and creatures is comparatively short in the case of God (Ps 90:4; 2 Pet 3:8[21]). Scripture affirms that God is able to know the future and human free participation in that future exhaustively, a fact which obviously goes beyond human possibilities (Dan 2:28; 11[22]).

---

20. This adaptation of God is not equivalent to Calvin's understanding of God's accommodation, which assumes the *via negativa* and consequently interprets spatio-temporal descriptions of God as spatial and temporal metaphors of God's timelessness and spacelessness. Regarding the spatio-temporal analogical interpretation of God in Scripture, see the following section. In connection with the knowledge about God in His immanence and His adaptation to the cognitive abilities of His finite creatures, E. G. White also understood that knowledge is progressive. "The years of eternity, as they roll, will bring richer and still more glorious revelations of God and of Christ. As *knowledge is progressive*, so will love, reverence, and happiness increase. The more men learn of God, the greater will be their admiration of His character." E. G. White, *The Great Controversy*, 478. Emphasis mine. Regarding the progressiveness of knowledge in general in E. G. White, see also ibid., 677.

21. Psalm 90:2, 4 does not suggest God's timeless eternity but a contrast between God's everlastingness and human transitory nature. Although God experiences time, He "is not vulnerable to the passage of time as are human beings. . . . The language is comparative, not absolute." Marvin E. Tate, *Psalms 51-100*, WBC 20 (Dallas, TX: Word, 1990), 440-441. In 2 Pet 3:8, it is also clear that "the intended contrast between man's perception of time and God's is not a reference to God's eternity in the sense of atemporality (Luther, Chaine). . . . The point is rather that God's perspective on time is not limited by a human life span. He surveys the whole of history and sets the times of events in accordance with his agelong purpose. His perspective is so much more comprehensive than that of men and women who, accustomed to short-term expectations, are impatient to see the Parousia in their own lifetime." Richard J. Bauckham, *2 Peter, Jude*, WBC 50 (Waco, TX: Word, 1983), 310. For the interpretation of these passages in Christian tradition, see footnotes 191 and 340 in Chapter 3; footnote 27 in Chapter 4.

22. Scripture affirms God's exhaustive knowledge of present—and consequently past—reality in general (Ps 147:4-5; Rom 11:33; Heb 4:13) and human reality and

A way to conceptualize these similarities and differences between God and His creation is to say that the relationship between them is one of likeness or analogy that requires an analogical or likeness language to talk about God.[23] God is neither completely different from His creation (equivocal view) nor is He the same as His creation (univocal view). This understanding of analogy, however, is not the same as the one of Aquinas. He understands analogy in connection with the application of the *via negativa*. Consequently, God is absolutely timeless and without direct relation to the world. Any affirmation about God's temporal reality or actions is metaphorical. For practical purposes, then, Aquinas's analogy tends to emphasize the equivocal element heavily in his understanding of God.[24]

From a biblical perspective, on the contrary, it is necessary to take biblical descriptions of divine reality and activity in a positive or affirmative way, without imposing alien ontological or epistemological presuppositions on the text. If Scripture describes God as temporal, there is no reason why such affirmation should not correspond with God's reality. Wolterstorff presents this interpretative principle regarding bib-

---

individual actions in particular (1 Chr 28:9; Pss 33:13-15; 139:1-6, 15-16). This exhaustive knowledge of past and present is in contrast to the fragmentary human knowledge of past and present. Scripture, moreover, affirms God's knowledge of the future in general (Daniel and Revelation) and of human free actions in particular (Ps 139:4; Luke 22:31-44, 54-62). The book of Daniel is a particularly interesting case where God predicts not only broad historical sceneries in the future but also multiple individual human free actions and interactions. This fact is especially true regarding Dan 11. See Bruce A. Ware, "Defining Evangelicalism's Boundaries Theologically: Is Open Theism Evangelical?" *Journal of the Evangelical Theological Society* 45, no. 2 (2002): 202. For a detailed discussion of several biblical texts affirming God's foreknowledge, see Millard J. Erickson, *What Does God Know and When Does He Know It? The Current Controversy Over Divine Foreknowledge* (Grand Rapids, MI: Zondervan, 2003), 39-57.

23. For an introductory discussion about the analogical language to talk about God, see Alan J. Torrance, "Analogy," *DTIB*, 38-40.

24. For a discussion of Aquinas's analogical language to talk about God, see pp. 79-80 in Chapter 3. Regarding the analogical language, Peckham clarifies, "There is a large spectrum of possible analogy between univocity and equivocity.... A strong case can be made that where Scripture does not appear to indicate the extent of similarity and dissimilarity (or where such indication is undetermined), it seems prudent to err toward the univocal end of the spectrum, in deference to the words of Scripture." Peckham, "Divine Passibility," 38, n. 24. For a similar statement, see ibid., 51. Peckham speaks about biblical analogical language as "partially univocal." Peckham, "The Concept of Divine Love," 23, 37, 38.

lical depictions of God by saying that "an implication of one's accepting Scripture as canonical is that one will affirm as literally true Scripture's representation of God unless one has good reason not to do so."[25] That *good reason*, of course, should come from Scripture itself.

This likeness or analogy is assumed in the biblical depiction of human beings as created in the image and likeness of God where similarities and differences between both are present (Gen 1:26-27).[26] These similarities entail that the biblical depictions of God in Scripture are not necessarily anthropomorphic.[27] The biblical authors are not describing God in purely human terms. Rather, they are describing humans as similar to God, who is the referent for understanding humanity—particularly in its original condition. In other words, human beings are theomorphic. Without some similarity between humanity and God, the human knowledge of God would be impossible.[28]

---

25. Wolterstorff, "Unqualified Divine Temporality," 188. Wolterstorff is not very explicit regarding the origin of the reason that could justify a non-literal interpretation of Scripture. Peckham, however, explains that Scripture can use metaphorical language or non-literal language to talk about God but in that case "language should be interpreted with careful attention to the genre, context, and other textual and contextual clues in order to avoid dismissing the exegetical content of the text (figurative or otherwise) based on extra-textual presuppositions and/or dogmatic pressures." John C. Peckham, "Theopathic or Anthropopathic? A Suggested Approach to Imagery of Divine Emotion in the Hebrew Bible," *Perspectives in Religious Studies* 42, no. 4 (2015): 343. See also Peckham, *Canonical Theology*, 232; Peckham, "The Concept of Divine Love," 25.

26. "The fact that Adam and Eve were created in the image of God without themselves being God presupposes a concept of analogy, minimally understood as entailing similarity and yet dissimilarity (or vice versa)." Peckham, "Divine Passibility," 39, n. 27.

27. The models in Christian theology in general and in Adventist theology in particular seem to imply this interpretation of the biblical depictions of God to a greater or lesser extent. See in Chapters 3 and 4 the discussion regarding the interpretation of God in every model.

28. In spite of the difficulties with John Sanders's understanding of God, it is possible to agree with him when he says, "If God is completely unlike anything in creation then nothing true can be said about God.... If God is like us in some respects, but not completely like us, then our language about God can be appropriate. We are different from God but no more different than God intended us to be. Following Abraham J. Heschel, instead of saying that God is like us we should say that we are like God since we are created in the divine image. Heschel says that God's concern for justice and love is not anthropomorphism, rather our concern for justice and love is a theomorphism." John Sanders, *The God Who Risks: A Theology of Divine Providence*, 2nd ed. (Downers Grove, IL: InterVarsity, 2007), 29. See also Vanhoozer, *Remythologizing Theology*, 64, 161. In order that knowledge be possible, there must be some similarity between the knower and the object. See Chapter 2, pp. 20-21. *Theomorphic*, though, does not refer to any kind of divinization.

The analogy between God and humanity does not involve only the similarities and differences regarding the experience of time or the cognitive abilities—such as knowledge.[29] Biblical references to God's feelings also require an analogical understanding. God's jealousy in Scripture, for example, does not imply envy.[30]

The analogical understanding of God's being also involves the fact that Scripture uses a language to talk about God in spatial-physical terms. This language is usually considered as anthropomorphic in Christian tradition and to some extent, in current Adventist theology. In contrast, Scripture clearly assumes that God has a spatial location (Exod 33:9-11; 1 Kgs 8:13, 30ff) although He is also omnipresent (1 Kgs 8:27; Jer 23:24; Ps 139:7-12). Similarly, His omnipresence does not prevent Him from having a physical appearance or form (John 5:37) that includes hands (Exod 33:22, 23), feet (24:10), back (33:23), and face (vv. 20, 23).[31] The biblical analogical language to talk about God,

---

29. For example, God and humans are able to know (similarity) and even reason together (Isa 1:18), but God's knowledge is complete and exhaustive, while humans only know in a fragmentary and incomplete way (difference). See footnote 22 in this chapter.

30. Compare, for example, Prov 3:31 with Exod 20:5 that use the same Hebrew term for *jealousy*. See the discussion in Peckham, "Theopathic or Anthropopathic?" 352; Peckham, "The Concept of Divine Love," 36. See also Vanhoozer, *Remythologizing Theology*, 77-78.

31. This fact was clear for the Adventist pioneers. Exodus 33:20-23, for example, was one of the typical texts (along with 24:9-11) used by the pioneers to affirm Gods corporeity. See pp. 131-132 in Chapter 3; Smith, *Mortal or Immortal?* 9-10; J. White, *Personality of God*, 1-2; Dudley M. Canright, "The Personality of God (*Continued*)," *The Adventist Review and Sabbath Herald*, September 5, 1878, 81-82. The Adventist pioneers clearly opposed the predominant classical tradition in their interpretation of God's corporeity. See Moon, "Quest for a Biblical Trinity," 145-147. However, it is still true that there is an "almost universal contention among scholars that God does not have an external form." Davidson, "Nature of the Human Being," 24. Thus, biblical interpreters discussing God's corporeity in Exod 33 usually interpret it as mere anthropomorphism. Nahum M. Sarna, for example, a Jewish interpreter, talks about a "daring anthropomorphism." Nahum M. Sarna, *Exodus*, The JPS Torah Commentary (Philadelphia, PA: JPS, 1991), 215. According to Godfrey Ashby, Exod 33 involves human imaginary that he qualifies as "anthropomorphisms." Godfrey Ashby, *Go Out and Meet God: A Commentary on the Book of Exodus*, International Theological Commentary (Grand Rapids, MI: Eerdmans, 1998), 134. See also Douglas K. Stuart, *Exodus*, The New American Commentary (NAC) 2 (Nashville, TN: Broadman & Holman, 2006), 710. Even Wolterstorff, who defends God's temporality based on biblical evidence, clearly denies that God has a spatial location and a corporeal aspect without invoking any biblical support. Wolterstorff, "Unqualified Divine Temporality," 208-209. Feinberg considers that if God is spirit, all biblical references to God's physical parts

then, involves God's temporality and physicality-spatiality. This analogical meaning of space and matter, in connection with the interpretation of God, should not be a problem in the same way in which the analogical meaning of time regarding God is not a problem either.[32]

The spatio-temporal analogical language that the Bible uses to talk about God implies that the description of God's presence and activities in heaven—as the dwelling place of God—requires a real-literal interpretation in contrast to a functional one. When Scripture says that Christ is seated at the right hand of the Father's throne in the heavenly sanctuary interceding for the believers (Rom 8:34; Eph 1:20; Heb 8:1-2), there is no reason to interpret Christ's and the Father's real sitting on a real throne in the context of a real intercessory activity in a way which is not literal.[33]

---

are anthropomorphisms, including Exod 33:20-23. See his discussion in Feinberg, *No One Like Him*, 214-223. Of course, he interprets *spirit* as opposed to *matter*. Feinberg, yet, has to admit that he does not know "what Matt 5:8 and Heb 12:14 exactly mean." Ibid., 223. The reason is simple: both verses affirm that those who are pure of heart or holy will see God. For a possible exception to the interpretation of God as bodiless, see Clark H. Pinnock, *Most Moved Mover: A Theology of God's Openness* (Grand Rapids, MI: Baker, 2001), 33-35. Clark H. Pinnock at least considers the possibility that God has a physical aspect. "In tradition, God is thought to function primarily as a disembodied spirit but this is scarcely a biblical idea." Ibid., 33.

32. There is no need to interpret space and matter in a univocal way, as in the case of Greek and modern philosophy, with their corresponding impact on theology. In this sense, it is probably better to say that God has a physical appearance—which is in some way part of His being—rather than saying that He takes a physical form, particularly in the context of biblical theophanies. In other words, biblical analogical language to talk about God implies that biblical depictions of God are analogically spatio-temporal. The idea of taking a form may imply a dualism—even if not intentional—between God's *being* and God's *manifestation* as if God's manifestation in time and space where not really God's spatio-temporal presence. Rice, for example, suggests distinguishing "between 'having a body' and 'assuming a physical form.' This enables us to say that God himself is not essentially physical, but he may assume a characteristic form from time to time when he manifests himself to physical creatures." Rice, *Reign of God*, 83. See also, with some qualifications, Peckham, "The Concept of Divine Love," 30, n. 72; Gulley, *Creation, Christ, Salvation*, 90. From a biblical perspective, however, God relates to His spatio-temporal creation as a spatio-temporal being, although He is not limited by His spatial location or physical appearance as the incarnated Christ in heaven demonstrates.

33. Interestingly, David M. Moffitt, a non-Adventist scholar, has realized that from the perspective of Hebrews, the fact that Christ ascended to heaven as a glorified human being has implications in the understanding of the ontology of heavenly realities, particularly the existence of a real heavenly sanctuary. "As one might expect with an account of a human [Jesus Christ] ascending into heaven where the heavenly

A last word in relation to the interpretation of God is in order here. Some biblical passages refer to God as transcending His creation (Gen 1:1; 2; 2 Chr 2:6) and they highlight His greatness, incomparability, and uniqueness regarding nature. However, as God's revelation, Scripture emphasizes God's relation to the world. Scripture focuses on God's immanence or self-adaptation to creation, without depicting any ontological overlap between both as the panentheistic models propose.[34] Consequently, the Bible does not claim to explain in detail issues related to God's transcendence. Even if Scripture reveals and affirms aspects about God's transcendence such as the unity of the three persons of the Godhead (Deut 6:4; cf. Matt 28:19), there is no clear explanation about how God is one in the sphere of His transcendence.[35] At the same time, while Scripture affirms God's foreknowledge or omnipresence, there is no clear elucidation about how that fact is possible in connection with human freedom or God's spatial location and physical appearance. Ultimately, any attempt to understand God's nature should keep in mind that there are aspects of His essence not revealed to His creatures (Deut 29:29).[36]

---

tabernacle that God pitched is thought to exist, the writer's language in [Heb] 9:11–12 encourages a *spatial and temporal conception* of Jesus entering and moving through a structure that actually exists in heaven in order to present his offering to God. This heavenly structure is the very one that Moses saw when he ascended from Sinai into heaven to receive the Law." David M. Moffitt, *Atonement and the Logic of Resurrection in the Epistle to the Hebrews*, Supplements to Novum Testamentum 141 (Leiden, The Netherlands: Brill, 2011), 225. Emphasis mine. See also David M. Moffitt, "Serving in Heaven's Temple: Sacred Space, Yom Kippur, and Jesus' Superior Offering in Hebrews," paper presented at the Annual Meeting of the Society of Biblical Literature, Chicago, IL, November 16-20, 2012.

34. Angel Manuel Rodríguez, quoting Isa 45:5, 6; 46:5, 9, underlines God's incomparability and uniqueness. "Since creation takes place outside God, there is, by nature, a distance between God and His creation. This idea is emphasized in the Bible through the concept of the incomparability of God." Angel Manuel Rodríguez, "God's Presence in the Sanctuary: A Theology of His Nearness," paper for the Biblical Research Institute, n.d., 2, accessed December 8, 2016, https://adventistbiblicalresearch.org/sites/default/files/pdf/God%27s%20presence%20in%20sanctuary.pdf. Moreover, Rodríguez also finds that the distance or transcendence of God regarding "His creation is radically affirmed when it is categorically stated that the 'heavens, even the highest heaven, cannot contain you' (1 Kings 8:27, NIV)." Ibid.

35. Of course, the unity of the three persons of the Godhead is part of the divine immanence as well, although even in this case, the ultimate nature of the unity is unrevealed. For a discussion of the doctrine of the Trinity from an Adventist perspective, see Whidden, Moon, and Reeve, *The Trinity*, 21-117. See also Gulley, *God as Trinity*, 3-32.

36. In the light of Gulley's emphasis on God's nature as love, Peckham's quali-

The Interpretation of the World

The world is a basic part of the biblical theological system whose interpretation is fundamental in order to understand the biblical interpretation of the principle of articulation. Without the world as something different from God, there is no need for articulation. From a biblical perspective, the world is God's creation (Gen 1:1; Neh 9:6). The world is not eternal or everlasting as in process theology. Creation (Gen 1-2) and preservation (Ps 147:9; Matt 6:26; Heb 1:3), then, are not the same (against Schleiermacher[37]). Moreover, the creation of the world is not a continuous still-in-process activity of God, as panentheistic evolution could imply (process theology, Guy). Creation is a finished work (Gen 2:1-3; Exod 20:11), accomplished in a specific period that establishes the starting point for the time and history of the world, as shared with, but distinguishable from, the time of the Godhead that exists from *before* (Gr. *pro*) the foundation of the world.[38]

Biblical creation, therefore, is a creation *ex nihilo* but not in the Thomistic sense of this expression that refers to Creation as a timeless and instantaneous activity of God. Creation is *ex nihilo* in the sense that God's creative activity does not depend on something else, different from His own power (Rom 4:17; Heb 11:3). From this perspective, it

---

fication regarding God's essence is timely. He warns that "it could be misleading to attempt to derive a divine ontology from one divine characteristic, even one as major as divine love." Peckham, "The Concept of Divine Love," 690. In consonance, he evaluates that "'God is love' is not necessarily intended to describe the divine essence as a whole (1 John 4:8, 16). Elsewhere, it is said that 'God is light' (1 John 1:5) and 'God is Spirit' (John 4:24). Many biblical scholars contend that the statement 'God is love' is not necessarily 'ontological' but descriptive of the divine character." Ibid., 705, n. 327. Peckham ultimately questions "whether it is possible to make any certain pronouncement(s) that correspond to the divine essence as a whole . . . which appears to be beyond not only divine revelation but also human cognizance." Ibid., 705.

37. Regarding Schleiermacher's interpretation of the world, see Chapter 3, pp. 114-115.

38. "Ten texts in the N[ew] T[estament] use 'foundation of the world' terminology to identify the starting point for this world's history. Six of these refer to events that have taken place 'since' or 'from' the foundation of the world (Matt. 13:35; 25:34; Luke 11:50; Heb. 4:3; 9:26; Rev. 17:8). Four refer to events that took place 'before' the foundation of the world (John 17:24; Eph. 1:4; 1 Peter 1:20; Rev. 13:8). Thus the N[ew] T[estament] writers knew Creation week as a finite point in time that divided the time and events before it from those that took place after it. As Bible writers referred to Creation, it was not vague or nebulous, but historically specific." William H. Shea, "Creation," in *Handbook of Seventh-day Adventist Theology*, ed. Raoul Dederen (Hagerstown, MD: Review & Herald, 2000), 437.

is probably more precise to say that God created through His powerful word (Gen 1; Ps 33:6, 9).[39]

God's creation *ex nihilo* is not kenotic as in the panentheistic modern Adventist model. Neither God is invested in the world nor is the world essential to God. God is still ontologically omnipotent (Gen 18:4; Matt 19:26; Luke 1:27). He only willingly limits His power regarding the free will of His intelligent creatures.[40]

Creation involves the universe in general and life and its organization on the earth in particular. The creation of the universe includes heavenly realities and angels (Ezek 28:15; Col 1:16; Heb 8:2; 9:11). The fact that angels were present at the time of the creation of the earth (Job 38:7) implies that Gen 1 does not necessarily describe the creation of the entire universe. The angels, heaven realities, and earth without life (Gen 1:2) are evidently part of a prior creation.[41] The creation of the life on the earth is consistently described as a historical and temporal creation of six literal consecutive days (Gen 1; Exod 20:11; 31:17) in a relatively recent time in the past.

This literal-temporal interpretation of the Creation account is in harmony with the narrative literary form of Gen 1-11 that includes the story of a universal flood.[42] Genesis 1-11 suggests that "the author intend-

---

39. In Aquinas, Creation has to be *ex nihilo* to avoid the possibility of change from something prior to something new. That change would imply time, which is irreconcilable with God's nature, according to Aquinas. See Chapter 3, p. 81.

40. Regarding the freedom of intelligent creatures, see pp. 265-266 in this chapter and the following section about the interpretation of the human being, p. 268ff.

41. As mentioned in Chapter 4, footnote 422, Davidson finds a passive gap between Gen 1:1 and 1:3 that would allow time for the creation of the angels in a prior creation. However, even if that gap is not admitted, it is still clear that Gen 1:2 assumes the existence of the earth at the beginning of the narrative of the Creation week. "The text acknowledges the fact that the inert earth was in a watery state before the events of Creation week, but it is not especially concerned with identifying how long it may have been in that state." Shea, "Creation," 419. The existence of the earth before the Creation week necessarily implies a previous creation that is consistent with the previous existence of intelligent creatures, such as angels and heavenly realities. In other words, this prior creation involves, at least, the earth, angels, and heaven (the abode of angels and God). This view of a Creation in at least two stages implies that heaven is part of the spatio-temporal creation, and not a timeless dimension. The idea of a heaven outside of the universe "would not seem cohere with the larger biblical context, in which other inhabited worlds . . . were in existence and actually watched the creation of this earth (Job 38:7)." Davidson, "The Genesis Account of Origins," 101, n. 121.

42. Regarding the historicity of the six-day Creation story and Gen 1-11 in gen-

ed to provide a historical narrative of earth's early history—not simply a theological statement, or a nonliteral, literary depiction of Creation such as poem, parable, saga, myth, etc."[43] A theological or non-literal interpretation of the Genesis Creation account involves "the presence of non-biblical-macro-hermeneutical presuppositions in the interpretation of Genesis 1."[44] These presuppositions are in line with the ontological and epistemological presuppositions of classical theism (the hierarchical model of Catholic theology, soteriological model of Protestant theology, and evangelical Adventist model) and modern theology (the panentheistic model of modern theology and modern Adventist theology).

The biblical interpretation of Creation is clearly not compatible with the notion of Creation through an evolutionary process or a progressive creation that requires millions of years of death, pain, and suffering, as part of the creative work. While Rom 5:12-14 along with 1 Cor 15:21 shows that the problem of death is the result of Adam's sin and exists since the time of Adam, Rom 8:19-23 clarifies that death and suffering exist in nature and involve the entire creation *as a result*

---

eral, there are several lines of evidence. Davidson mentions the narrative literary genre, the framing of this section in the *tōlĕdōt* (generations) structure of the whole book of Genesis, the use of the expression *evening* and *morning* in connection with the days of the Creation story, and the biblical references to Gen 1-2 in other parts of the canon (Exod 20:8-11). Davidson, "The Genesis Account of Origins," 73-80. Actually, "every chapter of Genesis 1 through 11 is referred to somewhere in the New Testament, and Jesus Himself refers to Genesis 1 through 7." Ibid., 80. An additional line of evidence comes from the use of the waw-consecutive in Gen 1-11, used in typical historical narratives such as Chronicles and Kings. See Younker, "How Can We Interpret," 75. See also Hasel, "The 'Days' of Creation in Genesis," 40-68. Regarding the recent chronological framework of Gen 1-11, see Davidson, "The Genesis Account of Origins," 102-104; Gerhard F. Hasel, "The Genealogies of Genesis 5 and 11 and Their Alleged Babylonian Background," *AUSS* 16, no. 2 (1978): 361-474. Randall W. Younker highlights that the books of Genesis and Exodus together "tell a continuous story from Creation, through Abraham, Joseph, the descent down to Egypt, and the Exodus." Younker, "How Can We Interpret," 75. If the text of Gen 1-11 is taken seriously, it is clear that the chronological framework does not allow the insertion of millions of years in the narrative.

43. Younker, "How Can We Interpret," 75. This conclusion opposes the interpretation of the Genesis account of Creation by modern and evangelical theology today. "Some biblical scholars, who reject a literal, six-day creation week, frankly admit that their ultimate criterion for such rejection is on the level of foundational presuppositions, in which the *sola Scriptura* principle is no longer maintained. . . . This is true of both liberal-critical and conservative-evangelical scholars." Davidson, "The Genesis Account of Origins," 83. Emphasis in original.

44. Davidson, "The Genesis Account of Origins," 84.

of human sin. Both humans and the rest of creation are waiting for a restoration (redemption) to the prior perfect condition lost for the sake of human sin.[45]

In consonance with this effect of sin in nature, it is also evident that nature in general does not possess a freedom or self-determination to contribute in the creation of its own reality, as process theology and modern Adventist model hold. As Paul states, "Creation was subjected to futility, not willingly" (Rom 8:20, NKJV).[46] Nature, instead, operates in obedience to the natural regularities established by God Himself (Acts 14:17; Job 38:4-39:30; Jer 10:13; 31:35-36). God has a "covenantal" relationship with nature in the sense that He has established the natural laws—legal order—that regulates its operation; nature obeys them in fulfillment of its purpose of service (Jer 33:20, 25) but does not have freedom to decide about the obedience to those laws.[47]

The origin of evil and sin in the world, then, is not a byproduct of a progressive creation or of an evolutionary process where the world has made wrong decisions. It is the result of a conscious and voluntary decision made by intelligent creatures in opposition to God's will and law. Thus, Scripture describes that at some point in the past, before the creation of the earth, one angel rebelled against God's government and tried to usurp His position (Isa 14:13-14). That angel is identified

---

45. See Chapter 4, footnote 171 and the references there. See also John T. Baldwin, "Progressive Creationism and Biblical Revelation: Some Theological Implications," *JATS* 3, no. 1 (1992): 105-119; John T. Baldwin, "The Geologic Column and Calvary: The Rainbow Connection—Implications for an Evangelical Understanding of the Atonement," in *Creation, Catastrophe, and Calvary: Why a Global Flood Is Vital to the Doctrine of Atonement*, ed. John T. Baldwin (Hagerstown, MD: Review & Herald, 2000), 112-113.

46. The implication of this text is "that creation was not party to Adam's failure but was drawn into it nonetheless." James D. G. Dunn, *Romans 1-8*, WBC 38A (Dallas, TX: Word, 1988), 470. See also Isa 24:5, where it becomes evident that humans defile the earth because of their sins. Samuel H. Widyapranawa, *The Lord Is Savior: Faith in National Crisis; A Commentary on the Book of Isaiah 1-39*, International Theological Commentary (Grand Rapids, MI: Eerdmans, 1990), 142-143.

47. Regarding the covenantal relationship between God and His creation, see pp. 293-295 in this chapter. See also, with some reservations, Frame, *Knowledge of God*, 12-13. E. G. White also affirms that "the harmony of creation depends upon the perfect conformity of all beings, of everything, animate and inanimate, to the law of the Creator. God has ordained laws for the government, not only of living beings, but of all the operations of nature. Everything is under fixed laws, which cannot be disregarded." E. G. White, *Patriarchs and Prophets*, 52.

as a guardian cherub (Ezek 28:14).[48] Because of this rebellion, this angel was cast out of heaven to earth (Isa 14:15; Ezek 28:16, 17). Several biblical passages echo this event.[49] This fallen angel is called Satan (Rev 12:9) and he did not fall alone. He persuaded many other angels who followed him in his rebellion (Rev 12:4, 7-9; 2 Pet 2:4; Jude 6). After the Creation week, Satan—that Rev 12:9 identifies with the serpent of Gen 3—succeeded in tempting Adam and Eve and, as a result, the problem of evil and sin spread to the earth with all their consequences (Gen 3).[50]

The fact that Satan and his followers committed sin in his rebellion against God reveals that they lived under the authority of a divine moral law (Ezek 28:15; John 8:44; 1 John 3:8). The disobedience to that law was an offense to God and a questioning of His character and government (Isa 14:13-15). In other words, before the Fall, the whole universe lived in harmony in a covenantal relationship with God that was broken through the sin (2 Pet 2:4). Angels were created to serve God (Ps 104:4; Ezek 26:14), but that obedience and service are evidently voluntary. The covenantal relationship between God and the angels was broken—at least with part of them—and put in danger the unity of the universe under God's authority.[51]

---

48. Isaiah 14 and Ezek 28 actually use the king of Babylon and the prince of Tyre as types of Satan. Both passages "portray the being who was the originator of evil and the propelling force behind every effort to disturb order in God's universe." José M. Bertoluci, "The Son of the Morning and the Guardian Cherub in the Context of the Controversy Between Good and Evil" (ThD diss., Andrews University, Berrien Springs, MI, 1985), 303. For an extensive explanation of the typological interpretation of Isa 14 and Ezek 28, see ibid., 288ff. Moreover, José M. Bertoluci's dissertation offers an excellent exegesis of Isa 14:12-15 and Ezek 28:12-19 in connection with the emergence of the problem of evil and sin. Regarding Ezek 28:12-19, see also Davidson, "Ezekiel 28:11-19."

49. See, for example, Luke 10:18; John 12:31; 2 Pet 2:4; Rev 9:1; 12:9, 10. For a partial list of passages, see Bertoluci, "The Son of the Morning," 282; Davidson, "Ezekiel 28:11-19," 63.

50. For additional discussion regarding the origin of evil and sin, see Holbrook, "The Great Controversy," 974-979; E. G. White, *Patriarchs and Prophets*, 33-42.

51. Regarding the covenantal relationship between God and angels, see p. 294 in this chapter. E. G. White implies the existence of a covenant between God and angels when she writes, "Everything in nature, from the mote in the sunbeam to the worlds on high, is under law. And upon obedience to these laws the order and harmony of the natural world depend. So there are great principles of righteousness to control the life of all intelligent beings, and upon conformity to these principles the well-being of the universe depends. Before this earth was called into being, God's law existed. Angels are governed by its principles." Ellen G. White, *Thoughts*

A last aspect regarding the biblical interpretation of the world is that the world is a spatio-temporal reality. The fact that creation involves heaven and earth, angels and humans, and that there is a spatio-temporal interaction between them shows that there is no such thing as a timelessness-temporality or spacelessness-spatiality ontological dualism. God's activities in heaven are in *synchronization* with human activities on earth. For example, human requests for forgiveness or other motives on earth induce a divine answer from heaven (1 Kgs 8:30-52). At the same time, although angels are described as spiritual creatures (Heb 1:7, 14), this fact is not in contradiction with their existence in space and time, having a physical aspect, in interaction with human beings (Gen 19:1-22; Heb 13:2).

What is spiritual, then, is not in contraposition to what is physical or material. Matter is not something negative as in Greek philosophy and classical theology. Material creation is good.[52] Time is also a valuable aspect of reality. One evidence of this biblical appreciation of time is the fact that at the end of the Creation week, God blessed and sanctified a day, the Sabbath (Gen 2:2-3), and that day remained holy even after the Fall (Exod 16:5, 22-30; 20:8-11). Time is not an illusion. It is a real linear succession past-present-future, as the time of the Creation week.[53]

From the Mount of Blessing (Mountain View, CA: Pacific Press, 1955), 48. See also E. G. White, *Patriarchs and Prophets*, 34.

52. See the sevenfold repetition that affirms the goodness of God's creation in Gen 1:4, 10, 12, 18, 21, 25, 31. In the first six references, God evaluates specific aspects of His creation as "good." In v. 31, however, God evaluates His entire creation as "very good." "The harmony and perfection of the completed heavens and earth express more adequately the character of their creator than any of the separate components can." Wenham, *Genesis 1-15*, 34. Regarding the goodness or original perfection of the world, Shea explains, "This view of the material world and its inhabitants was characteristically Hebrew." Shea, "Creation," 424. Similarly, E. G. White expresses, "All created things, in their original perfection, were an expression of the thought of God." E. G. White, *Education*, 16-17.

53. Cullmann contrasts the biblical conception of time with the Greek one in these terms: "We can clearly define the conception of the course of time which the New Testament presupposes by stating it in opposition to the typically Greek idea, and we must start from this fundamental perception, that the symbol of time for Primitive Christianity as well as for Biblical Judaism . . . is the *line*, while in Hellenism it is the *circle*." Cullmann, *Christ and Time*, 51. Emphasis in original. Regarding the Sabbath, it is important to clarify that it is not a temporal anticipation of a timeless eternity, as Heschel suggests. See Abraham J. Heschel, *The Sabbath: Its Meaning for Modern Man* (New York, NY: Noonday, 1994), 65-76. The eschatological expectation of Scripture clearly involves time and space (Isa 66:22-23; Rev 20-22).

The Interpretation of the Human Being

As angels, human beings are intelligent creatures who have the ability to know God and to communicate with Him (Gen 1:28-30; 2:15-17). As such, they are the culmination of the Creation week and not the product of an evolutionary process (Gen 1:26-27). The depiction of human beings as made in the image and likeness of God appears precisely in that setting. "The context surrounding the expression in Genesis 1:26, 27 associates this image with a position at the summit of all material creation."[54]

The concept of the image of God implies several things. "That the image of God, in which man and woman were created, includes a physical likeness is part of the conception conveyed by the original word used here."[55] This conclusion is only natural if the analogical understanding of God in Scripture involves temporality, spatiality, and physicality. As said in connection with the interpretation of God, human beings are theomorphic.[56] The image of God, however, includes other aspects. Based on Gen 1-2, it becomes clear that the image of God involves rationality, morality (especially in its original perfection), emotional life, freedom of choice (free will), a social dimension (including sexuality), and the human authority to rule over nature in general.[57]

---

54. Aecio E. Cairus, "The Doctrine of Man," in *Handbook of Seventh-day Adventist Theology*, ed. Raoul Dederen (Hagerstown, MD: Review & Herald, 2000), 207.

55. Shea, "Creation," 424. Shea clarifies that "moderns have shied away from the physical aspect of this phraseology. Ancient Hebrews did not." Ibid. See also Davidson, "Nature of the Human Being," 17. Gerhard von Rad also sees in the Hebrew word for *image* a physical resemblance. "This image is to correspond to the original image . . . to resemble it." Gerhard von Rad, *Genesis: A Commentary*, trans. John H. Marks, rev. ed. (London, UK: SCM, 1972), 58.

56. "Israel conceived even Jahweh himself as having human form. But the way of putting it which we use runs in precisely the wrong direction according to Old Testament ideas, for . . . it cannot be said that Israel regarded God anthropomorphically, but the reverse, that she considered man as theomorphic." Gerhard von Rad, *Old Testament Theology*, vol. 1, *The Theology of Israel's Historical Traditions*, trans. D. M. G. Stalker (Edinburgh, Scotland: Oliver & Boyd, 1962), 145. According to von Rad, Ezek 1:26 (that shows God with "the likeness as the appearance of a man", KJV) "is the theological prelude to the locus *classicus* for the *imago* doctrine in Gen I. 26." Ibid., 146. Emphasis in original.

57. Shea mentions several of these aspects. Shea, "Creation," 424. Aecio E. Cairus emphasizes the role of human beings as God's representatives, rulers over nature, and cooperators (Gen 1:26-27; 2:4-6, 15; Pss 8:3-8; 115:16). However, he does not exclude the aspect of resemblance. The representational role necessarily involves other aspects of the image of God. "Physical, intellectual, social, and spiritual endowments,

These elements are aspects or dimensions of the human being as a whole. The image of God does not refer to a supposedly separable aspect of human beings as the soul of Christian tradition (Augustine, Calvin). Human beings are a unitary entity, as the terminology used by Genesis reveals. God formed the first man by using dust. God breathed in him His breath of life and the man became a living soul (Gen 2:7; cf. Job 10:8-12). The text, then, shows that the living soul (Heb. *nepheš ḥayyâ*) is the whole person, including its physical dimension. The soul is not a timeless and bodiless conscious entity that can survive the extinction of the body.[58]

In consonance, Scripture describes death as the reverse process to the one described in Gen 2:7. According to Eccl 12:7, when a person dies, the dust returns to the ground (see also Gen 3:19; Job 34:15; Ps 146:4) and the breath of life (*rûah*) returns to God. "When God with-

---

as well as the ability to commune with God, are therefore integral to the concept of God's image." Cairus, "The Doctrine of Man," 208. Sarna also highlights the royal function of the image of God in connection with Ps 8 (see vv. 5-6). Nahum M. Sarna, *Genesis*, The JPS Torah Commentary (Philadelphia, PA: JPS, 1989), 12. Hans W. Wolff emphasizes virtually exclusively the dominion over creation. Hans W. Wolff, *Anthropology of the Old Testament*, trans. Margaret Kohl (Philadelphia, PA: Fortress, 1974), 159-164. Von Rad has a more integral perspective of the meaning of *imago Dei*. For him, it involves physical, spiritual, and intellectual dimensions, as well as the dominion on nature. von Rad, *Genesis*, 58-60. In a similar vein, Davidson shows that the image of God includes the physical aspect, free will (Gen 2:16, 17), rational abilities, memory, linguistic abilities, and aesthetic sensibilities (Gen 2:19-20; 3:1-6). Davidson, "Nature of the Human Being," 19. Moreover, Gen 1:26-28 and Ps 8:6-8 imply the relational-sexual-social aspect of the image of God as well as the royal-functional and ecological dimensions. Ibid., 20-22.

58. "This man . . . formed from the earth, becomes a living creature only when inspired with the divine breath of life. *Nᵉšāmā* corresponds to our 'breath.' This divine vital power is personified, individualized, but only by its entry into the material body; and only this breath when united with the body makes man a 'living creature.'" von Rad, *Genesis*, 77. Thus, in Gen 2:7, the breath of life seems to be the life itself given by God. This passage "distinguishes not body and 'soul' but more realistically body and life. The divine breath of life which unites with the material body makes man a 'living soul' both from the physical as well as from the psychical side. This life springs directly from God, as directly as the lifeless human body received breath from God's mouth when he bent over it." Ibid. Regarding the terminology of the New Testament about human being, see Ekkehardt Mueller, "The Nature of the Human Being in the New Testament," in *"What Are Human Beings That You Remember Them?" Proceedings of the Third International Bible Conference, Nof Ginosar and Jerusalem; June 11-21, 2012*, ed. Clinton Wahlen (Silver Spring, MD: Biblical Research Institute, 2015), 133-163.

draws his breath (Ps. 104.29 f.; Job 34.14 f.), man reverts to dead corporeity."[59] The thoughts of the person also disappear. There is no consciousness (Ps 146:4; Eccl 9:5-6).[60] Consequently, Scripture often refers to death as a sleep (Dan 12:2; John 11:11-14; 1 Thess 4:13-14).[61]

Death is not a natural condition (Eccl 3:11).[62] Humans beings were meant to live forever. Death in human experience is the result of human sin (Gen 3:17-19), the wrong use of human free will (Gen 2:17; 3:1-6). In spite of that reality, believers have a hope. That hope consists in the resurrection of the dead, not in the immortality of the soul (Job 19:25-27; Dan 12:2, 3; 1 Thess 4:15-17).[63]

---

59. von Rad, *Genesis*, 77. In Gen 2:7, the Hebrew expression for *breath of life* is *nĕšāmâ* while in Eccl 12:7 and Ps 104:29, the *breath* that God takes away from the human being is *rûah*. Yet, both words are frequently parallel terms, as Job 34:14 illustrates. See also Gen 7:22; Isa 42:5; 57:16. Wolff, *Anthropology of the Old Testament*, 33.

60. See also Pss 6:5; 115:17; 146:4. See Niels-Erik A. Andreasen, "Death: Origin, Nature, and Final Eradication," in *Handbook of Seventh-day Adventist Theology*, ed. Raoul Dederen (Hagerstown, MD: Review & Herald, 2000), 324-325.

61. See also Job 14:12; Acts 7:60; 1 Cor 15:51. For additional references and discussion, see Andreasen, "Death," 325. For additional discussion regarding the issue of death in the Old and the New Testament, see Félix H. Cortez, "Death and Future Hope in the Hebrew Bible," in *"What Are Human Beings That You Remember Them?" Proceedings of the Third International Bible Conference, Nof Ginosar and Jerusalem; June 11-21, 2012*, ed. Clinton Wahlen (Silver Spring, MD: Biblical Research Institute, 2015), 95-106; Félix H. Cortez, "Death and Hell in the New Testament," in *"What Are Human Beings That You Remember Them?" Proceedings of the Third International Bible Conference, Nof Ginosar and Jerusalem; June 11-21, 2012*, ed. Clinton Wahlen (Silver Spring, MD: Biblical Research Institute, 2015), 183-204.

62. "After sin, and in spite of death, humans maintain a strong sense of unending existence (Eccl. 3:11). Physically, mentally, and emotionally we all live with eternity in view and fight death with all our energies, will, and means." Miroslav M. Kiš, "Christian Lifestyle and Behavior," in *Handbook of Seventh-day Adventist Theology*, ed. Raoul Dederen (Hagerstown, MD: Review & Herald, 2000), 678. According to Eccl 3:11, God has put eternity (*'ôlām*) in the human heart. *Eternity* here refers to *duration* in contrast to a definite period. Roland E. Murphy, *Ecclesiastes*, WBC 23A (Dallas, TX: Word, 1992), 34.

63. See Isa 26:19; 1 Cor 15:51-55. For a discussion of the main texts about resurrection in the Old Testament, see Greg A. King, "Resurrection in the Old Testament: Hazy Hope or Certain Promise," in *The Great Controversy and the End of Evil: Biblical and Theological Studies in Honor of Ángel Manuel Rodríguez in Celebration of His Seventieth Birthday*, ed. Gerhard Pfandl (Silver Spring, MD: Biblical Research Institute, 2015), 217-227. Regarding the issue of resurrection in the New Testament see, with some qualifications, Oscar Cullmann, *Immortality of the Soul or Resurrection of the Dead? The Witness of the New Testament* (New York, NY: Macmillan, 1958).

While in normal circumstances all human beings participate in what the Bible calls the *first death*, the believers will resurrect in the *first resurrection* that takes place at the second coming of Christ, at the beginning of the millennium (Rev 20:6). Scripture, though, refers to a *second resurrection* at the end of the millennium that involves only those sinners who opposed God and rejected His salvation (v. 5). This resurrection allows the final punishment and annihilation of the wicked in a lake of fire, described as the *second death*. This death also entails the eradication of death in itself (2:11; 20:6, 14-15; 21:8). Scripture does not conceive the existence of a hell as an eternal place of torture for sinners. On the other hand, the saints are intended to enjoy an everlasting life as immortal and glorified human beings, starting with the millennium in heaven and the new earth after that period (1 Cor 15:51-54; Phil 3:21; Rev 20-22).[64]

The problem of sin entails not only disobedience to the divine will and commandments (Gen 2:17; 1 John 3:4). It is also a new condition in human nature (Ps 51:5) that has involved humanity since Adam (Rom 5:12ff) and produced broken relationships with God (Gen 3:8-11; cf. Isa 59:2), other humans (Gen 3:12-13), and even with nature (vv. 18-19). Moreover, human sin has affected nature by introducing the problem of suffering and death in general (Gen 3:17-19).[65] Sin "embraces the whole man . . . and its consequence, death, extends over all the rest of

---

64. "All human beings are subject to the first death, but its effect is merely to synchronize the rewards of those living in different ages; it will be unconditionally canceled by a resurrection. The second death is the penalty for personal sins, while the first is the effect of Adam's sin." Cairus, "The Doctrine of Man," 223. Regarding the first and second death and resurrection, as well as the final destiny of the wicked and saints, see Andreasen, "Death," 332-334; John C. Brunt, "Resurrection and Glorification," in *Handbook of Seventh-day Adventist Theology*, ed. Raoul Dederen (Hagerstown, MD: Review & Herald, 2000), 347-365; Cortez, "Death and Hell," 186-203. For additional references, see also the previous footnote. Scripture does not claim to explain how God preserves the identity of human beings between the first death and the resurrection. However, Scripture clearly assumes that identity is not lost with death. The resurrection, otherwise, would be a meaningless hope for the saints. Paul evidently understands that those who will resurrect at the second coming of Christ will be conscious of their identity (1 Thess 4:13-18). Even those who resurrect at the end of the millennium will remember who they are. Otherwise, the necessity of the judgment before the white throne would be incomprehensible.

65. Regarding the origin of sin in the human context, its nature, and consequences, see John M. Fowler, "Sin," in *Handbook of Seventh-day Adventist Theology*, ed. Raoul Dederen (Hagerstown, MD: Review & Herald, 2000), 237-239, 241-258.

creation."⁶⁶ The solution to the problem of sin is beyond human possibilities. It is a universal problem (Rom 3:23; 5:12), which necessarily requires divine intervention (Gen 3:15; Rom 5:6-11).⁶⁷

In spite of the problem of sin, the image of God did not disappear completely (Gen 9:6; 1 Cor 11:7; Jas 3:9). Human beings are still able to respond to God's initiative for salvation (John 16:8; Rom 5:6-8). They still have free will, although a much weakened one. The Holy Spirit awakens the sinful conscience that otherwise does not have spiritual discernment (1 Cor 2:14). The sinner has to hear Him with faith (Gal 3:1-5) and responds with repentance (Acts 2:38), confession (Prov 28:13; Jas 5:16), and conversion, before receiving forgiveness (Acts 3:19). These steps require the constant assistance of God. While the sinner has to exert faith, faith is also something that God stimulates through his Word (Rom 10:17). There is an interaction between God's initiative and human response (Mark 9:24).⁶⁸

A final aspect that is important to highlight regarding the interpretation of the human being is that as spatio-temporal beings, humans are relational creatures. "Being created in the image of God . . . means that we as humans find our ultimate identity in God, but also that our human identity in general is established in alterocentricity [the centrality of the others], not only in relation to God but in relation to fellow human beings as well."⁶⁹ The restoration of human identity, in harmony with the image of God as ideal, involves the restoration of these relations.⁷⁰

---

66. Cullmann, *Immortality of the Soul*, 30.

67. See also Fowler, "Sin," 258.

68. For additional discussion and biblical references about these steps, see Ivan T. Blazen, "Salvation," in *Handbook of Seventh-day Adventist Theology*, ed. Raoul Dederen (Hagerstown, MD: Review & Herald, 2000), 292-294; E. G. White, *Steps to Christ*, 23-55.

69. Paul B. Petersen, "'Unwholly' Relationships: Unity in a Biblical Ontology," in *"What Are Human Beings That You Remember Them?" Proceedings of the Third International Bible Conference, Nof Ginosar and Jerusalem; June 11-21, 2012*, ed. Clinton Wahlen (Silver Spring, MD: Biblical Research Institute, 2015), 246.

70. Of course, the restoration of the relationship with God is a priority. "In the brokenness of my life, I live in a double dependency: dependent on God as my Creator in whom alone, outside of myself, I find my true identity; and dependent on God to reveal Himself to me, a sinner, because I lack any hope of knowing Him on my own. It is the marvelous grace of God that He has revealed Himself to me as a person in God the Son, Jesus Christ, and that God the Holy Spirit through the Bible has painted the true picture of Jesus." Ibid., 247-248.

The Interpretation of the Articulating Agent

The reformers emphasized the centrality of Christ as articulating agent.[71] Calvin, in particular, held that Christ was a Mediator between God and the world in general but assuming a timeless ontology of God. From a biblical temporal ontology, Col 1:16-20 is a key passage in order to understand Christ's mediation role.[72] Verse 16 affirms the central role of Christ in divine creation in consonance with other texts of the New Testament (1 Cor 8:6; John 1:3, 10; Heb 1:3).[73] The phrase translated "in him" (NIV) at the beginning of the verse seems to involve the idea that Christ is the Designer of Creation. "It should be understood as *in his mind* or *in his sphere of influence and responsibility*. Practically, it means that Jesus conceived of creation and its complexities. . . . The phrase points to Jesus as the 'detailer' of creation."[74] Additionally, Christ is not only the Designer ("in him," NIV) of Creation. He is also the agent ("through him," NIV) and the goal ("for Him," NIV) of Creation. Creation finds in Christ its purpose and end, serving Him.[75]

---

71. See the discussion in Chapter 3, pp. 94-95, 104-105.

72. Calvin also identified texts referring to the unifying or articulating role of Christ, such as Eph 1:10, 22; Col 1:16-20. See, for example, Calvin, *Harmony of the Evangelists*, 1:206; Calvin, *Galatians and Ephesians*, 204-205; John Calvin, *Commentaries on the Epistles of Paul the Apostle to the Philippians, Colossians, and Thessalonians* (Edinburgh, Scotland: Calvin Translation Society, 1851), 150-157. See also Chapter 3, p. 104 and footnote 286 there. Of course, Calvin interpreted Christ's mediation assuming God's timelessness. He saw the necessity of this mediating role of Christ in general—not only regarding His incarnation—due to his view of the lowliness of God's creatures, including angels. See Chapter 3, p. 107. Based on Job 4:18, where an unidentified spirit talks to Eliphaz, Calvin says, "The Spirit [of God] declares there, that the greatest purity is vile, if it is brought into comparison with the righteousness of God. We must, therefore, conclude, that there is not on the part of angels so much of righteousness as would suffice for their being fully joined with God." Ibid., 156 (commentary on Col 1:20). In spite of Calvin's non-biblical ontological assumptions, his identification of biblical texts as referring to the general mediating or articulating role of Christ is still correct.

73. See Eduard Lohse, *Colossians and Philemon: A Commentary on the Epistles to the Colossians and to Philemon*, Hermeneia, trans. William R. Poehlmann and Robert J. Karris (Philadelphia, PA: Fortress, 1971), 50. Colossians 1:16 says, "For *in him* all things were created: things in heaven and on earth, visible and invisible, whether thrones or powers or rulers or authorities; all things have been created *through him* and *for him*" (NIV). Emphasis mine.

74. Richard R. Melick, *Philippians, Colossians, Philemon*, NAC 32 (Nashville, TN: Broadman, 1991), 217. Emphasis in original.

75. See the discussion in William Hendriksen, *Exposition of Colossians and Philemon*, New Testament Commentary (Grand Rapids, MI: Baker, 1965), 73-74; Melick,

The expression *all things* (*ta panta*), repeated several times in Col 1:16-18, 20, reveals the scope of creation. That creation does not include only what was created during the Creation week but also angels or heavenly intelligences.[76] This creation involves all things in *heaven* and *earth*. The use of these words entails a connection not only with Gen 1 but also with Prov 8, where Wisdom participates in the creation of heaven and earth (vv. 27-31).[77]

Something similar occurs with John 1:1-3 that combines Gen 1:1 and Prov 8:22-23.[78] The expression "in the beginning" (KJV) in John 1:1 obviously reminds the reader the same expression in Gen 1:1.[79] The Word (Christ) was already in the beginning with God. In the same way, Wisdom was already with God "in the beginning" (KJV) according to Prov 8:22, 23.[80] However, the *beginning* of John 1:1 is not the one of the Creation week. This beginning "relates . . . not to the act of creation [of the earth], but to what existed when creation came into being, namely the Word, who was with God and was God."[81]

In order to understand the temporal scope of the mediatorial role of Christ between God and creation, it is necessary to determine what the beginning in John 1:1 is, which is prior to the beginning of Gen 1:1. Proverbs 8:22, 23 mentions a beginning that is earlier in time to the appearance of God's works and the existence of the earth, in consonance with John 1:1 (cf. 17:5).[82] An understanding of that beginning requires

---

Philippians, Colossians, Philemon, 217-218. Richard R. Melick summarizes Paul's argument by saying, "Jesus is the central point of all of creation, and he rules over it." Ibid., 218.

76. See Lohse, *Colossians and Philemon*, 51. Paul's terminology referring to thrones, dominions, principalities, and powers may reflect the terminology of false teachers to talk about angels. Paul also believes in their existence (Eph 1:21, 22) and their influence, whether unfallen (1 Tim 5:21) or fallen (Eph 6:12) angels, but all of them are ultimately creatures that must be submitted to God's authority. Hendriksen, *Exposition of Colossians and Philemon*, 73-74.

77. For a connection between Col 1:16 and Prov 8:27-31, see Lohse, *Colossians and Philemon*, 50.

78. Davidson, "Proverbs 8," 34.

79. See George R. Beasley-Murray, *John*, WBC 36, 2nd ed. (Nashville, TN: Thomas Nelson, 1999), 10; Raymond E. Brown, *The Gospel According to John (I-XII)*, Anchor Bible (AB) 29 (Garden City, NY: Doubleday, 1966), 4.

80. See Brown, *Gospel According to John (I-XII)*, cxxiii.

81. Beasley-Murray, *John*, 10. "The 'beginning' [in John 1:1] refers to the period before creation." Brown, *Gospel According to John (I-XII)*, 4. Raymond E. Brown notices that the issue of Creation appears later in v. 3 of John 1. Ibid.

82. See Brown, *Gospel According to John (I-XII)*, cxxiii.

identifying the Wisdom of Prov 8. Davidson has persuasively demonstrated that Wisdom in that chapter refers to a divine person. The expression "I, Wisdom" in Prov 8:12 (NKJV) is actually "the common rhetorical self-asseverating form of 'divine self-praise' ('I am Wisdom') regularly reserved elsewhere in Scripture and in the ancient Near East for deity: 'I am Yahweh your God'; 'I am Ishtar of Arbela'; 'I am Isis the divine.'"[83] Moreover, Prov 8:36 refers to those who sin against Wisdom, something possible only if Wisdom is a divine person.[84]

More specifically, Michael V. Fox notices that the New Testament actually equates the Wisdom of Prov 8 with the *logos* of John 1:1-2 and the *prōtotokos* of Col 1:15-16—a text that he considers as evidently depending on Prov 8. In other words, from the New Testament perspective, Christ is the uncreated pre-existent Wisdom of Prov 8, the agent of Creation.[85] Paul's language in Col 1:16 evokes the language of Prov 8,

---

83. Davidson, "Proverbs 8," 42. "Biblical parallels to this 'divine self-praise' with the same grammatical structure can be found in Ezek 12:25; 35:12; Zech 10:6; Mal 3:6." Ibid., 42-43. In Prov 8:30, on the other hand, the appearance of the expression *I was* reinforces this divine identification of the master workman. The expression *I am* "recalls the mysterious revelation of Exod 3:14, where 'I am Who I am' occurs twice and 'I am' once more." Roland E. Murphy, *Proverbs*, WBC 22 (Nashville, TN: Thomas Nelson, 1998), 53.

84. Davidson does not mention this argument in particular. Roland E. Murphy says that the word *ḥāṭā* can mean *sin* or *miss the mark*. As R. E. Murphy does not believe that Wisdom is a divine person, he opts for the second translation: "Since sin can be directed only against the Lord, probably 'miss the mark' is a better translation." R. E. Murphy, *Proverbs*, 54. The text suggests, however, that *ḥāṭā* is parallel to the notion of hating Wisdom and connects with the ideas of treating one's own life with violence and loving death ("But he who sins against me wrongs his own soul; All those who hate me love death," NKJV). It is difficult not to see here a moral meaning for *ḥāṭā*. For additional evidence and discussion regarding the identification of Wisdom with a divine person, see Davidson, "Proverbs 8," 42-43.

85. Summarizing the history of the interpretation of the Wisdom of Prov 8 in early Christianity, Fox says, "In the New Testament, Sophia [Wisdom] was equated with and replaced by the Logos, which was for its part identified with the Christ.... According to John 1:1-2, the Logos was with God from the beginning.... According to Col 1:15-16 (a passage clearly dependent on Prov 8), the Christ is the 'firstborn' (*prōtotokos*) of creation, through whom all was created (cf. Heb 1:3)." Michael V. Fox, *Proverbs 1-9: A New Translation With Introduction and Commentary*, AB 18A (New York, NY: Doubleday, 2000), 279. Fox, however, does not believe himself that the Wisdom of Prov 8 is a divine person, although he admits that this is the New Testament interpretation of this text. Davidson finds allusions to Prov 8 in 1 Cor 1:24, 30, where Christ is "the wisdom of God." See Davidson, "Proverbs 8," 34, 47. Interestingly, E. G. White interprets the Wisdom of Prov 8 as referring to Christ, in connection with John 1 and Col 1. See E. G. White, *Patriarchs and Prophets*, 35.

implicitly identifying the *master workman* (master craftsman) or Wisdom in Prov 8:30 as "the personal, heavenly Christ."[86]

In relation to the beginning in John 1:1, Prov 8:22, 23 explains that in that beginning, before the creation of anything else, the Godhead begot, brought forth (vv. 22, 24, 25), installed, or established (v. 23; cf. Ps 2:6-7) a divine person, Christ, as the Wisdom, Designer, and Agent of Creation.[87] Wisdom personifies and implements the plan of God for Creation.[88] The divine Wisdom and Agent of Creation, then, assumes a mediating role between God and creation. "In Prov 8, Wisdom is portrayed as an entity proceeding from God . . . and intermediate between him and the world."[89] This role of Mediator, of course, became effective when Creation started but did not cease once it was completed. His mediation is not limited to the agency of Creation (John 1:3; Heb 1:2). Christ became a permanent Mediator between God and creation, prior to the problem of sin, as Col 1:16-17 also makes clear (see also Prov 8:30-31). It was part of the original plan of the Godhead installing or establishing Christ as Mediator, the articulating principle between the Godhead and the world. In fact, Christ's installation as the Wisdom of Creation also involves the inner-articulation of the world. From Creation, in Christ, "all things consist" (Col 1:17, NJKV). In other words, "'in him all things are held together,' [Col 1:17] asserts. He is the sustainer of the universe and the unifying principle of its life. Apart from his *continuous* sustaining activity . . . all would disintegrate."[90]

Why is a mediator necessary to articulate the relationship between God and His creation? Calvin saw the necessity of mediation in the

---

86. Peter T. O'Brien, *Colossians, Philemon*, WBC 44 (Waco, TX: Word, 1982), 46. Regarding the translation of *'āmôn* as *master workman* or *craftsman*, see Davidson, "Proverbs 8," 44-47.

87. "The language in Prov 8:22–25 for Wisdom's having been 'established/installed' and 'brought forth' before the creation of this world, is illuminated by parallel language in Ps 2:6–7, including, significantly, the only other biblical occurrence of the Hebrew word *nsk* III 'install.' Here Yahweh installs the Messianic king using the language of birth (=adoption)." Davidson, "Proverbs 8," 49. Emphasis in original.

88. "If Wisdom is here [Prov 8:30-31] an artisan, the message . . . is that principles of wisdom are woven into the fabric of the created order." Duane A. Garrett, *Proverbs, Ecclesiastes, Song of Songs*, NAC 14 (Nashville, TN: Broadman, 1993), 110.

89. Fox, *Proverbs 1-9*, 293. See also Davidson, "Proverbs 8," 51-52. The pre-incarnate Son, was "installed into the office of 'Mediator' between Yahweh and 'His inhabited world . . . the sons of men' (v. 30-31)." Davidson, "Earth's First Sanctuary," 86, n. 60.

90. O'Brien, *Colossians, Philemon*, 47. Emphasis in original.

lowliness of God's creatures even if they are not sinful creatures.[91] From a biblical perspective, that explanation is neither possible nor necessary. The Creator rejoices "in His inhabited world" (Prov 8:31, NKJV). Wisdom/the Word/Christ mediates God's actions in connection with His creation. As the Mediator, Christ articulates God's actions regarding the world.[92]

However, Col 1 not only points out that Christ is the Mediator between God and creation before the problem of sin as Agent of Creation, Sustainer, and unifying principle; Christ is also a Mediator in the sense that He is an agent of reconciliation between God and the world (v. 20). Colossians 1:15-20 does not directly explain the reason for that necessity of reconciliation. However, "although there has been no previous mention of it, it is presupposed here that unity and harmony of the cosmos have suffered a considerable disturbance, even a rupture. In order to restore the cosmic order reconciliation became necessary."[93]

The reason is, obviously, the problem of sin.[94] As Christ is the articulating agent of creation—the *all things (ta panta)* that are in heaven and on earth—He is also the articulating agent of reconciliation of *all things (ta panta)* that are on earth and in heaven (compare vv. 16 and 20). In other words, this reconciliation involves all that is part of creation: angels, human beings, and nature. The angelic society suffered disturbance and disruption for the sake of sin (Isa 14:12-14; Ezek 28:14-17; Rev 12:7-9; etc.) as well as humanity (Gen 3). Sin also resulted in the curse of nature and its submission to futility and cor-

---

91. See footnote 72 in this chapter.

92. Davidson seems to support the idea that Christ is the Mediator between God's transcendence and His creation. "There is described [in Prov 8] a time, before the creation of the universe, when, presumably by mutual consent, one Person of the Godhead is 'installed' . . . in a role of Mediator. While the Person we call the Father continued to represent the transcendent nature of the Godhead, the Person we know as the Son condescended . . . to represent the immanent aspect of divinity, coming close to His creation, mediating between infinity and finitude, even before sin." Davidson, "Proverbs 8," 54. It is clear in Scripture, however, that not only Christ but also the Father and the Holy Spirit act immanently in the world. All the members of the Deity are immanent and transcendent. God's transcendence is not available for creation. God is knowable only in connection with His creation, where He adapts Himself to the cognitive abilities of His creatures.

93. Lohse, *Colossians and Philemon*, 59.

94. "The real meaning of Col. 1:20 is probably as follows: Sin ruined the universe. It destroyed the harmony between one creature and the other, also between all creatures and their God." Hendriksen, *Exposition of Colossians and Philemon*, 81.

ruption (Gen 3:17; Rom 8:19-22).⁹⁵ Paul describes this reconciliation as done "by him [Christ] to reconcile all things unto himself" (Col 1:20, KJV). He means that Christ is not only the Agent of reconciliation but also the Object of it. Sin has severely affected and impacted the articulation between God and the world, and the inner articulation of the world itself. The restoration of the ideal situation prior to the problem of sin requires reconciliation with the articulating agent that ultimately implies reconciliation with God (Rom 5:10; 2 Cor 5:18-20).⁹⁶ In this sense, Christ's mediatorial role involves an additional aspect that was not included before the Fall. Christ has to mediate between God's holiness and His sinful creatures (Col 1:21-23; 2 Cor 5:18-19; Heb 10:19-22).

Scripture sees in Christ's sacrifice the base for this reconciliation (Col 1:18, 20). However, it is clear that the reconciliation aspect of the mediatorial or articulating role of Christ is a temporal process that does not conclude on the cross. Reconciliation with God has a greater scope that will culminate when *all things (ta panta)* be subject to Christ and through Him, to God (1 Cor 15:24-28; Eph 1:10, 21-22; cf. Phil 2:10-11).⁹⁷

In summary, then, Christ is the temporal divine articulating agent of the biblical system—and ultimately of reality as a whole that the biblical system interprets. He is the Designer, Agent, and Goal of Creation. He was installed by the Godhead as the Wisdom of Creation and the Mediator between God and the world before Creation. As the

---

95. See Melick, *Philippians, Colossians, Philemon*, 225.

96. See Hendriksen, *Exposition of Colossians and Philemon*, 80, n. 57. William Hendriksen clarifies that God is also the implicit subject in Col 1:19. Ibid. See also ibid., 78, n. 55. See also the useful discussion in Melick, *Philippians, Colossians, Philemon*, 224.

97. Regarding the gathering of *all things* in Christ in Col 1:20 and its thematic connection with 1 Cor 15:24-28; Eph 1:10, 22; Phil 2:10-11, see Hendriksen, *Exposition of Colossians and Philemon*, 82; O'Brien, *Colossians, Philemon*, 56, 57; Melick, *Philippians, Colossians, Philemon*, 228. According to Melick, "in this discussion of reconciliation, Paul had two basic reference points. First was the beginning of restoration, which occurred at the cross. The death of Christ provided the objective basis upon which all else followed. Thus Paul looked backward in time, resting his hopes on what was done in Christ. Second was the culmination of reconciliation which will take place in the future. Paul expressed by faith this necessary outworking of the death of Jesus. Thus Jesus died not only to provide individuals with salvation but also to restore a harmony to the universe. That harmony is an assured aspect of redemption." Ibid.

Wisdom of Creation, Christ personifies God's plan for the world, articulates the relation between God and the word, and sustains the world. In the context of the problem of sin, however, Christ also mediates between God's holiness and His sinful creatures. Still, He is not a Mediator only because of the problem of sin. He is a Mediator in general. There is an ontological necessity for articulation even before the Fall and after the restoration of the ideal conditions before the Fall. The reality is a complex temporal fact that involves God, the created world, and the intelligent creatures in the universe. Reality requires Christ's temporal articulation in order to preserve its harmony.

The Interpretation of the Articulating Action

As Scripture assumes a temporal ontology, the articulating action of the biblical system requires a temporal interpretation that recognizes the complexity of a temporal reality. The discussion of the biblical interpretation of the articulating action in this section involves three aspects. These are (1) the sanctuary/temple structural pattern of relationship, (2) the pre-articulating and general articulating actions, and (3) the specific articulating actions.

The Sanctuary/Temple Structural Pattern of Relationship

In Scripture, the sanctuary/temple (hereafter *sanctuary*) is an encompassing mediating structure through which Christ articulates the relationship between God and the world, including His intelligent creatures. The heavenly sanctuary structure is not only a physical place. It also operates as a pattern of relationship, a relational structure between God and the world.[98] It is God's central place from where He governs the universe. It is the place where God dwells in fellowship with His creatures, reveals Himself to them, and receives adoration. As such,

---

98. Roberto Ouro presents an extensive list of references in the Old and the New Testament showing the importance of the sanctuary in biblical theology. Although the list is not necessarily complete, it is possible to agree with him when he affirms "that the sanctuary plays an important role throughout all of Scripture. Just as the physical sanctuary in ancient Israel served as the centralized point around which the rest of the camp was situated, so the theological concept of the sanctuary is the point around which O[ld] T[estament] and N[ew] T[estament] theologies are structured." Roberto Ouro, "The Sanctuary: The Canonical Key of Old Testament Theology," *AUSS* 50, no. 2 (2012): 175.

it works as a model of all other dwellings of God with His creatures in the Garden of Eden, in the earthly sanctuaries, and in Christ's incarnation.[99] As God and the world-humanity are spatio-temporal, the sanctuary pattern of relationship is also spatio-temporal, and it is the structure of the articulating actions of Christ as the articulating agent since the Creation and throughout the history of the universe.

In consonance with the fact that Christ began His function as Mediator since the creation of the universe and before the introduction of the problem of sin, there is evidence that the sanctuary structure was already in operation before Satan's rebellion. Isaiah 14 and Ezek 28, for example, identify several motives that refer to a heavenly sanctuary existing before the problem of sin. These passages introduce the heavenly being typologically—that other texts more explicitly identify as Satan (Job 1, 2; Zac 3:1-2)[100]—in the context of a pre-existent heavenly sanctuary. In Isa 14:12-15, there is a scene, which is clearly located in a heavenly context.[101] The "mount of the congregation" (Isa 14:13) evokes Mount Zion, the location of Israel's temple, the place of worship par excellence.[102] This temple, though, is not on the earth because the text

---

99. This dwelling purpose becomes evident in connection with the earthly sanctuary. "In our traditional emphasis on the sacrificial aspect of the sanctuary, we often overlook the fact that even though the sacrifices were essential, they were not the primary reason for the existence of the sanctuary. The sacrifices were only a means to an end. The primary purpose of the sanctuary was to be the earthly dwelling place for God—a place where He could dwell among His people [cf. Exod 25:8] and remove whatever separated them from Him, and thus restore their relationship with Him." Gudmundur Olafsson, "Immanuel—God With Us," in *The Great Controversy and the End of Evil: Biblical and Theological Studies in Honor of Ángel Manuel Rodríguez in Celebration of His Seventieth Birthday*, ed. Gerhard Pfandl (Silver Spring, MD: Biblical Research Institute, 2015), 125, 123-124.

100. For the typological identification of the king of Babylon and the king of Tyre with Satan in these passages, see footnotes 48 and 49 in this chapter.

101. "It becomes apparent that Isa 14:12-15 deals with events transpiring in the heavenly realm. What emerges seems to be the attempt by one of the members of the divine council to overtake YHWH's position on the 'mount of the assembly,' or, in other words, to overtake the heavenly sanctuary/temple of YHWH." Elias Brasil de Souza, "The Heavenly Sanctuary/Temple Motif in the Hebrew Bible: Function and Relationship to the Earthly Counterparts" (PhD diss., Andrews University, Berrien Springs, MI, 2005), 257.

102. Winfried Vogel, *The Cultic Motif in the Book of Daniel* (New York, NY: Peter Lang, 2010), 26. "The close association of mountain, sanctuary, and Jerusalem is in fact evidenced throughout the Old Testament." Ibid., 27.

connects it with God's throne in heaven.[103] This reference to the mount of the congregation implies "the original worship function of the Sanctuary before sin. The heavenly sanctuary, on the holy mountain, was the location of the throne of God, and here the unfallen universe came to worship the Most High God."[104] This sanctuary is God's dwelling place and the meeting place of His cosmic council.[105]

Something similar occurs with Ezek 28. In v. 14, the heavenly being that rebelled against God is a "cherub who covers" (NKJV; cf. v. 16), "a description that (in light of the parallel with its earthly Sanctuary counterpart) ushers us into the Holy of Holies of the heavenly sanctuary, 'the holy mountain of God.'"[106] The vocabulary and several linguistic expressions in Ezek 28:13-16 point that the holy mountain refers to the heavenly sanctuary, prior to the introduction of sin in the universe, where God receives adoration. It is a heavenly Eden or "garden of God" (Ezek 28:13, KJV).[107]

As Rodríguez explains, the heavenly sanctuary is the specific place where God condescends to become immanent in the universe in general (Pss 11:4; 93:2; 103:19) and to enjoy fellowship with His angels.[108] The

---

103. See Rev 14:1-5; Heb 12:18-24. "On the basis of His presence on the earthly mount of Zion, the people of Israel had come to refer to God's dwelling place in heaven by the same name: 'Mount Zion.'" Jacques B. Doukhan, *Secrets of Revelation: The Apocalypse Through Hebrew Eyes* (Hagerstown, MD: Review & Herald, 2002), 121. It is clear from Ps 11:4; Isa 6:1, and other texts that "the throne of God is in his heavenly temple." Vogel, *The Cultic Motif*, 81. See ibid., 82 for additional references. Additional textual indicators such as "the stars of God" (Isa 14:13) and "the heights of the clouds" (v. 14) reinforce the idea that this temple is actually the heavenly sanctuary. de Souza, "The Heavenly Sanctuary/Temple Motif," 261-264.

104. Davidson, "Cosmic Metanarrative," 107-108.

105. Isaiah 6; Ps 82; Job 1:6-12; 2:1-7; Dan 7:9-10. See de Souza, "The Heavenly Sanctuary/Temple Motif," 260-261; 260, n. 3; 265.

106. Davidson, "Ezekiel 28:11-19," 67. In Ezek 1 and 10, cherubim are heavenly creatures at the service of the throne of God. They are "members of the divine entourage." de Souza, "The Heavenly Sanctuary/Temple Motif," 292.

107. The Garden of Eden in v. 13 is actually a reference to the heavenly sanctuary. The earthly Eden appeared later. Ezekiel 28:13-14 contains several allusions to Gen 2-3, where the Garden of Eden is described as an earthly sanctuary. For other connections between Ezek 28 and the motive of the sanctuary, see the discussion in de Souza, "The Heavenly Sanctuary/Temple Motif," 285-289.

108. Rodríguez, "God's Presence in the Sanctuary," 3. "God's localized presence within the space of His creatures is a unique fragment of space in the universe. It is a space within which God makes Himself accessible to His creatures; it assures intelligent life throughout the cosmos that God is indeed near." Ibid. See also Angel Manuel Rodríguez, "Sanctuary Theology in the Book of Exodus," *AUSS* 24, no. 2 (1986): 143.

fact that God has a specific location in a unique space of the universe does not restrict or limit Him to that space. It is actually because of His dwelling in the heavenly sanctuary that His presence—which is not different from His being—is felt in the whole universe. In His sanctuary, nothing is hidden from His presence (Jer 23:23-24).[109] The heavenly sanctuary is God's universal administrative center in space and time, where He instructs His angels, receives adoration, and meets His heavenly council to make decisions in agreement with its members (Pss 89:5-7; 103:19-22).[110]

Many texts illustrate this central role of the heavenly sanctuary. In Ps 29, for example, God does not only exert His kingship upon natural elements; He is also the object of worship by the sons of God (see v. 1), who are part of the heavenly court.[111] In 1 Kgs 22:19-22, God deliberates with His heavenly council in order to make a decision.[112] Through all these activities, God interacts with His creatures and reveals His char-

---

109. See Rodríguez, "God's Presence in the Sanctuary," 3. In spite of His location in the heavenly sanctuary, "nothing, absolutely nothing, takes place in the universe outside God's presence. The personal God who dwells in the heavenly temple at the same time rules from there over the totality of the space inhabited by His creatures (Ps. 139:7-16)." Ibid.

110. See ibid. According to Rodríguez, the sanctuary "is fundamentally a sacred space of meeting or encounter between God and His creation, a reference point that orients all other spaces." Ibid. According to Daegeuk Nam, the Hebrew Bible frequently describes God's throne as "the center of the universal administration of the divine Monarch." Daegeuk Nam, *The "Throne of God" Motif in the Hebrew Bible*, Korean Sahmyook University Monographs Doctoral Dissertation Series 1 (Seoul, Korea: Institute for Theological Research, Korean Sahmyook University, 1989), 462. Regarding the motif of the divine council in the Old Testament, see Merling K. Alomía, "Lesser Gods of the Ancient Near East and Some Comparisons With Heavenly Beings of the Old Testament" (PhD diss., Andrews University, Berrien Springs, MI, 1987), 333-375.

111. The expression *sons of God* is usually translated as "mighty ones" (NKJV), but in the light of Job 1:6; 2:1 (see also 38:7) it refers to God's divine assembly of angels in the heavenly sanctuary. See de Souza, "The Heavenly Sanctuary/Temple Motif," 384, 475. Although in Ps 29 God controls the forces of nature to punish the Caananites (see ibid., 387-388), theologically, the text sheds light on the general control of God upon nature from His heavenly sanctuary. Regarding God's control over nature, see also Ps 89:8-13. See Nam, *The "Throne of God" Motif*, 372-373.

112. "In Micaiah's vision, the host takes on the quality of attendants in the heavenly court, where the outcome of the battle is to be decided on; cf. the divine beings in Job 1:6 and the seraphs in Isa 6:2; cf. also Ps 103:21; 148:2." Mordechai Cogan, *I Kings: A New Translation With Introduction and Commentary*, AB 10 (Garden City, NY: Doubleday, 2001), 492.

acter to them, allowing harmony in the universe. "It was God's love that moved Him to be close and very near to those He loved."[113] In Ps 89, the members of the divine council praise the Lord for His faithfulness (vv. 5, 7). Verse 14 declares, "Righteousness and justice are the foundation of your throne; love and faithfulness go before you" (Ps 89:14, NIV; cf. Isa 6:3; Rev 4:8).[114] In the same way, in Ps 103:19, the God that "rules over all" (NKJV) from His heavenly throne in heaven is the same who demonstrates His love, mercy, righteousness, and grace (vv. 4, 6, 8, 17).[115]

The sanctuary, as the structural pattern of the relationship between God and the world, is replicated in the biblical description of the Garden of Eden. Genesis 2-3 depict the garden in terms of an earthly sanctuary, a location in space and time where God reveals Himself to human beings, has communion with them, and appoints them as their co-rulers and co-workers (Gen 2:15; cf. 1:26-30). The garden seems to be, in some way, a counterpart of the heavenly Eden (Ezek 28:13).[116] In

---

113. Rodríguez, "God's Presence in the Sanctuary," 3. According to Rodríguez, God's nearness through the heavenly sanctuary in the universe "satisfied the built-in need of His creatures to have fellowship with their Creator. The fragment of space in which God localized Himself—the heavenly sanctuary—provided for a divine nearness that was indispensable to the well-being of the universe, and in particular for that of His self-conscious intelligent creatures." Ibid.

114. *Righteousness* and *justice* are terms that express "the principles of divine government." Nam, *The "Throne of God" Motif*, 375. The other two terms, *love* and *faithfulness* (or *truth*), are parallel to the first two and reveal God's character. See ibid., 378, 379.

115. Ibid., 403, 304, 446.

116. Many authors support the idea that Eden operated as a first sanctuary. With some reservations see, for example, Gordon J. Wenham, "Sanctuary Symbolism in the Garden of Eden Story," in *Cult and Cosmos: Tilting Toward a Temple-Centered Theology*, ed. L. Michael Morales (Leuven, Belgium: Peeters, 2014), 161-166; L. Michael Morales, *The Tabernacle Pre-Figured: Cosmic Mountain Ideology in Genesis and Exodus* (Leuven, Belgium: Peeters, 2012); Gregory K. Beale and Mitchell Kim, *God Dwells Among Us: Expanding Eden to the End of the Earth* (Downers Grove, IL: InterVarsity, 2014), 17-28. See also the bibliography referred to in Davidson, "Earth's First Sanctuary," 65, n. 1. While it is possible to interpret the Eden's sanctuary language as an anticipation of the language used regarding the tabernacle, it is better to interpret the language used in connection with the building and operation of the tabernacle as reminiscent of Eden's language. See ibid., 68. In other words, Eden represents the ideal pattern of relationship between God and the world-humanity that God tried to re-establish through His dwelling in the earthly sanctuary. Regarding Eden as the first sanctuary from a more Adventist perspective, see, with some qualifications, ibid., the entire article, particularly pp. 68-80; Davidson, "Cosmic Metanarrative," 108-112. For a summary of the main

this context, God even sanctifies a specific time, the seventh day as a day of communion, a "palace in time."[117] The presence of cherubim at the entrance of the Garden of Eden after the Fall reinforces the idea of the garden as a sanctuary (Gen 3:24), in the entrance of which God occasionally appeared (cf. Exod 33:9-10; Num 12:5) and where sacrifices were offered.[118]

Of course, the problem of sin introduces a modification in the pattern of relationship between God and the world. Direct communion is restricted. After the Fall, the pattern reflects the necessity of reconciliation between God and the world, including particularly God's intelligent creatures.[119] God inaugurated in Eden a sacrificial system (Gen

---

parallels that Davidson observes between Eden and the tabernacle in these articles, see footnote 466 in Chapter 4. See also Ángel Manuel Rodríguez, "Genesis 1 and the Building of the Israelite Sanctuary," *Ministry*, February 2002, 9-11; Ángel Manuel Rodríguez, "Eden and the Israelite Sanctuary: A Study in God's Abiding Interest in Harmony and Restoration," *Ministry*, April 2002, 11-13, 30; Jorge E. Rico, *Conexiones teológicas del santuario* (Burleson, TX: Biblical Foundations, 2011), 59-67.

117. "The seventh day is like a palace in time." Heschel, *The Sabbath*, 21. There is no need to subscribe, however, to the idea that holiness of time and holiness of space are two separate things, as Heschel suggests. Ibid., 8-10. God's presence in Eden to enter in communion with the first human beings evidently sanctified that place (cf. Exod 3:4-5).

118. Joaquim Azevedo explains that in Gen 4:7 the word usually translated as *sin* (*ḥaṭṭā't*), is better translated as *sin/purification offering* (Lev 4:3, 8, 14, 20-21, etc.), referring to the sacrifice that Cain had to bring at the door of Eden in order to receive forgiveness for his inappropriate sacrifice. Cain was the firstborn but because of his inappropriate sacrifice, he probably lost his firstborn right. As a result, he became angry with Abel. In order to receive forgiveness, Cain had to offer a sin/purification offering at the door of the garden. In that way, Cain could have ruled again over Abel as the firstborn. Joaquim Azevedo, "At the Door of Paradise: A Contextual Interpretation of Gen. 4:7," in *Cult and Cosmos: Tilting Toward a Temple-Centered Theology*, ed. L. Michael Morales (Leuven, Belgium: Peeters, 2014), 173-181.

119. It is possible to argue that the sanctuary is a structure designed mainly to deal with intelligent creatures, and consequently, it does not resolve the issue of a general reconciliation with the world. However, the problem of sin started with intelligent creatures and then affected the rest of creation. Thus, in order to reconcile *all things* with God it is necessary to start with the reconciliation between God and His intelligent creatures, which will lead to the reconciliation of *all things*. That is why nature is also waiting "for the revealing of the sons of God" (Rom 8:19, NKJV). The revelation of God's sons points out the moment of the final glorification. "Paul is affirming a solidarity of the nonhuman world with the human world in the redemption that Christ has wrought. In its own way it echoes Yahweh's promise to Noah of the covenant to be made 'between myself and you and every living creature' (Gen

3:21) that would have continuity throughout the patriarchal era, in the Israelite tabernacle of the wilderness, and in the temple of Jerusalem. In the patriarchal era, the focus of the religious activity became the altar, a miniature version of what it would become later the sacrificial system of the tabernacle.[120] "The liturgy of the genuine altars of the patriarchal era identified the true worshipers of Yahweh and prefigured typologically the vicarious sacrifice of Christ for the redemption of the human race."[121]

Through the tabernacle—and later through the temple in Jerusalem—God showed to Israel that He wanted to restore the original harmony and fellowship of Eden, prior to the introduction of sin.[122] The sanctuary was built according to the particular pattern or model that God provided to Moses and David (Exod 25:8, 40; Heb 8:5; cf. 1 Chr 28:11-19) in spatial and functional correspondence with the heavenly sanctuary.[123] This sanctuary was not only an illustration of the activities related to the heavenly sanctuary or a mere illustration of the Gospel. It was not just a teaching device or a visual aid.[124] It was a clear application of the sanctuary pattern, articulating the relationship between God and the people of Israel through Christ's real presence. "By asking the Israelites to build Him a sanctuary, God was showing them that in spite of sin He was still near to them; that even though they did not have access to the heavenly dwelling, He was willing to localize

---

9:12–13)." Joseph A. Fitzmyer, *Romans: A New Translation With Introduction and Commentary*, AB 33 (New York, NY: Doubleday, 1993), 506.

120. For Abraham's altars, see Gen 12:7, 8; 13:18; 22:9. Abraham's descendants built altars in a similar way. See Gen 26:25 (Isaac); 33:20; 35:7 (Jacob). Alberto R. Timm, "The Sanctuary Motif Within the Framework of the Great Controversy," *The Cosmic Battle for the Planet Earth: Essays in Honor of Norman R. Gulley*, ed. Ron du Preez and Jiří Moskala (Berrien Springs, MI: Old Testament Department, SDA Theological Seminary, Andrews University), 70-72.

121. Ibid., 72.

122. "The Israelite sanctuary seems to have pointed back to the original harmony of God and humans and forward to its full restoration." Rodríguez, "Eden and the Israelite Sanctuary," 30. The sacrificial system had the same purpose. "The sacrificial system served the purpose of initiating, preserving, and restoring the state of order and harmony recreated by God in the tabernacle." Rodríguez, "Building of the Israelite Sanctuary," 11.

123. For an excellent discussion regarding the heavenly sanctuary as ultimately the pattern or model for the earthly one, see Richard M. Davidson, *Typology in Scripture: A Study of Hermeneutical Typos Structures*, AUSDDS 2 (Berrien Springs, MI: Andrews University Press, 1981), 367-388. See also Rodríguez, "Sanctuary Theology," 142-144.

124. See Chapter 4, pp. 239-240 and footnote 500 in the same chapter.

Himself within a world of sin to reveal His gracious disposition to be close to them."[125] Just as God became immanent within the universe in the heavenly sanctuary and in Eden before the Fall, He also became immanent within this sinful planet in the structure of the earthly sanctuary/temple in order to reveal Himself.[126]

---

125. Rodríguez, "God's Presence in the Sanctuary," 3. Rodríguez also mentions the illustration role of the earthly sanctuary but it seems that for him, the earthly sanctuary is more than that. It is part of a more general pattern of relationship between God and the world. See ibid., 4. It is useful to differentiate here between an illustration and a typological structure as the earthly sanctuary. An illustration is disposable. The sanctuary, as a *typos* structure, is not. It is a real pattern of relationship between God and humanity, ontologically grounded in its correspondence with the heavenly antitype. It is not a symbol or metaphor. God's being is actually present there. It is interesting to notice that even before the building of the earthly tabernacle, the sanctuary pattern of relationship was already operative between God and Israel. Rodríguez suggests that God's revelation to the people of Israel at Mount Sinai when they received the Law follows the sanctuary pattern in the context of sin. God revealed Himself with restrictions. Sinai had bounds or fences that the people could not pass through (Exod 19:12), and at the foot of Sinai, Moses built an altar (24:4). Aaron, Nadab, Abihu, and the 70 elders could go up to some point that allowed them to see God (or at least His feet) from afar (24:1, 9-11). Only Moses, however, was able to enter the cloud, into the very presence of God (vv. 12-18). The fence with the altar parallels the court of the tabernacle with its altar that would be built later. The second place, where the priests and the elders could go, parallels the Holy Place of the tabernacle, while Moses was able to enter into the place that is equivalent to the Most Holy Place. See Rodríguez, "Sanctuary Theology," 132-134. Actually, it is clear that even before the building of the definitive tabernacle, some kind of tent or tabernacle was already operative ("tabernacle of the meeting," according to Exod 33:7, NKJV) where Moses met God (vv. 7-11). In spite of the restrictions, God wanted to walk again with His people (Lev 26:10-11; Deut 23:14; 2 Sam 7:6) as He used to do in the Garden of Eden (Gen 3:8). Olafsson, "Immanuel—God With Us," 124.

126. "The sanctuary is, therefore, a proclamation of God's immanence, rooted in his loving grace." Rodríguez, "Sanctuary Theology," 131. Evidently, the earthly sanctuary/temple was not always operative during the time of the Old Testament. However, the pattern of relationship as such did not disappear because it was ultimately always available from the heavenly sanctuary. Consequently, "even when the people pray in the earthly sanctuary, God hears their prayers in his heavenly sanctuary (cf. 1 Kgs 8:30). When the psalmist, in his distress, prays to God, God hears from his heavenly temple and descends from heaven to help his servant (Ps 18:6, 9-10). Elsewhere in the Psalter, as well as in the prophetic books, we find further references to God's heavenly temple (e.g., Pss 11:4; 60:6; 102:18-19; Isa 6:1-7; Mic 1:2)." Rodríguez, "Sanctuary Theology," 143. See multiple additional examples in de Souza, "The Heavenly Sanctuary/Temple Motif," 83-482. De Souza also points out that when the earthly and the heavenly sanctuary existed simultaneously, there was a dynamic interaction between them, as it is evident in 1 Kgs 8:22-53; 2 Chr 30:27, where God listens in the heavenly sanctuary the prayers elevated in the earthly temple. See a summa-

In the context of sin, the essential facet in the implementation of the sanctuary pattern of relationship between God and the world is Christ's incarnation and His work as the result of that incarnation. In fulfillment of the antitypes of the earthly sanctuary in the context of sin, the Mediator became flesh, dwelt among human beings in a specific place and time, and supremely revealed God's glory, according to John 1:14.[127] Through Christ, the God-man and only "mediator between God and mankind" (1 Tim 2:5, NIV), human beings could have access to God in the heavenly sanctuary. Christ's life and ministry on earth, His atoning sacrifice, and His posterior work of intercession and atonement in the heavenly sanctuary provided that access (John 14:1-11; Rom 8:34-39; Heb 7:25).[128]

As the role of Christ as Mediator began before the problem of sin and involves His role as articulating agent of the divine actions regarding the world, it should not be assumed that after the problem of sin that role would disappear. Only the mediation of God's holiness will not be necessary anymore. The redeemed humans will see God again face to face in the restored Garden of Eden (Rev 22:4). The sanctuary structure patterning the relationship between God and His creation will continue. Only the soteriological aspect of this pattern of relationship will disappear but not the pattern itself.[129] "The throne of God and of the Lamb" (Rev 22:1, 3, NIV) in the New Jerusalem, the heart of the sanctuary structure, will still preserve its role as the center of rul-

---

rized discussion of these texts and others in ibid., 491-493.

127. This dwelling, literally translated, means that Christ "'tabernacled' or 'tented,' which reminds us of Israel's wilderness experience of God's presence in the tabernacle or tent of meeting (cf. Exod 25:8–9; 35:7–16; 40:1–38)." Gerald L. Borchert, *John 1-11*, NAC 25A (Nashville, TN: Broadman & Holman, 2006), 119. Of course, this fact does not mean that Christ was already incarnated in the earthly sanctuary.

128. See Rodríguez, "God's Presence in the Sanctuary," 4-6. See also Heb 4:14-16; 8:1-2; 9:23-28; etc. The literature about the work of Christ in the heavenly sanctuary is too numerous to be quoted here. For extensive references and discussion, especially—but not exclusively—by Adventist authors, see Denis Kaiser, "The Biblical Sanctuary Motif in Historical Perspective," in *Scripture and Philosophy: Essays Honoring the Work and Vision of Fernando Luis Canale*, ed. Tiago Arrais, Kenneth Bergland, and Michael F. Younker (Berrien Springs, MI: Adventist Theological Society, 2016), 167-186. Much of the Adventist literature about the sanctuary discuss it from the perspective of a theological *motif* of Scripture. The interpretation of the sanctuary in this discussion, however, goes far beyond that. The sanctuary here refers to an ontological reality through which Christ structures the relationship between God and the world.

129. See Timm, "The Sanctuary Motif," 83.

ership, adoration, and communion where the saved will come to serve and worship God.[130] God will fulfill His desire to dwell with His people in a context of open access to His presence (Rev 7:15; 21:3; 21:22). They will learn more of His character under the leading or shepherding of the Lamb (7:15-17; cf. 14:4). That Revelation refers to Christ as *the Lamb* even after the end of the great controversy suggests that the prior experience of that controversy, where God revealed Himself through His Son (John 14:6-9), will enrich the process of learning about God's character (Rev 3:21; 15:1-4; 19:1-7).[131]

In fact, Christ as the articulating agent between God and the world

---

130. See Laszlo Gallusz, *The Throne Motif in the Book of Revelation* (London, UK: Bloomsbury, 2014), 172-174; Davidson, "Cosmic Metanarrative," 119. Ranko Stefanovic has suggested a distinction between the heavenly tabernacle (*skēnē*) and the heavenly temple (*naos*) of the book of Revelation. For him, the temple is a temporary structure, only designed to solve the problem of sin, while the tabernacle refers to the permanent dwelling of God, whether before the rise of the problem of sin or after its eradication. The temple will disappear after the eradication of sin and no mediation will exist anymore. Ranko Stefanovic, "The Heavenly Sanctuary and Its Services in the Book of Revelation: Its Reality and Meaning" (MA thesis, Adventist International Institute of Advanced Studies, Silang, Cavite, Philippines, 1990), 48-50. This position, however, is untenable considering that the heavenly sanctuary/temple is clearly preexistent to the problem of sin as Isa 14 and Ezek 28 show. Some of its functions actually are not necessarily related to the problem of sin, such as rulership and the preservation of nature. On the other hand, from the perspective of Revelation itself, the distinction between the tabernacle as merely God's dwelling and the temple as a real structure is questionable. The verbal form of *skēnē*, *skēnoō*, appears in connection with the temple and the throne of God. Revelation 7:15 says, "They [the multitude coming from the great tribulation] are before the throne of God; and they serve Him day and night in His temple; and He who sits on the throne shall *spread His tabernacle* [*skēnoō*] over them" (NASB). Emphasis mine. In 13:6, the *skēnē* blasphemed by the beast from the sea clearly refers to God's heavenly temple in the context of the problem of sin. In fact, in Rev 15:5, the temple and tabernacle seem to be equivalents. "The **temple** is called the **tabernacle of testimony** because it is the heavenly equivalent of the tabernacle of testimony, which was in Israel's presence in the wilderness." Gregory K. Beale and David H. Campbell, *Revelation: A Shorter Commentary* (Grand Rapids, MI: Eerdmans, 2015), 322. Bold type in original.

131. Regarding the references to Christ as the Lamb after the end of the great controversy, see Rev 21:9, 14, 22-23, 27; 22:1-3; compare with 5:6, 8, 12, 13, 6:1, 16. E. G. White also explains the importance of Christ in revealing God's character after the end of the problem of sin: "The more men learn of God, the greater will be their admiration of His character. As Jesus opens before them the riches of redemption and the amazing achievements in the great controversy with Satan, the hearts of the ransomed thrill with more fervent devotion, and with more rapturous joy they sweep the harps of gold." E. G. White, *The Great Controversy*, 678.

has a central role in the city. He does not only share the throne with His Father, He is also the husband of the city (Rev 21:9), the founder (the names of His apostles are on the foundations, v. 14), His lamp (v. 23), and the keeper of the Book of Life with the name of the citizens (v. 27). "Christ is the center of the New Jerusalem. He is the king. . . . In the Lamb of the New Jerusalem we have 'the summing up of all things.' (Eph 1:10, NASB)."[132]

John says that He saw no temple in the New Jerusalem "for the Lord God Almighty and the Lamb are the temple of it" (Rev 21:22, KJV). God's direct dwelling with His people is the temple in the sense that the redeemed have direct access to God's presence (21:3). At the same time, God has a specific place in the city where His throne is located and from where He rules and receives adoration. In Revelation, the structure of the temple (Rev 22:1, 3) is integrated into the structure of the city.[133] In the earthly Jerusalem, God dwelt in His temple but the access to His presence was restricted because of the problem of sin. In contrast, in the New Jerusalem, the redeemed will periodically appear before the throne of God and the Lamb.[134]

---

132. Roberto Badenas, "New Jerusalem—The Holy City," in *Symposium on Revelation*, vol. 2, *Exegetical and General Studies*, ed. Frank B. Holbrook (Silver Spring, MD: Biblical Research Institute, GC of SDAs, 1992), 269-270.

133. As said, the mention of the throne of God in Rev 22:1, 3—clearly connected with God's temple in the book of Revelation (7:15)—suggests that the sanctuary pattern will exist after the end of the problem of sin. John's "mention of the throne-as-temple affords John the opportunity to reflect briefly on the relationship between God and the people of God: *and his servants will serve him. They will see his face, and his name will be on their foreheads.*" J. Ramsey Michaels, *Revelation*, The IVP New Testament Commentary Series 20 (Downers Grove, IL: InterVarsity, 1997), 248. Emphasis in original. Several facts suggest that there is an integration of the temple with the New Jerusalem. There is a measurement of the city as there was a measure of the temple (Rev 22:15; cf. 11:1; Ezek 40:3ff), and the city has a cube structure that resembles the shape of the Most Holy Place of Jerusalem's temple (1 Kgs 6:20). See Badenas, "New Jerusalem," 260. Moreover, the city is a restored Eden, which originally operated as an earthly sanctuary, where God has His throne. Regarding the New Jerusalem as a new Eden, see ibid., 265-267.

134. "It seems that the temple as much as the city will be a place to which the redeemed will go weekly, monthly and yearly to worship the Creator and to partake of the tree of life (Isa 66:23; Ezek 47:12; Rev 22:2; Zech 14:16; cf. Rev 21:24-27; 22:3-5)." Alberto R. Treiyer, *The Day of Atonement and the Heavenly Judgment: From the Pentateuch to Revelation* (Siloam Springs, AR: Creation Enterprises, 1992), 641, n. 649. See also Alberto R. Treiyer, *The Seals and the Trumpets: Biblical and Historical Studies* (n.p.: Distinctive Messages, 2005), 394-397.

Pre-Articulating and General Articulating Actions

In the general context of the sanctuary as the structural pattern of the relationship between God and the world, it is necessary to clarify the specific ways in which Christ's actions articulate God's relationship with the world. However, some actions before the creation of the world should be considered in order to understand the way in which Christ articulates that relationship. They can be called *pre-articulating actions* because they are prior to the existence of the world, whose existence is a requirement for the articulation. At the same time, there are general actions that God performs since the Creation in order to make the specific articulating actions possible. They can be called *general articulating actions*. It is necessary to clarify them before detailing God's specific articulating actions.

The fact that the Godhead established Christ as the creative Word, the Wisdom of Creation, its Designer, and Implementer, as well as the Mediator between God and the world, means that Christ created the world and assumed His articulating role in harmony with a plan shared with the Godhead (Prov 8:22, 23, 30; Col 1:16, 19; John 1:3).[135] The planning of the divine design for Creation and God's installation of Christ as the Wisdom of Creation/Mediator between God and the world are not articulating actions because they are prior to the existence of the world—one of the elements to be articulated. However, these actions still condition the way of the articulation of the entire reality since Creation. Therefore, they are pre-articulating actions.

The fact that Scripture affirms God's foreknowledge of future events[136] implies that although God had an ideal plan for His creation, He also knew about the emerging of the problem of sin that would take place after Creation. While His ideal plan involved communion and fellowship with His intelligent creatures (Prov 8:31), those creatures also had free will and they eventually would rebel against Him. In consequence, the Godhead also decided that Christ would become the Mediator between God's holiness and His sinful creatures. Christ's soteriological mediation and sacrifice, then, were not an improvisation but part of the Godhead's plan established "before the foundation of the world" (1 Pet 1:20, NKJV; cf. Rev 13:8). In harmony with His salv-

---

135. For additional discussion, see pp. 273-277 in this chapter.
136. See p. 256 and footnote 22 in this chapter.

ific purpose, God made a provision of grace through Christ "before the world began" (2 Tim 1:9, KJV; cf. Titus 1:2). Before Creation, Christ became not only the Wisdom of Creation but also the Wisdom of God's salvation plan (1 Cor 1:24, 30; cf. 2:7).[137] This plan entailed that Christ would become God's Lamb, offering His life in order to give human beings the possibility of salvation (John 1:29; 1 Pet 1:19-20). At the same time, this plan predestined those human beings who would believe in Christ (John 3:16; Eph 1:12) to be restored for salvation (Eph 1:4, 5, 10-11) in conformity to God's original plan of Creation (Rom 8:29). This predestination, though, does not determine the future decisions of human beings. It is a part of God's plan which expresses His purpose because He "desires all men to be saved" (2 Tim 2:4; cf. Titus 2:11; 2 Pet 3:9). However, human beings still can reject God's offer of salvation. Salvation involves all humanity in terms of intention but is effective only for all those who decide to believe (1 Tim 4:10; John 1:12; Acts 2:21).[138]

This understanding of predestination assumes God's temporality and temporal foreknowledge of the future. From a biblical perspective, "God's predestination is based on foreknowledge"[139] (Rom 8:29; cf. 1 Pet 1:2). This foreknowledge, however, is not causative (as it is for Aquinas), nor is it based on an unchangeable and immutable will of God (as it is for Calvin). God's foreknowledge and predestination are compatible with human free will.[140] Thus, while God's intention is to implement

---

137. In the context of his discussion about Pauline texts such as 1 Cor 1:24, 30; 2:7, James D. G. Dunn affirms that "Paul talks of what might be called a 'pre-existent wisdom' (2.7). . . . In I Cor. 1-2 Christ is the fulfilment [sic] or embodiment of God's wise intention 'to bring us to glory' (2.7)." James D. G. Dunn, *Christology in the Making: A New Testament Inquiry Into the Origins of the Doctrine of the Incarnation*, 2nd ed. (London, UK: SCM, 1989), 178. Dunn finds in Prov 8:22-31 an antecedent of the Pauline understanding of Christ as Wisdom. See ibid., 168. Dunn considers, along with 1 Cor 1, 2, other Wisdom texts in Paul (such as Col 1:15-20) before concluding that "granted that we can speak meaningfully of the Wisdom of God active in creation, revelation and salvation, then it is meaningful to identify Jesus as this Wisdom. . . . Jesus is to be seen as the wise activity of God, as the expression and embodiment of God's wisdom." Ibid., 196.

138. For a broader discussion of predestination from a biblical systematic perspective, see Canale, *Basic Elements of Christian Theology*, 155-166.

139. Gulley, *God as Trinity*, 550.

140. Ibid. As part of his discussion of biblical texts referring to predestination, Gulley explains the connection between God's foreknowledge, will, and predestination in these terms: "Foreknowledge is important to the process of predestination. . . . God knows how people will freely respond to His universal gospel—some accepting it,

His predestination as part of His plan through Christ "who works all things according to the counsel of His will" (Eph 1:11, NKJV), this plan grants free choice to human beings. In interaction with human free will, the last purpose of this plan involves "the summing up of all things in Christ, things in the heavens and things upon the earth" (Eph 1:10, NASB; cf. Rev 21:5; 1 Cor 15:24-29).[141]

The general plan of God to save humanity implies an intra-divine covenant by which the members of the Godhead agree that Christ would be the Mediator of God's holiness in the context of the appearance of the problem of sin. This covenant is usually named the *everlasting covenant*, using the expression of Heb 13:20 and other texts. In Hebrews, the everlasting covenant is evidently equivalent to the *new covenant* of Heb 8:8-13, which finds confirmation through Christ's blood or sacrifice (Heb 9:20; 10:29). Christ's sacrifice was already part of God's plan of salvation established in God's council before Creation (1 Pet 1:20; cf. Eph 1:4-5, 7). "This means that the everlasting covenant is primarily a covenant between the Father and Christ that Christ would take humanity and shed His blood to redeem humans from sin."[142] This everlasting covenant, therefore, is a pre-articulating action that asserted God's plan, indicating the general path that He

---

others rejecting it. . . . Foreknowledge guides His will, but His will does not determine human destinies (without any input from human wills). Thus predestination isn't arbitrary (dependent solely on God's will) but relational (God allowing human free will)." Ibid., 546.

141. In other words, predestination does not determine in detail every aspect of human history. Rather, the implementation of this plan, which pertains to God's providence, implies an interaction between the divine and the human will, although in general, God will finally fulfill His purpose in Christ. See Canale, *Basic Elements of Christian Theology*, 163-164. The possibility of this interaction is implicit in Rom 8:29-30. Commenting on this text, John H. Wright says, "Out of this regard God *predestines* what his love intends: from eternity he decides that people should be made like Christ. To implement this decision he *calls* them by grace. The people who accept this call through faith he *justifies*, that is, he forgives their sins, adopts them as his sons and daughters, and thus makes them initially like Christ. When they persevere in a life of love he *glorifies* them by granting them eternal salvation, making them definitively like Christ. Paul does not imply here that those who are predestined and called cannot fall away, for he warns them of this danger (see Rom 11:22)." John H. Wright, "Predestination," *The New Dictionary of Theology*, ed. Joseph A. Komonchak, Mary Collins, and Dermot A. Lane (Collegeville, MN: Liturgical, 1987), 797. Emphasis in original.

142. Peter M. van Bemmelen, "The Everlasting Covenant," *JATS* 24, no. 1 (2013): 104. See ibid., 103-104.

would follow through Christ's mediatorial work in order to save humanity from the problem of sin.¹⁴³

In summary, God's pre-articulating actions involve Christ's installation to be the Wisdom of Creation and the Mediator between God and the world. These pre-articulating actions also include God's foreknowledge of the problem of sin, and the working out of the plan of salvation. This plan entails the appointment of Christ as Wisdom and Mediator of salvation in the context of the everlasting covenant among the members of the Godhead.

The general articulating actions are those that God performs, once the world was created, in order to sustain His creation. As discussed above, God preserves the universe and rules it from His spatio-temporal location in the heavenly sanctuary.¹⁴⁴ Without this general rulership and sustaining activity, the world would disappear, making the relationship between God and the world impossible (Col 1:17). In the context of the problem of sin, the general sustaining work implies that God allows the existence of evil in order to provide time for the development and culmination of the great controversy (Matt 5:45; Acts 14:16-17; 17:30). This conflict involves the process leading to the reunion of all things in Christ and their final reconciliation with God (Heb 1:3; 2 Cor 5:17-19).

Specific Articulating Actions

In order that God may tabernacle or dwell with His creatures, Christ performs specific articulating actions. First, God's tabernacling with His creatures requires entering in a covenantal relationship with them.¹⁴⁵ While the everlasting covenant as an intra-divine activity prior to Creation is a pre-articulating action, after Creation the covenant becomes a specific articulating action by which Christ articulates the

---

143. Hans K. LaRondelle also affirms that according to the biblical evidence, this everlasting covenant took place between the Father and the Son *"before* the creation of the world, as stated in Ephesians 1:4 ('He chose us in him [Christ] before the creation of the world'; cf. 2 Tim. 1:9; 1 Pet. 1:20; Rev. 13:8)." Hans K. LaRondelle, *Our Creator Redeemer: An Introduction to Biblical Covenant Theology* (Berrien Springs, MI: Andrews University Press, 2005), 5. Emphasis in original.

144. See pp. 279-280, 281-283 in this chapter. See Nam, *The "Throne of God" Motif*, 445, 446, 448, 449, 461-462.

145. For a general introduction to the issue of covenant in Scripture, see George E. Mendenhall, "Covenant Forms in Israelite Tradition", *The Biblical Archeologists* 17, no. 3 (1954): 50-76; LaRondelle, *Our Creator Redeemer* (the whole book is an introduction to the topic).

relationship between God and His creatures in the context of the sanctuary structure.

Scripture does not explain in detail the covenantal relationship between God and the angels. However, the fact that the judgment of the guardian cherub (Satan) in Ezek 28 has the structure of a covenant lawsuit entails that cherub had broken the terms of a covenant that was already in existence at the time of his fall. This action implies that the guardian cherub questioned God's fairness because those terms constitute the legal principles that regulate God's government and make the dwelling of God with the angelic community and with the universe in general possible (Pss 89:5, 7, 14; 103:6-8, 19-22, etc.).[146]

The importance of the covenant as a requirement for God to tabernacle or dwell with His creatures even before the problem of sin becomes clearer in connection with the so-called *Creation covenant*. As the Garden of Eden works as God's sanctuary on the earth, Christ the Creator periodically comes to meet human beings (Gen 3:8). "The garden in Eden is characterised [*sic*] by the presence of God. There God comes to meet man at the cool of the day."[147] In this context, God, through Christ's mediation, established a covenant with Adam and Eve that includes some privileges and obligations (Gen 1:28-30; 2:15-17), allowing God's dwelling in personal interrelationship with them.[148]

---

146. For the illegal actions of the guardian cherub/Satan against God and His sanctuary in Ezek 28:11-19, see de Souza, "The Heavenly Sanctuary/Temple Motif," 291-292. Compare to the illegal actions of Lucifer/Satan in Isa 14:12-15. See ibid., 264-265. For Ezek 28:11-19 as a covenant lawsuit against the guardian cherub, see Richard M. Davidson, "The Divine Covenant Lawsuit Motif in Canonical Perspective," *JATS* 21, nos. 1-2 (2010): 80; Richard M. Davidson, "The Chiastic Literary Structure of the Book of Ezekiel," in *To Understand the Scripture: Essays in Honor of William H. Shea*, ed. David Merling (Berrien Springs, MI: Institute of Archaeology, Siegfried H. Horn Archaeological Museum, Andrews University, 1997), 71-93, particularly pp. 75, 87-89. See also Davidson, "Cosmic Metanarrative," 116.

147. Peter J. Gentry and Stephen J. Wellum, *Kingdom Through Covenant: A Biblical-Theological Understanding of the Covenants* (Wheaton, IL: Crossway, 2012), 211. "Eden was the first place of worship, since it was where God's presence dwelt and the only place where satisfaction in God could be found." Beale and Kim, *God Dwells Among Us*, 28.

148. LaRondelle, *Our Creator Redeemer*, 3-4, 6. Although the context of Gen 1-2 does not explicitly mention the word *covenant*, Hos 6:7 suggests, in an implicit reference to Gen 2, that Adam broke a covenant. See Gulley, *God as Trinity*, 314. Meredith G. Kline also considers that "Hosea 6:7 probably refers to Adam as the breaker of a covenant." Meredith G. Kline, *Kingdom Prologue: Genesis Foundations for a Covenantal Worldview* (Overland Park, KS: Two Age, 2000), 14.

The sign of this covenant was the Sabbath, destined to be the palace in time where God would meet Adam and Eve (Gen 2:2-3; Mark 2:27).[149] As they were created in God's image, they were also His representatives in taking care of, and ruling over, this planet.[150] In consonance, the covenant had implications for the creation that they had to rule. Human obedience or disobedience to the terms of the covenant would affect the rest of creation.

This involvement of the entire planet in the covenant that God made with humanity also becomes evident after the Fall when, in the Eden sanctuary setting, God makes a new covenant with Adam and Eve through Christ's mediation. In this new covenant, human beings and nature would suffer the consequences of human sin. God's curses encompass the experience of suffering, conflict, and death (Gen 3:14-19) by humans but also by nature as the result of human sin (v. 17). At the same time, the covenant includes the promise of a Savior, the Seed of the woman (v. 15), who would defeat the seed of the serpent and would "restore humankind in Paradise. This is God's covenant of grace with Adam and the human race."[151]

In the covenant of God with Noah, once again God involves humanity (Gen 6:18; 9:9) and nature (9:10-11, 13, 16-17). Nature is inseparable from the covenant that God is making with humanity (vv. 12, 15). Therefore, the human transgression of this covenant has negative consequences for the earth in general (cf. Isa 24:5).[152]

God's covenant with Adam after the Fall and with Noah are applications of God's everlasting covenant. The covenant with Noah, which is a confirmation of the prior covenant with Adam,[153] is called *everlasting*

---

149. Regarding the Sabbath as a sign of the covenant of Creation, see LaRondelle, *Our Creator Redeemer*, 7-9; Kline, *Kingdom Prologue*, 39.

150. LaRondelle, *Our Creator Redeemer*, 7.

151. Ibid., 16. Genesis 3 does not mention the word *covenant* but the language in Gen 6:18; 9:9, 11, 17, suggests that God is confirming with Noah a previous covenant, not that He is initiating a completely new one. In this way, Gen 6 and 9 imply that there is a previous covenant in Genesis. Gentry and Wellum, *Kingdom Through Covenant*, 154-155. See also LaRondelle, *Our Creator Redeemer*, 19. LaRondelle correctly interprets that there are two previous covenants: the Creation covenant and the covenant with Adam after the Fall. See ibid., 3-4, 6, and compare with ibid., 11, 15-16.

152. In this sense, it is possible to agree with John M. Frame, who says, "In a broad sense, all of God's dealings with creation are covenantal in character." Frame, *Knowledge of God*, 12. For additional discussion of the covenant with Noah, see LaRondelle, *Our Creator Redeemer*, 18-22; Gulley, *God as Trinity*, 315-316.

153. See footnote 151 in this chapter.

covenant (Gen 9:16). The same happens with the covenant with Abraham and his descendants (17:7, 13, 19), which clearly includes the people of Israel (cf. 15:18-21; Exod 2:24; 6:4). God's covenants with Adam, after the Fall, as well as with Noah, Abraham, and his descendants, comprise God's appearances and the offering of sacrifices, in anticipation of God's manifestation in Sinai and the building of a permanent place for God's dwelling and the functioning of the sacrificial system.[154] God's theophany in Sinai—where He made the covenant with Israel in harmony with the sanctuary pattern[155]—"should become permanent in the tabernacle. So the glory of Yahweh that appears on Mount Sinai found its permanent dwelling in the tabernacle as described in Exodus 40:34."[156]

Posterior biblical covenants, the one with David (2 Sam 7:4-17), and the new covenant announced by Jeremiah (Jer 31:31-34), are also implementations of the everlasting covenant.[157] In these covenants, God's desire to dwell among His people in a permanent way in His sanctuary is evident (2 Sam 7:13; Ezek 37:26-27). The unfolding of the everlasting covenant reaches a culminating point with the ratification of that covenant through the sacrifice of Christ on the cross. The new covenant of Heb 8:8-13 (cf. Luke 22:20; 1 Cor 11:25; 2 Cor 3:6) is the renewal of God's everlasting covenant with the remnant of Israel: the church (Rom 9-11).[158]

---

154. See Gen 3:8, 21 (where an animal sacrificed by God Himself is implied); 8:20-21; 12:7-8; 15:1, 17-18; 17:1-2. The earthly liturgy of patriarchal "altars would be expanded and enriched significantly through the priestly ministration of the tabernacle built after the Israelites were liberated by Yahweh from the bondage of Egypt." Timm, "The Sanctuary Motif," 72. For additional discussion regarding the covenants of God with Abraham and Israel (the nation), see LaRondelle, *Our Creator Redeemer*, 22-27; Gulley, *God as Trinity*, 316-317.

155. See footnote 125 in this chapter.

156. Elias Brasil de Souza, "Sanctuary: Cosmos, Covenant, and Creation," *JATS* 24, no. 1 (2013): 31.

157. The covenant with David and the new covenant of Jeremiah are part of the everlasting covenant. See 2 Sam 23:5; Jer 32:40; 50:5; cf. Isa 55:3; 61:8; Ezek 16:60; 36:26-28; Heb 13:20.

158. For the relationship between the old and new covenants, see LaRondelle, *Our Creator Redeemer*, 74-88; Gulley, *God as Trinity*, 339-363. For a discussion about the elements of continuity and discontinuity between Israel and the church, considering the covenantal element, see Richard M. Davidson, "Israel and the Church: Continuity and Discontinuity—I," in *Message, Mission, and Unity of the Church*, ed. Ángel Manuel Rodríguez (Silver Spring, MD: Biblical Research Institute, 2013), 375-400; Richard M. Davidson, "Israel and the Church: Continuity and Discontinuity—II," in *Message, Mission, and Unity of the Church*, ed. Ángel Manuel

Christ is the Mediator of this covenant (Heb 8:6; 9:15; 12:24). As this covenant is a renovation of all previous redemptive covenants in the Old Testament, Christ is ultimately the Mediator of all of them—understood as a Mediator between God and humanity. Christ is the Angel of the Lord. He identifies Himself as Yahweh, the One who articulates the relationship between God and His people, the *I Am* of Exod 3:14.[159]

The essential stipulations of the covenant are those that constitute the foundation of God's throne/government from His sanctuary. They are a reflection of God's character (Ps 89:14). These stipulations find their clearer expression in the Decalogue (Exod 20:1-11) that God delivered to Israelites at Sinai, "to whom pertain . . . the covenants" (Rom 9:4, NKJV). The sign of the Sinaitic covenant was also the Sabbath (Exod 31:13-17; cf. Ezek 20:12, 20). The Sabbath unites the Edenic covenant with the redemptive covenants through the history of salvation and it is a sign of the present and future rest of the redeemed (Heb 4:3, 9-11), an institution that will continue in the context of the new heaven and the new earth (Isa 66:22-23; cf. Rev 21:1).[160]

Rodríguez (Silver Spring, MD: Biblical Research Institute, 2013), 401-427.

159. "The divine covenants with Adam (Gen. 2:2-3, 15-17; 3:15), Abraham (Gen. 12; 15; 17), Israel through Moses (Exod. 19-34), and David (2 Sam. 7), along with the promised 'new covenant' to Israel (Jer. 31; Ezek. 36), can be viewed as successive stages of God's single covenant of redeeming grace that is fulfilled in Jesus Christ." LaRondelle, *Our Creator Redeemer*, 5. See also Davidson, "Continuity and Discontinuity—I," 398-399; Gudmundur Olafsson, "God's Eternal Covenant and the Sabbath," *JATS* 16, nos. 1-2 (2005): 158, n. 13. Regarding Christ as a Mediator of the new covenant, see LaRondelle, *Our Creator Redeemer*, 86-87. In relation to Christ as the Angel of the Lord, see Davidson, "Proverbs 8," 52; Gulley, *God as Trinity*, 281; Fernando L. Canale, "Doctrine of God," in *Handbook of Seventh-day Adventist Theology*, ed. Raoul Dederen (Hagerstown, MD: Review & Herald, 2000), 122. About Christ as the *I Am*, see Whidden, Moon, and Reeve, *The Trinity*, 28-30, 52-54.

160. "The connecting link of God's covenant of creation with His covenant of redemption is God's Sabbath rest." LaRondelle, *Our Creator Redeemer*, 11. See also Kline, *Kingdom Prologue*, 19-20; Gerhard F. Hasel, "The Sabbath in the Pentateuch," in *The Sabbath in Scripture and History*, ed. Kenneth A. Strand (Washington, DC: Review & Herald, 1982), 21, 35-37. Compare the version of the fourth commandment in Exod 20:8-11 (that emphasizes God's resting at the end of Creation as the reason to keep the Sabbath) with Deut 5:13-15 (that emphasizes God's deliverance of Israel from Egypt as the reason). See LaRondelle, *Our Creator Redeemer*, 37; Hasel, "The Sabbath in the Pentateuch," 37. Regarding the Sabbath as a sign of the present and future rest of the redeemed, see LaRondelle, *Our Creator Redeemer*, 12-13; Samuele Bacchiocchi, *Divine Rest for Human Restlessness: A Theological Study of the Good News of the Sabbath for Today* (Rome, Italy: Pontifical Gregorian University Press, 1980), 165-170; Sigve K. Tonstad, *The Lost Meaning of the Seventh Day* (Ber-

The covenant, in connection with the sanctuary, is an articulating action in operation even before the problem of sin, although the implementation of the everlasting covenant is post-fall. In the context of the sanctuary pattern of relationship, the covenant—in its successive manifestations—gradually unfolds God's plan through Christ that reveals more about God's loving character and promotes the lost harmony and fellowship between the Creator and the creatures.[161] Those who enter in a covenantal relationship with God become God's people, whether they are Adam and Eve, Israel, or the church.[162]

After the Fall, the basic mission of God's people is to communicate His revelation to others and persuade them to participate in God's covenantal community.[163] God's people are an instrument for the manifestation of His holiness to the world (Ezek 36:22-23)[164] and for the fulfillment of the mission of gathering all things in Christ, the head of God's people (Eph 1:10; Col 1:16, 18). Thus, the ultimate goal of the covenant is the restoration of the original harmony and fellowship between God and His creation,[165] and the restoration of "the original covenant of creation with humanity,"[166] by which God will tabernacle forever with

---

rien Springs, MI: Andrews University Press, 2009), 290-293. The Sabbath anticipates God's dwelling with His people in the new earth. "God shall finally dwell among men forever, they shall be his people, and he will be their God (Rev 21:3, 7), a fellowship they will commemorate weekly 'from sabbath to sabbath [as] all mankind will come to bow down before [him]' (Isa 66:23) in eternal thankfulness." Olafsson, "Eternal Covenant and the Sabbath," 162-163. See also Kline, *Kingdom Prologue*, 35-36; Bacchiocchi, *Divine Rest*, 170.

161. See LaRondelle, *Our Creator Redeemer*, xi-xii, 5-6, 11.

162. The typical covenantal formula suggests precisely this idea. "As God introduced his plan of redemption to Moses, he expressed the essence of the covenant—'I will take you for my people and I will be your God' (Exod 6:7). This expression and variations of it is repeated more than thirty times in the Bible, usually with the concept of the covenant being either explicit or implied in the context." Olafsson, "Eternal Covenant and the Sabbath," 156.

163. See Scot McKnight, "Covenant," *DTIB*, 143.

164. LaRondelle, *Our Creator Redeemer*, 3-4. God's holiness manifests "itself visibly *through* the covenant people of Yahweh before the eyes of the world." Ibid., 4. Emphasis in original.

165. In Gen 9:8-17, God reaffirms His covenant with *all living creatures* and with *all flesh*. In Col 1:15-20, "by confessing that in Jesus God reconciles all of creation to himself, Paul is reaffirming God's most foundational covenantal promise to be faithful to all of creation." Sylvia C. Keesmaat, "Colossians, Book of," *DTIB*, 120.

166. LaRondelle, *Our Creator Redeemer*, 14. See ibid., 152-154. "The ultimate purpose of the covenant will be achieved when God completes the re-creation of the earth at the end of the age (Rev 21:7)." Olafsson, "Eternal Covenant and the Sabbath," 158.

His people without the barrier of sin. The covenant, then—as a specific articulating action linked to the sanctuary pattern of relationship—is the instrument to constitute God's people and originates the mission of that people. Sanctuary, covenant, people of God, and mission are inseparable.

In the context of sin, the covenantal relationship between God and His creatures would be impossible without Christ's work of reconciliation-atonement, which is also developed within the sanctuary pattern. In contrast to the understanding of atonement as reduced to the cross (D. Ford), the biblical view of Christ and His actions as temporal leads to an understanding of atonement in terms of a historical process, following the pattern of relationship of the heavenly sanctuary. The foundation of that historical process is Christ's substitutionary atoning sacrifice on the cross (Rom 3:25; 1 John 2:2; 4:10).[167] This event is the base for the implementation of the rest of God's plan of Atonement. In the sacrificial services of the sanctuary in the Old Testament, it is clear that atonement is a process that involves the sacrifices through the year, along with the intercession of the priest who was responsible to make atonement for the sinner (Lev 4:20, 26, 31, 35, etc.), and the final atonement in the Day of Atonement (Lev 16).[168] In a similar way, in the antitypical fulfillment of the types of the earthly sanctuary, "the Bible clearly shows that atonement did not end at the cross; atonement is a grand process which began at the cross and which continues until we are completely separated from sin and united with God."[169] The cross is the fundamental event in a process by which Christ would draw all things to Himself (John 12:32). This process follows with Christ's intercession in the heavenly sanctuary (Heb 7:25; 8:1-2; Rom 8:34; 1 John 2:2) and the final judgment or antitypical Day of Atonement where the final destiny of every believer—and eventually, every person—will be

---

167. "The cross represents the one and only, once for all, truly efficacious atoning death (Heb 9:28)." Roy Gane, "Temple and Sacrifice," *JATS* 10, nos. 1-2 (1999): 370.

168. Gerhard F. Hasel, "Studies in Biblical Atonement II: The Day of Atonement," in *The Sanctuary and the Atonement: Biblical, Historical, and Theological Studies*, ed. Arnold V. Wallenkampf and Richard Lesher (Washington, DC: Review & Herald, 1981), 120; Roy Gane, *Cult and Character: Purification Offerings, Day of Atonement, and Theodicy* (Winona Lake, IN: Eisenbrauns, 2005), 267-284; Treiyer, *The Day of Atonement*, 207-210; Gane, "Temple and Sacrifice," 371, 373.

169. Gane, "Temple and Sacrifice," 371. See Treiyer, *The Day of Atonement*, 207. See also, with some qualifications, R. Adams, *The Sanctuary*, 56.

decided and God's character will be vindicated.[170]

Christ's temporal intercessory work in the heavenly sanctuary makes the personal dimension of Atonement possible. Without Christ's intercession, there is no possibility of justification and sanctification. Since Christ's intercession and the final judgment are temporal processes, justification and sanctification are also temporal processes. Justification is essentially forgiveness of sin (Rom 4:1-8).[171] As such, justification cannot be once and forever as in the case of Luther, Calvin, or D. Ford. Forgiveness is required every time that a person commits sin (1 John 2:1). In consequence, justification is something that can be forfeited. In Old Testament terms, an Israelite who was guilty or impure "could not simply do nothing and maintain the covenant connection."[172] Christians are in covenantal relationship with God. The commission of sin implies a tension with the terms of the covenant that requires resolution through additional forgiveness that Christ's intercession in the sanctuary provides.[173] As part of the general experience of salvation, then, justification is a continuous fact throughout the life of the believer.[174]

---

170. See Dan 7:9-14, 22, 26-27; 8:14; Matt 16:27; 25:31-46; Rom 14:10; 1 Cor 6:3; 2 Cor 5:10; Rev 14:7; 20:4, 11-15; etc. Regarding the final judgment and its phases, see Treiyer, *The Day of Atonement*, which covers the topic throughout the whole Scripture as an antitypical fulfillment of the typical Day of Atonement. See also Gerhard F. Hasel, "Divine Judgment," in *Handbook of Seventh-day Adventist Theology*, ed. Raoul Dederen (Hagerstown, MD: Review & Herald, 2000), 830-848. In harmony with the types of the Old Testament and biblical texts about the pre-Advent phase of the final judgment, it is clear that this phase is not only vindicatory of God's character but also "investigative and evaluative in regard to all who have made a profession to be believers. One of the accomplishments of the pre-Advent judgment is the determination of those among the professed people who will inherit the kingdom." Ibid., 844. In other words, there is a real decision-making process in the investigative judgment. E. G. White clearly supported this position. See footnotes 148 and 477 in Chapter 4.

171. Blazen, "Salvation," 281-283.

172. Gane, "Temple and Sacrifice," 368.

173. It is possible to talk about a *daily justification*. See George R. Knight, *Sin and Salvation: God's Work for and in Us*, rev. ed. (Hagerstown, MD: Review & Herald, 2008), 88. Knight clarifies that "some scholars prefer to think of ongoing justification as 'continued forgiveness,' since their standing with God was corrected at the time of their conversion and initial justification, but in essence the difference is largely semantic." Ibid.

174. "In harmony with the O[ld] T[estament], where salvation is past, present, and future, a person who experiences God's salvation was saved (Rom. 8:24; Eph. 2:5, 8), is being saved (1 Cor. 1:18; 15:2), and shall be saved (Matt. 24:13; Rom. 5:9, 10)." Blazen, "Salvation," 272. In the same line, Knight adds, "Salvation . . . is a continuing process rather than being a once-save-always-saved event. That means that to retain

This understanding of justification implies that justification by faith and sanctification are inseparable. "While we might separate faith and works for purpose of academic discussion, in daily life you cannot have one without the other, since both are part of the same covenant relationship."[175] Abandoning sanctification as a moral growth through the assistance of the Holy Spirit[176] necessarily puts justification at risk (Col 1:21-23), which involves the covenant relationship with Christ in the context of the sanctuary. "In Christ we have abundant assurance as long as we accept and keep on accepting each wave of His transforming atonement."[177]

In the final judgment, which is part of the cosmic dimension of Atonement, justification by faith and sanctification are still inseparable. That is why James can say that "Abraham was justified by works" (Jas 2:21, NKJV) and Paul can say that in the judgment, "the doers of the law will be justified" (Rom 2:13, NKJV). Judgment entails a complete evaluation of the life of the believer in the light of the terms of the covenant or God's law.[178] Justification, thus, is not God's definitive judgment of believers. They find their final vindication in the context of the eschatological judgment.[179]

The connection between justification/sanctification and covenant implies that Atonement has a social dimension. The justified person

---

the assurance of salvation, one must continue to remain in covenant relationship with God through Christ." Knight, *Sin and Salvation*, 84.

175. Knight, *Sin and Salvation*, 84.

176. See Rom 15:16; 1 Cor 6:11; 1 Pet 1:2; 2 Thess 2:13; Gal 5:16-17, 22-23. Sanctification is "a progressive process of moral change by the power of the Holy Spirit in cooperation with the human will." Blazen, "Salvation," 296.

177. Gane, "Temple and Sacrifice," 369. "God cannot save a person who does not really have faith or who abandons faith after receiving forgiveness." Ibid., 377. "Christ imputes his perfection and righteousness to the believing sinner when he does not continue in sin, but turns from transgression to obedience of the commandments." Ellen G. White, "The Law Exalted by Christ," *The Advent Review and Sabbath Herald*, May 23, 1899, 321.

178. This is already observable in the antitypical Day of Atonement. "The Day of Atonement functioned as a judgment which reviewed and renewed the covenant relationship between God and the Israelites." Roy Gane, "Judgment as Covenant Review," *JATS* 8, nos. 1-2 (1997): 188.

179. It is useful to notice that James's affirmation about justification by faith and works (Jas 2:14-26) appears in a judgment context. See Jas 2:8-13 and 3:1-2, which clearly refer to judgment. Roy E. Graf Maiorov, "El uso de Génesis 15:6 por Pablo y Santiago: Implicaciones hermenúticas" (MTh thesis, Universidad Peruana Unión, Lima, Perú, 2012), 124-127.

becomes part of God's people.[180] Thus, it is clear that "God is working out salvation at various levels: the individual, social, and cosmic."[181] Atonement operates in the individual (justification-sanctification), social (belonging to the covenant-people of God), and cosmic dimensions (cross-intercession-judgment). The last makes the first two possible. Christ's continuous work following the sanctuary structural pattern leads to God's vindication and, ultimately, makes God's continuous dwelling or tabernacling with His people possible.[182]

The fact that Christ acts in history through the covenant and Atonement in harmony with the sanctuary pattern entails that He operates as a historical cause in the flow of historical events. Christ articulates human history providentially, implementing through the structure of the sanctuary God's plan established before Creation. Providence refers precisely to the implementation of God's plan before Creation.[183] Christ governs history leading it to the fulfillment of God's purpose. The biblical prophecies clearly show this providential action. From His immanent presence in the sanctuary (Ps 11:4), God through Christ "changes the times and the seasons; He removes kings and raises up kings" (Dan 2:21, NKJV). The apocalyptic prophecy demonstrates how the great prophetic periods that organize human history relate in a systematic way to the sanctuary activity in its interaction with the human will. The 70 weeks of Dan 9:24-27, for example, involve the atoning sacrifice of the Messiah the Prince (vv. 24, 26), the confirmation of His covenant (v. 27; cf. Heb 8:7-13), the end of the sacrificial system in the earthly temple (Dan 9:27; cf. Matt 27:51), and the inauguration of the heavenly sanctuary (v. 24). These events are part of a precise prophetic calendar.[184] The 2,300 days-years

---

180. "Justification has a corporate as well as individual dimension. It creates the people of God. As persons are set right with God they are also brought into a right relationship with each other and become one body (Rom. 12:4; 15:7; 1 Cor. 12:12, 13; Eph. 4:4, 5)." Blazen, "Salvation," 284.

181. Canale, "Doctrine of God," 119.

182. See Gane, "Temple and Sacrifice," 377; Gane, "Judgment as Covenant Review," 188.

183. See, with some qualifications, Erickson, *Christian Theology*, 365. Erickson understands God's plan as timeless although executed in time. Compare with Canale, "Doctrine of God," 118-119; Canale, *Basic Elements of Christian Theology*, 163, 221; Kerbs, *El problema de la identidad*, 247.

184. Regarding the content and the chronology of this prophecy see, for example, William H. Shea, "The Prophecy of Daniel 9:24:27," in *70 Weeks, Leviticus, and the Nature of Prophecy*, ed. Frank B. Holbrook (Washington, DC: Biblical Research

of Dan 8:14, connected with the 70 weeks prophecy predict a continuous intercessory work in the heavenly sanctuary as well as the time of the purification/vindication of the heavenly sanctuary or antitypical Day of Atonement.[185] Moreover, the 3½ times of Dan 7:25; 12:7; and Rev 12:14, which are the 42 months of Rev 11:2; 13:5, and the 1,260 days-years of Rev 11:3; 12:6, are a period during which God allowed the development of a false system of intercession, competing with the heavenly sanctuary until the time of its vindication (Dan 8:14).[186]

Institute, GC of SDAs, 1986), 75-118; Brempong Owusu-Antwi, *The Chronology of Daniel 9:24-27*, Adventist Theological Society Dissertation Series 2 (Berrien Springs, MI: Adventist Theological Society, 1993). Gane, *Who's Afraid of the Judgment?* 51-58. For a discussion about the biblical evidence for the year-day principle involved in the prophetic periods mentioned in this paragraph, see William H. Shea, *Selected Studies on Prophetic Interpretation* (n.p.: GC of SDAs, 1982), 56-88; Alberto R. Timm, "Miniature Symbolization and the Year-Day Principle of Prophetic Interpretation," *AUSS* 42, no. 1 (2004): 149-167.

185. For an introduction to the study of this prophecy see, for example, Gerhard F. Hasel, "The 'Little Horn,' the Heavenly Sanctuary and the Time of the End: A Study of Daniel 8:9-14," in *Symposium on Daniel: Introductory and Exegetical Studies*, ed. Frank B. Holbrook (Washington, DC: Biblical Research Institute, GC of SDAs, 1986), 378-461; Clifford Goldstein, *1844 Made Simple* (Boise, ID: Pacific Press, 1988); Gane, *Who's Afraid of the Judgment?* 36-45, 59-67.

186. The 1,290 days-years and 1,335 days-years of Dan 12:11-12 seem to connect the 3½ or 1,260 days-years with the 2,300 days-years. There is a systematic interrelationship among the main prophetic periods of Daniel and Revelation, where the sanctuary is always the articulating element. For a discussion regarding the 1,260 days-years from a biblical and historical perspective, see C. Mervyn Maxwell, "An Exegetical and Historical Examination of the Beginning and Ending of the 1260 Days of Prophecy With Special Attention Given to A.D. 538 and 1798 as Initial and Terminal Dates" (MA thesis, SDA Theological Seminary, Washington, DC, 1951). Regarding the time of initiation of the prophetic periods of Dan 7:25; 12:7, 11, 12 and its historical fulfillment, see Alberto R. Timm, "Algunas consideraciones breves en torno a los años 508 y 538 en relación con el establecimiento de la supremacía papal," *Theologika* 19, no. 2 (2004): 254-283; Treiyer, *The Seals and the Trumpets*, 88-118. For the interrelationship among the main prophetic periods of Daniel and Revelation, see William H. Shea, "Time Prophecies of Daniel 12 and Revelation 12-13," in *Symposium on Revelation*, vol. 1, *Introductory and Exegetical Studies*, ed. Frank B. Holbrook (Silver Spring, MD: Biblical Research Institute, GC of SDAs, 1992), 327-360; Treiyer, *The Day of Atonement*, 364-366; Treiyer, *The Seals and the Trumpets*, 111-114. Possible prophetic periods also connected to the sanctuary are the five months of Rev 9:5, 10 and the hour, day, month, and year of Rev 9:15. They appear in the context of the seven trumpets of Rev 8-9, which are historical judgments coming from the heavenly sanctuary (Rev 8:2-6). See possible interpretations of these prophecies in ibid., 309-314, 324-343.

This providential, historical-temporal involvement of God in human history that Christ systematically articulates through the sanctuary structural pattern is consistent with the historicist approach to the interpretation of the biblical prophecy (particularly Daniel and Revelation), which is in continuity with biblical history in general. God's participation in history is not restricted to some specific point in the past or in the future, as some approaches to apocalyptic prophetic interpretation suggest—preterism or futurism. From the perspective of His spatio-temporal immanence in the sanctuary, God through Christ's articulating action permanently participates in human history as a temporal cause from Eden to the final establishment of His eternal kingdom in the new earth. Christ is historically involved in all redemptive events, such as the Exodus (1 Cor 10:4) and the first and second coming of Christ, to mention only some.[187]

God's interventions in history through Christ's articulating action, then, are not from "outside" of the historical sequence of events. God does not perform miracles through a timeless intervention in time, breaking His own natural laws or the sequence of cause-effect. Rather He participates in history as a personal cause, which is different from the world and not ontologically limited by it. Whether this participation is observable—as in miracles—or not, God leads history from the advantageous position of His sanctuary.

Although God's participation in history responds to His general plan, this plan gives space for the freedom of His intelligent creatures. In the human realm, Christ's providential action in history does not overrule human free will. Believers, for example, can express their will and petitions to God in prayer and expect that He will consider them from the heavenly sanctuary (Matt 7:7-11; Rev 8:3-4).[188] From this perspective, it is possible to agree with process theology that God acts persuasively (Isa 1:18) in the sense that He exhausts the possibilities

---

187. From a historicist perspective, then, "the prophecies of Daniel and Revelation provide a divinely inspired, descriptive overview and evaluation of some of the most theologically significant events of this era. The Christian era is seen to stand in continuity with the historical description and prophetic evaluation of events in the O[ld] T[estament] era. The same God has been active in a similar way in both of these dispensations." Shea, *Prophetic Interpretation*, 57.

188. Humans, though, are not completely free in the sense that they can reject God's plan without consequences. God's intention to dwell in harmony with His people will finally prevail, and those who do not want to participate in the reenacting of the Creation covenant will be destroyed (see Rev 20-22).

to convince His creatures to accept His plan for them and to recognize the fairness of His character and government without forcing them.[189] It is not surprising, then, that God allows the participation of intelligent creatures in the pre-advent and millennial phases of the eschatological judgment (Dan 7:9, 10, 26; 1 Cor 6:2-3; Rev 20:4). Only this procedure can ensure that God will not deal a second time with the problem of evil and sin, and He will tabernacle with His creatures in harmony forever.[190]

In a broad perspective that includes pre-fall reality and the future reality after the end of the great controversy, the articulating action can be conceptualized as Christ's mediation between God and the world-humanity through the sanctuary/temple structural pattern of relationship—God's dwelling with His creatures in a spatio-temporal location. In one word, this articulating action is *tabernacling*. The pattern of relationship is *sanctuary-form*. God's dwelling with His creatures is Christ's essential articulating action that explains all the others. God's tabernacling or dwelling requires a covenantal relationship between God and human beings who become His people with a mission when they participate in the covenant. Ultimately, the covenant involves the entire universe, which exists in solidarity with intelligent creatures. More particularly in the context of the great controversy, Christ also mediates between God's holiness and His sinful creatures. God's dwelling requires a work of Atonement that Christ implements by means of His providential action in history (as demonstrated in apocalyptic prophecy). The sanctuary structural pattern of relationship entails a progressive revelation of God's character and plans. This revelation promotes, through loving persuasion, an increasing higher level of harmony, joy, and fellowship in the world and in reality as a whole.

---

189. God's persuasive action, however, is only applicable to intelligent creatures and not to every entity in the world.

190. See E. G. White, *The Great Controversy*, 504. In Dan 7:9-10, 26, for example, it is clear that God ("the Ancient of days" in v. 9) sits on His throne in order to preside the judgment that involves other heavenly beings that also sit on their own thrones (in plural in v. 9). They constitute the heavenly court (vv. 10, 26) of intelligent creatures that participate in the judicial process (cf. Ps 82:1; 1 Kgs 22:19). Louis F. Hartman and Alexander A. Di Lella, *The Book of Daniel*, AB 23 (Garden City, NY: Doubleday, 1978), 217. In fact, "it is probably the associate judges in the celestial court by whom 'the books were opened.'" Ibid., 218.

The Interpretation of the Whole

As the articulating action is historical-temporal in nature, the articulated reality can change over time. Hence, it is useful to consider two different but complementary approaches to describe the whole—the entire reality articulated by the articulating action—in its different aspects: a diachronic approach and a synchronic one.[191] The diachronic approach considers the whole from the perspective of its changes throughout its existence. From a biblical perspective, reality as a whole involves God, the world, and the intelligent creatures that inhabit the world. Christ is the articulating agent of that whole, articulating the relationship between God and the world through the sanctuary structure. He is also the one who provides inner articulation to the world.[192]

This whole started to exist since Creation. To the extent that creation reflected the original plan of God, the whole can be described as a condition of complete harmony and perfection (Gen 1:31; cf. Ezek 28:12-15). That original harmony, however, suffered a serious disruption as a result of the introduction of the problem of sin: the rebellion

---

191. Diachronic and synchronic approaches are usual expressions in linguistics and the conceptualization of the distinction between both can be found in Ferdinand de Saussure, *Course in General Linguistics*, trans. Wade Baskin (New York, NY: Philosophical Library, 1959). In biblical studies, diachronic and synchronic have become expressions naming the different approaches in the study of the meaning of biblical terms. The diachronic approach emphasizes the etymology and historical development of terms, while the synchronic approach emphasizes the literary context. See John H. Walton, "Etymology," *DTIB*, 200. Probably more frequently, however, these terms refer to different approaches in the study of the biblical text in a more general way. The diachronic approach usually refers to the historical development of the text under study (frequently understood from a historical-critical perspective), and the diachronic approach refers to the study of the text from the perspective of its final form. See Koog P. Hong, "Synchrony and Diachrony in Contemporary Biblical Interpretation," *The Catholic Biblical Quarterly* 75, no. 3 (2013): 521-528. It is also possible to apply the distinction between diachronic and synchronic in biblical theology to the study of a topic throughout its historical development in the Bible (diachronic) in contrast to the study of the topic in a specific delimited section of Scripture (synchronic). Guy, *Thinking Theologically*, 214-215. Here, however, the approaches do not refer to the interpretation of the biblical text but to the interpretation of an ontological reality, the principle of articulation, from the perspective of the biblical text, assuming the biblical temporality of the principle, whether in the diachronic or the synchronic approach. Of course, the following diachronic and synchronic depiction of the whole is just an outline in the context of the proposal of this chapter—which requires additional development and expansion.

192. See, for example, 1 Cor 15:27-28; Eph 1:10-11; Col 1:16-20; Heb 1:3.

of some creatures against the Creator. Given the fact that God has decided to deal with the problem of sin and evil using persuasion rather than coercion, reality became what Adventists have usually named the great controversy (as E. G. White calls it) or cosmic controversy (as Gulley calls it).

During this conflict, Christ has articulated the relationship between God and the world through His mediatorial work following the sanctuary structural pattern of relationship. In the context of the problem of sin, that pattern involves Christ's mediation of God's holiness, in addition to His mediation in general between God and the world. The sanctuary pattern of relationship involves—without claiming to be exhaustive—the redemptive covenants with Adam, Noah, Abraham, Israel, and David. It also includes the dwelling of the *I Am* in the earthly tabernacle/temple of the Old Testament. It comprises the following activities of Christ: incarnation, sacrificial substitutionary atonement and ratification of the new covenant on the cross, resurrection, intercession in the heavenly sanctuary, pre-Advent investigative judgment, and Second Coming. It also encompasses the millennial judgment and the executive judgment at the end of the millennium. Through all this process, God has been revealing His desire and purpose to dwell with His creatures, restoring the original harmony prior to the beginning of the great controversy. Revelation 21-22 disclose the restoration of that original condition in the context of the new heavens and the new earth (cf. Isa 66:22; 2 Pet 3:13, etc.). Thus, from a diachronic approach, the whole or the articulated reality can be described in its extension as *original harmony → great controversy → new heavens and new earth*.[193]

On the other hand, Christ articulates reality as a whole at more than one level: cosmic, social, and individual. Thus, in the context of the great controversy, the synchronic approach allows visualizing the operation of the articulating action at specific moments of the process of articulation and the coordinated interrelationship of the three levels at a particular time. For instance, since His ascension after the Resurrection, Christ intercedes in the heavenly sanctuary (cosmic level) for

---

193. The Adventist pioneers emphasized the whole as a reality in conflict, from the perspective of the problem of sin and their expectation of the final events. They did not ignore, though, the original harmony and Christ's action to achieve a total restoration of that perfect condition at the end of the great controversy. Compare p. 138 in Chapter 3 with E. G. White, *Patriarchs and Prophets*, 35; E. G. White, *The Great Controversy*, 674-678.

those who pertain to His covenantal missionary people (social level) whose members have a daily experience of justification and sanctification (individual level). During the time of the pre-advent judgment, in turn, the cosmic level adds the investigative activity to the one of intercession. This change at the cosmic level implies changes at the other levels. At the social level, an end-time remnant emerges, faithful to the stipulations of the covenant, with the mission to announce the coming of the judgment and its consequences for those who falsify or reject the articulating action of Christ (Rev 12:17; 14:7-12).[194] At the individual level, Christ encourages believers to examine their own lives in the light of the final events and to participate in the final mission (2 Pet 3:11-12, 14; Rev 3:14-21).

It is also possible to visualize the operation of the articulating action at the three levels even before or after the problem of sin. At the cosmic level, for example, God revealed (before the sin) and will progressively reveal (in the new earth) His character through His fair rulership and His interaction with His intelligent creatures in a way that is observable for the entire universe. At the social level, God had a covenantal relationship with Adam and Eve, and He will still have a covenantal relationship with His people in the new earth. Those who do not honor the stipulations of the covenant will not be in the New Jerusalem (Rev 21:7-8, 27; 22:15).[195] At the individual level, Adam and Eve had the possibility of character development in harmony with the divine model. Their free will implied that possibility. The same will be possible for those dwelling in communion with God in the new earth (cf. Rev 22:4; cf. 14:1), where freedom of choice will still be a reality for those restored to the image of God.[196]

Diachronic and synchronic approaches, then, complement each

---

194. See Davidson, "Continuity and Discontinuity—II," 423-424.

195. The expression "I will be his God, and he shall be my son" in Rev 21:7 (cf. v. 3) refers to the covenantal relationship between God and His people in the New Jerusalem. See Olafsson, "Immanuel—God With Us," 120. Actually, "God has always worked with humanity within the context of a covenant, from the time of Adam at Creation (Hos 6:7) to the Earth made new (Rev 21:7)." Olafsson, "Eternal Covenant and the Sabbath," 157. In contrast, Rev 21:8 (cf. 21:27, 22:15) refers to those who have rejected the terms of the covenant and were excluded from God's people.

196. There is no reason to assume that freedom of choice will disappear in the new earth. Free will is the reason why God has decided to deal with the problem of sin in a persuasive way—within some limits. The image and likeness of God involve free will.

other to better understand the biblical interpretation of the articulated reality as a whole. There is a horizontal dimension (original harmony-controversy-restoration) and a vertical one (cosmic, social, and individual level) of the articulated whole. In the present time, the whole is still a reality in conflict. This reality, however, moves toward the resolution of this controversy and the restoration of the original harmony.

Conclusion

This chapter has outlined a proposal to interpret the principle of articulation in Adventist theology from a biblical perspective that comprises an interpretation of the ontological and epistemological presuppositions of the principle, as well as an interpretation of God, the world, the human being, the articulating agent, the articulating action, and the articulated whole. The interpretation of the principle of articulation suggested in this chapter took into consideration the contributions of the models analyzed and evaluated in Chapter 4. It suggested, however, possible ways to be more consistent with the biblical data, in harmony with the *sola Scriptura* principle. By way of conclusion, then, some comparative remarks are useful here. First, regarding the ontological and epistemological presuppositions, as well as the interpretation of God, this proposal avoids the implicit or explicit application of the *via negativa*—that entails an ontological dualism—observable especially in the evangelical and modern Adventist models. This proposal shares with the Adventist theodicy model a similar understanding of God's temporality, but does not consider the physical descriptions of God in the Bible as anthropomorphisms (as Gulley suggests). It recognizes the spatio-temporal analogical or likeness language of the Bible to talk about God. This affirmative way allows the understanding of the articulating action as God's dwelling or tabernacling with His creatures in the world in a spatio-temporal location, while it avoids speculation regarding the mystery of God's transcendence.

Second, in connection with the interpretation of the world and the human being, this proposal departs from the evangelical and the modern Adventist models regarding the understanding of origins. It is clearly closer to the creationist position of the Adventist theodicy model. At the same time, it shares with the three models the unitary understanding of the human being.

Third, in relation to the interpretation of the articulating agent and the articulating action, this proposal emphasizes the fundamental role of Christ in a way that goes beyond the other models—to the extent that they have granted that role to Christ. From the perspective of this proposal, Christ's temporal articulating role through the sanctuary structural pattern of relationship meet the epistemological necessity for articulation in the Adventist cognitive theological system. At the same time, as epistemology assumes ontology, this perspective of the Adventist cognitive theological system assumes that there is an ontological necessity for articulation that Christ's temporal articulating action through the sanctuary is able to explain. Christ's articulating action through the sanctuary fills the ontological necessity for articulation. This ontological articulating role encompasses the mediatorial role in the context of sin but goes beyond that. Christ's mediation or articulating role is not limited to the problem of sin or His incarnation. Christ is the articulating agent performing the articulation of reality as a whole.

Fourth, in consonance with the articulating role of Christ, the proposal of the sanctuary structural pattern of relationship—God's dwelling in the world—does not ignore the importance of justification emphasized by the evangelical Adventist model. This proposal, though, interprets justification as part of the temporal experience of salvation in the broader context of the general temporal-historical process of Atonement that follows the sanctuary pattern of relationship. This proposal also considers the importance of persuasion, pointed out by the modern Adventist model, but not in the light of a panentheistic ontology. Persuasion is part of the process of articulation in the general context of the biblical understanding of God's providential action in history. Moreover, this proposal also recognizes the importance of the vindication of God's character, that the theodicy Adventist model highlights, but as part of the process of Atonement that allows the complete restoration of God's dwelling with His creatures.

Finally, concerning the interpretation of the whole, this proposal agrees with the theodicy model that the present reality as a whole is a reality in conflict. A cosmic controversy is unfolding. At the same time, this proposal highlights that the whole in its temporal extension includes the past harmony as well as the future restored harmony. The controversy in itself does not provide unity for reality as a whole. The articulating-mediating role of Christ through the sanctuary structural pattern of relationship is the unifying element of the entire reality.

CHAPTER SIX

Summary, Conclusions, and Recommendations

Summary

The purpose of this study was to (1) explain the notion of the principle of articulation in theology; (2) describe, analyze, and evaluate the main interpretations of the principle of articulation in current Adventist theology; and (3) propose an interpretation of the principle of articulation for Adventist theology. Chapter 1 offered a preliminary introduction to the notion of principle of articulation and the difficulties for its interpretation in the context of Adventist theology. This principle is a systematic presupposition of mind that is always operative not only in knowledge in general but also in theological knowledge in particular. It is the structuring element in any theological system. In theology, the principle of articulation always refers to God. However, in Christian theology in general, and in Adventist theology in particular, the identification of the principle has been problematic. It is usually conceptualized as a *center*. Adventist theology has claimed to operate based on the *sola Scriptura* principle. This epistemological claim, though, has not avoided multiple interpretations regarding what constitutes the center or articulating principle of Adventist theology.

The diverse suggested centers operate at the micro (exegetical) or meso (doctrinal-theological) hermeneutical level of interpretation. Canale has proposed to study the interpretation of the principle of articulation from the perspective of the macro hermeneutical presuppositions of the knower: ontological, epistemological, and systematic (or metaphysical) assumptions. The systematic assumption, that assumes the first two, is the principle of articulation. This approach entails that the interpretation of this principle should involve the application of the *sola Scriptura* principle at the level of the presuppositions based on which theology interprets doctrines. Furthermore, this approach offers the opportunity to analyze and evaluate the current interpretations of the principle (centers), as well as to elaborate an interpretation proposal that takes into consideration the application of the *sola Scriptura* principle at the level of the basic presuppositions of knowledge.

In order to undertake this task, then, Chapter 1 also offered other introductory remarks, including a preliminary clarification of the methodology of the study. This methodology includes three aspects. First, it requires a phenomenological description of the principle of articulation in theology. Second, it involves the application of the hermeneutical method to determine the ontological and epistemological presuppositions underlying the diverse interpretations of the principle of articulation. Third, it entails the use of the model method, in order to typify the main interpretations of the principle in Christian theology in general and in current Adventist theology in particular. This methodology is systematic rather than historical, although the order of presentation of the models is historical. The chapter concluded with an explanation of the procedure followed in the subsequent chapters of this study.

Chapter 2 of this study presented the necessary methodological considerations to face the rest of the study. First, the chapter introduced the notion of principle of articulation from the perspective of the structure of knowledge in interaction with Kant, Heidegger, and Gadamer. The principle of articulation is the presupposition that allows the knower to integrate or systematize the new knowledge of an object external to the mind with the previous knowledge (of which the principle is a part). It is an *a priori* principle that provides unity, systematicity, and wholeness to knowledge. At the same time, it is modifiable due to the circular structure of knowledge.

Second, the chapter elaborated a phenomenological description of the principle of articulation in theology. This description reveals four operative components of every theological system. These are (1) the basic parts or doctrines of the system that involve God, the world, and the human being; (2) the articulating agent that, in theology, refers always to God; (3) the articulating action that is always an action of God articulating the relationship between God Himself and the world; and (4) the whole that results from the articulating action.

Third, the chapter explained the role of the hermeneutical method in order to understand the principle of articulation. The method allows disclosing the ontological and epistemological presuppositions underlying the interpretation of the principle of articulation. Ultimately, the interpretation of being (ontology), knowledge (epistemology), and articulation (principle of articulation) can be essentially timeless or temporal. The same is valid for the interpretation of the being of God. An interpretation of God as timeless—as in classical theology—requires a denial of any temporal-spatial characteristic in God (*via negativa*). A temporal interpretation of God—as in Scripture—requires an affirmative way to interpret God's being. In consonance, the interpretation of the principle of articulation in theology—related to God's being and actions—can be timeless or temporal. Whatever be the interpretation of the principle, though, it is always an interpretation of an ontological reality, external to the mind, which is also articulated. At the same time, the interpretation of the principle of articulation depends on the epistemological sources admitted in a given theological system, such as Scripture, tradition, or culture. The hermeneutical method helps to clarify the origin of the presuppositions involved in the system.

Fourth, the chapter also indicated the criteria for the selection of the representative models of interpretation of the principle of articulation discussed in Chapter 3 (the historical chapter) and Chapter 4 (current Adventist theology). They exemplify different attitudes toward the *sola Scriptura* principle. In both chapters, the discussion of each model follows the outline provided for the phenomenological description of the principle of articulation and is preceded by an analysis of the ontological and epistemological presuppositions implied in the model.

Fifth, Chapter 2 ended by explaining the criterion for the evaluation of the models. The basic criterion is the *sola Scriptura* principle, which assumes the consistency and coherence of Scripture as a whole. The evaluation involves the presuppositions underlying the interpretations of the principle of articulation.

Chapter 3 reviewed the main interpretations of the principle of articulation in Christian history. In this way, the chapter provided the necessary historical background to evaluate the potential connections between the Adventist models described in Chapter 4 and Christian tradition in general. The chapter also briefly reviewed the interpretations of the principle of articulation among the Adventist pioneers, considering early attempts to change that interpretation. In the first section, then, the chapter offered a brief introduction to the Greek philosophical background that has affected Christian tradition in general. Second, the chapter discussed the hierarchical model of interpretation of the principle of articulation in Catholic medieval theology—Augustine and Aquinas. In this model, following the influence of Greek philosophy, being in general is timeless. God is also timeless, immutable. The knowledge about God implies the application of the *via negativa*. God created the world in a timeless way (*ex nihilo*). Heaven, the realm of God, is timeless and God does not relate directly to the temporal part of creation. Human beings are a soul-body dichotomy. Only the immortal soul reflects God's image. God articulates reality through a hierarchy of being, similar to the one of Greek philosophy, where He is the ultimate unmoved cause of motion in harmony with His causative timeless knowledge and His deterministic providential plan. God knows particular things in the world only through the timeless ideas of those things included in His mind. Things actually exist by participation in their unchangeable essences in God's mind. Predestination is part of God's immutable plan that includes Christ's incarnation. The reality as a whole is a hierarchy, where everything tends toward God's immutability.

Third, the chapter also analyzed the soteriological model of Protestant Reformation. Luther and Calvin maintain an ontological dualism in continuity with medieval theology. They also apply the *via negativa* to the knowledge about God, who is considered as timeless, immutable, and spaceless. For the reformers, God's will is the supreme cause of everything that happens. What God wills is the cause of His knowledge. The world is God's creation, involving a timeless spiritual heaven and a spatio-temporal transient world. The human being is also a duality of body and soul, corrupted by the problem of sin, and without free will. God's timeless will predestines humans for salvation or damnation. The articulating agent is Christ, the Mediator between God and the world. His essential articulating action is the implementation of God's timeless providence-predestination according to His immutable will. God determines from eternity every aspect of reality. Salvation is a timeless action, essentially reduced to justification, which is a manifestation of predestination. It covers the past, present, and future sins of the believer. Reality as a whole is a simplified version of the medieval hierarchy. It finds its unity in Christ and it will find final realization in a spiritualized eschatology where all creatures will be one with God.

Fourth, the chapter discussed the panentheistic model of modern theology—Schleiermacher and process theology. Modern liberal theology still preserves an ontological dualism. Regarding the knowledge of God, modern theology holds that there is some *a priori* element in religious experience. Revelation is an immanent and universal experience where the community of faith is the arbiter of beliefs. God is dipolar, with a timeless and a temporal pole. The temporal pole is essentially the world. The world is everlasting. God introduces changes in the world through an immanent process of evolution. There is no personal immortality or resurrection. Salvation is the strengthening of God's consciousness (Schleiermacher) or the actualization in the individual of His initial aim. God's articulation of the world is completely immanent. For Schleiermacher, God articulates reality through His absolute causality. In process theology, God articulates the world through persuasion. The world has some self-determination and can introduce change in God. Both views, though, see the entire reality in terms of panentheism. Reality is still seen as a hierarchy but adapted to the mindset of modern science.

Finally, the chapter reviewed the interpretation of the principle of articulation among the Adventist pioneers. The discovery of the heavenly sanctuary led early Sabbatarian Adventists to realize that heaven and earth were part of the same spatio-temporal creation. Consequently, in their writings, they reject any ontological dualism and apply a literal-temporal hermeneutics to the interpretation of heavenly realities in consonance with a deeper commitment to the *sola Scriptura* principle. They also reject any spiritualized interpretation of God. He is a temporal being, acting in human history but transcendent to the world. He is a personal being, Creator and Sustainer of the universe, although different from it. The biblical account of Creation in six days is literal. God also created human beings in His image including the outward resemblance and character. The Adventist pioneers hold a unitary view of the human being, rejecting the belief in an immortal soul and an eternal hell. Human beings possess free will, and the problem of sin is the result of their conscious disobedience to God. Since its inception, sin produced a separation between God and humanity and introduced suffering and death in the world.

Christ is the articulating agent. His work of redemption is part of His general work of mediation between God and the world—articulating action. The Deity established Christ as the Mediator of the everlasting covenant that went through successive implementations with human beings. Christ ratified that covenant by His incarnation and atoning sacrifice that allowed a fuller revelation of God's character and offered to humanity the possibility of salvation. Christ's atoning work continues in the heavenly sanctuary, making justification, sanctification, and the whole process of salvation possible. The sanctuary is the key to the biblical system of truth. Reality as a whole is a great controversy that started with Satan's rebellion and is still in progress. Adventist theology faced some early challenges in its interpretation of the principle of articulation. Waggoner tried to interpret the principle from a more soteriological perspective while Kellogg tried to do the same from a modern theological view.

Chapter 4 described, analyzed, and evaluated the three main models of the interpretation of the principle of articulation in current Adventist theology. The first one is the evangelical Adventist model, whose main representative is D. Ford, though other authors are discussed. This model entails an adaptation of Adventist theology to the soteriological model of Protestant theology. Although it claims to support *sola Scriptura*, in practice, this model reintroduces in Adventist theology the ontological and epistemological dualism of classical theology, which implies the application of the *via negativa* in the interpretation of God and His actions. God is timeless and without any physical appearance. The Bible uses anthropomorphic language to talk about God. The heavenly sanctuary is a functional reality, not a literal one. This application of the *via negativa* allows, in the case of D. Ford, interpreting the world and human reality from the perspective of progressive creationism. There is a dualism between spiritual and scientific knowledge. D. Ford does not accept a literal interpretation of the Genesis account. Although he still holds the Adventist unitary view of the human being, he also introduces the idea that humans were seminally present in Adam when he sinned. His belief in free will is inconsistent with his interpretation of God as timeless, immutable, and unchangeable.

The evangelical Adventist model identifies Christ as the articulating agent, emphasizing His salvific role. Justification by faith is the essential articulating action. It is a punctiliar timeless decision, as in Protestant theology, that covers the past, present, and future sins of the believer. It implicitly assumes the timeless view of predestination that is inconsistent with the affirmation of free will. The model tends to reduce judgment to justification, and justification, to the cross—the place of final atonement. Salvation is essentially equivalent to justification, a punctiliar fact. Sanctification is a process that is not part of salvation. The cross works as a microcosm where timelessness and temporality find their unity and wholeness. D. Ford's view of the Gospel is an abstractive center that tends to ignore or reinterpret metaphorically biblical information that does not coincide with his view of justification by faith.

Second, the chapter discussed the modern Adventist model of interpretation of the principle of articulation in current Adventist theology. Guy is its main representative, though other authors appear. This model entails an adaptation of Adventist theology to the interpretation of the principle of articulation in modern theology. Theoretically, this model holds a temporal ontology of becoming. Reality is in constant change. Knowledge is interpretation, a temporal action that is never finished. In practice, however, modern Adventist theology applies the *via negativa*—which implies an ontological dualism—as part of its critical realism. Theological truth is timeless, spiritual. Scientific truth is temporal, empirical. Scripture expresses theological truth rather than empirical facts. There are other sources of theology such as science, culture, and experience. This model rejects *sola Scriptura*. The task of theology is to interpret the faith of the religious community in the light of its tradition. Doctrines are symbolic manifestations of the experience of the religious community. All theological language is symbolic (*via symbolica*), anthropomorphic, including the belief in a heavenly sanctuary.

In this model, God is dipolar, as in process theology. The future is open for God. His character and existence are linked to His timeless pole. His temporal pole experiences the world, which is essential to Him. Yet, the world has a beginning. God created the entire world with some freedom of choice. Freedom of choice is not only a human prerogative. This general freedom implies that the world participates in its own creation through an evolutionary process. Natural evil is the result of this freedom rather than of moral decisions by intelligent creatures. God leads the evolutionary process through His persuasive love. Creation is kenotic. God limits Himself to ensure freedom for the world and He is self-invested in the world. He is the articulating agent, whose character of love finds its supreme revelation in Christ. God's loving persuasive action in the world articulates reality in an immanent way, which is not discernible from natural causation. God does not use coercive power in the world. This interpretation of reality as a whole is consistent and virtually identifiable with the so-called kenotic Trinitarian panentheism. This way of panentheism adapts process theology to the notion of *creatio ex nihilo*.

Third, the chapter discussed the Adventist theodicy model. The main representative is Gulley but the section includes other names. This model adopts a temporal ontology in clear detachment from classical theology. Knowledge is also a temporal activity, always in progress. Theological knowledge should build upon the *sola Scriptura* principle through a hermeneutical spiral. God is a temporal relational Trinity, whose nature is love. His temporality is qualitatively and quantitatively different from the one of the world. Gulley also rejects the *via negativa* although he inconsistently interprets biblical descriptions of God's appearance and emotions as anthropomorphisms. However, he believes that God dwells in a spatio-temporal place—the heavenly sanctuary.

Regarding the interpretation of the world and humanity, this model accepts that God created life on earth in six literal days. There is a prior creation of the angels and the universe in general. God created the entire human being in His image, which involves physical appearance and free will. There is no anthropological dualism. The problem of sin began in heaven, originating a cosmic controversy that moved to the earth when Adam and Eve sinned. Sin introduced suffering and death. God's image suffered severe damage though it did not disappear. It is not completely clear, however, to what extent human free will was preserved after the Fall, according to Gulley.

The theodicy model uses the cosmic controversy theme as a conceptual center in its theological system. As a result, the model emphasizes the vindication of God's character as the articulating action. This emphasis is particularly evident in connection with the understanding of the investigative judgment that becomes an exhibition of evidence or audit. The decisions about the destiny of believers or unbelievers have been already made, in a way that resembles the evangelical Adventist understanding of judgment and its assimilation of the judgment of believers to justification. From the perspective of the phenomenological description of the principle of articulation in theology, though, the articulating agent requires a divine agent. Although the cosmic controversy theme involves divine actions, it also involves other agents acting in opposition to God. The cosmic controversy theme operates as an imprecise way to articulate the theological system. This center seems to be a better description of the whole of the system in the context of sin.

Chapter 5 outlined a proposal for a biblical Adventist interpretation of the principle of articulation consistent with the *sola Scriptura* principle. The chapter takes into account prior research in the fields of biblical studies, systematic theology, and the presuppositions of theology, as well as the discussion in the previous chapters. In Scripture, the interpretation of God determines the interpretation of being. Since in Scripture God is temporal, created entities are temporal too. Time is an intrinsic characteristic of being although it is analogically understood in the case of God. The knowledge of God is also temporal, which entails a temporal epistemology and the rejection of the *via negativa*. Theological knowledge is based on Scripture alone (*sola Scriptura*) because it is the only inspired record of God's revelation of His presence and actions in the world. Since it is temporal, theological knowledge is always open, in progress. Scripture uses a spatio-temporal analogical or likeness language to talk about God. Scripture, however, does not describe God with the limitations of His creatures.

In Scripture, the world is a spatio-temporal reality, ontologically different from God and not essential for Him. God created first the universe in general and then life on earth in six literal days, as described in Gen 1-2. Evil and death in the world are the results of sin. The originator of sin is Satan, who rebelled against God, questioned His character and government, and induced Adam and Eve to commit sin as well. Originally, humans were theomorphic creatures—created in the image of God. Sin, however, seriously affected that image and weakened original free will. Only the divine initiative allows humans a new opportunity to restore their broken relationship with God.

From a biblical perspective, Christ is the articulating agent of the entire reality (Prov 8; Col 1; John 1). The Godhead appointed Him for that function before Creation. He is the Agent of Creation and the Mediator between God and the world. He articulates the actions of the Deity in connection with the world. After the introduction of the problem of sin, however, Christ also became the Mediator between God's holiness and His sinful creatures. Scripture interprets the articulating action in the light of the sanctuary/temple spatio-temporal structural pattern of relationship. Sanctuary is God's dwelling place and administrative center from where He relates to His creation. This structure existed before the problem of sin (Isa 14; Ezek 28). Eden conformed to that structure. The problem of sin, however, restricted communion with God and the sanctuary pattern reflected that situation. The earthly tabernacle/temple, erected in spatial and functional correspondence with the heavenly model, demonstrated that although God wanted to dwell with His creatures, a process of reconciliation was necessary. Christ's work of reconciliation after the Fall—including His incarnation, sacrifice, and intercession—follows the same pattern. Even if the soteriological aspect of this pattern will conclude with the end of sin, the pattern in general will not disappear (Rev 7, 21-22).

Christ's specific articulating actions in the context of the sanctuary pattern require pre-articulating actions before Creation and general articulating actions since Creation. Before Creation, the Godhead installed Christ as the Wisdom of Creation and as a Mediator between God and the world. God foreknew the problem of sin and designed a plan of salvation that included the predestination for salvation of those who would willingly believe in Christ (Eph 1). The Godhead also appointed Christ as the Wisdom and Mediator of salvation in the context of an intra-divine covenant, the everlasting covenant. Moreover, Christ's specific articulating actions require Christ's general articulating actions since Creation: particularly His task of preservation and sustenance of the universe.

The essential specific articulating action of Christ is His mediation between God and the world-humanity in harmony with the sanctuary pattern of relationship. This mediation adopts the fundamental way of God's tabernacling with His creatures in a spatio-temporal location. This sanctuary-form relationship requires, first, a covenant between God and His intelligent creatures in order to make God's dwelling among them possible. Christ is the Mediator of all the covenants between God and His creation. The covenantal relationship originates God's people and mission. Second, in the context of sin, the covenant is only possible through Christ's work of atonement. This work is a historical process, developed in the general frame of the sanctuary, which has several dimensions: cosmic (atoning sacrifice, intercession), social (belonging to God's covenantal people), and individual (justification-sanctification). Third, Christ's articulating action through the sanctuary pattern requires and structures the implementation of God's covenants and the work of Atonement by means of a temporal providential action in history. Christ acts in history as a historical cause, implementing God's pre-Creation plan. Apocalyptic prophecies and prophetic periods reveal this providential action in history that Christ articulates through the sanctuary pattern, in interaction with God's free-will creatures. Christ's s action through the sanctuary pattern, then, requires and structures the covenantal relationship between God and His people, the process of Atonement in its different aspects, and the divine providential actions. Ultimately, Christ's action through the sanctuary pattern of relationship is the articulating action that explains all the others. It promotes the revelation of God's character and plans, allowing an increase of harmony and fellowship between God and His creatures.

In understanding the whole from a biblical perspective, it is possible to describe the articulated whole using a diachronic and a synchronic approach. The whole, in its historical development, encompasses the original harmony, great controversy, and new heavens and new earth (the restoration of the original harmony). From a synchronic approach, the whole comprehends the cosmic, social, and individual levels of operation.

Conclusions

This study addressed the description, analysis, and evaluation of the multiple models of interpretation of the principle of articulation in current Adventist theology in the wider context of Christian tradition, including the ontological and epistemological presuppositions that condition its interpretation. This task required a prior phenomenological description of the principle of articulation in theology in its basic operative components. The basic criterion for the evaluation of the models was the *sola Scriptura* principle. This evaluation focused on the interpretation of the basic components of the principle in connection with the ontological and epistemological presuppositions assumed by each model. In this way, the study paved the way to propose an outline interpretation of the principle of articulation that took into account the previous discussion, but at the same time tried to be more consistent with *sola Scriptura*.

As a result, this study has shown that it is possible to arrive at the following conclusions: First, it is important to notice, based on the phenomenological analysis of the principle of articulation in theology and its validation in the analysis of the diverse models in Chapters 3 and 4, that the core of the principle of articulation in theology is the articulating agent and the articulating action. Both elements, however, cannot be properly understood disconnected from the other operative components of the principle. The interpretations of God, the world, and the human being are essential to the interpretation of the articulating agent and the articulating action because these two elements depend on the interpretation of God's ontology and actions. Moreover, there is no way to know God separately from the world-humanity in the context of which God always reveals Himself. Thereby, the principle of articulation in its operative components constitutes a complex structure in a theological system, the identification of which is essential in order to understand the system and its interpretation of reality as a whole.

Second, all the models of interpretation of the principle of articulation in current Adventist theology reflect, in different degrees, the influence or impact of Christian tradition that early adopted and adapted the ontological, epistemological, and even metaphysic presuppositions coming from philosophy rather than from Scripture. This fact is more evident in the evangelical Adventist model and in the modern Adventist model. Although evangelical Adventism claims to follow *sola Scriptura*, in practice it still assumes essentially the same ontological and epistemological presuppositions of the soteriological model of Protestant Reformation. It also follows a similar interpretation of the nature of God as timeless and spaceless. The interpretation of the world allows seeing the influence of the scientific theories of origins (progressive creationism), which conceals an ontological dualism as well. The interpretation of the articulating action is essentially the one of the Protestant reformers: justification by faith as a punctiliar timeless fact. This understanding of justification also entails a simplified version of the hierarchical interpretation of reality as a whole, ultimately traceable to the hierarchical model of medieval Christianity.

On the other hand, the modern Adventist model willingly adopts *prima Scriptura* instead of *sola Scriptura*. This fact makes Adventist theology even more vulnerable to the influence of Christian tradition, particularly to the impact of the panentheistic model of modern theology. Modern Adventism applies the *via negativa* (or *via symbolica*) that assumes a dualistic ontology. Its dipolar interpretation of God, the interpretation of the world and its relationship to God, as well as the interpretation of the articulating action—God's immanent persuasive participation in a world that evolved—are an adaptation of elements of process theology and the ontology of becoming to Adventist theology. At the end, the virtually panentheistic view of reality as a whole in modern Adventism still maintains the medieval hierarchy, in a way adapted to the scientific mindset.

The Adventist theodicy model strongly endorses the *sola Scriptura* principle. In a lesser extent, however, the model also reflects some impact of Christian tradition, particularly the influence of the soteriological model of Protestant theology. Its interpretation of God's physical appearance and emotions as anthropomorphisms, as well as the classification of God's attributes in incommunicable and communicable are examples in this sense. The tendency to assimilate the investigative judgment to an exhibition of evidence or audit, where God has already decided the destiny of individuals in connection with their reaction to the cross during their lives, is also significant in this model.

Third, the models reflect some inner inconsistencies. These contradictions are the result of adapting elements of Christian tradition to biblical data in a way that is incompatible with the *sola Scriptura* principle. The evangelical Adventist model, for example, supports the belief in free will while at the same time adopts an understanding of justification that implicitly assumes the Protestant view of a timeless predestination. The modern Adventist model affirms in theory a temporal ontology that its adoption of the *via negativa* denies in practice. The Adventist theodicy model rejects the *via negativa* but still understands that the biblical descriptions of God are anthropomorphic. In the case of the evangelical Adventist model and the Adventist theodicy model, moreover, these inconsistencies suggest that the affirmation of the *sola Scriptura* principle does not ensure its real application in the interpretation of the principle of articulation. This fact requires a vigilant attitude toward the potential interference of extra-biblical assumptions. While it is not possible to read Scripture without presuppositions, it is possible to become aware of those presuppositions, contrast them with those of Scripture, and modify them more in harmony with it.

Fourth, and in connection with the previous remark, the fact that Scripture adopts a temporal theological epistemology implies that the biblical understanding of the principle of articulation is always incomplete, unfinished, and in progress or perfectible. This fact requires a cautious and humble approach to the study of this issue in Scripture. The knowledge of the principle is, as the knowledge of the Bible in general, inexhaustible. It requires successive approaches to Scripture in order to increase the understanding of the principle in the light of Scripture itself. The progressive knowledge of the principle of articulation, however, will be biblical to the extent that it is developed within the boundaries of Scripture itself. Any attempt to facilitate the progress of its knowledge through extra-biblical sources will face the problem of lack of inner consistency due to the different presuppositions assumed by the different sources.

Fifth, in general, the proposed interpretation of the principle of articulation in Chapter 5 has more in common with the Adventist theodicy model than with the other models. The elements in common include similarities regarding the interpretation of the ontological and epistemological presuppositions, as well as a similar interpretation of the world and the human being. In spite of some inconsistencies already mentioned, the Adventist theodicy model agrees with the proposal of Chapter 5 in a temporal interpretation of God and in the importance of the great/cosmic controversy in order to understand reality as a whole in the present context of the problem of sin. Of course, some differences remain. Undoubtedly, the most important difference refers to the way to articulate the system—articulating agent and action. Still, the similarities are important and find an explanation in the serious effort of the Adventist theodicy model to follow the *sola Scriptura* principle.

Sixth, the background of the introductory chapter mentioned possible central themes or motifs of Adventist theology, usually suggested in the literature by biblical and systematic theologians. These themes or topics include God, the Trinity, Christ, the sanctuary, the sanctuary-covenant, Atonement, justification by faith, and the great controversy. The outline interpretation of Chapter 5 has the advantage of integrating most part of these topics—if not all of them—while taking into account the contributions of the main models considered in Chapter 4 as part of a more complex interpretation of the principle of articulation that is more consistent with the biblical data. The outline interpretation avoids simplification and the tendency to see the principle of articulation as a mere center or motif, which relegates as peripheral biblical material that does not harmonize with the center or even ignores biblical material that is part of the biblical theological system. In other words, the outline interpretation considers biblical data that the other models minimize or ignore. Moreover, in consonance with the concern expressed in the statement of the problem, the outline interpretation of Chapter 5 explains the principle of articulation in a biblical-systematic way and the relationship among its diverse structural elements. At the same time, it goes beyond the usual exegetical or doctrinal approach in order to include also in the interpretation of the principle the basic presuppositions of the mind—the macro hermeneutical level of interpretation—in harmony with the interpretation of those presuppositions in Scripture itself.

Seventh, the discussion of the interpretation of the principle of articulation in Adventist theology has some practical implications, as mentioned in the justification of the study. Against the background of this study, it is timely to remark the most important ones. The diverse interpretations of this principle imply that the Adventist Church faces the problem of theological disunity. This situation entails difficulties with the theological identity of the church. Different interpretations of the principle of articulation represent different understandings of Adventist theology as a whole, given the basic structuring role of the principle. This study, however, suggests that theological unity is possible. It is possible to find a unity of meaning in Scripture—using Gadamer's terminology—in spite of the diverse philosophical, cultural, and educational backgrounds of the members of the church.

At the same time, this unity is not only possible but also highly desirable. The different interpretations of the principle of articulation entail different ways of understanding spirituality and the mission of the church. The diverse interpretations regarding the nature of God, the world, and humanity, as well as the different interpretations regarding the way in which God relates to the world and humanity have a significant impact on the understanding of the personal relationship of the believer with God, the understanding of worship, and ultimately of salvation itself. Concerning mission, different interpretations of the principle of articulation entail that the church is proclaiming different messages that in turn contribute to increasing its theological disunity. This study contributes to a better understanding of what is involved in the unity of the theology and message of the church, grounded on Scripture.

Recommendations

This dissertation does not claim to exhaust the study of the principle of articulation in Adventist theology. Moreover, several aspects of the topic and related issues require further research. Few of them are mentioned here. First, the outline interpretation of Chapter 5, as said, requires additional discussion, construction, and expansion. Additional research about the biblical interpretation of the principle of articulation in general with the tools of biblical theology is necessary. Chapter 5 has followed a more systematic-synthetic approach. It is possible to enrich and complement this approach, with an in-depth study of the diverse operative components of the principle of articulation in Scripture through a more analytical-exegetical approach as usual in biblical studies. This study should take into consideration the phenomenological description of the principle of articulation as well as the biblical presuppositions underlying the interpretation of this principle in Scripture. At the same time, it is necessary to develop an Adventist systematic theology based on the biblical interpretation of the principle of articulation outlined in Chapter 5 in interaction with the findings of biblical studies.

Second, an important issue that requires additional clarification relates to the interpretation of God. This study has suggested taking the spatio-temporal analogical or likeness language to talk about God in Scripture seriously. The Adventist pioneers understood the importance of this issue in connection with their interpretation of the sanctuary. Recent Adventist literature, however, does not reflect the same certainty. A comprehensive study from a biblical and systematic perspective is necessary, considering the centrality of the understanding of the nature of God and His actions regarding the interpretation of the principle of articulation in Adventist theology.

A third question in need of attention is the ontology of the sanctuary in Adventist theology and Scripture. This issue is relevant, given the importance of the sanctuary in order to understand Christ's articulating actions according to the proposed interpretation of the principle of articulation in Chapter 5. Adventist theology is divided regarding the interpretation of the ontology of the sanctuary. The evangelical Adventist model does not support the belief in a real heavenly sanctuary. Additionally, the modern Adventist model does not interpret the existence of a heavenly sanctuary in literal terms. On the other hand, the Adventist theodicy model and the proposal of Chapter 5 hold the existence of a real heavenly sanctuary, a viewpoint considered in harmony with the biblical ontological and epistemological presuppositions. However, the different positions deserve additional comparative study in the light of Scripture. This study should include an analysis and a biblical evaluation of the ontological and epistemological presuppositions underlying the different interpretations of the heavenly sanctuary.

A fourth question relates to the necessity of additional study about the possible impact of the Protestant and evangelical Adventist view of justification by faith on the understanding of judgment—particularly the investigative judgment—in Adventist theodicy model. This model seems to depart from the Adventist pioneers' historical view of the judgment as a decision-making process by interpreting it as a simple exhibition of evidence or audit. This audit is still a process but only for vindicatory purposes. The soteriological dimension is neglected. Apparently, the real judgment of individuals takes place during their lives. Does it mean for the Adventist theodicy model that the real judgment of believers is equivalent to justification by faith? The view of judgment as an audit deprives angelical or heavenly intelligences of any active role in the investigative judgment. They would be only witnesses that confirm decisions already made. This position seems to be in tension with the description of the judgment in Dan 7 and with the general way in which God proceeds in governing the world from the sanctuary, where He shares His decisions with the heavenly council (cf. 1 Kgs 22:19-22).

Finally, this study has possible implications for missiology that require additional exploration and study. If the principle of articulation is a basic presupposition of mind, as explained in Chapter 2, it means that every culture with its own view of reality as a whole has its own implicit interpretation of that principle. It is necessary to explore how the identification of the principle of articulation in diverse cultural contexts can help to communicate the biblical message with its own identification of the same principle in a relevant way for those contexts. The principle of articulation is the structuring element of every system of thought. Its identification in the context of a given community can facilitate the comparison with the biblical interpretation of the principle and the development of missionary strategies that take into account similarities and differences between both interpretations. Of course, this task is possible only if Adventist theology reflects an important level of agreement regarding the interpretation of its own principle of articulation.

BIBLIOGRAPHY

Adams, Robert M. "Faith and Religious Knowledge." In *The Cambridge Companion to Friedrich Schleiermacher*, edited by Jacqueline Mariña, 35-51. Cambridge, UK: Cambridge University Press, 2005.

Adams, Roy. *The Sanctuary: Understanding the Heart of Adventist Theology*. Hagerstown, MD: Review & Herald, 1993.

──────. *The Sanctuary Doctrine: Three Approaches in the Seventh-Day Adventist Church*. Andrews University Seminary Doctoral Dissertation Series 1. Berrien Springs, MI: Andrews University Press, 1981.

Agustín. *Del Génesis a la letra*. Edited by Balbino Martín. *Obras Completas de San Agustín: Edición Bilingüe*. Vol. 15, *De la doctrina cristiana; Del Génesis contra los maniqueos; Del Génesis a la letra, incompleto; Del Génesis a la letra*. Madrid, España: Biblioteca de Autores Cristianos, 1957. 577-1271.

──────. *Del libre albedrío*. Translated by Evaristo Seijas. *Obras de San Agustín en Edición Bilingüe*. Vol. 3, *Obras Filosóficas*. 3rd ed. Madrid, España: Biblioteca de Autores Cristianos, 1963. 200-409.

──────. *Ochenta y tres cuestiones diversas*. Translated by Teodoro C. Madrid. *Obras Completas de San Agustín: Edición Bilingüe*. Vol. 40, *Escritos varios (2.°)*. Madrid, España: Biblioteca de Autores Cristianos, 1995. 65-297.

Alomía, Merling K. "Lesser Gods of the Ancient Near East and Some Comparisons With Heavenly Beings of the Old Testament." PhD diss., Andrews University, Berrien Springs, MI, 1987.

Althaus, Paul. *The Theology of Martin Luther*. Translated by Robert C. Schultz. Philadelphia, PA: Fortress, 1979.

Andreasen, Niels-Erik A. "Death: Origin, Nature, and Final Eradication." In *Handbook of Seventh-day Adventist Theology*, edited by Raoul Dederen, 314-346. Hagerstown, MD: Review & Herald, 2000.

A[ndrews], John N. "The Sanctuary." *Advent Review and Sabbath Herald*, June 18, 1867, 12.

Aquinas, Thomas. *Concerning Being and Essence*. Translated by George G. Leckie. New York, NY: Appleton-Century, 1937.

_____. *Summa Contra Gentiles, Book 1: God*. Translated by Anton C. Pegis. Garden City, NY: Image, 1955.

_____. *Summa Contra Gentiles, Book 2: Creation*. Translated by James F. Anderson. Garden City, NY: Images, 1956.

_____. *Summa Contra Gentiles, Book 3: Providence; Part 1*. Translated by Vernon J. Bourke. Garden City, NY: Image, 1956.

_____. *Summa Theologica*. Translated by Fathers of the English Dominican Province. 5 vols. New York, NY: Benziger, 1948. Reprint. Westminster, MD: Christian Classics, 1981.

Aristotle. *The Categories*. In *Aristotle in Twenty-Three Volumes*. Vol. 1, *The Categories; On Interpretation; Prior Analytics*. Translated by Harold P. Cooke [*The Categories; On Interpretation*] and Hugh Tredennick [*Prior Analytics*]. Cambridge, MA: Harvard University Press, 1983. 12-109.

_____. *Metaphysics*. In *Aristotle*. Vol. 17, *Metaphysics: Books I-IX*. Translated by Hugh Tredennick. Cambridge, MA: Harvard University Press, 1996.

_____. *Metaphysics*. In *Aristotle*. Vol. 18, *Metaphysics, X-XIV; Oeconomica; Magna Moralia*. Translated by Hugh Tredennick [*Metaphysics*] and Cyril Armstrong [*Oeconomica; Magna Moralia*]. Cambridge, MA: Harvard University Press, 1990. 3-303.

_____. *On the Heavens*. In *Aristotle in Twenty-Three Volumes*. Vol. 6, *On the Heavens*. Translated by William K. C. Guthrie. Cambridge, MA: Harvard University Press, 1986.

_____. *On the Soul*. In *Aristotle in Twenty-Three Volumes*. Vol. 8, *On the Soul; Parva Naturalia; On Breath*. Translated by Walter S. Hett. Cambridge, MA: Harvard University Press, 1986. 8-203.

_____. *The Physics*. In *Aristotle in Twenty-Three Volumes*. Vol. 5, *The Physics II: Books V-VIII*. Translated by Philip H. Wicksteed and Francis M. Cornford. Cambridge, MA: Harvard University Press, 1980.

Arnold, Matthieu. "Luther on Christ's Person and Work." In *The Oxford Handbook of Martin Luther's Theology*, edited by Robert Kolb, Irene Dingel, and L'ubomír Batka, 274-293. New York, NY: Oxford University Press, 2014.

Ashby, Godfrey. *Go Out and Meet God: A Commentary on the Book of Exodus*. International Theological Commentary. Grand Rapids, MI: Eerdmans, 1998.

Augustin. *The City of God*. Translated by Marcus Dods. Edited by Philip Schaff. The Nicene and Post-Nicene Fathers. Edinburgh, Scotland: T. & T. Clark, 1887. 2:1-511.

_____. *The Confessions*. Translated by Joseph G. Pilkington. Edited by Philip Schaff. The Nicene and Post-Nicene Fathers. Edinburgh, Scotland: T. & T. Clark, 1886. 1:33-207.

_____. *On Christian Doctrine*. Translated by James F. Shaw. Edited by Philip Schaff. The Nicene and Post-Nicene Fathers. Edinburgh, Scotland: T. & T. Clark, 1886. 2:517-597.

_____. *On the Trinity*. Translated by Arthur W. Haddan. Edited by Philip Schaff. The Nicene and Post-Nicene Fathers. Edinburgh, Scotland: T. & T. Clark, 1886. 3:17-228.

_____. *A Treatise on the Gift of Perseverance*. Translated by Peter Holmes and Robert E. Wallis. Edited by Philip Schaff. The Nicene and Post-Nicene Fathers. Edinburgh, Scotland: T. & T. Clark, 1887. 5:525-552.

_____. *A Treatise on the Grace of Christ, and on Original Sin*. Translated by Peter Holmes and Robert E. Wallis. Edited by Philip Schaff. The Nicene and Post-Nicene Fathers. Edinburgh, Scotland: T. & T. Clark, 1887. 5:217-254.

_____. *A Treatise on the Predestination of the Saints*. Translated by Peter Holmes and Robert E. Wallis. Edited by Philip Schaff. The Nicene and Post-Nicene Fathers. Edinburgh, Scotland: T. & T. Clark, 1887. 5:497-520.

_____. *A Treatise on the Soul and Its Origin*. Translated by Peter Holmes and Robert E. Wallis. Edited by Philip Schaff. The Nicene and Post-Nicene Fathers. Edinburgh, Scotland: T. & T. Clark, 1887. 5:315-371.

Aulén, Gustaf. *Christus Victor: An Historical Study of the Three Main Types of the Idea of the Atonement*. Translated by Arthur G. Hebert. New York, NY: Macmillan, 1969.

Azevedo, Joaquim. "At the Door of Paradise: A Contextual Interpretation of Gen. 4:7." In *Cult and Cosmos: Tilting Toward a Temple-Centered Theology*, edited by L. Michael Morales, 167-181. Leuven, Belgium: Peeters, 2014.

Bacchiocchi, Samuele. *Divine Rest for Human Restlessness: A Theological Study of the Good News of the Sabbath for Today*. Rome, Italy: Pontifical Gregorian University Press, 1980.

Badenas, Roberto. "New Jerusalem—The Holy City." In *Symposium on Revelation*. Vol. 2, *Exegetical and General Studies*, edited by Frank B. Holbrook, 243-270. Silver Spring, MD: Biblical Research Institute, GC of SDAs, 1992.

Baldwin, Dalton D. "Creation and Time: A Biblical Reflection." In *Understanding Genesis: Contemporary Adventist Perspectives*, edited by Brian Bull, Fritz Guy, and Ervin Taylor, 35-51. Riverside, CA: Adventist Today, 2009.

Baldwin, John T. "The Geologic Column and Calvary: The Rainbow Connection—Implications for an Evangelical Understanding of the Atonement." In *Creation, Catastrophe, and Calvary: Why a Global Flood Is Vital to the Doctrine of Atonement*, edited by John T. Baldwin, 108-123. Hagerstown, MD: Review & Herald, 2000.

──────. "Progressive Creationism and Biblical Revelation: Some Theological Implications." *Journal of the Adventist Theological Society* 3, no. 1 (1992): 105-119.

Barrio Maestre, José María. *El Dios de los filósofos*. Madrid, España: Ediciones Rialp, 2013.

Barth, Karl. *The Theology of John Calvin*. Translated by Geoffrey W. Bromiley. Grand Rapids, MI: Eerdmans, 1995.

Battistone, Joseph. *The Great Controversy Theme in E. G. White Writings*. Berrien Springs, MI: Andrews University Press, 1978.

Battles, Ford L. "God Was Accommodating Himself to Human Capacity." In *Readings in Calvin's Theology*, edited by Donald K. McKim, 21-42. Grand Rapids, MI: Baker, 1984.

Bauckham, Richard J. *2 Peter, Jude*. Word Biblical Commentary 50. Waco, TX: Word, 1983.

Bavinck, Herman. *Reformed Dogmatics*. Vol. 2, *God and Creation*. Translated by John Vriend. Grand Rapids, MI: Baker, 2004.

Beale, Gregory K., and David H. Campbell. *Revelation: A Shorter Commentary*. Grand Rapids, MI: Eerdmans, 2015.

Beale, Gregory K., and Mitchell Kim. *God Dwells Among Us: Expanding Eden to the End of the Earth*. Downers Grove, IL: InterVarsity, 2014.

Beasley-Murray, George R. *John*. Word Biblical Commentary 36. 2nd ed. Nashville, TN: Thomas Nelson, 1999.

Bertoluci, José M. "The Son of the Morning and the Guardian Cherub in the Context of the Controversy Between God and Evil." ThD diss., Andrews University, Berrien Springs, MI, 1985.

Beutel, Albrecht. "Luther's Life." In *The Cambridge Companion to Martin Luther*, edited by Donald K. McKim, 3-19. Cambridge, UK: Cambridge University Press, 2003.

Billings, J. Todd. *Calvin, Participation, and the Gift: The Activity of Believers in Union With Christ*. New York, NY: Oxford University Press, 2007.

———. *Union With Christ: Reframing Theology and Ministry for the Church*. Grand Rapids, MI: Baker, 2011.

Blazen, Ivan T. "Justification and Judgment." In *70 Weeks, Leviticus, and the Nature of Prophecy*, edited by Frank B. Holbrook, 339-388. Washington, DC: Biblical Research Institute, GC of SDAs, 1986.

———. "Salvation." In *Handbook of Seventh-day Adventist Theology*, edited by Raoul Dederen, 271-313. Hagerstown, MD: Review & Herald, 2000.

Bliss, Sylvester. *Memoirs of William Miller: Generally Known as a Lecturer on the Prophecies, and the Second Coming of Christ*. Boston, MA: Joshua V. Himes, 1853.

Borchert, Gerald L. *John 1-11*. The New American Commentary 25A. Nashville, TN: Broadman & Holman, 2006.

Boyd, Gregory A. *God at War: The Bible and Spiritual Conflict*. Downers Grove, IL: InterVarsity, 1997.

———. *Satan and the Problem of Evil*. Downers Grove, IL: InterVarsity, 2001.

Brand, Leonard R. "A Biblical Perspective on the Philosophy of Science." *Origins* 59 (2006): 6-42.

Brierley, Michael W. "Naming a Quiet Revolution: The Panentheistic Turn in Modern Theology." In *In Whom We Live and Move and Have Our Being: Panentheistic Reflections on God's Presence in a Scientific World*, edited by Philip Clayton and Arthur Peacocke, 1-15. Grand Rapids, MI: Eerdmans, 2004.

Brown, Raymond E. *The Gospel According to John (I-XII)*. Anchor Bible 29. Garden City, NY: Doubleday, 1966.

Brunt, John C. "Resurrection and Glorification." In *Handbook of Seventh-day Adventist Theology*, edited by Raoul Dederen, 347-374. Hagerstown, MD: Review & Herald, 2000.

Bull, Brian. "Living in Incommensurate Worlds." *Spectrum* 31, no. 2 (2003): 17-23.

Bull, Brian, and Fritz Guy. "Then a Miracle Occurs." In *Understanding Genesis: Contemporary Adventist Perspective*, edited by Brian Bull, Fritz Guy, and Ervin Taylor, 53-69. Riverside, CA: Adventist Today, 2009.

Bull, Brian, Fritz Guy, and Ervin Taylor, eds. *Understanding Genesis: Contemporary Adventist Perspectives*. Riverside, CA: Adventist Today, 2009.

Bull, Malcolm, and Keith Lockhart. *Seeking a Sanctuary: Seventh-day Adventism and the American Dream*. 2nd ed. Bloomington, IN: Indiana University Press, 2007.

Cairus, Aecio E. "The Doctrine of Man." In *Handbook of Seventh-day Adventist Theology*, edited by Raoul Dederen, 205-232. Hagerstown, MD: Review & Herald, 2000.

Calvin, John. *Commentaries on the Book of the Prophet Daniel*. Vol. 2. Translated by Thomas Myers. Edinburgh, Scotland: Calvin Translation Society, 1853.

―――. *Commentaries on the Catholic Epistles*. Translated by John Owen. Edinburgh, Scotland: Calvin Translation Society, 1855.

―――. *Commentaries on the Epistles of Paul the Apostle to the Philippians, Colossians, and Thessalonians*. Edinburgh, Scotland: Calvin Translation Society, 1851.

―――. *Commentaries on the Epistles of Paul to the Galatians and Ephesians*. Translated by William Pringle. Edinburgh, Scotland: Calvin Translation Society, 1854.

―――. *Commentaries on the Four Last Books of Moses, Arranged in the Form of a Harmony*. Vol. 3. Translated by Charles William Bingham. Edinburgh, Scotland: Calvin Translation Society, 1854.

———. *Commentary on a Harmony of the Evangelists Matthew, Mark, and Luke*. 3 vols. Translated by William Pringle. Edinburgh, Scotland: Calvin Translation Society, 1845.

———. *Institutes of the Christian Religion* [two vols. in one]. Translated by Henry Beveridge. Grand Rapids, MI: Eerdmans, 1989.

Campbell, Michael W. "Great Controversy Vision." *The Ellen G. White Encyclopedia*. Edited by Denis Fortin and Jerry Moon. 2nd ed. Hagerstown, MD: Review & Herald, 2013. 853-854.

Canale, Fernando L. *Basic Elements of Christian Theology: Scripture Replacing Tradition*. Berrien Springs, MI: Andrews University, 2005.

———. *The Cognitive Principle of Christian Theology: A Hermeneutical Study of the Revelation and Inspiration of the Bible*. Berrien Springs, MI: Andrews University Lithotech, 2010.

———. *Creación, evolución y teología: Una introducción a los métodos científico y teológico*. Libertador San Martín, Entre Ríos, Argentina: Editorial Universidad Adventista del Plata, 2009.

———. *A Criticism of Theological Reason: Time and Timelessness as Primordial Presuppositions*. Andrews University Seminary Doctoral Dissertation Series 10. Berrien Springs, MI: Andrews University Press, 1987.

———. "Deconstrucción y teología: Una propuesta metodológica." *DavarLogos* 1, no. 1 (2002): 3-26.

———. "Deconstructing Evangelical Theology?" *Andrews University Seminary Studies* 44, no. 1 (2006): 95-130.

———. "Doctrine of God." In *Handbook of Seventh-day Adventist Theology*, edited by Raoul Dederen, 105-159. Hagerstown, MD: Review & Herald, 2000.

———. "Evangelical Theology and Open Theism: Toward a Biblical Understanding of the Macro Hermeneutical Principles of Theology?" *Journal of the Adventist Theological Society* 12, no. 2 (2001): 16-34.

———. "From Vision to System: Finishing the Task of Adventist Theology Part I; Historical Review." *Journal of the Adventist Theological Society* 15, no. 2 (2004): 5-39.

_____. "From Vision to System: Finishing the Task of Adventist Biblical and Systematic Theologies—Part II." *Journal of the Adventist Theological Society* 16, nos. 1-2 (2005): 114-142.

_____. "From Vision to System: Finishing the Task of Adventist Theology; Part III Sanctuary and Hermeneutics." *Journal of the Adventist Theological Society* 17, no. 2 (2006): 36-80.

_____. "The Message and the Mission of the Remnant: A Methodological Approach." In *Message, Mission, and Unity of the Church*, edited by Angel Manuel Rodríguez, 261-286. Silver Spring, MD: Biblical Research Institute, 2013.

_____. "Philosophical Foundations and the Biblical Sanctuary." *Andrews University Seminary Studies* 36, no. 2 (1998): 183-206.

Canright, Dudley M. "The Personality of God (*Continued*)." *The Adventist Review and Sabbath Herald*, September 5, 1878, 81-82.

Chartier, Gary. "From La Sierra to Cambridge: Growing Up Theologically." *Spectrum* 20, no. 2 (1989): 2-10.

Christian, C. W. *Friedrich Schleiermacher*. Waco, TX: Word, 1979.

Christoffel, Larry. "Evangelical Adventism—*Questions on Doctrine*'s Legacy." Paper presented at the Question on Doctrine 50th Anniversary Conference, Andrews University, Berrien Springs, MI, October 24-27, 2007.

_____. "'I, if I Be Lifted Up'—A Response." *Ministry*, December 1992, 12-13.

Cilliers, Paul. *Complexity and Postmodernism: Understanding Complex Systems*. London, UK: Routledge, 1998.

Clark, David K. *To Know and Love God: Foundation of Evangelical Theology; Method for Theology*. Wheaton, IL: Crossway, 2003.

Clayton, Philip. "Kenotic Trinitarian Panentheism." *Dialog: A Journal of Theology* 44, no. 3 (2005): 250-255.

_____. "Systematizing Agency: Toward a Panentheistic-Participatory Theory of Agency." In *Schleiermacher and Whitehead: Open Systems in Dialogue*, edited by Christine Helmer, 215-233. Berlin, Germany: Walter de Gruyter, 2004.

Cobb, John B., Jr. *A Christian Natural Theology: Based on the Thought of Alfred North Whitehead*. Philadelphia, PA: Westminster, 1965.

_____. *God and the World*. 1998. Reprint. Eugene, OR: Wipf & Stock, 2000.

———. *Whitehead Word Book: A Glossary With Alphabetical Index to Technical Terms in Process and Reality*. Claremont, CA: P. & F. Press, 2008.

Cobb, John B., Jr., and David R. Griffin. *Process Theology: An Introductory Exposition*. Philadelphia, PA: Westminster, 1976.

Cogan, Mordechai. *I Kings: A New Translation With Introduction and Commentary*. Anchor Bible 10. Garden City, NY: Doubleday, 2001.

Cooper, John W. *Panentheism: The Other God of the Philosophers; From Plato to the Present*. Grand Rapids, MI: Baker, 2006.

Copleston, Frederick. *A History of Philosophy* [three vols. in one book]. Vol. 1, *Greece and Rome*. Garden City, NY: Image, 1985.

———. *A History of Philosophy* [three vols. in one book]. Vol. 2, *Augustine to Scotus*. Garden City, NY: Image, 1985.

Coppedge, Allan. *The God Who Is Triune: Revisioning the Christian Doctrine of God*. Downers Grove, IL: InterVarsity, 2007.

Corson, Ron. "Progressive and Traditional Adventists Examined." *Adventist Today*, November-December, 2002, 18-19.

Cortez, Félix H. "Death and Future Hope in the Hebrew Bible." In *"What Are Human Beings That You Remember Them?" Proceedings of the Third International Bible Conference, Nof Ginosar and Jerusalem; June 11-21, 2012*, edited by Clinton Wahlen, 95-106. Silver Spring, MD: Biblical Research Institute, 2015.

———. "Death and Hell in the New Testament." In *"What Are Human Beings That You Remember Them?" Proceedings of the Third International Bible Conference, Nof Ginosar and Jerusalem; June 11-21, 2012*, edited by Clinton Wahlen, 183-204. Silver Spring, MD: Biblical Research Institute, 2015.

Cottrell, Raymond F. "Extend of the Genesis Flood." In *Creation Reconsidered: Scientific, Biblical, and Theological Perspectives*, edited by James L. Hayward, 265-277. Roseville, CA: Association of Adventist Forums, 2000.

———. "Welcome to *Adventist Today*." *Adventist Today*, May-June 1993, 2.

Craig, William L. *Time and Eternity: Exploring God's Relationship to Time*. Wheaton, IL: Crossway, 2001.

Crandall, Alan. "Whither Evangelical Adventism?" *Evangelica*, May

1982 [n.p.]. Quoted in Larry Christoffel, "Evangelical Adventism—*Questions on Doctrine*'s Legacy." Paper presented at the Question on Doctrine 50th Anniversary Conference, Andrews University, Berrien Springs, MI, October 24-27, 2007.

Crosier, Owen R. L. "The Law of Moses." *The Day-Star Extra*, February 7, 1846, 37-44.

Cullmann, Oscar. *Christ and Time: The Primitive Christian Conception of Time and History*. Translated by Floyd V. Filson. 3rd ed. London, UK: SCM, 1962.

⎯⎯⎯⎯. *Immortality of the Soul or Resurrection of the Dead? The Witness of the New Testament*. New York, NY: Macmillan, 1958.

Daily, Steve. "What Is Progressive Adventism?" *Adventist Today*, May-June 2002, 16-17.

Damsteegt, P. Gerard. "Among Sabbatarian Adventists (1845-1850)." In *Doctrine of the Sanctuary: A Historical Survey*, edited by Frank B. Holbrook, 17-55. Silver Spring, MD: Biblical Research Institute, 1989.

Daniells, Arthur G. *Christ Our Righteousness: A Study of the Principles of Righteousness by Faith as Set Forth in the Word of God and the Writings of the Spirit of Prophecy*. Washington, DC: Review & Herald, 1941.

Davidson, Richard M. "Back to the Beginning: Genesis 1-3 and the Theological Center of Scripture." In *Christ, Salvation, and the Eschaton: Essays in Honor of Hans K. LaRondelle*, edited by Daniel Heinz, Jiří Moskala, and Peter M. van Bemmelen, 5-29. Berrien Springs, MI: Old Testament Department, SDA Theological Seminary, Andrews University, 2009.

⎯⎯⎯⎯. "Biblical Evidence for the Universality of the Genesis Flood." In *Creation, Catastrophe, and Calvary*, edited by John T. Baldwin, 79-92. Hagerstown, MD: Review & Herald, 2000.

⎯⎯⎯⎯. "Biblical Interpretation." In *Handbook of Seventh-day Adventist Theology*, edited by Raoul Dederen, 58-104. Hagerstown, MD: Review & Herald, 2000.

⎯⎯⎯⎯. "The Chiastic Literary Structure of the Book of Ezekiel." In *To Understand the Scripture: Essays in Honor of William H. Shea*, edited by David Merling, 71-93. Berrien Springs, MI: Institute of Archaeology, Siegfried H. Horn Archaeological Museum, Andrews University, 1997.

―――――. "Cosmic Metanarrative for the Coming Millennium." *Journal of the Adventist Theological Society* 11, nos. 1-2 (2000): 102-119.

―――――. "The Divine Covenant Lawsuit Motif in Canonical Perspective." *Journal of the Adventist Theological Society* 21, nos. 1-2 (2010): 45-84.

―――――. "Earth's First Sanctuary: Genesis 1-3 and Parallel Creation Accounts." *Andrews University Seminary Studies* 53, no. 1 (2015): 65-89.

―――――. "The Eschatological Literary Structure of the Old Testament." In *Creation, Life, and Hope Creation, Life, and Hope: Essays in Honor of Jacques B. Doukhan*, edited by Jiří Moskala, 349-366. Berrien Springs, MI: Old Testament Department, SDA Theological Seminary, Andrews University, 2000.

―――――. "Ezekiel 28:11-19 and the Rise of the Cosmic Conflict." *The Great Controversy and the End of Evil: Biblical and Theological Studies in Honor of Ángel Manuel Rodríguez in Celebration of His Seventieth Birthday*, edited by Gerhard Pfandl, 57-69. Silver Spring, MD: Review & Herald, 2015.

―――――. "The Genesis Account of Origins." In *The Genesis Creation Account and Its Reverberations in the Old Testament*, edited by Gerald A. Klingbeil, 59-129. Berrien Springs, MI: Andrews University Press, 2015.

―――――. "The Genesis Account of Origins." In *He Spoke and It Was: Divine Creation in the Old Testament*, edited by Gerald A. Klingbeil, 39-71. Nampa, ID: Pacific Press, 2015.

―――――. "The Genesis Flood Narrative: Crucial Issues in the Current Debate." *Andrews University Seminary Studies* 42, no. 1 (2004): 49-77.

―――――. "The Good News of Yom Kippur." *Journal of the Adventist Theological Society* 2, no. 2 (1991): 4-27.

―――――. "Inauguration or Day of Atonement? A Response to Norman Young's 'Old Testament Background to Hebrews 6:19-20 Revisited.'" *Andrews University Seminary Studies* 40, no. 1 (2002): 69-88.

_____. "Israel and the Church: Continuity and Discontinuity—I." In *Message, Mission, and Unity of the Church*, edited by Ángel Manuel Rodríguez, 375-400. Silver Spring, MD: Biblical Research Institute, 2013.

_____. "Israel and the Church: Continuity and Discontinuity—II." In *Message, Mission, and Unity of the Church*, edited by Ángel Manuel Rodríguez, 401-427. Silver Spring, MD: Biblical Research Institute, 2013.

_____. "The Nature of the Human Being From the Beginning: Genesis 1-11." In *"What Are Human Beings That You Remember Them?" Proceedings of the Third International Bible Conference, Nof Ginosar and Jerusalem; June 11-21, 2012*, edited by Clinton Wahlen, 11-42. Silver Spring, MD: Biblical Research Institute, 2015.

_____. "Proverbs 8 and the Place of Christ in the Trinity." *Journal of the Adventist Theological Society* 17, no. 1 (2006): 33-54.

_____. "Sanctuary Typology." In *Symposium on Revelation*. Vol. 1, *Introductory and Exegetical Studies*, edited by Frank B. Holbrook, 99-130. Silver Spring, MD: Biblical Research Institute, GC of SDAs, 1992.

_____. *Typology in Scripture: A Study of Hermeneutical Typos Structures*. Andrews University Seminary Doctoral Dissertation Series 2. Berrien Springs, MI: Andrews University Press, 1981.

_____. "Understanding the 'When' of Creation in Genesis 1-2." In *In the Beginning: Science and Scripture Confirm Creation*, edited by Bryan W. Ball, 97-113. Nampa, ID: Pacific Press, 2012.

Davis, Brian. *The Thought of Thomas Aquinas*. New York, NY: Oxford University Press, 1992.

Dederen, Raoul, ed. *Handbook of Seventh-day Adventist Theology*. Commentary Reference Series 12. Hagerstown, MD: Review & Herald, 2000.

Dembski, William A. *The End of Christianity: Finding a Good God in an Evil World*. Nashville, TN: B & H, 2009.

De Preester, Helena. "Part-Whole: Metaphysics Underlying Issues of Internality/ Externality." *Philosophica* 73 (2004): 27-50.

de Saussure, Ferdinand. *Course in General Linguistics*. Translated by

Wade Baskin. New York, NY: Philosophical Library, 1959.

de Souza, Elias Brasil. "The Heavenly Sanctuary/Temple Motif in the Hebrew Bible: Function and Relationship to the Earthly Counterparts." PhD diss., Andrews University, Berrien Springs, MI, 2005.

_____. "Sanctuary: Cosmos, Covenant, and Creation." *Journal of the Adventist Theological Society* 24, no. 1 (2013): 25-41.

Dionysius the Areopagite. *On the Divine Names and the Mystical Theology*. Translated by Clarence E. Rolt. 1920. Reprint. N.p. MT: Kessinger, 1992.

Doan, Ruth Alden. *The Miller Heresy, Millennialism, and American Culture*. Philadelphia, PA: Temple University Press, 1987.

Douglass, Herbert E. "The Great Controversy Theme: What It Means to Adventists." *Ministry*, December 2000, 5-7.

_____. *Messenger of the Lord: The Prophetic Ministry of Ellen G. White*. Nampa, ID: Pacific Press, 1998.

Douglass, Herbert E., comp. *The Heartbeat of Adventism: The Great Controversy Theme in the Writings of Ellen G. White*. Nampa, ID: Pacific Press, 2010.

Doukhan, Jacques B. *Secrets of Revelation: The Apocalypse Through Hebrew Eyes*. Hagerstown, MD: Review & Herald, 2002.

Duah, Martha O. "A Study of Warfare Theodicy in the Writings of Ellen G. White and Gregory A. Boyd." PhD diss., Andrews University, Berrien Springs, MI, 2012.

Dulles, Avery. *The Craft of Theology: From Symbol to System*. New York, NY: Crossroad, 1992.

_____. *Models of Revelation*. New York, NY: Doubleday, 1983.

_____. *Models of the Church*. Expanded ed. New York, NY: Doubleday, 1987.

Dunn, James D. G. *Christology in the Making: A New Testament Inquiry Into the Origins of the Doctrine of the Incarnation*. 2nd ed. London, UK: SCM, 1989.

_____. *Romans 1-8*. Word Biblical Commentary 38A. Dallas, TX: Word, 1988.

Dussel, Enrique D. *El dualismo en la antropología de la cristiandad*. Buenos Aires, Argentina: Editorial Guadalupe, 1974.

Ebeling, Gerhard. *The Study of Theology*. Translated by Duane A. Priebe. Philadelphia, PA: Fortress, 1978.

Edmondson, Stephen. *Calvin's Christology*. New York, NY: Cambridge University Press, 2004.

Epperly, Bruce G. *Process Theology: A Guide for the Perplexed*. London, UK: T. & T. Clark, 2011.

Erickson, Millard J. *Christian Theology*. 3rd ed. Grand Rapids, MI: Baker, 2013.

――――――. *God the Father Almighty: A Contemporary Exploration of the Divine Attributes*. Grand Rapids, MI: Baker, 1998.

――――――. *What Does God Know and When Does He Know It? The Current Controversy Over Divine Foreknowledge*. Grand Rapids, MI: Zondervan, 2003.

Feinberg, John S. *No One Like Him: The Doctrine of God*. Wheaton, IL: Crossway, 2001.

Finger, Thomas N. *Christian Theology: An Eschatological Approach*. Vol. 1. Nashville, TN: Thomas Nelson, 1985.

Fitzmyer, Joseph A. *Romans: A New Translation With Introduction and Commentary*. Anchor Bible 33. New York, NY: Doubleday, 1993.

Fockner, Sven. "Reason and Theology: A Comparison of Fernando Canale and Wolfhart Pannenberg." MA thesis, Andrews University, Berrien Springs, MI, 2008.

Folkenberg, Robert S. "Will the Real Evangelical Adventist Please Stand Up." *Adventist Review*, April 1996, 16-19.

Ford, Desmond. *Answers on the Way: Scriptural Answers to Your Questions*. Mountain View, CA: Pacific Press, 1977.

――――――. *The Coming Worldwide Calvary: Christ Versus Antichrist*. Bloomington, IN: iUniverse, 2009.

――――――. *Crisis! A Commentary on the Book of Revelation*. Vol. 2, *A Verse by Verse Commentary*. Newcastle, CA: Desmond Ford, 1982.

――――――. "Daniel 8:14, the Day of Atonement, and the Investigative Judgment." Paper presented at the Sanctuary Review Committee, Glacier View, CO, August 10-15, 1980.

――――――. *Genesis Versus Darwinism: Abridged for Adventists*. N.p.: Desmond Ford, 2015.

_____. *Genesis Versus Darwinism: The Case for God in a Scientific World*. N.p.: A&S, 2014.

_____. *Right With God Right Now: How God Saves People as Shown in the Bible's Book of Romans*. Newcastle, CA: Desmond Ford, 1999.

_____. *Physicians of the Soul: God's Prophets Through the Ages*. Nashville, TN: Southern Pub. Assn., 1980.

_____. *The Time Is at Hand! An Introduction to the Book of Revelation*. Bloomington, IN: iUniverse, 2009.

Ford, Desmond, and Gillian Ford. *The Adventist Crisis of Spiritual Identity*. Newcastle, CA: Desmond Ford, 1982.

Ford, Lewis S. "Tillich and Thomas: The Analogy of Being." *The Journal of Religion* 46, no. 2 (1966): 229-245.

"Fourteenth Business Meeting: Fifty-Third General Conference Session; April 25, 1980, 9:30 A.M." *Adventist Review*, May 21, 1980, 16-19.

Fowler, John M. "Sin." In *Handbook of Seventh-day Adventist Theology*, edited by Raoul Dederen, 233-270. Hagerstown, MD: Review & Herald, 2000.

Fox, Michael V. *Proverbs 1-9: A New Translation With Introduction and Commentary*. Anchor Bible 18A. New York, NY: Doubleday, 2000.

Frame, John M. *The Doctrine of the Knowledge of God*. Phillipsburg, NJ: Presbyterian & Reformed, 1987.

Froom, LeRoy E. *Movement of Destiny*. Washington, DC: Review & Herald, 1971.

Fuller, Benjamin A. G. *A History of Philosophy*. Vol. 2. Rev. ed. New York, NY: Henry Holt, 1947.

Gadamer, Hans-Georg. *Truth and Method*. Revised by Joel Weinsheimer and Donald G. Marshall. 2nd rev. ed. London, UK: Continuum, 2004.

Gage, Kenneth. "What Human Nature Did Jesus Take? Fallen." *Ministry*, June 1985, 9-21.

Gale, Richard M. "Time, Temporality, and Paradox." In *The Blackwell Guide to Metaphysics*, edited by Richard M. Gale, 66-86. Oxford, UK: Blackwell, 2002.

Gallusz, Laszlo. *The Throne Motif in the Book of Revelation*. London, UK: Bloomsbury, 2014.

Gane, Roy. *Cult and Character: Purification Offerings, Day of Atonement, and Theodicy*. Winona Lake, IN: Eisenbrauns, 2005.

⸺. "Judgment as Covenant Review." *Journal of the Adventist Theological Society* 8, nos. 1-2 (1997): 181-194.

⸺. "Temple and Sacrifice." *Journal of the Adventist Theological Society* 10, nos. 1-2 (1999): 357-380.

⸺. *Who's Afraid of the Judgment? The Good News About Christ's Work in the Heavenly Sanctuary*. Nampa, ID: Pacific Press, 2006.

Garrett, Duane A. *Proverbs, Ecclesiastes, Song of Songs*. The New American Commentary 14. Nashville, TN: Broadman, 1993.

Geisler, Norman L. *Thomas Aquinas: An Evangelical Appraisal*. Grand Rapids, MI: Baker, 1991.

Geisler, Norman L., and Paul D. Feinberg. *Introduction to Philosophy: A Christian Perspective*. Grand Rapids, MI: Baker, 1980.

General Conference of Seventh-day Adventists. *Seventh-day Adventist Church Manual*. 19th ed. Silver Spring, MD: GC of SDAs, 2016.

⸺. *Seventh-day Adventist Church Manual*. Silver Spring, MD: GC of SDAs, 1981.

⸺. *Yearbook of the Seventh-day Adventist Denomination: The Official Directories*. Washington, DC: Review & Herald, 1931.

General Conference of Seventh-day Adventists and the Lutheran World Federation. "Adventists and Lutherans in Conversation: 1994-1998; Report of the Bilateral Conversations Between the Lutheran World Federation and the Seventh-day Adventist Church." In *Lutherans & Adventists in Conversation: Report and Papers Presented: 1994-1998*. Silver Spring, MD: GC of SDAs, 2000.

Gentry, Peter J., and Stephen J. Wellum. *Kingdom Through Covenant: A Biblical-Theological Understanding of the Covenants*. Wheaton, IL: Crossway, 2012.

George, Timothy. *Theology of the Reformers*. Nashville, TN: Broadman, 1988.

Geraty, Lawrence T. "Archaeology of the Flood." In *Understanding Genesis: Contemporary Adventist Perspective*, edited by Brian Bull, Fritz Guy, and Ervin Taylor, 167-195. Riverside, CA: Adventist Today, 2009.

Gilkey, Langdon. *Maker of Heaven and Earth: A Study of the Christian Doctrine of Creation*. New York, NY: Anchor, 1965.

Gilsdorf, Joy. *The Puritan Apocalypse: New England Eschatology in the Seventeenth Century*. Outstanding Studies in Early American History. New York, NY: Garland, 1989.

Gladson, Jerry. "Taming Historical Criticism: Adventist Biblical Scholarship in the Land of the Giants." *Spectrum* 18, no. 4 (1988): 19-34.

Glanz, Oliver. "Investigating the Presuppositional Realm of Biblical-Theological Methodology, Part I: Dooyeweerd on Reason." *Andrews University Seminary Studies* 47, no. 1 (2009): 5-35.

————. "Investigating the Presuppositional Realm of Biblical-Theological Methodology, Part II: Canale on Reason." *Andrews University Seminary Studies* 47, no. 2 (2009): 217-240.

————. "Investigating the Presuppositional Realm of Biblical-Theological Methodology, Part III: Application and Comparison." *Andrews University Seminary Studies* 48, no. 1 (2010): 55-79.

————. "Investigating the Presuppositional Realm of Biblical-Theological Methodology, Part IV: Critique and Transformation." *Andrews University Seminary Studies* 48, no. 2 (2010): 257-285.

Goldstein, Clifford. *1844 Made Simple*. Boise, ID: Pacific Press, 1988.

————. "Investigating the Investigative Judgment." *Ministry*, February 1992, 6-9.

————. "Two Adams, Two Eves?" *Adventist Review*, February 3, 2016. Accessed July 21, 2016. http://www.adventistreview.org/two-adams,-two-eves.

González, Justo L. *Historia del pensamiento cristiano*. Barcelona, España: Clie, 2010.

Goñi, Carlos. *Breve historia de la Filosofía*. Madrid, España: Ediciones Palabra, 2010.

Goodwin, George L. "The Openness of God: A Compromised Position?" *Spectrum* 12, no. 1 (1981): 62-63.

Graf Maiorov, Roy E. "El uso de Génesis 15:6 por Pablo y Santiago: Implicaciones herménuticas." MTh thesis, Universidad Peruana Unión, Lima, Perú, 2012.

Grenz, Stanley J. *The Named God and the Question of Being: A Trinitarian Theo-Ontology*. Louisville, KY: Westminster John Knox, 2005.

_____. *A Primer on Postmodernism*. Grand Rapids, MI: Eerdmans, 1996.

_____. *Revisioning Evangelical Theology: A Fresh Agenda for the 21st Century*. Downers Grove, IL: InterVarsity, 1993.

_____. *Theology for the Community of God*. Grand Rapids, MI: Eerdmans, 1994.

Grenz, Stanley J., and John R. Franke. *Beyond Foundationalism: Shaping Theology in a Postmodern Context*. Louisville, KY: Westminster John Knox, 2001.

Grenz, Stanley J., and Roger E. Olson. *Who Needs Theology: An Invitation to the Study of God*. Downers Grove, IL: InterVarsity, 1996.

Griffin, David R. "Process Theology and the Christian Good News: A Response to Classical Free Will Theism." In *Searching for an Adequate God: A Dialogue Between Process and Free Will Theists*, edited by John B. Cobb Jr. and Clark H. Pinnock, 1-38. Grand Rapids, MI: Eerdmans, 2000.

Griffith Thomas, William H. *The Catholic Faith: A Manual of Instruction for Members of the Church of England*. New ed. London, UK: Longmans, 1920.

Grossi, Vittorino, Luis F. Ladaria, Philippe Lécrivain, and Bernard Sesboüé. *Historia de los dogmas*. Vol. 2, *El hombre y su salvación*. Translated by Alfonso Ortiz García. Salamanca, España: Secretariado Trinitario, 1996.

Guarino, Thomas G. *Foundations of Systematic Theology*. New York, NY: T. & T. Clark, 2005.

Gulley, Norman R. *Christ Is Coming! A Christ-Centered Approach to Last-Day Events*. Hagerstown, MD: Review & Herald, 1998.

_____. "The Cosmic Controversy: World View for Theology and Life." *Journal of the Adventist Theological Society* 7, no. 2 (1996): 82-124.

_____. *Systematic Theology*. Vol. 1, *Prolegomena*. Berrien Springs, MI: Andrews University Press, 2003.

_____. *Systematic Theology*. Vol. 2, *God as Trinity*. Berrien Springs, MI: Andrews University Press, 2011.

———. *Systematic Theology*. Vol. 3, *Creation, Christ, Salvation*. Berrien Springs, MI: Andrews University Press, 2012.

———. *Systematic Theology*. Vol. 4, *The Church and the Last Things*. Berrien Springs, MI: Andrews University Press, 2016.

———. "Why the Sanctuary Is So Important." *Ministry*, August 2014, 22-23.

Guthrie, William K. C. *A History of Greek Philosophy*. Vol. 6, *Aristotle: An Encounter*. Cambridge, UK: Cambridge University Press, 1981.

Guy, Fritz. "Change, Scripture, and Science: Good News for Adventist Thinking in the Twenty-First Century." *Spectrum* 39, no. 3 (2009): 50-55.

———. "Comments on a Recent Whiteheadian Doctrine of God." *Andrews University Seminary Studies* 4, no. 2 (1966): 107-134.

———. "Confidence in Salvation: The Meaning of the Sanctuary." *Spectrum* 11, no. 2 (1980): 44-53.

———. "Divine Forgiveness as Experienced Event." *Andrews University Seminary Studies* 5, no. 2 (1967): 87-100.

———. "God's Time: Infinite Temporality and the Ultimate Reality of Becoming." *Spectrum* 29, no. 1 (2001): 19-28.

———. "Interpreting Genesis One in the Twenty-First Century." *Spectrum* 31, no. 2 (2003): 5-16.

———. "Man and His Time: Three Contemporary Theological Interpretations." PhD diss., University of Chicago, IL, 1971.

———. "Negotiating the Creation-Evolution Wars." *Spectrum* 20, no. 1 (1989): 40-46.

———. "The Presence of Ultimacy." *Spectrum* 9, no. 1 (1977): 48-54.

———. "The Purpose and Function of Scripture: Preface to a Theology of Creation." In *Understanding Genesis: Contemporary Adventist Perspective*, edited by Brian Bull, Fritz Guy, and Ervin Taylor, 86-101. Riverside, CA: Adventist Today, 2009.

———. *Thinking Theologically: Adventist Christianity and the Interpretation of Faith*. Berrien Springs, MI: Andrews University Press, 1999.

———. "The Ultimate Triumph of Love." *Southern Asia Tidings*, February 1989, 3-4.

Hagen, Kenneth. "Luther on Atonement–Reconfigured." *Concordia Theological Quarterly* 61, no. 4 (1997): 251-276.

Haldane, John J. "A Thomist Metaphysics." In *The Blackwell Guide to Metaphysics*, edited by Richard M. Gale, 87-109. Oxford, UK: Blackwell, 2002.

Halper, Edward C. *One and Many in Aristotle's Metaphysics: The Central Books*. 2nd ed. Las Vegas, NV: Parmenides, 2005.

Harmon, Ellen G. "Letter From Sister Harmon." *The Day-Star*, January 24, 1846, 31-32.

———. "Letter From Sister Harmon." *The Day-Star*, March 14, 1846, 7.

Hartman, Louis F., and Alexander A. Di Lella. *The Book of Daniel*. Anchor Bible 23. Garden City, NY: Doubleday, 1978.

Hartshorne, Charles. *A Natural Theology for Our Time*. La Salle, IL: Open Court, 1967.

Hartshorne, Charles, and William L. Reese. *Philosophers Speak of God*. Chicago, IL: University of Chicago Press, 1953.

Hasel, Gerhard F. "The 'Days' of Creation in Genesis 1: Literal 'Days' or Figurative 'Periods/Epochs' of Time?" In *Creation, Catastrophe, and Calvary*, edited by John T. Baldwin, 40-68. Hagerstown, MD: Review & Herald, 2000.

———. "Divine Judgment." In *Handbook of Seventh-day Adventist Theology*, edited by Raoul Dederen, 815-856. Hagerstown, MD: Review & Herald, 2000.

———. "The Genealogies of Genesis 5 and 11 and Their Alleged Babylonian Background." *Andrews University Seminary Studies* 16, no. 2 (1978): 361-474.

———. "The 'Little Horn,' the Heavenly Sanctuary and the Time of the End: A Study of Daniel 8:9-14." In *Symposium on Daniel: Introductory and Exegetical Studies*, edited by Frank B. Holbrook, 378-461. Washington, DC: Biblical Research Institute, GC of SDAs, 1986.

———. *New Testament Theology: Basic Issues in the Current Debate*. 1975. Reprint. Grand Rapids, MI: Eerdmans, 1993.

———. *Old Testament Theology: Basic Issues in the Current Debate*. 4th ed. Grand Rapids, MI: Eerdmans, 1995.

———. "Proposal for a Canonical Biblical Theology." *Andrews University Seminary Studies* 34, no. 1 (1996): 23-33.

———. "The Sabbath in the Pentateuch." In *The Sabbath in Scripture and History*, edited by Kenneth A. Strand, 21-43. Washington, DC: Review & Herald, 1982.

———. "Studies in Biblical Atonement II: The Day of Atonement." In *The Sanctuary and the Atonement: Biblical, Historical, and Theological Studies*, edited by Arnold V. Wallenkampf and Richard Lesher, 115-133. Washington, DC: Review & Herald, 1981.

Hatch, Edwin. *The Influence of Greek Ideas and Usages Upon the Christian Church*. 6th ed. London, NY: Williams & Norgate, 1897.

Hayward, James L., ed. *Creation Reconsidered: Scientific, Biblical, and Theological Perspectives*. Roseville, CA: Association of Adventist Forums, 2000.

Heide, Gale. *Timeless Truth in the Hands of History: A Short History of System in Theology*. Princeton Theological Monograph Series 178. Eugene, OR: Pickwick, 2012.

Heidegger, Martin. *Being and Time*. Translated by John Macquarrie and Edward Robinson. Oxford, UK: Blackwell, 2001.

———. "The Onto-theo-logical Constitution of Metaphysics." In *Identity and Difference*, 42-74. Translated by Joan Stambaugh. New York, NY: Harper & Row, 1969.

———. *Schelling's Treatise on the Essence of Human Freedom*. Translated by Joan Stambaugh. Athens, OH: Ohio University Press, 1985.

Heinz, Daniel. "Introduction: Seventh-day Adventists in Europe; Heirs of the Reformation." In *Heirs of the Reformation: The Story of Seventh-day Adventists in Europe*, edited by Hugh Dunton, Daniel Heinz, Dennis Porter, and Ronald Strasdowsky, 11-16. Grantham, England: Stanborough, 1997.

Hendriksen, William. *Exposition of Colossians and Philemon*. New Testament Commentary. Grand Rapids, MI: Baker, 1965.

Heppenstall, Edward. *Our High Priest: Jesus Christ in the Heavenly Sanctuary*. Washington, DC: Review & Herald, 1972.

———. "The Pre-Advent Judgment." *Ministry*, December 1981, 12-15.

Herr, Larry G. "Genesis One in Historical-Critical Perspective." *Spectrum* 13, no. 2 (1982): 51-62.

Heschel, Abraham J. *The Sabbath: Its Meaning for Modern Man.* New York, NY: Noonday, 1994.

Hodgson, Peter C. *Winds of the Spirit: A Constructive Christian Theology.* Louisville, KY: Westminster John Knox, 1994.

Holbrook, Frank B. "The Great Controversy." In *Handbook of Seventh-day Adventist Theology*, edited by Raoul Dederen, 969-1009. Hagerstown, MD: Review & Herald, 2000.

Holbrook, Frank B., ed. *Doctrine of the Sanctuary: A Historical Survey.* Daniel and Revelation Committee Series 5. Silver Spring, MD: Biblical Research Institute, 1989.

Hong, Koog P. "Synchrony and Diachrony in Contemporary Biblical Interpretation." *The Catholic Biblical Quarterly* 75, no. 3 (2013): 521-539.

Huijgen, Arnold. *Divine Accommodation in John Calvin's Theology: Analysis and Assessment.* Göttingen, Germany: Vandenhoeck & Ruprecht, 2011.

Ickert, Scott S. "Luther on the Timelessness of God." *Lutheran Quarterly* 7, no. 1 (1993): 45-66.

Illanes Maestre, José Luis. *Sobre el saber teológico.* Madrid, España: Rialp, 1978.

Inbody, Tyron. *The Faith of the Christian Church: An Introduction to Theology.* Grand Rapids, MI: Eerdmans, 2005.

Johns, Warren H. "Theology and Geology of the Flood: Moving Beyond Flood Geology." In *Understanding Genesis: Contemporary Adventist Perspective*, edited by Brian Bull, Fritz Guy, and Ervin Taylor, 151-166. Riverside, CA: Adventist Today, 2009.

Johnson, Douglas. "The Word of Life: A Study of the Relationship Between the Doctrines of Revelation and Redemption, With Reference to the Theology of John Calvin and Contemporary Thought Concerning Speech and Action." PhD thesis, Roehampton University, London, UK, 2013.

Johnsson, William G. "The Heavenly Sanctuary—Figurative or Real?" In *Issues in the Book of Hebrews*, edited by Frank B. Holbrook, 35-51. Silver Spring, MD: Biblical Research Institute, 1989.

Johnston, Robert M. "The Case for a Balanced Hermeneutic." *Ministry*, March 1999, 10-12.

"Joint Statement of the World Evangelical Alliance and the Seventh-day

Adventist Church." Accessed June 17, 2016. http://www.worldevangelicals.org/news/WEAAdventistDialogue20070809d.pdf.

Jones-Haldeman, Madelynn. "Progressive Adventism: Dragging the Church Forward." *Adventist Today*, January-February, 1994, 9-11.

Kaiser, Denis. "The Biblical Sanctuary Motif in Historical Perspective." In *Scripture and Philosophy: Essays Honoring the Work and Vision of Fernando Luis Canale*, edited by Tiago Arrais, Kenneth Bergland, and Michael F. Younker, 154-193. Berrien Springs, MI: Adventist Theological Society, 2016. 167-186.

Kaiser, Walter C., Jr. "Putting It All Together: The Theological Use of the Bible." In *An Introduction to Biblical Hermeneutics: The Search for Meaning*, edited by Walter C. Kaiser Jr. and Moisés Silva, 193-206. Grand Rapids, MI: Zondervan, 1994.

Kant, Immanuel. *Critique of Pure Reason*. Translated by Max Müller. London, UK: Macmillan, 1922.

──────. *Kant's Critique of the Practical Reason and Other Works on the Theory of Ethics*. Translated by Thomas K. Abbott. 6th ed. London, UK: Longmans, Green, 1903.

Kärkkäinen, Veli-Matti. *Constructive Christian Theology for the Pluralistic World*. Vol. 2, *Trinity and Revelation*. Grand Rapids, MI: Eerdmans, 2014.

──────. *The Doctrine of God: A Global Introduction; A Biblical, Historical and Contemporary Survey*. Grand Rapids, MI: Baker, 2004.

Kassay, Laurent B. "Richard Rice's Anticipatory Theory of Divine Foreknowledge: A Critical Evaluation." PhD diss., Adventist International Institute of Advanced Studies, Silang, Cavite, Philippines, 2001.

Keesmaat, Sylvia C. "Colossians, Book of." *Dictionary for Theological Interpretation of the Bible*. Edited by Kevin J. Vanhoozer. Grand Rapids, MI: Baker, 2005. 119-123.

Kellogg, John H. *The Living Temple*. Battle Creek, MI: Good Health, 1903.

Kenney, John P. "Augustine and Classical Theism." In *Models of God and Alternative Ultimate Realities*, edited by Jeanine Diller and Asa Kasher, 125-132. London, UK: Springer, 2013.

Kerbs, Raúl. "La crítica del Pentateuco y sus presuposiciones filosóficas." In *Inicios, paradigmas y fundamentos: Estudios teológicos y exegéticos en el Pentateuco*, edited by Gerald A. Klingbeil, 3-43. Libertador San Martín, Entre Ríos, Argentina: Editorial Universidad Adventista del Plata, 2004.

──────. "El método histórico crítico en teología: En busca de su estructura básica y de las interpretaciones filosóficas subyacentes (Parte I)." *DavarLogos* 1, no. 2 (2002): 105-123.

──────. "El método histórico crítico en teología: En busca de su estructura básica y de las interpretaciones filosóficas subyacentes (Parte II)." *DavarLogos* 2, no. 1 (2003): 1-27.

──────. "Observaciones epistemológicas e históricas preliminares sobre la relación fe-razón desde una perspectiva cristiana adventista." Paper presented at the 14th Institute for Christian Teaching, Universidad Adventista del Plata, Argentina, January 16-28, 1994.

──────. "Philosophical Assumptions of the Church Fathers: God and Creation." *Enfoques* 26, no. 1 (2014): 31-55.

──────. *El problema de la identidad bíblica del cristianismo: Las presuposiciones filosóficas de la teología cristiana; desde los presocráticos al protestantismo*. Libertador San Martín, Entre Ríos, Argentina: Editorial Universidad Adventista del Plata, 2014.

Kierkegaard, Søren. *Concluding Unscientific Postscript to the Philosophical Crumbs*. New York, NY: Cambridge University Press, 2009.

King, Greg A. "Resurrection in the Old Testament: Hazy Hope or Certain Promise." In *The Great Controversy and the End of Evil: Biblical and Theological Studies in Honor of Ángel Manuel Rodríguez in Celebration of His Seventieth Birthday*, ed. Gerhard Pfandl, 217-227. Silver Spring, MD: Biblical Research Institute, 2015.

Kirk, Geoffrey S., John E. Raven, and Malcolm Schofield. *The Presocratic Philosophers: A Critical History With a Selection of Texts*. 2nd ed. Cambridge, UK: Cambridge University Press, 1983.

Kiš, Miroslav M. "Christian Lifestyle and Behavior." *Handbook of Seventh-day Adventist Theology*. Edited by Raoul Dederen, 675-723. Hagerstown, MD: Review & Herald, 2000.

Kline, Meredith G. *Kingdom Prologue: Genesis Foundations for a Covenantal Worldview*. Overland Park, KS: Two Age, 2000.

Klingbeil, Gerald A. "El santuario, el ritual y la teología: En busca del centro de la teología adventista." *Theologika* 27, no. 2 (2012): 66-85.

Knight, George R. *The Apocalyptic Vision and the Neutering of Adventism: Are We Erasing Our Relevancy?* Hagerstown, MD: Review & Herald, 2008.

──────. *A Brief History of Seventh-day Adventists*. Hagerstown, MD: Review & Herald, 1999.

──────. "The Rise of Sabbatarian Doctrines." In *1844 and the Rise of Sabbatarian Adventism*. Edited and compiled by George R. Knight, 143-145. Hagerstown, MD: Review & Herald, 1994.

──────. *A Search for Identity: The Development of Seventh-day Adventist Beliefs*. Hagerstown, MD: Review & Herald, 2000.

──────. *Sin and Salvation: God's Work for and in Us*. Rev. ed. Hagerstown, MD: Review & Herald, 2008.

──────. *A User-Friendly Guide to the 1888 Message*. Hagerstown, MD: Review & Herald, 1998.

Küng, Hans. *Theology for the Third Millennium: An Ecumenical View*. Translated by Peter Heinegg. New York, NY: Doubleday, 1988.

Kwiram, Alvin L. "Introduction." *Spectrum* 1, no. 1 (1969): 4-5.

Lăiu, Florin G. "The Sanctuary Doctrine: A Critical-Apologetic Approach." Paper presented at the Biblical Research Committee, Cernica-Bucharest, Romania, November 16, 2011.

Landeen, William M. *Martin Luther's Religious Thought*. Mountain View, CA: Pacific Press, 1971.

LaRondelle, Hans K. *Our Creator Redeemer: An Introduction to Biblical Covenant Theology*. Berrien Springs, MI: Andrews University Press, 2005.

Larson, David R. "Coercive or Persuasive Power: Which Is Stronger?" David R. Larson, July 21, 2007. Accessed August 29, 2016. http://www.davidrlarson.com/2007/07/coercive-or-per.html.

──────. "Jesus and Genocide: Another Alternative." *Spectrum* 34, no. 3 (2006): 66-69.

──────. "The Moral Danger of Miracles." *Spectrum* 18, no. 4 (1988): 13-18.

―――――. "Necessarily, Essentially, Neither or Both: How Does God Love the Universe?" Paper presented at the Annual Meeting of the American Academy of Religion, San Antonio, TX, November 20-23, 2004.

―――――. "The Omnipotence Fallacy and Beyond." *Spectrum* 23, no. 3 (1993): 39-43.

―――――. "On Openness of God." *Spectrum* 12, no. 3 (1982): 61-62.

―――――. "'Panentheism' Is Not a Four-Letter Word!" *Spectrum*, July 30, 2010. Accessed August 18, 2016. http://spectrummagazine.org/article/column/2010/07/30/%E2%80%9Cpanentheism%E2%80%9D-not-four-letter-word.

―――――. "Process Theology and Me." *Spectrum*, February 25, 2008. Accessed August 18, 2016. http://spectrummagazine.org/article/column/2008/02/25/process-theology-and-me.

―――――. "Think Less of God Intervening, Think More of God Participating." *Spectrum*, September 1, 2008. Accessed August 28, 2016. http://spectrummagazine.org/article/column/2008/09/01/think-less-god-intervening-think-more-god-participating.

―――――. "Traditional Free Will Theism and the Ten Core Doctrines of Process Philosophy." David. R. Larson, July 14, 2010. Accessed August 18, 2016. http://www.davidrlarson.com/2010/07/traditional-free-will-theism-and---the-ten-core-doctrines-of-process-philosophy--by-david-r-larson----how-much-difference-pe.html#more.

―――――. "Was Spinoza Right About Miracles?" *Spectrum* 32, no. 2 (2004): 47-51.

Leaders, Bible Teachers, and Editors. *Seventh-day Adventist Answer Questions on Doctrine*. Washington, DC: Review & Herald, 1957.

Lewis, Clive S. *Mere Christianity*. Rev. ed. New York, NY: Macmillan, 1952.

Liddell, Henry George, and Robert Scott. *A Greek English Lexicon*. 8th rev. ed. New York, NY: American, 1901.

Litch, Josiah. *An Address to the Public, and Especially to Clergy, on the Near Approach of the Glorious, Everlasting Kingdom of God on Earth, as Indicated by the Word of God, the History of the World and Signs of the Present Times*. Boston, MA: Joshua V. Himes, 1841.

———. *Prophetic Expositions; Or a Connected View of the Testimony of the Prophets Concerning the Kingdom of God and the Time of Its Establishment*. Vol. 1. Boston, MA: Joshua V. Himes, 1842.

Lohse, Eduard. *Colossians and Philemon: A Commentary on the Epistles to the Colossians and to Philemon*. Hermeneia. Translated by William R. Poehlmann and Robert J. Karris. Philadelphia, PA: Fortress, 1971.

Lonergan, Bernard. *Método en Teología*. Translated by Gerardo Temolina. 4th ed. Salamanca, España: Ediciones Sígueme, 2006.

Luther, Martin. *Luther's Works*. Vol. 1, *Lectures on Genesis: Chapters 1-5*. Edited by Jaroslav Pelikan and George V. Schick. Saint Louis, MO: Concordia, 1958.

———. *Luther's Works*. Vol. 2, *Lectures on Genesis: Chapters 6-14*. Edited by Jaroslav Pelikan, Daniel E. Poellot, and George V. Schick. Saint Louis, MO: Concordia, 1960.

———. *Luther's Works*. Vol. 3, *Lectures on Genesis: Chapters 15-20*. Edited by Jaroslav Pelikan and George V. Schick. Saint Louis, MO: Concordia, 1961.

———. *Luther's Works*. Vol. 4, *Lectures on Genesis: Chapters 21-25*. Edited by Jaroslav Jan Pelikan and Walter A. Hansen. Translated by George V. Schick. Saint Louis, MO: Concordia, 1964.

———. *Luther's Works*. Vol. 5, *Lectures on Genesis: Chapters 26-30*. Edited by Jaroslav Pelikan and Walter A. Hansen. Saint Louis, MO: Concordia, 1968.

———. *Luther's Works*. Vol. 12, *Selected Psalms I*. Edited by Jaroslav Pelikan. Saint Louis, MO: Concordia, 1955.

———. *Luther's Works*. Vol. 16, *Lectures on Isaiah: Chapters 1-39*. Edited by Jaroslav Pelikan and Hilton C. Oswald. Translated by Herbert J. A. Bouman. Saint Louis, MO: Concordia, 1969.

———. *Luther's Works*. Vol. 23, *Sermons on the Gospel of St. John: Chapters 6-8*. Edited by Jaroslav Pelikan and Daniel E. Poellot. Translated by Martin H. Bertran. Saint Louis, MO: Concordia, 1959.

———. *Luther's Works*. Vol. 24, *Sermons on the Gospel of St. John: Chapters 14-16*. Edited by Jaroslav Pelikan and Daniel E. Poellot. Translated by Martin H. Bertram. Saint Louis, MO: Concordia, 1961.

_____. *Luther's Works*. Vol. 25, *Lectures on Romans*. Edited by Hilton C. Oswald. Saint Louis, MO: Concordia, 1972.

_____. *Luther's Works*. Vol. 26, *Lectures on Galatians, 1535, Chapters 1-4*. Edited by Jaroslav Pelikan and Walter A. Hansen. Translated by Jaroslav Pelikan. Saint Louis, MO: Concordia, 1963.

_____. *Luther's Works*. Vol. 27, *Lectures on Galatians, 1535, Chapters 5-6; Lectures on Galatians, 1519, Chapters 1-6*. Edited by Jaroslav Pelikan and Walter A. Hansen. Saint Louis, MO: Concordia, 1964.

_____. *Luther's Works*. Vol. 28, *1 Corinthians 7, 1 Corinthians 15, Lectures on 1 Timothy*. Edited by Hilton C. Oswald. Saint Louis, MO: Concordia, 1973.

_____. *Luther's Works*. Vol. 29, *Lectures on Titus, Philemon, and Hebrews*. Edited by Jaroslav Pelikan and Walter A. Hansen. Saint Louis, MO: Concordia, 1968.

_____. *Luther's Works*. Vol. 30, *The Catholic Epistles*. Edited by Jaroslav Pelikan and Walter A. Hansen. Saint Louis, MO: Concordia, 1967.

_____. *Luther's Works*. Vol. 31, *Career of the Reformer I*. Edited by Harold J. Grimm and Helmut T. Lehmann. Philadelphia, PA: Fortress, 1957.

_____. *Luther's Works*. Vol. 32, *Career of the Reformer II*. Edited by George W. Forell and Helmut T. Lehmann. Philadelphia, PA: Fortress, 1958.

_____. *Luther's Works*. Vol. 33, *Career of the Reformer III*. Edited by Philip S. Watson and Helmut T. Lehmann. Philadelphia, PA: Fortress, 1972.

_____. *Luther's Works*. Vol. 34, *Career of the Reformer IV*. Edited by Lewis W. Spitz and Helmut T. Lehmann. Philadelphia, PA: Fortress, 1960.

_____. *Luther's Works*. Vol. 35, *Word and Sacrament I*. Edited by E. Theodore Backmann and Helmut T. Lehmann. Philadelphia, PA: Fortress, 1960.

_____. *Luther's Works*. Vol. 37, *Word and Sacrament III*. Edited by Robert Fischer and Helmut T. Lehmann. Philadelphia, PA: Fortress, 1961.

———. *Luther's Works*. Vol. 40, *Church and Ministry II*. Edited by Conrad Bergendoff and Helmut T. Lehmann. Philadelphia, PA: Fortress, 1958.

———. *Luther's Works*. Vol. 48, *Letters I*. Edited by Gottfried G. Krodel and Helmut T. Lehmann. Philadelphia, PA: Fortress, 1963.

———. *Luther's Works*. Vol. 51, *Sermons I*. Edited by John W. Doberstein and Helmut T. Lehmann. Philadelphia, PA: Fortress, 1959.

———. *Luther's Works*. Vol. 52, *Sermons II*. Edited by Hans J. Hillerbrand and Helmut T. Lehmann. Philadelphia, PA: Fortress, 1974.

———. *Luther's Works*. Vol. 54, *Table Talk*. Edited by Theodore G. Tappert and Helmut T. Lehmann. Philadelphia, PA: Fortress, 1967.

Lyotard, Jean-François. *The Postmodern Condition: A Report on Knowledge*. Translated by Geoff Bennington and Brian Massumi. Manchester, UK: Manchester University Press, 1984.

Macquarrie, John. *Principles of Christian Theology*. 2nd ed. New York, NY: Charles Scribner, 1977.

Madges, William. *God and the World: Christian Texts in Perspective*. Maryknoll, NY: Orbis, 1999.

Marías, Julián. *History of Philosophy*. Translated by Stanley Appelbaum and Clarence C. Strawbridge. New York, NY: Dover, 1967.

———. *Idea de la metafísica*. Buenos Aires, Argentina: Editorial Columba, 1954.

Martínes, Carmelo. "Principios epistemológicos para la comprensión de la doctrina del santuario." *DavarLogos* 11, no. 1 (2012): 1-17.

Martínez Marzoa, Felipe. *Historia de la Filosofía II*. Madrid, España: Ediciones Istmo, 2003.

Mattes, Mark. "Luther's Use of Philosophy." *Lutherjahrbuch* 80 (2013): 110-141.

Matthews, Gareth B. *Augustine*. Oxford, UK: Blackwell, 2005.

Maxwell, C. Mervyn. "An Exegetical and Historical Examination of the Beginning and Ending of the 1260 Days of Prophecy With Special Attention Given to A.D. 538 and 1798 as Initial and Terminal Dates." MA thesis, SDA Theological Seminary, Washington, DC, 1951.

McGrath, Alister E. *Christian Theology: An Introduction*. 2nd ed. Oxford, UK: Blackwell, 1997.

———. *A Scientific Theology*. Vol. 1, *Nature*. Grand Rapids, MI: Eerdmans, 2001.

McKnight, Scot. "Covenant." *Dictionary for Theological Interpretation of the Bible*. Edited by Kevin J. Vanhoozer. Grand Rapids, MI: Baker, 2005. 141-143.

Melick, Richard R. *Philippians, Colossians, Philemon*. The New American Commentary 32. Nashville, TN: Broadman, 1991.

Mendenhall, George E. "Covenant Forms in Israelite Tradition." *The Biblical Archeologists* 17, no. 3 (1954): 50-76.

Metzger, Bruce M., and Bart D. Ehrman. *The Text of the New Testament: Its Transmission, Corruption, and Restoration*. 4th ed. New York, NY: Oxford University Press, 2005.

Michaels, J. Ramsey. *Revelation*. The IVP New Testament Commentary Series 20. Downers Grove, IL: InterVarsity, 1997.

Miller, William. "Cleansing of the Sanctuary." *Signs of the Times*, April 6, 1842, 1-2.

———. *Evidence From Scripture and History of the Second Coming of Christ About the Year 1843: Exhibited in a Course of Lectures*. Boston, MA: Joshua V. Himes, 1842.

———. *Miller's Works*. Vol. 1, *Views on the Prophecies and Prophetic Chronology*. Boston, MA: Joshua V. Himes, 1842.

———. *William Miller's Apology and Defence*. Boston, MA: J. V. Himes, 1845.

Miralbell, Ignacio. "La teoría aristotélica de la abstracción y su olvido moderno." *Sapientia* 63, no. 223 (2008): 3-27.

Moffitt, David M. *Atonement and the Logic of Resurrection in the Epistle to the Hebrews*. Supplements to Novum Testamentum 141. Leiden, The Netherlands: Brill, 2011.

———. "Serving in Heaven's Temple: Sacred Space, Yom Kippur, and Jesus' Superior Offering in Hebrews." Paper presented at the Annual Meeting of the Society of Biblical Literature, Chicago, IL, November 16-20, 2012.

Moltmann, Jürgen. *God in Creation: An Ecological Doctrine of Creation; The Gifford Lectures 1984-1985*. Translated by Margaret Kohl. London, UK: SCM, 1985.

———. *The Trinity and the Kingdom: The Doctrine of God*. Translated by Margaret Kohl. Minneapolis, MN: Fortress, 1993.

Moon, Jerry. "The Quest for a Biblical Trinity: Ellen White's 'Heavenly Trio' Compared to the Traditional Doctrine." *Journal of the Adventist Theological Society* 17, no. 1 (2006): 140-159.

Moore, Marvin. *The Case for the Investigative Judgment: Its Biblical Foundation*. Nampa, ID: Pacific Press, 2010.

Morales, L. Michael. *The Tabernacle Pre-Figured: Cosmic Mountain Ideology in Genesis and Exodus*. Leuven, Belgium: Peeters, 2012.

Moreland, James P., and William L. Craig. *Philosophical Foundations for a Christian Worldview*. Downers Grove, IL: InterVarsity, 2003.

Moskala, Jiří. "Toward a Biblical Theology of God's Judgment: A Celebration of the Cross in Seven Phases of Divine Universal Judgment (An Overview of a Theocentric-Christocentric Approach)." *Journal of the Adventist Theological Society* 15, no. 1 (2004): 138-165.

Mueller, Ekkehardt. "The Nature of the Human Being in the New Testament." In *"What Are Human Beings That You Remember Them?" Proceedings of the Third International Bible Conference, Nof Ginosar and Jerusalem; June 11-21, 2012*, edited by Clinton Wahlen, 133-163. Silver Spring, MD: Biblical Research Institute, 2015.

Muller, Richard A. *Christ and the Decree: Christology and Predestination in Reformed Theology From Calvin to Perkins*. Grand Rapids, MI: Baker, 1988.

Murphy, James G. *A Critical and Exegetical Commentary on the Book of Genesis*. Andover, MA: Warren F. Draper, 1866.

Murphy, Nancey. *Beyond Liberalism and Fundamentalism: How Modern and Postmodern Philosophy Set the Theological Agenda*. Harrisburg, PA: Trinity Press International, 2007.

Murphy, Roland E. *Ecclesiastes*. Word Biblical Commentary 23A. Dallas, TX: Word, 1992.

———. *Proverbs*. Word Biblical Commentary 22. Nashville, TN: Thomas Nelson, 1998.

Nam, Daegeuk. *The "Throne of God" Motif in the Hebrew Bible*. Korean Sahmyook University Monographs Doctoral Dissertation

Series 1. Seoul, Korea: Institute for Theological Research, Korean Sahmyook University, 1989.

Nash, Ronald H. *Faith and Reason: Searching for a Rational Faith*. Grand Rapids, MI: Zondervan, 1988.

Nichol, Francis D. "Scientific Ideas Are Not Infallible." *Review & Herald*, January 7, 1965, 6-8.

Nichol, Francis D., ed. *Seventh-day Adventist Bible Commentary*. Rev. ed. Washington, DC: Review & Herald, 1957.

O'Brien, Peter T. *Colossians, Philemon*. Word Biblical Commentary 44. Waco, TX: Word, 1982.

Olafsson, Gudmundur. "God's Eternal Covenant and the Sabbath." *Journal of the Adventist Theological Society* 16, nos. 1-2 (2005): 155-163.

_____. "Immanuel—God With Us." In *The Great Controversy and the End of Evil: Biblical and Theological Studies in Honor of Ángel Manuel Rodríguez in Celebration of His Seventieth Birthday*, edited by Gerhard Pfandl, 119-126. Silver Spring, MD: Biblical Research Institute, 2015.

Olson, Roger E. *Arminian Theology: Myths and Realities*. Downers Grove, IL: InterVarsity, 2006.

_____. *The Journey of Modern Theology: From Reconstruction to Deconstruction*. Downers Grove, IL: InterVarsity, 2013.

Oord, Thomas J. "Free Process Defense." *Encyclopedia of Science and Religion*. Edited by J. Wentzel V. van Huyssteen. New York, NY: Macmillan, 2003. 339.

Osborne, Grant R. *The Hermeneutical Spiral: A Comprehensive Introduction to Biblical Interpretation*. 2nd ed. Downers Grove, IL: InterVarsity, 2006.

Our Firm Foundation: A Report of the Seventh-day Adventist Bible Conference Held September 1-13, 1952, in the Sligo Seventh-day Adventist Church Takoma Park, Maryland. 2 vols. Washington, DC: Review & Herald, 1953.

Ouro, Roberto. "The Sanctuary: The Canonical Key of Old Testament Theology." *Andrews University Seminary Studies* 50, no. 2 (2012): 159-177.

Owen, Gwilym E. L. "Plato and Parmenides on the Timeless Present." *The Monist* 50 (1966): 317-340.

Owusu-Antwi, Brempong. *The Chronology of Daniel 9:24-27*. Adventist Theological Society Dissertation Series 2. Berrien Springs, MI: Adventist Theological Society, 1993.

Pannenberg, Wolfhart. *Metaphysics and the Idea of God*. Translated by Philip Clayton. Edinburgh, Scotland: T. & T. Clark, 1990.

―――――. *Systematic Theology*. Vol. 1. Grand Rapids, MI: Eerdmans, 1991.

Partee, Charles B. *Calvin and Classical Philosophy*. Leiden, Netherlands: Brill, 1977.

Patrick, Arthur N. "Are Adventists Evangelicals?" *Ministry*, February 1995, 14-17.

Paxton, Geoffrey J. *The Shaking of Adventism*. Wilmington, DE: Zenith, 1977.

Peckham, John C. "The Analogy of Scripture Revisited: A Final Form Canonical Approach to Systematic Theology." *Mid-America Journal of Theology* 22 (2011): 41-53.

―――――. "The Canon and Biblical Authority: A Critical Comparison of Two Models of Canonicity." *Trinity Journal* 28, no. 2 (2007): 229-249.

―――――. *Canonical Theology: The Biblical Canon, Sola Scriptura, and Theological Method*. Grand Rapids, MI: Eerdmans, 2016.

―――――. "The Concept of Divine Love in the Context of the God-World Relationship." PhD diss., Andrews University, Berrien Springs, MI, 2012.

―――――. "Divine Passibility, Analogical Temporality, and Theo-Ontology: Implications of a Canonical Approach." In *Scripture and Philosophy: Essays Honoring the Work and Vision of Fernando Luis Canale*, edited by Tiago Arrais, Kenneth Bergland, and Michael F. Younker, 32-53. Berrien Springs, MI: Adventist Theological Society, 2016.

―――――. "An Investigation of Luther's View of the Bondage of the Will With Implications for Soteriology and Theodicy." *Journal of the Adventist Theological Society* 18, no. 2 (2007): 274-304.

―――――. "*Sola Scriptura*: Reductio ad Absurdum?" *Trinity Journal* 35, no. 2 (2014): 195-223.

―――――. "Theopathic or Anthropopathic? A Suggested Approach to Imagery of Divine Emotion in the Hebrew Bible." *Perspectives in Religious Studies* 42, no. 4 (2015): 341-355.

Pelikan, Jaroslav. *Christianity and Classical Culture: The Metamorphosis of Natural Theology in the Christian Encounter With Hellenism*. New Haven, CT: Yale University Press, 1993.

Petersen, Paul B. "'Unwholly' Relationships: Unity in a Biblical Ontology." In *"What Are Human Beings That You Remember Them?" Proceedings of the Third International Bible Conference, Nof Ginosar and Jerusalem; June 11-21, 2012*, edited by Clinton Wahlen, 235-248. Silver Spring, MD: Biblical Research Institute, 2015.

Pinnock, Clark H. *Most Moved Mover: A Theology of God's Openness*. Grand Rapids, MI: Baker, 2001.

_____. "Systematic Theology." In *The Openness of God: A Biblical Challenge to the Traditional Understanding of God*, 101-125. Downers Grove, IL: InterVarsity, 1994.

Placher, William C. *A History of Christian Theology: An Introduction*. Philadelphia, PA: Westminster, 1983.

Plato. *Parmenides*. In *Plato in Twelve Volumes*. Vol. 4, *Cratylus; Parmenides; Greater Hippias; Lesser Hippias*. Translated by Harold N. Fowler. Cambridge, MA: Harvard University Press, 1977. 193-331.

_____. *Phaedo*. In *Plato*. Vol. 1, *Euthyphro; Apology; Crito; Phaedo; Phaedrus*. Translated by Harold N. Fowler. Cambridge, MA: Harvard University Press, 1995. 193-403.

_____. *Phaedrus*. In *Plato*. Vol. 1, *Euthyphro; Apology; Crito; Phaedo; Phaedrus*. Translated by Harold N. Fowler. Cambridge, MA: Harvard University Press, 1995. 405-579.

_____. *The Republic*. In *Plato in Twelve Volumes*. Vol. 6, *The Republic II: Books VI-X*. Translated by Paul Shorey. Cambridge, MA: Harvard University Press, 1980.

_____. *Timaeus*. In *Plato in Twelve Volumes*. Vol. 9, *Timaeus; Critias; Cleitophon; Menexenus; Epistles*. Translated by Robert G. Bury. Cambridge, MA: Harvard University Press, 1989. 1-253.

Pöhler, Rolf J. "Does Adventist Theology Have, or Need, a Unifying Center?" In *Christ, Salvation, and the Eschaton: Essays on Honor of Hans K. LaRondelle*, edited by Daniel Heinz, Jiří Moskala, and Peter M. van Bemmelen, 17-32. Berrien Springs, MI: Andrews University, 2009.

Polkinghorne, John. *Belief in God in an Age of Science.* New Haven, CT: Yale University Press, 1998.

———. *Beyond Science: The Wider Human Context.* Cambridge, UK: Cambridge University Press, 1996.

———. *Science and Religion in Quest of Truth.* New Haven, CT: Yale University Press, 2011.

———. *Science and the Trinity: The Christian Encounter With Reality.* New Haven, CT: Yale University Press, 2004.

———. *Science and Providence: God's Interaction With the World.* Philadelphia, PA: Templeton Foundation, 2005.

Prescott, William W. *The Doctrine of Christ: A Series of Bible Studies for Use in Colleges and Seminaries.* Washington, DC: Review & Herald, 1920.

Rader, Michelle, David VanDenburgh, and Larry Christoffel. "Evangelical Adventism: Clinging to the Old Rugged Cross." *Adventism Today,* January-February 1994, 6-8.

Rand, Benjamin. "What Human Nature Did Jesus Take? Unfallen." *Ministry,* June 1985, 8, 10-21.

Rescher, Nicholas. *Kant and the Reach of Reason: Studies in Kant's Theory of Rational Systematization.* Cambridge, UK: Cambridge University Press, 2000.

Rice, Richard. "Biblical Support for a New Perspective." In *The Openness of God: A Biblical Challenge to the Traditional Understanding of God,* 11-58. Downers Grove, IL: InterVarsity, 1994.

———. *God's Foreknowledge and Man's Free Will.* Minneapolis, MN: Bethany, 1985.

———. "Process Theism and the Open View of God: The Crucial Difference." In *Searching for an Adequate God: A Dialogue Between Process and Free Will Theists,* edited by John B. Cobb Jr. and Clark H. Pinnock, 163-200. Grand Rapids, MI: Eerdmans, 2000.

———. Professor of Theology at Loma Linda University. Interview by Laurent B. Kassay, Silang, Cavite, Philippines, July 4, 2001. In Laurent B. Kassay, "Richard Rice's Anticipatory Theory of Divine Foreknowledge: A Critical Evaluation," 277-280. PhD diss., Adventist International Institute of Advanced Studies, Silang, Cavite, Philippines, 2001.

_____. *Reason and the Contours of Faith*. Riverside, CA: La Sierra University Press, 1991.

_____. *Reign of God: An Introduction to Christian Theology From a Seventh-day Adventist Perspective*. 2nd ed. Berrien Springs, MI: Andrews University Press, 1997.

_____. "The Relevance of the Investigative Judgment." *Spectrum* 14, no. 1 (1993): 32-38.

_____. "Why I Am a Seventh-day Adventist." *Spectrum* 24, no. 1 (1994): 34-45.

Rico, Jorge E. *Conexiones teológicas del santuario*. Burleson, TX: Biblical Foundations, 2011.

Rodríguez, Ángel Manuel. "Eden and the Israelite Sanctuary: A Study in God's Abiding Interest in Harmony and Restoration." *Ministry*, April 2002, 11-13, 30.

_____. "Genesis 1 and the Building of the Israelite Sanctuary." *Ministry*, February 2002, 9-11.

_____. "God's Presence in the Sanctuary: A Theology of His Nearness." Paper for the Biblical Research Institute, n.d. Accessed December 8, 2016. https://adventistbiblicalresearch.org/sites/default/files/pdf/God%27s%20presence%20in%20sanctuary.pdf.

_____. "Justification and the Cross." Paper for the Biblical Research Institute, 2002. Accessed July 22, 2016. https://www.adventistbiblicalresearch.org/sites/default/files/pdf/Rom%205_12-21_0.pdf.

_____. "Sanctuary Theology in the Book of Exodus." *Andrews University Seminary Studies* 24, no. 2 (1986): 127-145.

Rolston, Holmes, III. "Does Nature Need to Be Redeemed?" *Zygon* 29, no. 2 (1994): 205-229.

Ross, David. *Aristotle*. 6th ed. London, UK: Routledge, 1995.

Ross, Hugh. *The Creator and the Cosmos: How the Greatest Scientific Discoveries of the Century Reveal God*. 2nd ed. Colorado Springs, CO: NavPress, 1995.

Sanctuary Review Committee. "Christ in the Heavenly Sanctuary." Consensus Document, Glacier View Ranch, CO, August 10-15, 1980. *Ministry*, October 1980, 16-19.

_____. "Statement on Desmond Ford Document." *Ministry*, October 1980, 20-22.

Sanders, John. *The God Who Risks: A Theology of Divine Providence*. 2nd ed. Downers Grove, IL: InterVarsity, 2007.

Sarna, Nahum M. *Exodus*. The JPS Torah Commentary. Philadelphia, PA: JPS, 1991.

―――. *Genesis*. The JPS Torah Commentary. Philadelphia, PA: JPS, 1989.

Schleiermacher, Friedrich. *The Christian Faith*. London, UK: T. & T. Clark, 1999.

―――. *On Religion: Speeches to Its Cultured Despisers*. Translated by John Oman. London, UK: K. Paul, Trench, Trubner, 1893.

Schwarz, Hans. *True Faith in the True God: An Introduction to Luther's Life and Thought*. Rev. ed. Minneapolis, MN: Fortress, 2015.

Schwarz, Richard W. *Light Bearers to the Remnant*. Mountain View, CA: Pacific Press, 1979.

Schüssler Fiorenza, Francis. "Systematic Theology: Task and Methods." In *Systematic Theology: Roman Catholic Perspectives*, edited by Francis Schüssler Fiorenza and John P. Galvin, 1:1-78. 2nd rev. ed. Minneapolis, MN: Fortress, 2011.

Sharrock, Graeme. "Faith Development in a Scientific Culture." In *Creation Reconsidered: Scientific, Biblical, and Theological Perspectives*, edited by James L. Hayward, 323-335. Roseville, CA: Association of Adventist Forums, 2000.

She, King L. *The Use of Exodus in Hebrews*. Studies in Biblical Literature 142. New York, NY: Peter Lang, 2011.

Shea, William H. "Creation." In *Handbook of Seventh-day Adventist Theology*, edited by Raoul Dederen, 418-456. Hagerstown, MD: Review & Herald, 2000.

―――. Foreword to *The Case for the Investigative Judgment: Its Biblical Foundation* by Marvin Moore, 7-8. Nampa, ID: Pacific Press, 2010.

―――. "The Prophecy of Daniel 9:24:27." In *70 Weeks, Leviticus, and the Nature of Prophecy*, edited by Frank B. Holbrook, 75-118. Washington, DC: Biblical Research Institute, GC of SDAs, 1986.

―――. *Selected Studies on Prophetic Interpretation*. N.p.: GC of SDAs, 1982.

―――. "Time Prophecies of Daniel 12 and Revelation 12-13." In *Symposium on Revelation*. Vol. 1, *Introductory and Exegetical*

Studies, edited by Frank B. Holbrook, 327-360. Silver Spring, MD: Biblical Research Institute, GC of SDAs, 1992.

Siggins, Jan D. Kingston. *Martin Luther's Doctrine of Christ*. New Haven, CT: Yale University Press, 1970.

Silva, Moisés. "Systematic Theology and the Apostle to the Gentiles." *Trinity Journal* 15, no. 1 (1994): 3-26.

Silva, Moisés, ed. "*Aiōn, aiōnios.*" *New International Dictionary of New Testament Theology and Exegesis*. Rev. ed. Grand Rapids, MI: Zondervan, 2014. 1:193-200.

S[mith], U[riah]. "The Judgment of Rev. 14:7." *The Advent Review and Herald of the Sabbath*, January 13, 1874, 36.

[Smith, Uriah]. *A Declaration of the Fundamental Principles Taught and Practiced by the Seventh-day Adventists*. Battle Creek, MI: Steam Press of the SDA Pub. Assn., 1872.

[Smith, Uriah]. "Our Righteousness." *The Advent Review and Sabbath Herald*, June 11, 1889, 376-377.

Smith, Uriah. *An Appeal to the Youth*. Battle Creek, MI: Steam Press of the SDA Pub. Assn., 1864.

———. *Daniel and the Revelation: Thoughts, Critical and Practical, on the Book of Daniel and the Revelation; Being an Exposition, Text by Text, of These Important Portions of the Holy Scriptures*. Nashville, TN: Southern Pub. Assn., 1897.

———. *Looking Unto Jesus: Or Christ in Type and Antitype*. Chicago, IL: Review & Herald, 1898.

———. *Man's Nature and Destiny: Or the State of the Dead, the Reward of the Righteous and the End of the Wicked*. Oakland, CA: Pacific Press, 1884.

———. *Mortal or Immortal? Which? Or an Inquiry Into the Present Constitution and Future Condition of Man*. Battle Creek, MI: Steam Press of the Review & Herald Office, 1860.

———. *The State of the Dead and the Destiny of the Wicked*. Battle Creek, MI: Steam Press of the SDA Pub. Assn., 1873.

Smith, Uriah, and George I. Butler. *Replies to Elder Canright's Attacks on Seventh-day Adventists*. Battle Creek, MI: Review & Herald, 1895.

Snider, Andy. "Story and System: Why We Should Not Categorize the Attributes of God." Paper presented at the 64th Annual Meeting of the Evangelical Theological Society, Milwaukee, WI, November 14-16, 2012.

Spalding, Arthur W. *Captains of the Host: First Volume of a History of Seventh-day Adventists Covering the Years 1945-1900.* Washington, DC: Review & Herald, 1949.

Spence, Martin. "The Renewal of Time and Space: The Missing Element of Discussions About Nineteenth Century Premillennialism." *The Journal of Ecclesiastical History* 63, no. 1 (2012): 81-101.

Sprague, Stuart R. "Shaping a Process Theology: The Theological Method of John B. Cobb, Jr." PhD diss., Southern Baptist Theological Seminary, Louisville, KY, 1975.

Stefanovic, Ranko. "The Heavenly Sanctuary and Its Services in the Book of Revelation: Its Reality and Meaning." MA thesis, Adventist International Institute of Advanced Studies, Silang, Cavite, Philippines, 1990.

Stokes, Michael C. *One and Many in Presocratic Philosophy.* Washington, DC: Center for Hellenic Studies, 1971.

Strobel, Lee. *The Case for a Creator: A Journalist Investigates Scientific Evidence That Points Toward God.* Grand Rapids, MI: Zondervan, 2004.

Strohl, Jane E. "Luther's Eschatology." In *The Oxford Handbook of Martin Luther's Theology*, edited by Robert Kolb, Irene Dingel, and L'ubomír Batka, 353-362. Oxford, UK: Oxford University Press, 2014.

Stuart, Douglas K. *Exodus.* The New American Commentary 2. Nashville, TN: Broadman & Holman, 2006.

Stump, Eleonore. "Augustine on Free Will." In *The Cambridge Companion to Augustine*, edited by Eleonore Stump and Norman Kretzmann, 124-147. Cambridge, UK: Cambridge University Press, 2001.

Tarán, Leonardo. "Perpetual Duration and Atemporal Eternity in Parmenides and Plato." *The Monist* 62 (1979): 43-53.

Tate, Marvin E. *Psalms 51-100.* Word Biblical Commentary 20. Dallas, TX: Word, 1990.

Taylor, Ervin. "Death Before Sin?—Yes." *Adventist Today*, Fall 2010, 10-13.

―――. "Progressive Adventism: A Nonfundamentalist Vision." *Adventist Today*, September-October 2001, 14.

Terreros, Marco T. "Death Before the Sin of Adam: A Fundamental Concept in Theistic Evolution and Its Implications for Evangelical Theology." PhD diss., Andrews University, Berrien Springs, MI, 1994.

_____. "What Is an Adventist? Someone Who Upholds Creation." *Journal of the Adventist Theological Society* 7, no. 2 (1996): 142-167.

TeSelle, Eugene. *Augustine: The Theologian*. London, UK: Burns & Oates, 1970.

Tillich, Paul. *Dynamics of Faith*. New York, NY: Harper, 1957.

_____. *A History of Christian Thought: From Its Judaic and Hellenistic Origins to Existentialism*. New York, NY: Simon & Schuster, 1968.

_____. *Systematic Theology: Three Volumes in One*. Chicago, IL: The University of Chicago Press, 1967.

Timm, Alberto R. "Algunas consideraciones breves en torno a los años 508 y 538 en relación con el establecimiento de la supremacía papal." *Theologika* 19, no. 2 (2004): 254-283.

_____. "Miniature Symbolization and the Year-Day Principle of Prophetic Interpretation." *Andrews University Seminary Studies* 42, no. 1 (2004): 149-167.

_____. *The Sanctuary and the Three Angels' Messages: Integrating Factors in the Development of Seventh-day Adventist Doctrines*. Adventist Theological Society Dissertation Series 5. Berrien Springs, MI: Adventist Theological Society, 1995.

_____. "The Sanctuary Motif Within the Framework of the Great Controversy." *The Cosmic Battle for the Planet Earth: Essays in Honor of Norman R. Gulley*, edited by Ron du Preez and Jiří Moskala, 59-84. Berrien Springs, MI: Old Testament Department, SDA Theological Seminary, Andrews University.

Tonstad, Sigve K. *The Lost Meaning of the Seventh Day*. Berrien Springs, MI: Andrews University Press, 2009.

Torrance, Alan J. "Analogy." *Dictionary for Theological Interpretation of the Bible*. Edited by Kevin J. Vanhoozer. Grand Rapids, MI: Baker, 2005. 38-40.

Torreblanca, Jorge. "Construyendo sobre Hasel y Davidson: Una posible definición del centro teológico en el Pentateuco." *TheoBiblica* 1 (2013): 1-14.

Tracy, David. *Blessed Rage for Order: The New Pluralism in Theology.* Minneapolis, MN: Winston-Seabury, 1975.

Treiyer, Alberto R. *The Day of Atonement and the Heavenly Judgment: From the Pentateuch to Revelation.* Siloam Springs, AR: Creation Enterprises, 1992.

———. *The Seals and the Trumpets: Biblical and Historical Studies.* N.p.: Distinctive Messages, 2005.

Troeltsch, Ernst. *Christian Thought: Its History and Application.* London, UK: University of London Press, 1923.

———. *Religion in History.* Translated by James Luther Adams and Walter F. Bense. Minneapolis, MN: Fortress, 1991.

Tutsch, Cindy. "Ellen White on Eschatology and the End of Evil." In *The Great Controversy and the End of Evil: Biblical and Theological Studies in Honor of Ángel Manuel Rodríguez in Celebration of His Seventieth Birthday,* edited by Gerhard Pfandl, 285-295. Silver Spring, MD: Review & Herald, 2015.

van Bemmelen, Peter M. "The Everlasting Covenant." *Journal of the Adventist Theological Society* 24, no. 1 (2013): 92-106.

———. "Revelation and Inspiration." In *Handbook of Seventh-day Adventist Theology,* edited by Raoul Dederen, 22-57. Hagerstown, MD: Review & Herald, 2000.

van de Fliert, J. R. "Fundamentalism and the Fundamentals of Geology." *Journal of the American Scientific Affiliation* 21 (1969): 69-81.

Vanhoozer, Kevin J. *First Theology: God, Scripture and Hermeneutics.* Downers Grove, IL: InterVarsity, 2002.

———. *Remythologizing Theology: Divine Action, Passion, and Authorship.* New York, NY: Cambridge University Press, 2010.

Vogel, Winfried. *The Cultic Motif in the Book of Daniel.* New York, NY: Peter Lang, 2010.

von Rad, Gerhard. *Genesis: A Commentary.* Translated by John H. Marks. Rev. ed. London, UK: SCM, 1972.

———. *Old Testament Theology.* Vol. 1, *The Theology of Israel's Historical Traditions.* Translated D. M. G. Stalker. Edinburgh, Scotland: Oliver & Boyd, 1962.

[Waggoner, Ellet J.] "A Present Salvation." *The Present Truth,* May 18, 1893, 145-146.

Waggoner, Ellet J. "Bible Study: Letter to the Romans—.No. 1." General Conference Daily Bulletin, March 8, 1891, 33-34.

———. "Bible Study: Letter to the Romans—No. 13." General Conference Daily Bulletin, March 22, 1891, 199-204.

———. *Christ and His Righteousness*. Oakland, CA: Pacific Press, 1890.

Wallenkampf, Arnold V. "A Brief Review of Some of the Internal and External Challengers to the Seventh-day Adventist Teachings on the Sanctuary and the Atonement." In *The Sanctuary and the Atonement: Biblical, Historical, and Theological Studies*, edited by Arnold V. Wallenkampf and Richard Lesher, 582-603. Washington, DC: Review & Herald, 1981.

Walton, John H. "Etymology." *Dictionary for Theological Interpretation of the Bible*. Edited by Kevin J. Vanhoozer. Grand Rapids, MI: Baker, 2005. 200-202.

Ward, Keith. *God: A Guide for the Perplexed*. London, UK: Oneworld, 2002.

———. *God, Faith and the New Millennium: Christian Belief in an Age of Science*. Oxford, UK: Oneworld, 1998.

Ware, Bruce A. "Defining Evangelicalism's Boundaries Theologically: Is Open Theism Evangelical?" *Journal of the Evangelical Theological Society* 45, no. 2 (2002): 193-212.

Wartofsky, Marx W. *Models: Representation and the Scientific Understanding*. Boston, MA: Reidel, 1979.

Watson, Timothy. "The Meaning and Function of System in Theology." PhD diss., Andrews University, Berrien Springs, MI, 2011.

Weiss, Herold. "Revelation and the Bible: Beyond Verbal Inspiration." *Spectrum* 7, no. 3 (1976): 49-54.

Wendel, François. *Calvin: The Origins and Development of His Religious Thought*. Translated by Philip Mairet. New York, NY: Harper & Row, 1963.

Wenham, Gordon J. *Genesis 1-15*. Word Biblical Commentary 1. Waco, TX: Word, 1987.

———. "Sanctuary Symbolism in the Garden of Eden Story." In *Cult and Cosmos: Tilting Toward a Temple-Centered Theology*, edited by L. Michael Morales, 161-166. Leuven, Belgium: Peeters, 2014.

Westphal, Merold. "Onto-theology." *Dictionary for Theological Inter-

pretation of the Bible. Edited by Kevin J. Vanhoozer. Grand Rapids, MI: Baker, 2005. 546-549.

Whidden, Woodrow W., II. *Ellen White on Salvation*. Hagerstown, MD: Review & Herald, 1995.

_____. "The Triumph of God's Love: The Optimistic, Theological Theodicy of Ellen G. White." *Andrews University Seminary Studies* 53, no. 1 (2015): 197-214.

Whidden, Woodrow, Jerry Moon, and John W. Reeve. *The Trinity: Understanding God's Love, His Plan of Salvation, and Christian Relationships*. Hagerstown, MD: Review & Herald, 2002.

White, Ellen G. *The Acts of the Apostles*. Mountain View, CA: Pacific Press, 1911.

_____. "Build on a Sure Foundation." *Advent Review and Sabbath Herald*, September 24, 1908, 7-8.

_____. "Chosen in Christ." *Signs of the Times*, January 2, 1893, 134.

_____. *Christian Education*. Battle Creek, MI: International Tract Society, 1894.

_____. *Counsels to Parents, Teachers, and Students*. Mountain View, CA: Pacific Press, 1943.

_____. *The Desire of Ages*. Mountain View, CA: Pacific Press, 1940.

_____. *Education*. Mountain View, CA: Pacific Press, 1952.

_____. *The Ellen G. White 1888 Materials* (1987). Ellen G. White Writings Comprehensive Research Edition [CD ROM]. Silver Spring, MD: Ellen G. White Estate, 2008.

_____. *Faith and Works*. Nashville, TN: Southern Pub. Assn., 1979.

_____. *Fundamentals of Christian Education*. Nashville, TN: Southern Pub. Assn., 1923.

_____. "The Gospel for Both Jews and Gentiles." *The Signs of the Times*, August 5, 1889, 465-466.

_____. *Gospel Workers*. Washington, DC: Review & Herald, 1948.

_____. "The Grace of God Manifested in Good Works." *The Advent Review and Sabbath Herald*, January 29, 1895, 65-66.

_____. *The Great Controversy Between Christ and Satan*. Mountain View, CA: Pacific Press, 1950.

_____. "The Law Exalted by Christ." *The Advent Review and Sabbath Herald*, May 23, 1899, 321-322.

_____. *Life Sketches of Ellen G. White*. Mountain View, CA: Pacific Press, 1943.

_____. *Manuscript Releases*. Vol. 2. Silver Spring, MD: Ellen G. White Estate, 1987.

_____. *Manuscript Releases*. Vol. 11. Silver Spring, MD: Ellen G. White Estate, 1990.

_____. *Manuscript Releases*. Vol. 12. Silver Spring, MD: Ellen G. White Estate, 1990.

_____. *Manuscript Releases*. Vol. 14. Silver Spring, MD: Ellen G. White Estate, 1990.

_____. *Manuscript Releases*. Vol. 19. Silver Spring, MD: Ellen G. White Estate, 1990.

_____. *Maranatha*. Washington, DC: Review & Herald, 1976.

_____. *Patriarchs and Prophets*. Washington, DC: Review & Herald, 1958.

_____. "The Plan of Salvation." *Signs of the Times*, February 13, 1893, 230-231.

_____. *Prophets and Kings*. Mountain View, CA: Pacific Press, 1943.

_____. "The Revelation of God." *The Advent Review and Sabbath Herald*, November 8, 1898, 709-710.

_____. *Selected Messages*. Vol. 1. Washington, DC: Review & Herald, 1958.

_____. *A Sketch of the Christian Experience and Views of Ellen G. White*. Saratoga Springs, NY: James White, 1851.

_____. *Spiritual Gifts*. Vol. 3. Battle Creek, MI: SDA Pub. Assn., 1864.

_____. *Steps to Christ*. Mountain View, CA: Pacific Press, 1956.

_____. "Surpassing Love Revealed in His Plan." *Signs of the Times*, December 15, 1914, 769, 777.

_____. *Testimonies for the Church Containing Messages of Warning and Instruction to Seventh-day Adventists: Regarding Dangers Connected With the Medical Missionary Work*. Series B no. 7. N.p.: Published for the author [1906].

_____. *Testimonies for the Church*. Vol. 6. Mountain View, CA: Pacific Press, 1948.

_____. *Testimonies for the Church*. Vol. 8. Mountain View, CA: Pacific Press, 1948.

---. *Thoughts From the Mount of Blessing*. Mountain View, CA: Pacific Press, 1955.

---. "The True Standard of Righteousness." *Adventist Review and Sabbath Herald*, August 25, 1895, 529-530.

---. "The Way of Life." *Advent Review and Sabbath Herald*, November 4, 1890, 673.

---. "The Word Made Flesh." *The Advent Review and Sabbath Herald*, April 5, 1906, 8-9.

White, Ellen G., to Ole A. Olsen, May 1, 1895. In Ellen G. White, *Manuscript Releases*, 14:114-135. Silver Spring, MD: Ellen G. White Estate, 1990.

---., to the Teachers in Emmanuel Missionary College, September 23, 1903. In *Spalding and Magan Collection (1985)*, 324-325. Ellen G. White Writings Comprehensive Research Edition [CD ROM]. Silver Spring, MD: Ellen G. White Estate, 2008.

White, James. *Appeal on Immortality*. Battle Creek, MI: SDA Pub. Assn., n.d.

---. "The Cause." *Advent Review, and Sabbath Herald*, October 29, 1861, 172.

---. *Personality of God*. Battle Creek, MI: SDA Pub. Assn., [1861?].

Whitehead, Alfred North. *Process and Reality: An Essay in Cosmology*. Corrected ed. London, UK: Free, 1978.

---. "Religion and Science." In *Creation Reconsidered: Scientific, Biblical, and Theological Perspectives*, edited by James L. Hayward, 337-343. Roseville, CA: Association of Adventist Forums, 2000.

---. *Religion in the Making: Lowell Lectures 1926*. New York, NY: Macmillan, 1926. Reprint. New York, NY: Fordham University Press, 1996.

Widyapranawa, Samuel H. *The Lord Is Savior: Faith in National Crisis; A Commentary on the Book of Isaiah 1-39*. International Theological Commentary. Grand Rapids, MI: Eerdmans, 1990.

Williams, Robert R. *Schleiermacher: The Theologian; The Construction of the Doctrine of God*. Philadelphia, PA: Fortress, 1978.

Wilson, Brian C. *Dr. John Harvey Kellogg and the Religion of Biologic Living* Bloomington, IN: Indiana University Press, 2014.

Wolff, Hans W. *Anthropology of the Old Testament*. Translated by Margaret Kohl. Philadelphia, PA: Fortress, 1974.

Wolterstorff, Nicholas. *Inquiring About God: Selected Essays, Volume I*. Edited by Terence Cuneo. Cambridge, UK: Cambridge University Press, 2010.

──────. "Unqualified Divine Temporality." In *God & Time: Four Views*, edited by Gregory E. Ganssle, 187-213. Downers Grove, IL: InterVarsity, 2001.

Wood, Kenneth H. "The Mother of Us All: Mainstream Adventism." *Adventist Today*, January-February 1994, 4-5.

Wright, John H. "Predestination." *The New Dictionary of Theology*. Edited by Joseph A. Komonchak, Mary Collins, and Dermot A. Lane. Collegeville, MN: Liturgical, 1987. 797-798.

Wyman, Walter E., Jr. "Sin and Redemption." In *The Cambridge Companion to Friedrich Schleiermacher*, edited by Jacqueline Mariña, 129-149. Cambridge, UK: Cambridge University Press, 2005.

Young, Norman H. "The Alpha and the Omega Heresy: Kellogg and the Cross." *Adventist Heritage* 12, no. 1 (1987): 33-42.

──────. "The Day of Dedication or the Day of Atonement? The Old Testament Background to Hebrews 6:19-20 Revisited." *Andrews University Seminary Studies* 40, no. 1 (2002): 61-68.

──────. "The Gospel According to Hebrews 9." *New Testament Studies* 27, no. 2 (1981): 198-210.

──────. "'Where Jesus Has Gone as a Forerunner on Our Behalf' (Hebrews 6:20)." *Andrews University Seminary Studies* 39, no. 2 (2001): 165-173.

Younker, Randall W. "How Can We Interpret the First Chapters of Genesis? In *Understanding Creation: Answers to Questions on Faith and Science*, edited by L. James Gibson and Humberto M. Rasi, 69-77. Nampa, ID: Pacific Press, 2011.

www.ingramcontent.com/pod-product-compliance
Lightning Source LLC
Chambersburg PA
CBHW030850170426
43193CB00009BA/552